SCHOOL FINANCE

Its Economics and Politics

Austin D. Swanson • Richard A. King

State University of New York
at Buffalo

University of
Northern Colorado

Longman
New York & London

School Finance: Its Economics and Politics

Longman, 95 Church Street, White Plains, N.Y. 10601

Associated companies:
Longman Group Ltd., London
Longman Cheshire Pty., Melbourne
Longman Paul Pty., Auckland
Copp Clark Pitman, Toronto

Senior editor: Naomi Silverman
Production editor: Ann P. Kearns
Cover design: Anne M. Pompeo
Text art: Fine Line Inc.
Production supervisor: Kathleen M. Ryan

Library of Congress Cataloging-in-Publication Data

Swanson, Austin D.
    School finance : its economics and politics / Austin D. Swanson.
  Richard A. King.
        p.   cm.
    Includes bibliographical references (p.) and index.
    ISBN 0-8013-0296-X
    1. Public schools—United States—Finance. 2. State aid to
education—United States. 3. Federal aid to education—United
States. 4. Education—United States—Aims and objectives.
I. King, Richard A. II. Title.
LB2825.S739 1991
379.1'22'0973—dc20   90-43878
                                                       CIP

ABCDEFGHIJ–DO–99 98 97 96 95 94 93 92 91

Contents

PART IV: Improving School Finance Structures and Use of Resources

---

PART V: Synthesis

Preface

We enter the 1990s with great expectations. After fifty years of hot and cold wars, there appears to be a willingness among nations, East and West, to direct more of their attention and resources to improving the conditions of humankind. The possibility of peaceful coexistence is stronger now than at any time since World War II.

In his annual address to Congress, January 6, 1941, President Franklin Delano Roosevelt formulated "The Four Freedoms," which became a battle cry of the Allied Forces during World War II. Roosevelt said,

> In the future days, which we seek to make secure, we look forward to a world founded on four essential human freedoms.
>
> The first is freedom of speech and expression everywhere in the world.
>
> The second is freedom of every person to worship God in his own way everywhere in the world.
>
> The third is freedom from want, which, translated into world terms, means economic understandings which will secure to every nation a healthy peacetime life for its inhabitants everywhere in the world.
>
> The fourth is freedom from fear—which, translated into world terms, means a worldwide reduction of armaments to such a point and in such a thorough fashion that no nation will be in a position to commit an act of physical aggression against any neighbor—anywhere in the world.

Roosevelt believed that the freedoms were obtainable by his generation, but we are now fully aware of how painfully elusive the obtainment—and retention—of those freedoms are. Our generation, also, may fall short of the ultimate goal, but we enter the 1990s with an optimism that has been absent since the close of World War II.

What does the beating of swords into plowshares have to do with school finance? A great deal! For one thing, when a nation is spending eight to ten percent of its gross national product on defense, as the United States has for decades, there is less to spend on human services such as education.

But beyond the financial aspect, it is clear that international events influence domestic policy. We, indeed, have become a global village. A primary concern launching the educational reform movement of the 1980s was the potential loss of economic competitiveness by the United States. While American businesses and industries were making their productive processes more efficient and monitoring quality more closely, strong public pressure was brought against the public schools to do likewise because an efficient economy depends upon a highly skilled work force. Beginning in 1992, the economic challenges will be not only from Japan and the Pacific basin but also from the European Common Market as most restrictions on the movement of goods, persons, and capital among member nations are abolished. If Gorbachev's "perestroika" is successful, there may even be serious economic competition from Eastern Europe as the Iron Curtain parts.

The threat of external powers, be they economic or military, was not a primary factor leading to the establishment of a free public school system in the United States, however; rather, it was concern over potential internal aggressors. No nation can remain free and uneducated, and the greatest threat to freedom has always been the ineptitude of a nation's citizens. In our quest to maintain economic and military competitiveness, we must not lose sight of the importance of education to domestic and personal tranquillity.

Aside from national defense, the pursuit of equity among the nation's citizens has been a primary public concern in the period since World War II. The Depression of the 1930s had shattered confidence in the free market and people looked increasingly to government as a vehicle for realizing their aspirations. The theories of Marx and total state supremacy were tested in the East. The West moved more cautiously toward a division of power between the state and the market. The East discovered that the state could be as oppressive as the bourgeoisie or aristocracy, and both East and West learned that bureaucracies were as capable of failure as free markets.

As we enter the 1990s, we do so with a new respect for market mechanisms along with an appreciation of the practical limits of governmental intervention. The strategies followed during the past fifty years in search of equity exacted a heavy toll on personal freedom and liberty. There now appears to be a willingness to experiment with new strategies which respect personal as well as societal privilege. A major policy issue of the 1990s is this: Can we enjoy both liberty and equity in a fiercely competitive and frequently hostile world?

The schools have been affected directly by the current social, political, economic, and ideological ferment. It is within the context of ferment and change that this book examines the relevance of traditional theories and practice of school finance and evaluates possible alternatives. Drawing on political and economic models, the book begins with a discussion of the educational decision-making process in a political–economic system divided between public and private sectors. The discussion then shifts to the impact of public and private values, including equality, liberty, fraternity, efficiency, and economic growth, on decisions made about education. It is demonstrated how changes in priorities given to values require corresponding changes in public policy. The shift in public priorities from equity in the 1960s and 1970s to excellence, efficiency, accountability, and liberty in the 1980s serves as a case in point. Part I concludes with a brief description of the history and existing structure of school governance and finance in the United States.

Part II examines the origin of resources used in support of education. It begins with an overview of the federated tax structure in the United States and presents criteria that can be used for evaluating the impact of tax policies. Because of its unique importance in the financing of public education, and because a thorough understanding is necessary for the competent administration of local school districts, the property tax is singled out for special treatment. Part II concludes with a discussion of nontax resources for education, including borrowing, investments, foundations, partnerships with other organizations, and the use of volunteers.

Part III deals with state and federal aid issues. The merits and structure of general and categorical aid programs are examined. Several constructs for measuring the educational need, the wealth or revenue-generating ability, and the fiscal effort made by school districts are presented in relation to state policy. Strategies for monitoring the use of aid monies and their impact are discussed, including program and financial audits. Federal finance policy is discussed within several themes that capture the rationale for federal involvement in public education.

In Part IV, existing and proposed school finance structures and decision-making strategies for the use of resources are evaluated, using as criteria of success several objectives of public policy. The first chapter in the section looks at how various school finance plans have withstood judicial scrutiny. Subsequent chapters examine school finance policy, using constructs of economists and other policy analysts. The integration of state-of-the-art information and communication technologies into instructional systems is examined along with its impact on staffing (and, thus, financial) decisions. Personnel remuneration strategies and career ladders are examined in the light of higher standards for teachers and a growing teacher shortage. Financial implications of inducing marketlike incentives into the public schooling structure through family-choice plans and school-based management are analyzed.

The 1990s will see dramatic changes in the financing of elementary and secondary schools, reflecting the organizational changes that are likely to take place within them as a result of the school reform movement. The book concludes by bringing together its themes into an integrated discussion of the challenges these changes pose for school finance policy and to assess some of the more promising alternatives before us.

The book is designed as a primary text for graduate courses in public school finance and the economics of education, although analysts of educational policy should find it a valuable reference. Several features distinguish this book from other texts on the market. It treats the financial implications of the school reform movement, it emphasizes political as well as economic models of analysis, and it includes many cross-national references.

The strategy of the book is to respect the importance of economic theory in analyzing the impact of existing and alternative policies, but it recognizes that such theories do little to help understand the forces shaping school finance legislation and the process through which financial policy is developed. To understand fully what has happened in school finance legislation, and what is likely to happen, the field must also be studied by drawing on concepts from political science. The text strives for a balanced approach.

ACKNOWLEDGMENTS

The ideas and conceptualizations presented in this text have evolved over the years. They have been shaped and sharpened by the insights and criticisms of colleagues past and present. Interest in school finance as a field of study was first stimulated by Paul R. Mort many decades ago at Teachers College, Columbia University. His genius and mentorship provided a firm foundation on which to build understanding of the forces shaping school finance policy and the conditions to which school finance policy must respond.

As authors of this text, we assume full responsibility for its contents. However, a number of colleagues and independent reviewers assisted us in developing related manuscripts, sharing documents, and/or critiquing early drafts of the manuscript. We acknowledge the helpful insights of many individuals—among them are: Hedley Beare, University of Melbourne; Carvin L. Brown, University of Georgia; Daniel J. Brown, University of British Columbia; William Crocoll, Chittenden South School District, Vermont; William J. Fowler, National Center for Education Statistics; R. Oliver Gibson, State University of New York at Buffalo; Marjorie Hanson, Dade County, Florida, School District; Richard V. Hatley, University of Missouri at Columbia; G. Alfred Hess, Chicago Panel on Public School Policy and Finance; Thomas H. Jones, University of Connecticut; Robert E. Lamitie, New York and Connecticut State Education Departments; Eugene P. McLoone, University of Maryland; Bettye MacPhail-Wilcox, North Carolina State University; Betty Malen, University of Washington; Eugene A. Nelson, Virginia State Education Department; David Nyberg, State University of New York at Buffalo; William E. Sparkman, Texas Tech University; Ulysses V. Spiva, Old Dominion University; Edward J. Willett, Houghton College; and R. Craig Wood, University of Florida. We sincerely appreciate the efforts of Naomi Silverman, Ann Kearns, and Karen Philippidis of Longman Publishing Group in preparing the manuscript for publication.

Finally, we acknowledge former students, who have challenged us in past teaching, and future students, who provided the inspiration to write a textbook for their use in understanding school finance policy and practice.

PART I

The Context of School Finance

CHAPTER 1

Educational Decision Making in a Mixed Economy

Education is big business. By 1993, $180 billion will be spent annually on public elementary and secondary schools, making expenditures for education the largest single budgetary component of state and local governments (National Center for Education Statistics, 1989). These expenditures will represent about 4 percent of the gross national product. Forty-five million children attend these schools and they employ nearly 7 million professional educators and support personnel (U.S. Department of Commerce, 1988). No matter how one looks at it, schooling involves a highly significant portion of the nation's human and economic resources.

But education is much more than big business. Education deals with matters that relate to the heart and soul of the individual citizen and, at the same time, is critical to the political and economic welfare of the nation and its military security. Education's fundamental importance was the central theme of the report of the National Commission on Excellence in Education (1983), to which many attribute the launching of the Educational Reform Movement of the 1980s. The commissioners wrote,

> Our nation is at risk. Our once unchallenged preeminence in commerce, industry, science, and technological innovation is being overtaken by competitors throughout the world. This report is concerned with only one of the causes and dimensions of the problem, but *it is one that undergirds American prosperity, security and civility*. We report to the American people that while we can take justifiable pride in what our schools and colleges have historically accomplished and contributed to the United States and the well-being of its people, the educational foundations of our society are presently being eroded by a rising tide of mediocrity that threatens our very future as a Nation and a people. (Emphasis added.)

Although one may take exception to the hyperbole of the report's rhetoric, it nevertheless states forcefully and with authority the centrality of schools, public schools in particular, to the welfare of the nation and its citizens.

3

Making decisions about how much should be spent on schooling, how schools should be organized, what they should teach, and to whom is an important and complex process. One cannot fully understand the financing of elementary and secondary schooling without also understanding how decisions about school finance are made and how those funds are transformed into the realization of societal and individual aspirations. It is the purpose of this chapter to provide a basis for such understanding by describing the functioning of the economic and political arenas in which those decisions are made and implemented. The issues of when and how governments should become involved in the process are also considered.

EDUCATION: A PUBLIC AND A PRIVATE GOOD

Education is considered to be both a public and a private good because it brings with it important benefits to the individual and society. If public benefits were simply the sum of individual benefits, this would not constitute a problem; but this is not the case. Frequently there are substantial differences between societal and individual interests. Full public interest would not be realized if provision of education were left solely to private vendors and to the ability of individuals to pay for education; and it is unlikely that the full private or individual interest would be satisfied if education were left solely to public provision.

Private goods are divisible and their benefits are left primarily to their owners. If an individual desires a particular item or service, he or she can legally obtain the item by negotiating an agreed-upon price with the current owner. The new owner can enjoy the item or service whereas those unable or unwilling to pay the price cannot. A good is "private" if someone who does not pay for it can be excluded from its use and enjoyment. This is known as the exclusion principle. Such goods are readily provided through the market system, that is, the private sector.

The private (or individual) benefits of both publicly and privately provided education include the ability to earn more money and to enjoy a higher standard of living and a better quality of life. As part of this, educated persons are likely to be employed at more interesting jobs than are less educated persons. Schooling opens up the possibility of more schooling, which in turn leads to even better employment possibilities; long-term unemployment is much less likely. Similarly, educated persons, through knowledge and understanding of the arts and other manifestations of culture, and with greater resources at their disposal, are likely to have more options for the use of leisure time and are likely to use such time in more interesting ways. As informed consumers, they are likely to get more mileage out of their resources. Finally, better educated persons are likely to enjoy a better diet and have better health practices. This results in less sickness and a longer productive life.

Public goods are indivisible, yielding large and widespread benefits to the community and to society as a whole. Because these benefits are such that they cannot be limited to individuals willing to pay the price, it is unlikely that they would be provided fully through the market system in a satisfactory fashion. In other words, "public" or "collective" goods are those which violate the exclusion principle. The public (or societal) benefits of publicly and privately provided education include enlightened citizenship, which is particularly important to a democratic form of government. In projecting a common set of values and knowledge, schools can foster a sense of community and national identity and loyalty among a diverse population. A public school system can provide an effective network for talent identification and development, spurring the creation of both cultural and technological innovations and providing the skilled work force required for the efficient functioning of society. This results in more rapid economic growth and in a generally more vital and pleasant quality of life for everyone.

Structuring the decision-making process for education is particularly complex because education is both a public and a private good. Procuring educational services incurs costs and produces benefits which accrue to individuals independently, and at the same time, incurs social costs and produces benefits which accrue to society collectively. Levin (1987) concludes that there is a potential dilemma when schools are expected to provide both public and private benefits:

> Public education stands at the intersection of two legitimate rights: the right of a democratic society to assure its reproduction and continuous democratic functioning through providing a common set of values and knowledge and the right of families to decide the ways in which their children will be molded and the types of influences to which their children will be exposed. To the degree that families have different political, social, and religious beliefs and values, there may be a basic incompatibility between their private concerns and the public functions of schooling. (p. 629)

To ensure that both individual and societal demands for schooling are met, decisions about the provision of education are made in both the public and private sectors. Decisions in the public sector are made through political processes by governments, whereas decisions in the private sector are made by individuals using market mechanisms. Easton (1965a) described politics as the process by which *values* are allocated within society. Economics, on the other hand, is the study of the allocation of *scarce resources* within society. Economics is concerned with production, distribution, and consumption of commodities. Efficiency in the use of resources is the objective—efficiency being defined as securing the highest level of societal satisfaction at the least cost of scarce resources.

Obviously, one's value priorities strongly influence one's judgment as to what is an efficient allocation of material resources. Thus, there is continuing interaction between economics and politics. Public finance of education is one point of interaction. Decisions about the public finance of education will be made in political arenas; but the decisions made in those arenas will have strong economic implications for individuals and for businesses as well as for communities, states, and the nation. Individuals and businesses will respond independently to political decisions by deciding whether or not to participate in government programs or to supplement or substitute for government programs by purchasing services provided through the private sector. We now proceed to examine the process from both economic and political perspectives.

DECISION MAKING IN THE MARKETPLACE

Any society has to make certain fundamental economic decisions:

> What shall be produced?
> How shall it be produced?
> For whom shall it be produced? (Samuelson, 1980, p. 16)

In a capitalistic economy, the preference is to make such decisions through unrestrained or self-regulating markets. Figure 1.1 illustrates the circular flow of a monetary economy between two sets of actors, households and producers. It is assumed that households own all resources, whereas producers have the capacity of converting resources into finished goods and services. Resources are traditionally grouped into three categories called *factors of production:* land, labor, and capital. *Land* refers not only to the dry surface area of the earth but also to its vegetation, wildlife, and mineral content. *Labor* represents the human resource that goes into production. Originally, economic analysts defined labor in quantitative terms as the number of workers and the time they worked. With the advent of human capital theory (T. W. Schultz, 1963), the quality of labor has been considered an important economic characteristic of labor also. Formal education is, of course, an important means of improving the quality of the work force. *Capital* refers to the produced means of production such as machinery, factory buildings, and computers. Households may own land and capital outright or as shareholders in a corporation, and they also control the availability of their individual labor.

The households and the producers each have something the other wants and needs. Producers need the resources controlled by households in order to produce finished goods and services. Households need the goods and services provided by the producers for survival in the case of food and shelter and for improved quality of life in the case of many other goods. To facilitate the exchange, markets provide a means of communication. Producers acquire the resources they need through resource markets by making money income available to households in the form of wages, rents, interest, and profits. Households in turn use the money acquired through the sale of resources to purchase finished goods and services in product markets. It is these sales which provide producers with money to purchase resources from the households. And so the cycle continues.

Through markets, households and producers negotiate prices to be paid for resources and finished goods and services. The outcomes of these negotiations ultimately determine the answers to the three economic questions raised above. Resources are scarce and unevenly distributed among households, whereas household wants are unlimited. This

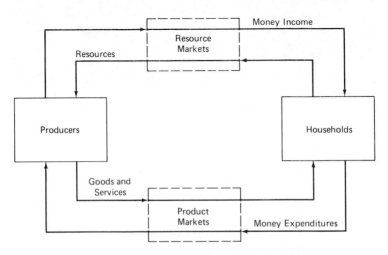

Figure 1.1. The Circular Flow of Resources in a Monetary Economy

means that each household must prioritize its wants and satisfy as many of them as possible within the constraints of the resources it controls and their value. The value or price of resources depends upon supply and demand. As illustrated in Figure 1.2, if the demand for labor among producers (Q_3), for example, exceeds the available supply (Q_1), the wage (P_1) producers are willing to pay increases to P_2. The higher wages entice more and more persons to make their labor available to producers (moving from Q_1 to Q_2). At the same time, higher costs dissuade some producers from employing as much labor; for example, they may invest instead in more efficient technology. The process leads to equilibrium, the point where supply matches demand.

Producers will produce only that on which they can make a reasonable profit. Profit depends on the amount of a good or a service that is sold, the price, and the cost of production. If the demand for a product is not sufficient to sell all units produced at a price above the cost of production, no profit can be made. Under such circumstances, the producer has three options: reduce the cost of production by adopting more efficient means of production, shift production to another product which can be sold for a profit, or go out of business. When conditions permit an above-average profit for producing a given good, more producers are attracted into the field. The number of units produced increases to the point where supply equals demand. Competition forces prices down, returning the rate of profit to a normal range.

Each dollar controlled by each consuming household is a potential vote to be cast in favor of the production of one good or service over another or the product of one producer over the product of a competitor. The influence of a household over producers is directly proportional to the value of the resources controlled by the household. This poses ethical dilemmas about the distribution of wealth. The rich make expenditures for improving the quality of life, whereas the poor lack basic necessities. Or new manufacturing technologies may be so efficient as to reduce the demand for labor, causing a reduction in wages and/ or widespread unemployment.

We do not rely solely on market mechanisms to make economic decisions, however.

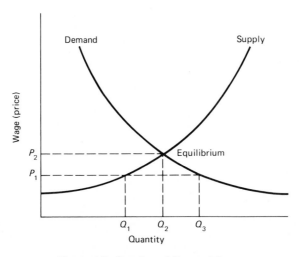

Figure 1.2. Supply and Demand Curves

Approximately one-third of our gross national product (GNP) is distributed according to political decisions made by governments, for example, municipalities and school districts. Important differences distinguish governmental units from households and producers in the ways they answer economic questions and the criteria they use. Downs (1957, p. 282) identifies government as that agency in the division of labor which has as its proper function the maximization of social welfare. When results generated by free markets are ethically or economically unsatisfactory, government can be used as a tool of intervention to set things right (p. 292). Governments have the unique power to extract involuntary payments, called taxes, from households and producers alike, and the federal government controls the money supply upon which both public and private sectors depend. Governmental programs and agencies are not profit-oriented and they rarely "go out of business." When they do go out of business, it is the result of political decisions and not of market forces, although conditions in the market may influence the political decision. Efficiency has not traditionally been an overriding objective of the public sector.

Figure 1.3 inserts government (the public sector) into the center of the circular flow of a monetary economy. As noted, government obtains money for its operations through taxes on producers and households. With this money, government acquires resources through resource markets and goods and services through product markets. There are no separate markets for the private and public sectors; government demands are factored into the resource and product markets in establishing prices. Thus, there is not a unique market for school personnel, for example; school districts compete with businesses, professions, and other governmental units for desired human services.

Governments produce some goods and services which are desired by households and producers. These include public schooling, national defense, fire and police protection, airports, harbor facilities, and roads. Governments also redistribute wealth through transfer payments and subsidies. These include social security and welfare payments, unemployment insurance, and subsidies to farmers and businesses.

Public sector decisions are political, and ideally, political power is distributed evenly among the electorate, that is, one person, one vote. In the private sector, influence is

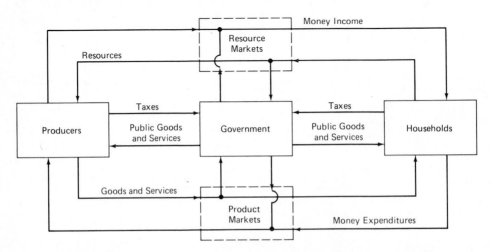

Figure 1.3. The Circular Flow of Resources, including Government (the public sector)

distributed in proportion to the amount of resources controlled; that is, the rich have much influence and the poor have little. Because of the difference in the distribution of influence over decisions made in the public and private sectors, there are marked differences between the sectors in the answers given to the three economic questions. The greater relative power of the poor in the public sector when compared with the private sector leads to an equalitarian bias in decisions made in the public sector. The private sector has a libertarian bias to permit the exercise of individual preferences.

Thus, in making decisions about education, natural tensions exist among households, members of the teaching profession, and society. To the extent that decisions are made in the private sector, individuals and families can maximize their personal aspirations within the limits of their economic resources and according to individual value preferences. Professionals are free to provide or to withhold services and to determine their nature. But when decisions are made through the political process, individuals and groups of varying value orientations must negotiate a single solution, and their value preferences may be compromised in the process.

POLITICAL DECISION MAKING

There are a number of ways of looking at the public policy-making process. Among the most useful for understanding policy relating to school finance are

    systems theory
    institutionalism
    incrementalism
    group theory
    elite theory
    rationalism

These theories and models are complementary to one another. Each emphasizes a particular aspect of the policy-making process. Taken together, they provide a rather complete picture of the total process.

The most comprehensive of the models is systems theory. A system is made up of a number of elements which are interrelated. An open system, which is characteristic of political systems, draws resources from its environment, processes them in some fashion, and returns the processed resources to the environment. All systems tend toward entropy or disorganization, and they must consciously combat this tendency in order to maintain equilibrium. A key function for combating entropy is feedback, that is, continual monitoring of a system's internal operations and its relationship with its environment. Accurate feedback is particularly critical to a system's health in that the system depends upon the environment for resources without which the system would shrink or die. Equilibrium is maintained by modifying or adapting system structures and processes based on analyses of feedback. Maintaining equilibrium is a dynamic process leading to growth and evolution of the system in harmony with its environment.

Easton (1965b) adapted general systems theory to political systems. His model, illustrated in Figure 1.4, conceptualizes public policy as a response of a political system

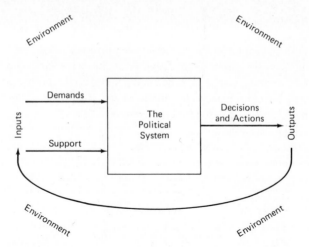

Figure 1.4. A Simplified Model of a Political System. (*Source:* D. Easton. [1965]. *A Systems Analysis of Political Life.* Chicago: University of Chicago Press, p. 32. Copyright 1965 by University of Chicago Press. Reprinted by permission.)

to forces from the environment. Environmental pressures or inputs come in the forms of (1) demands for public action and (2) support of government by obeying laws, paying taxes, and accepting outcomes of elections. The inputs are processed through the political system and transformed into policy outputs. Political systems consist of sets of identifiable and interrelated institutions and activities. With respect to school finance, these would include everything from the local school board and teachers' union or association through the Congress and the Supreme Court. Feedback in a political system is both formal and informal. Formal feedback is provided through elections, referenda, hearings, and policy analysis. Informal feedback occurs through interactions with constituents and others.

Institutionalism focuses on the structure of the policy-making process (Elazar, 1972; Grodzins, 1966; Walker, 1981). Unlike most of the rest of the world, where education is a function of the national government, educational governance in the United States is characterized by its decentralized nature. State governments hold the responsibility for education, and they in turn delegate significant amounts of authority to local school districts—usually including the authority to levy taxes. On the positive side, this arrangement has produced educational systems that are quite diverse, dynamic, and responsive to local conditions. On the negative side, decentralization has resulted in gross financial and curricular inequities. Some districts spend several times as much per pupil as do other districts. Some districts operate schools which are unequaled in quality throughout the world, whereas others operate schools which are an embarrassment to the profession and to the nation. Decentralized school governance impeded state and federal efforts during the 1960s, 1970s, and 1980s to equalize educational opportunities in finance; curriculum; and the integration of students and staff with respect to race, ethnicity, and national origin.

The change in the structure of educational governance over the years is reflected in the revenue statistics reported in Table 1.1. During the early part of the twentieth century, state governments on average paid less than 20 percent of the cost of elementary and secondary education; the rest was provided by school districts and/or local governments.

TABLE 1.1. Revenue Sources for Public Elementary
and Secondary Schools

Year	Total Revenues* (in thousands)	Sources		
		Local	State	Federal
		(percentage of total)		
1920	$ 970,121	83.2	16.5	0.3
1930	2,088,557	82.7	16.9	0.4
1940	2,260,527	68.0	30.3	1.8
1950	5,437,044	57.3	39.8	2.9
1960	14,746,618	56.5	39.1	4.4
1970	40,266,923	52.1	39.9	8.0
1980	96,881,165	43.4	46.8	9.8
1987[†]	160,908,262	43.8	50.0	6.2

*In current dollars.
†Preliminary data. (*Source:* National Center for Education Statistics.
[1988]. *The Condition of Education* [Vol. 1]. Washington, DC: U.S.
Government Printing Office, p. 94.)

The state share has been growing steadily since then. In 1986 total aggregate state aid of the 50 states exceeded 50 percent of school revenues for the first time; school districts provided 44 percent. Federal participation grew from virtually nothing at the beginning of the century to nearly 10 percent in 1980. Federal aid has since declined to 6 percent of all revenues for public schools (National Center for Education Statistics, 1988, p. 34). Although most financial support for schools is now provided by state governments, schools are still operated by local school districts. But grants-in-aid are a significant source of state and federal influence over local school policies.

The growing participation by state and federal governments in the financing of schools parallels their growing interest in and influence over educational policy. State governments have become particularly active in the prescription of basic curricula, monitoring student progress through mandatory testing programs and the certification of teachers (Darling-Hammond & Barry, 1988; Elmore & McLaughlin, 1988). State education departments and the U.S. Education Department have increased in size and influence (Moore, Goertz, & Hartle, 1983; Murphy, 1982). Less discretion has been left to school districts.

Other structural changes in political institutions are taking place which will affect the decision-making process and the ultimate nature of decisions made. Small districts have consolidated and large districts have decentralized. Progress is being made toward the professionalization of teaching, school site decision making, and parental choice of schools. Adoption of policies such as educational vouchers and tax credits would further change the face of educational governance, increasing the role of private providers.

Lindblom (1959) first described the public policy process in the United States as a continuation of past government activities with only incremental modifications. He insightfully labeled the process as "muddling through." Although some deplore his exaltation of the process, most credit him with presenting "a well considered theory fully geared to the actual experience of practicing administrators" (Dror, 1964, p. 153). Lindblom (1968, p. 32) takes issue with the popular view that politics is a process of conflict resolution. He argues that "governments are instruments for vast tasks of social cooperation" and that "conflicts are largely those that spring from the opportunities for cooperation that have evolved once political life becomes orderly." Within this context, he describes the play of power as a process of cooperation among specialists. It is gamelike, normally proceeding according to implicitly accepted rules. "Policy analysis is incorporated as an instrument or weapon into the play of power, changing the character of analysis as a result" (p. 30).

The focus of the play of power is on means (policy), not ends (goals or objectives). This, according to Lindblom, is what permits the political system to work. Because of the overlap in value systems among interested groups and the uncertainty of the outcomes of any course of action, partisans across the value spectrum are able to come to agreement on means where agreement on ends would be impossible.

Since the agreement on goals is impossible in a pluralistic society, according to Lindblom (1968, p. 33), the type of analysis appropriate to the political process is termed "partisan analysis." It is analysis conducted by advocates of a relatively limited set of values and/or ends such as teacher associations, taxpayer groups, and patriotic organizations. Comprehensiveness is provided by the variety of partisans participating in the political process. The responsibility for promoting specific values thus lies in the hands of advocates of those values (pressure groups and lobbyists) and not in the hands of some "impartial" analyst.

The net result of this advocacy process is incremental rather than revolutionary changes in policy. In the light of our grand state of ignorance about the relationships between public policy and human behavior, Lindblom views incremental policy decisions as being well justified. Incrementalism permits the expansion of policies which prove successful while limiting the harm caused by unsuccessful policies. Incrementalism preserves the system while changing it.

Group theory and elite theory give further insight into how incremental progressions may develop. Truman (1951), a leading proponent of group theory, sees politics as the interaction among groups (as opposed to individuals) in the formulation of public policy. Individuals band together into formal or informal groups, similar to Lindblom's partisans, to confront government with their demands. The group is the vehicle through which individuals can influence government action. Even political parties are viewed as coalitions of interest groups. Elected and appointed officials are seen as being continually involved in bargaining and negotiating with relevant groups to work out compromises that balance interests.

Group theory, as portrayed by Dye (1987), is illustrated in Figure 1.5. Public policy at any time represents the equilibrium of the balance of power among groups. Because the power alignment is continually shifting (e.g., toward Group B as it gains influence), the equilibrium also shifts, leading to incremental changes in policy. Stability in the system is attributed to a number of factors. First, most members of the electorate are latent supporters of the political system and share in its inherent values. This latent group is generally inactive but can be aroused to defend the system against any group which attacks it. Second, there is a great deal of overlap in the membership of groups; a given individual is likely to be a member of several. This tends to have a dampening effect on any group taking an extreme position because although the group may be focused on a single issue, its membership is much more broadly oriented. The third factor promoting system stability results from group competition. No single group constitutes a majority in American

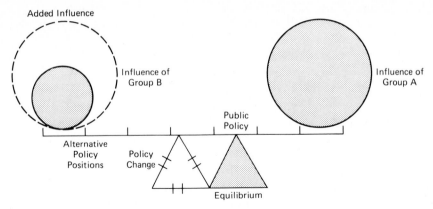

Figure 1.5. Group Theory Model. (*Source:* T. R. Dye. [© 1987]. *Understanding Public Policy* [6th ed.]. Englewood Cliffs, NJ: Prentice Hall, p. 27. Reprinted by permission of Prentice Hall, Inc., Englewood Cliffs, NJ.)

society. Coalitions are easily formed to counter the influence of any group appearing to gain undue influence.

Elite theory focuses on actions by a select group of influential elites. Elite theory (Dye & Zeigler, 1981) characterizes the general public as apathetic, ill informed, and uninterested about public policy—not unlike the characterization of the latent group in group theory. This leaves a power vacuum, which is happily filled by an elite. The elites do more to shape the opinion of the masses on public issues than the general public does to shape the opinions of the elite, although influence is reciprocal. According to this theory, policy is developed by the elites among the trappings of democratic government.

Elites tend to be drawn from upper socioeconomic levels. They are not necessarily against the general welfare of the masses but approach their welfare through a sense of *noblesse oblige*. Although not agreeing on all issues, the elite share a consensus on basic social values and on the importance of preserving the system. The masses give superficial support to this consensus, which provides a basis for elite rule. When events occur which threaten the system, elites move to take corrective action. According to elite theory, changes in public policy come about as the result of elites redefining their own positions, although this redefinition may be a function of external pressures. Because of elites' conservative posture with respect to preserving the system, policy changes tend to be incremental.

Adherents of rationalism seek to shape the policy-making process in such a fashion as to ensure the enactment of policies which maximize social gain. According to Dror (1968, p. 132), the assumptions of pure rationality are deeply rooted in modern civilization and culture and are the basis of certain economic theories of the free market and political theories of democracy. He characterizes the pure-rationality model as having six phases:

1. establishing a complete set of operational goals, with relative weights allocated to the different degrees to which each may be achieved;
2. establishing a complete inventory of other values and of resources, with relative weights;

3. preparing a complete set of alternative policies open to the policymaker;
4. preparing a complete set of valid predictions of the costs and benefits of each alternative, including the extent to which each will achieve the various operational goals, consume resources, and realize or impair other values;
5. calculating the net expectation of each alternative by multiplying the probability of each benefit and cost for each alternative by the utility of each, and calculating the net benefit (or cost) in utility units;
6. comparing the net expectations and identifying the alternative (or alternatives, if two or more are equally good) with the highest net expectation (p. 132).

These phases are organized sequentially in Figure 1.6.

In theory, rationalism involves all individual, social, political, and economic values, not just those that can be converted to dollars and cents. In reality, the measurement difficulties make inclusion of other than economic values unlikely. Thus this model elevates economic efficiency above other potential societal objectives.

To select a policy "rationally," policymakers, ideally, should know all of society's value preferences and relative weights and all available policy alternatives and the consequences of each. To "know" all this would require what Lindblom (1959, p. 88) terms "superhuman comprehensiveness." In essence, rationalism attempts the impossible by quantifying all elements of the political process and human behavior and expressing the decision-making function in mathematical terms. Although imperfect, the representative legislature (e.g., school boards) is a social mechanism for knowing "all of society's value preferences and relative weights."

Rational techniques that are based on economic principles and procedures should be an important factor in budget development. However, Cibulka (1987) acknowledges that budgetary decisions are not actually made on the basis of rationality. Wildavsky (1964) also argues that pure rationality is an illusion. He emphasizes the political nature of the budgetary process:

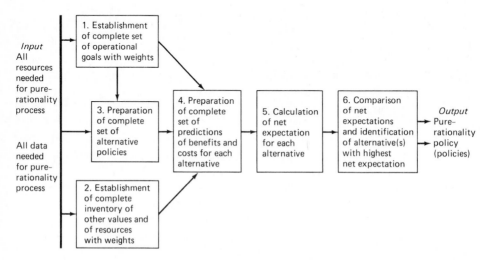

Figure 1.6. The Phases of Pure-Rationality Policy-Making. (*Source:* Y. Dror. [1968]. *Public Policymaking Reexamined.* San Francisco: Chandler, p. 134.)

> If one looks at politics as a process by which the government mobilizes resources to meet pressing problems, then the budget is the focus of these efforts. . . . In the most integral sense, the budget lies at the heart of the political process. (pp. 4–5)

Political realists argue that decisions in the public sector, including public education, are made on the basis of political rationality rather than economic rationality. To them, "rationalism" is at best irrelevant and can be downright dysfunctional to the political process (C. L. Schultz, 1968).

Nevertheless, rationalistic philosophy has had an important impact on policy analysis and indirectly on policy decision making. Its bias of economic efficiency is a value that is all too frequently neglected in the traditional political process. The spirit of rationalism has fostered such management devices as planning programming budgeting systems (PPBS), zero-based budgeting (ZBB), management by objectives (MBO), and operations research (OR) as well as cost-benefit and cost-effectiveness analysis. The terms "accountability" and "assessment" are now a part of the schooling vernacular, and teacher, pupil, and program evaluations are accepted procedures. Local school boards and state and federal governments are adding to their long-standing concerns over the quantity and quality of school inputs a similar concern over school outputs through mandatory evaluation and testing programs.

Although tools of systematic analysis have had some effect on the educational decision-making process, rationalistic approaches have fallen short of the expectations of their supporters and have met with strong opposition from some segments of the traditional educational decision-making process. A major source of resistance to the use of analysis in schools is the teaching profession. In addition to their vested interest, teachers are acutely aware of the almost impossible task of quantitatively measuring the complex variables associated with educational inputs and outputs and with the learning process itself.

The most ardent supporters of systematic analysis are economic purists who unbendingly seek economic efficiency in the public sector. Within the private sector powerful mechanisms exist to weed out inefficiencies. Indeed, one of the roles of government is to police the marketplace, keeping in check those forces which would impede the functioning of these mechanisms. Few, if any, similar mechanisms function in the public sector, making efficiency advocates very uncomfortable with the allocation process. When government was small, inefficiency could be tolerated; however, with one-third of the national economy being allocated through the political process of the public sector, 4 percent by school districts alone, inefficient use of resources can be extremely harmful to the general welfare.

WHEN SHOULD GOVERNMENTS INTERVENE?

To this point, we have sketched the functioning of the economic and political systems separately and have indicated likely differences in decisions made in the two sectors. Each sector is capable of answering the three allocation questions posed; but we, as individuals and as a society, would probably be quite unhappy with the results if all decisions were made through one sector. Given the general preference of a capitalistic society for the private sector, we would like now to address the issues of when governments should intervene and how they should intervene.

Eckstein (1967) has identified four situations where market mechanisms fail and where government intervention is necessary:

collective goods
divergence between private and social costs or benefits
extraordinary risks
natural monopolies

The case of collective or "public" goods has already been discussed, along with markets and the circular flow of resources in a monetary economy. Education was described as both a private and a public good, justifying governmental involvement in its provision. Other examples of collective goods are national defense and flood control.

The market works well when the prices charged reflect the total costs involved in producing goods or services. There are instances, however, when a producer can escape paying the full cost of production, with the consumer benefiting in terms of lower prices, or when a producer cannot charge the full value of that which is produced. These are known as external economies or diseconomies. When external economies occur, the good or service is not fully provided by the private sector; education is a case in point. There are few profit incentives to provide for education in the private sector.

External economies are illustrated by paper manufacturing. Until environmental protection legislation, paper manufacturers dumped highly toxic waste generated by the manufacturing process into neighboring rivers and streams, killing wildlife and fouling the air. Requiring the detoxification of waste prior to returning it to the environment increased the cost of production and raised the cost of paper to the consumer. Before protective legislation, manufacturers were able to escape paying a portion of the costs of production. The price was paid by those living in the environs of the paper mill in the form of low quality of life and low property values because of the pollution.

Similarly, when pupils drop out or are forced out of school, there is a high probability that they will become wards of society in one form or another. They are much less likely to be regularly employed than are persons completing their schooling and are more likely to receive governmental assistance in the form of unemployment insurance, welfare, and Medicaid. School dropouts are also more likely to turn to lives of crime and be incarcerated in penal institutions. The resources saved by society by not fully educating such persons may be lost many times over in providing social services to them later in life.

Until intervention by the federal government, many persons with severe mental and physical handicaps were denied access to schooling because of the high cost of special education. This meant that they were institutionalized their entire lives. Now, having access to schooling, many are able to work and live independently or with minimal supervision. The increased expenditures for education are paying dividends in terms of lower costs for social services and a better quality of life for persons with handicaps.

Extraordinary risks refers to situations where the probable payoff on investment is low. The development of atomic energy, space exploration, and cancer research are examples. Investments in research on learning and curriculum may also fall into this category.

A natural monopoly is an enterprise enjoying a continually falling cost curve. In other words, the cost to produce a unit becomes less and less as the number of units produced or served increases. Thus, because of economies of scale, the largest firm has a distinct competitive advantage, eventually driving smaller firms out of business. Electricity, gas, and water utilities are examples. The technology governing most businesses and industries is such that economies of scale are realized only up to a point, where diseconomies of scale set in; that is, the cost per unit increases as the number of units produced or serviced increases. This produces a U-shaped cost curve, nullifying any advantage of large firms over small ones and preserving competition. Although economies of scale are realized quite quickly in elementary and secondary schools (as is discussed in Chapter 13), schooling has been organized as a near public monopoly for noneconomic reasons.

Governmental intervention also takes place for other reasons. The federal government has assumed a responsibility for controlling business cycles and inflation, and to a limited extent, the redistribution of wealth. All governments use the power of eminent domain, by which they can force the sale of private property for public use. There are also just plain convenience and low cost, although most of these situations fall under natural monopolies.

HOW SHOULD GOVERNMENT INTERVENE?

Once the decision for intervention is made, there are numerous ways to do so. Public schools are owned and operated by government. So are police and fire departments and the U.S. armed forces. Ownership is not the typical type of governmental intervention, however. Governments may also oversee the public interest through regulation and licensure, taxation, subsidies, transfer payments, and contracts.

Most communication systems, utilities, and intercity transportation enterprises in the United States are privately owned, yet they are carefully monitored and regulated. Restaurants are regularly inspected for health code violations. Professionals are licensed by governments although most professionals, an important exception being teachers, work in the private sector.

Governments can attempt to influence human behavior by changing the price paid for specific items through subsidies or taxation. Consumption of cigarettes, alcoholic beverages, and gasoline is discouraged through excise taxes, increasing the cost to consumers with the intent of reducing demand. On the other hand, the government may pay subsidies to farmers to encourage them to increase production or to businesses to enable them to remain in operation in the face of foreign competition. Similarly, subsidies and scholarships that reduce the cost of higher education encourage families and individuals to pursue education beyond high school.

Governments also contract for services from private companies. Federal, state, and local governments rely on contractors to build their buildings, highways, and parks. Although the federal government coordinates space exploration, private vendors under contract conduct research and development and manufacture space vehicles. During periods of rapid increases in enrollment, school districts may rent space from private vendors. Contracting for transportation, cleaning, and cafeteria services is a common practice among school districts.

Many governmental responsibilities are met through transfer payments to individuals. Social Security, Aid for Dependent Children, unemployment insurance, food stamps, and educational vouchers are examples. Through transfer payments, the government can equalize the distribution of resources while permitting the individual maximum discretion as to how the funds are used. For example, prior to Social Security, elderly indigents were institutionalized in facilities owned and operated by local government. Now, with monthly payments from the Social Security system, recipients have many options, such as living in their own homes, smaller apartments, retirement communities in the sun belt, residences for the elderly, nursing homes, and living with relatives. The public policy of providing all citizens with at least a subsistence living standard is realized without prescribing their life styles.

THE ECONOMICS AND POLITICS OF EDUCATION

Since the publication of Adam Smith's (1976) *Wealth of Nations* in 1776, economists have recognized the linkages between education and economic growth and development. It was not until after World War II, however, that some economists, concerned with the growing gap between predicted and actual growth of national economies, turned their attention to studying these linkages intensely. Human capital theory emerged and was successful in explaining a substantial portion of the unexplained gap (Becker, 1964; Denison, 1962; T. W. Schultz, 1963). Human capital theory treated education as investment rather than as consumption, as had prior economic analyses. (Chapter 13 develops the issues involved more thoroughly.) About the same time, another group of economists applied their talents to broad educational issues, and the economics of education emerged as a subspecialization. Included in this group are Charles Benson (1961), Mark Blaug (1970), Elchanan Cohn (1979), Henry Levin (1987), and John Vaizey (1962).

The 1960s also saw the tools of political scientists being applied to develop a better understanding of school governance and the adoption and implementation of educational policy (Burlingame, 1988; Kimbrough, 1964; Wirt & Kirst, 1982). The development of a subspecialization known as the politics of education resulted. More recently, this subspecialization has shifted its primary focus onto what has come to be known as policy analysis. Mitchell (1988) distinguishes between the two thrusts: "Where political research focuses on who wins and who loses in the effort to control the schools, policy research draws attention to the extent to which particular actions reliably produce specific results."

Policy analysis has been strongly influenced by the political science theory of rationalism and the economic paradigm of cost-benefit analysis. The early optimism that policy analysis would bring about radical change has shifted to more realistic expectations of incremental change; policy analysis is currently considered more an art or craft than a science. Analysis has become highly concerned with context and implementation as well as potential impact (Wildavsky, 1965). Boyd (1988) sees policy analysis as having the potential "(a) to bridge the perennial gap between theory and practice and (b) to link organizational and administrative processes to organizational outcomes, countering the troublesome tendency toward goal displacement in educational organizations" (p. 518).

In analyzing social policies, it is necessary to apply the tools and concepts of several social sciences. In this book, we emphasize economics and politics in discussing school finance policy.

SUMMARY

We have shown that elementary and secondary schools consume a significant amount of the nation's resources and that these resources bring benefits to individuals and to society collectively. Resources are derived from both the public and private sectors, and educational services are produced by both sectors. The decision-making processes of markets and of governments were described. Criteria for governmental intervention in resource allocation decisions were presented and means of governmental intervention were discussed. In the next chapter, the allocation of resources to education is considered from five value perspectives: liberty, equality, fraternity, efficiency, and economic growth.

ACTIVITIES

1. Education as a public and private good:
   a. List separately the public and private benefits of education.
   b. Are any public benefits derived from private schools? If so, (1) What are they? (2) Can public financing of private schools be justified to the extent of the value of those public benefits?
2. Fundamental economic decisions about education:
   a. How are the fundamental economic decisions listed on page 5 made with respect to education?
   b. How might schools be organized to serve more efficiently:
      • students with no severe impediments to learning?
      • children with handicapping conditions?
      • gifted children?
      • adults?
      • preschool children?
3. Governmental intervention:
   a. Do conditions anticipated for the twenty-first century justify the continuation of today's near public monopoly in the provision of elementary and secondary education? List separately the arguments supporting affirmative and negative responses to the question.
   b. What alternative structures have been proposed for organizing elementary and secondary education in the future? Which, if any, do you consider the most viable? Why?
4. Political decision making:
   a. Interview your superintendent of schools and/or members of your board of education about how educational policy is developed in your school district.
   b. On the basis of information gathered from these interview(s), describe situations which illustrate each of the policy-making models listed on page 9.

5. Extraordinary risks:
  a. What is the professional knowledge base of education?
  b. Does research on learning and curriculum development represent an activity in which the probable payoff of private investment is so low as to justify governmental involvement? List the arguments in support of your response.
  c. Ideally, how should research on learning and curriculum development be organized and financed?

REFERENCES

Becker, G. S. (1964) *Human capital: A theoretical and empirical analysis, with special reference to education.* New York: National Bureau of Economic Research.

Benson, C. S. (1961). *The economics of public education.* Boston: Houghton Mifflin.

Blaug, M. (1970). *An introduction to the economics of education.* Middlesex, England: Penguin Books, Harmondsworth.

Boyd, W. L. (1988). Policy analysis, educational policy, and management: Through a glass darkly? In N. J. Boyan (Ed.), *Handbook of research on educational administration* (pp. 501–522). White Plains, NY: Longman.

Burlingame, M. (1988). The politics of education and educational policy: The local level. In N. J. Boyan (Ed.), *Handbook of research on educational administration* (pp. 439–451). White Plains, NY: Longman.

Cibulka, J. G. (1987). Theories of education budgeting: Lessons from the management of decline. *Educational Administration Quarterly, 23,* 7–40.

Cohn, E. (1979). *The economics of education:* (Rev. ed.). Cambridge, MA: Ballinger.

Darling-Hammond, L., & Barry, B. (1988). *The evolution of teacher policy* (Report No. JRE-01). Santa Monica, CA: Rand Corporation.

Denison, E. F. (1962). *The sources of economic growth in the United States.* New York: Committee for Economic Development.

Downs, A. (1957). *An economic theory of democracy.* New York: Harper & Row.

Dror, Y. (1964). Muddling through—"science" or inertia? *Public Administration Review, 24,* 153–157.

Dror, Y. (1968). *Public policymaking reexamined.* San Francisco: Chandler.

Dye, T. R. (1987). *Understanding public policy* (6th ed.). Englewood Cliffs, NJ: Prentice Hall.

Dye, T. R., & Zeigler, H. (1981). *The irony of democracy.* Monterey, CA: Brooks/Cole.

Easton, D. A. (1965a). *A framework for political analysis.* Englewood Cliffs, NJ: Prentice Hall.

Easton, D. A. (1965b). *A systems analysis of political life.* Chicago: University of Chicago Press.

Eckstein, O. (1967). *Public finance* (2nd ed.). Englewood Cliffs, NJ: Prentice Hall.

Elazar, D. J. (1972). *American federalism.* New York: Harper & Row.

Elmore, R. F., & McLaughlin, M. W. (1988). *Steady work: Policy, practice, and the reform of American education* (Report No. R-3574-NIE/RC). Santa Monica, CA: Rand Corporation.

Grodzins, M. (1966). *The American system.* Skokie, IL: Rand McNally.

Kimbrough, R. B. (1964). *Political power and educational decision-making.* Skokie, IL: Rand McNally.

Levin, H. M. (1987). Education as a public and private good. *Journal of Policy Analysis and Management, 6,* 628–641.

Lindblom, C. E. (1959). The science of muddling through. *Public Administration Review, 19,* 79–88.

Lindblom, C. E. (1968). *The policy-making process.* Englewood Cliffs, NJ: Prentice Hall.

Mitchell, D. E. (1988). Educational politics and policy: The state level. In N. J. Boyan (Ed.), *Handbook of research on educational administration* (pp. 453–466). White Plains, NY: Longman.

Moore, M. K., Goertz, M., & Hartle, T. (1983). Interaction of federal and state programs. *Education and Urban Society, 4,* 452–478.

Murphy, J. (1982). The paradox of state government reform. In A. Lieberman & M. McLaughlin (Eds.), *Educational policy-making.* The 81st Yearbook of the National Society for the Study of Education. Chicago: University of Chicago Press.

National Center for Education Statistics. (1988). *The condition of education* (Vol. 1). Washington, DC: U.S. Government Printing Office.

National Center for Education Statistics. (1989). *Targeted forecast* (No. CS 89-639). Washington, DC: U.S. Department of Education.

National Commission on Excellence in Education. (1983). *A nation at risk: The imperative of educational reform.* Washington, DC: U.S. Government Printing Office.

Samuelson, P. A. (1980). *Economics* (11th ed.). New York: McGraw-Hill.

Schultz, C. L. (1968). *The politics and economics of public spending.* Washington, DC: The Brookings Institution.

Schultz, T. W. (1963). *The economic value of education.* New York: Columbia University Press.

Smith, A. (1976). *An inquiry into the nature and cause of the wealth of nations.* Chicago: University of Chicago Press.

Truman, D. B. (1951). *The governmental process.* New York: Knopf.

U.S. Department of Commerce, Bureau of the Census. (1988). *Statistical abstract of the United States, 1988.* Washington, DC: U.S. Government Printing Office.

Vaizey, J. (1962). *The economics of education.* New York: Free Press.

Walker, D. B. (1981). *Toward a functioning federalism.* Cambridge, MA: Winthrop Press.

Wildavsky, A. (1964). *The politics of the budgetary process.* Boston: Little, Brown.

Wildavsky, A. (1965). The once and future school of public policy. *The Public Interest, 79,* 25–41.

Wirt, F. M., & Kirst, M. W. (1982). *Schools in conflict: The politics of education.* Berkeley, CA: McCutchan.

CHAPTER 2

The Impact of Public
and Private Values
on Decisions about Education

In Chapter 1, we discussed processes by which decisions about education and its financing are made in the public and private sectors. That the consequences of those decisions have quite different effects on individuals, singly, and society, collectively, was noted. The chapter concluded with a discussion of when and how governments should become involved in social issues. Although general guides were provided for governmental interventions, determining the appropriate nature of specific interventions is a political process—one that yields different answers over time and circumstances.

This chapter presents a framework for conceptualizing the allocation of authority for making decisions about education among interested parties. The framework places a decision matrix in the midst of a network of social values or policy objectives consisting of liberty, equality, fraternity, economic growth, and efficiency. The conceptualization is useful in highlighting relationships between characteristics of governance structures and the nature of decisions made, in designing new educational governance structures, and in evaluating the relative effectiveness of alternative structures under differing value priorities. Historical events in the United States are discussed within the context of the model. The model is also used to examine the restructuring of school governance now taking place in England and Australia.

TENSIONS AMONG FIVE VALUES
AFFECTING SOCIAL POLICY

Five values or objects of policy that have been historically prominent in shaping Western societies and are also particularly relevant to making decisions about the provision and consumption of educational services are liberty, equality, fraternity, efficiency, and economic growth. Each has experienced ascendance and descendance in priority with changing social circumstances, but none has ever lost its relevance entirely. The current shift in priorities placed on these five values underlies much of the controversy surrounding education today.

Liberty, equality, and fraternity are ethical values derived from the doctrine of natural rights expressed as early as 1690 by John Locke (1956) in his *Second Treatise of Government*. These are intrinsic values associated with human nature and human rights, whereas efficiency and economic growth are practical or derived values that enhance the realization of the former. Efficiency and economic growth have become primary objectives of public policy only during the twentieth century.

Liberty is the right to act in the manner of one's own choosing, not subject to undue restriction or control. *Equality* refers to the state, ideal, or quality of being equal, as in the state of enjoying equal social, political, and economic rights. In modern times, within the sociopolitical context, operational definitions of equality also include factors of condition, placing emphasis on the *appropriateness* of treatment. As such, "equality" has taken on connotations of "equity," "the state, ideal, or quality of being just, impartial and fair" (W. Morris, 1969, p. 443). "Equality" and "equity" are used in terms of civil rights and not of personal characteristics and abilities.

Nyberg (1981) cautions that "freedom" (or liberty) derives its meaning at least in part from the times in which it is used. He points out that between 1787 and 1947, a transformation took place in the United States from "freedom as natural rights (rights *against* the government, rights of independence), to civil rights (rights to *participate* in civil government), to human freedoms (rights to the *help* of government in achieving protection from fear and want)" (pp. 97–98).

Parallel transformations took place in the meaning of equality. Initially, equality was viewed in terms of rights only and not of conditions; people were to be treated the same by law, custom, and tradition. When considered as such, equality was the instrument for guaranteeing liberty as originally defined. In recent times, the operational definitions of equality have expanded to include factors of condition also. It has become accepted that some persons are handicapped in enjoying liberty because of circumstances beyond their control such as minority status, gender, poverty, and physical and psychological impairments. Education has become a principal instrument of social policy for removing or reducing the liabilities of these conditions (e.g., compensatory education programs). With a broadened definition of equality, the value comes into direct conflict with the value of liberty as originally defined because the policies of remediation involve not only the disadvantaged person but also all others. Liberty requires an opportunity for expression through individual freedom (e.g., educational vouchers and family choice of schooling), whereas equality of condition requires some curbing of individual freedom (e.g., desegregation, mainstreaming, and expenditure caps).

Fraternity refers to a common bond that produces a sense of unity, community, and nationhood. Building a sense of national identity is today a primary mission of schools in developing countries. This was a mission of schooling in the United States as it broke away from its identity with England and emerged from its war of independence as thirteen independent states. The need for the schools to be a force for welding together the nation continued in the nineteenth and early twentieth centuries as immigrants poured into the country from all parts of the world. The school became an important instrument of the "melting-pot" strategists (Ravitch, 1985, Chap. 14; Tyack, 1974).

Like equality, fraternity (or community) imposes constraints upon liberty. Cremin (1976) notes an inescapable and obvious relationship between the concepts of education and community. Referring to Dewey's (1916) *Democracy and Education,* Cremin writes, "There must be ample room in a democratic society for a healthy individualism and a healthy pluralism, but that individualism and that pluralism must also partake of a continuing quest for community" (p. 72). Nyberg (1977, p. 217) characterizes the historical and social functions of a school as "a method by which individuals become communities, and through which these communities describe themselves."

Efficiency, the ratio of outputs to inputs, is of more recent concern in education. Efficiency is increased by increasing desired outcomes secured from available resources or by maintaining a given level of outcomes while using fewer resources. As institutions functioning largely in the public sector, schools do not face the stringent discipline for efficient operations (internal efficiency) imposed by the market on institutions operating in the private sector (Benson, 1978, p. 14; Guthrie, Garnes, & Pierce, 1988, pp. 30–33). By the very nature of capitalistic countries, those things of social necessity which would not be done well if left to the incentives of the private sector fall to government (Downs, 1957; Eckstein, 1979). Governments in such countries tend to deal with issues in which economic concerns are not overriding. Efficiency comes into play when all other things are equal—which they rarely are. In the educational lexicon, efficiency concerns are expressed in terms of "accountability" and "standards."

Increasing the aggregate national production of goods and services (*economic growth*) involves the development of skills needed in the work force to support the economy so that it will expand at a desired pace. This objective is also of relatively recent interest. When public education was developing in the nineteenth century, the general skill requirements of the work force were minimal, and where special skills were required, they were usually developed through apprenticeship-type programs in the private sector. As entry skills required by business, industry, and the professions became more sophisticated, the connection between economic growth and educational enterprises became apparent. Public schools increasingly took on vocational responsibilities. More recently, concerns over linkages between poor schooling and inadequate economic growth were expressed in a number of reform reports, including the National Commission on Excellence in Education (1983), cited in Chapter 1; the Committee for Economic Development (1985); and the Carnegie Forum on Education and the Economy (1986). Concern over economic growth will continue to gain in importance as a criterion for evaluating educational policy as international competition and the level of skills demanded in the labor market increase further.

Because of the conceptual inconsistencies among the five social values, it is not possible to emphasize all at the same time in public policy—or in individual lives—as desirable as each may be. Priorities must be established among them by individuals and by society. This is a dynamic process in that priorities of individuals change with circumstances, and when there has been a sufficient shift among individuals, shifts in public priorities follow (Ravitch, 1985, Chap. 5). Agreement upon priorities is not necessary for private or market sector decisions beyond the aggregation of the family. In the public sector, however, a singular decision is required, thereby involving negotiation and compromise among interested partisans and generating significant social stress in the process. The higher the level of aggregation, the more difficult agreement becomes because of the greater amount of heterogeneity introduced. Friedman (1962) analyzed the situation:

The widespread use of the market reduces the strain on the social fabric by rendering conformity unnecessary with respect to any activities it encompasses. The wider the range of activities covered by the market, the fewer are the issues on which explicit political decisions are required and hence on which it is necessary to achieve agreement. In turn, the fewer issues on which agreement is necessary, the greater the likelihood of getting agreement while maintaining a free society. (p. 24)

With respect to education, driven by a priority concern for equity, the trend during the 1960s and 1970s was toward centralizing decisions at the state and federal levels. In seeking higher educational standards, the first wave of reform in the early 1980s produced further centralization; the second wave, however, was directed toward greater decentralization. It appears that some decisions about education may best be made by central authorities, particularly those involving equity, but others are best left to those with professional expertise at the school level or to those having a personal stake in the happiness and welfare of a specific child, the family (Coleman & Hoffer, 1987; Coons & Sugarman, 1978; Cremin, 1976; McNeil, 1986; Wise, 1979, 1988). Determining the optimal allocation of authority in education is a complex and unending process. The next section presents a model designed to help analyze the complexity of that process.

THE MODEL

The allocation of authority for making decisions about education among interested parties appears to shape the nature of the decisions made and the effectiveness with which they are implemented. Determining a satisfactory pattern of allocation of authority is a continuing problem that changes along with priorities placed on fundamental social values. In studying the merits of alternative decision-making structures for education within the context of specific policy objectives, it is useful to examine the type of issues needing to be addressed according to the interests and expertise of the potential decision makers, that is, individuals (or families), the profession, and society (through governments). Figure 2.1 presents one way of portraying the decision-making process. It consists of a decision matrix surrounded by a network representing the three intrinsic values of liberty, equality, and fraternity and the two derived values of efficiency and economic growth.

The five types of educational policy issues included in the matrix are

1. setting goals and objectives for the educational enterprise;
2. allocating resources to and among educational services;
3. determining the means by which educational services are provided;
4. determining for whom educational services are provided;
5. determining the level of investment in population quality to promote economic growth.

These are elaborations of the three fundamental economic decisions presented in Chapter 1.

The potential concern of each set of decision makers extends to each of the issues, although the actual level of interest and expertise of a given set will vary from issue to

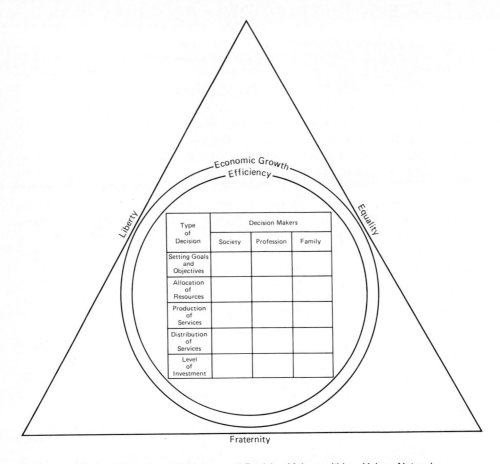

Figure 2.1. Matrix of Educational Decisions and Decision Makers within a Values Network

issue. Societal concerns are expressed by individuals and interest groups and moderated through the political process of government as described in Chapter 1. They become paramount over family and professional concerns for those issues in education where there is significant spillover of benefits (i.e., "collective" or "public" goods) and where there are redistributive considerations. The teaching profession holds the technical expertise of schooling and teachers are employees of the system. Parents are the guardians of the interests and needs of individual children. The family holds the most intimate knowledge about and caring concern for the child. It is through the family that the child's voice is heard (Bridge, 1976; Coons & Sugarman, 1978).

Within any given context, significantly different patterns of allocation of authority can be structured depending upon the relative priorities given to policy objectives (Kirst, 1988). Extreme centralization of authority is characterized by public officials making all decisions collectively and by administering them through public institutions. This approximates the current arrangement for schooling in the United States, tempered modestly by placing the locus of decision making at the state level (rather than federal), devolving some authority to school districts, and permitting unsubsidized private schools to function. This arrangement permits the family to make only one basic decision: whether to participate in "free" public schools or to opt for private schools and substantial tuition fees. If the decision is to go with public schools, there is a related family decision which can be made by those who can afford it, the purchase of a home or renting of an apartment in a school district of choice.

Centralization of authority has been motivated largely by the desire to promote equity and fraternity; but judging from the flood of national criticism during the 1980s, liberty, efficiency, and economic growth have suffered. To promote liberty and efficiency while retaining considerable control over equality and fraternity, some districts have moved toward open enrollment and magnet school policies (Raywid, 1985). Raising student academic standards and standards for entering the teaching profession; improving working conditions; providing differentiated career ladders, school-site decision making, and teacher empowerment have all been proposed in the interest of promoting greater efficiency—and through efficiency, economic growth.

Extreme decentralization of authority is characterized by having no public schools and no subsidies, leaving the production and distribution of educational services entirely to markets. This position may enhance some definitions of efficiency and liberty but has severely negative implications for equality, fraternity, and probably economic growth (because of the underinvestment in education which would result). In a modified configuration of decentralization, equity concerns can be accommodated by maintaining public financing through a regulated voucher system, leaving the production of services to the private and/or public sectors (Center for the Study of Public Policy, 1970; Wise & Darling-Hammond, 1984). With full public financing, fraternity concerns could be met with public regulation of student intake in order to ensure an appropriate mix of ethnic groups. Economic growth concerns can be attended to in part by determining the level of public financing. To meet societal concerns fully, some curricular regulations would be needed. These issues are developed more fully in Chapters 16 and 17.

McGinn and Street (1986) characterize centralization and decentralization as a dyad.

> Decentralization is not primarily an issue of control by government of individual citizens. Instead it is a question of the distribution of power among various groups in society. A highly participatory society—one in which all citizens actually do participate—is likely to require a competent and powerful state that actively and continuously seeks to redistribute power among groups and individuals in the society. The location of authority in local government does not protect the local citizen from tyranny, and the redistribution of power through the market mechanism in a society that currently is highly inequitable is a guarantee that inequities will persist and worsen. On the other hand, competition and markets can contribute to social justice in circumstances where there is a relatively equitable balance of powers among the participants in the competition or market. . . . A strong state must first achieve some minimal degree of social equity so that decentralization can lead to genuine participation. (pp. 489–490)

McGinn and Street's analysis is wholly compatible with Nyberg's (1981) concept of freedom. Whether authority over education is to be centralized or decentralized is not the issue. Centralization and decentralization of authority are means toward desired ends, not ends in themselves (Hanson, 1986).

DISCUSSION: THE UNITED STATES

At the origin of public education in the United States, control was largely decentralized and in the hands of families (using Figure 2.1 as a point of reference) through the town-meeting format. The teaching profession was weak, and the larger society, as represented by the state, was relatively inactive other than to provide enabling legislation. The principles of liberty, fraternity (among socioeconomic classes but not races), and equality of opportunity within the community were dominant. Efficiency and economic growth were not yet concerns of the schools.

With the growing sophistication of the teaching profession, especially its administrators, professional control and bureaucratization took over near the beginning of the twentieth century (Callahan, 1962)—a shift of authority to the left (i.e., from family to profession) in Figure 2.1. States became more involved by enacting compulsory attendance laws; setting certain basic standards, as for teacher certification; and providing some financing, including equalization aid, that is, the allocation of aid in inverse relation to local property wealth. The federal government entered the scene by providing aid for vocational education. Liberty was less a concern than before, efficiency came into play for the first time, equity was beginning to take on a statewide dimension, and linkages between education and economic growth were beginning to be noticed.

Following World War II, there was a rapid expansion of suburban school systems and a decline in the quality of services provided in urban centers. During the 1950s and through the 1970s, in an attempt to correct the inequities which resulted from a still highly decentralized system, society became deeply involved in decisions about the distribution of services through litigation in federal courts. These actions concerned civil rights and affirmative action (Levin, 1987). Court-ordered desegregation, hiring quotas, limits on disciplinary discretion of educators, and curricular change resulted. This litigation was followed by state and federal legislation, which had the effect of making specific court decisions universal and centralizing educational decision making.

In the 1960s and 1970s, society's influence was also enlarged with respect to the allocation of resources, again through litigation followed by legislation (Berne & Stiefel, 1983). States increased their participation in financing school operations, school buildings, and transportation. The federal role in school finance became a significant factor for the first time as categorically funded programs for disadvantaged, bilingual, and handicapped children. State education departments grew in size and influence. Concurrently, student achievement declined, and along with it, the credibility of the teaching profession. The principle of equity was a dominant concern and its definition came to include conditions as well as rights. Fraternity began to be defined in racial and ethnic rather than socioeconomic terms. Economic growth remained an important consideration (e.g., the War on Poverty), but liberty and efficiency suffered as the constraints placed on local school districts by state and federal governments grew. The dominant decision makers had become the state and federal governments (Guthrie, 1980; Ravitch, 1983), representing society in Figure 2.1.

The deterioration which had taken place in the educational system was nationally recognized with the publication of numerous reports on the state of education, beginning with the report of the National Commission on Excellence in Education (1983), *A Nation at Risk: The Imperative for Educational Reform*. The educational reform movement of the 1980s followed. To arrest the decline in standards, most states intervened with mandated curricula, competency examinations for both students and teachers, and stiffer requirements for teacher certification and student diplomas. This initial phase of the reform movement severely constrained what remained of the discretionary authority of educational officials at the school district level, creating in many communities a substantial mismatch between local aspirations for their schools and the reality of those schools. The locus of authority had clearly moved from the family and the profession to society.

But legislating higher standards did not necessarily produce higher standards (Iannaccone, 1985), and state governors, among others, were quick to notice. Governor Lamar Alexander of Tennessee, commenting on the National Governors' Association's report on education reform, *Time for Results* (Alexander & Kean, 1986), wrote,

> We're not ready to bargain away the minimum standards that some states are just now setting. But, we have learned that real excellence cannot be imposed from a distance. Governors don't create excellent schools; communities—local school leaders, teachers, parents, and citizens—do. (p. 203)

Alexander, who was chair of the association when its report was issued, described the bargaining he foresaw:

> The kind of horse trading we are talking about will dramatically change the way most schools work. First, the governors want to help establish clear goals and better report cards—ways to measure what students know and can do. Then we're ready to give up a lot of state regulatory control—even to fight for changes in the law to make that happen—if schools and school districts will be accountable for the results. These changes will require more rewards for successes and consequences for failure for teachers, school leaders, schools, and school districts. They will mean giving parents more choice in the public schools their children attend as one way of insuring higher quality without heavy-handed state control. (Alexander, 1986, p. 203)

Parental empowerment is recognized in Alexander's reference to giving parents the right to choose the public schools their children attend. Choice would shift some aspects of the decision process concerning the distribution of services (Figure 2.1) back to families. Choice is becoming a reality in Minnesota, Iowa, and Arkansas, and many other states are considering "choice" proposals (Snider, 1989c). President Bush has characterized the expansion of parents' rights to choose public schools as a "national imperative" (Snider, 1989b). Boston is moving toward school-based management and family choice (Snider, 1989a) and Chicago is operating under a school-based governance structure dominated by parents (Hess, 1990). Issues concerning family choice of schooling are the focus of Chapter 17.

Teachers also are gaining in authority. Many school districts have negotiated contracts with their teachers' unions which greatly enlarge teachers' roles in educational decision making. A privately funded board for setting national professional teaching standards has been established with a majority of its members being teachers. These issues are considered more fully in Chapter 14.

Governor Alexander's comments suggest that there is a willingness to return to the profession decisions over how educational services are to be provided. But he is perfectly clear that the governors (society) want to remain closely involved in the setting of goals and the monitoring of standards (Education Commission of the States, 1987). As we enter the 1990s, liberty and efficiency (excellence) are once again policy concerns (Iannaccone, 1988). There is a strong desire to retain equity and fraternity as guiding principles, but there is considerable doubt as to the probability of doing so in the presence of liberty and efficiency. Economic growth remains a priority concern, as even a cursory reading of *A Nation at Risk* or other reform documents would indicate (Carnegie Forum on Education and the Economy, 1986; Committee for Economic Development, 1985; National Commission on Excellence in Education, 1983).

AN INTERNATIONAL PERSPECTIVE

Most other nations are also in states of transition. Some are decentralizing centralized systems whereas others are centralizing decentralized systems. But even within nations, changes are not unidimensional—resulting in an intriguing patchwork of authority allocations among potentially interested educational decision makers. In this section, an overview of the educational governance transitions taking place in England and Australia are presented. Each is discussed within the context of the model in Figure 2.1.

England

England offers a particularly interesting case at the moment, one in which centralization and decentralization forces are at work simultaneously. England has long had one of the world's most decentralized educational systems. Its Department of Education and Science (1978) has described the system as a national system, locally administered. Financial constraints are set by the national government and Local Education Agencies (LEAs); but until the Education Reform Act (1988), most pedagogical decisions, including curriculum, were made at the school-building level, with the headmaster or mistress being the key decision maker. This led to markedly dissimilar educational programs even within the same LEA.

In the 1987 general election, all of the major political parties advocated a national curriculum for the schools. The victorious Thatcher government moved decisively in that direction by legislating the Education Reform Act of 1988. The act provides for a nationally mandated core curriculum and the preparation of study guides for each core subject to define minimum content and competencies. A national system of assessment is authorized to measure pupil performance in core subjects at ages 7, 11, 14, and 16.

Although the act expands the national government's authority over curriculum, it leaves to the schools complete discretion over the implementation of the curriculum and the determination of offerings beyond the core. In other areas, the scope of the schools' authority, through their boards of governors, is increased by granting the boards control over admissions, budget allocations, and appointment and dismissal of teaching and nonteaching staffs. Schools are funded by a direct appropriation from their LEAs based on the number of pupils enrolled. These funds can be dispersed by school-building authorities as they feel appropriate to implement their program philosophy, stripping LEAs of their former allocative powers. This funding scheme, coupled with parental choice of schooling, generates marketlike incentives for schools. Fewer pupils served means less money; more pupils served means more money. Under this arrangement, schools could become financially bankrupt as well as educationally bankrupt.

The LEAs have been the big losers in the power shuffle. They had previously been able to establish enrollment ceilings and control budget allocations. The final reduction of their former powers is the granting to schools with more than 300 registered pupils the authority to withdraw from the LEA to which they belong and to apply directly to the national government for financial maintenance grants.

In studying the implications of these proposed reforms, Thomas and Ranson (1988) observe,

> The Education Reform Bill is a centerpiece in the constituting of a new moral and political order of individual rights and private choice, where the public accountability of government is to the private individual as consumer not citizen. (p. 16)
>
> . . . The idea that general well-being of society is best served when private individuals are allowed to pursue their self-interest leads to a rejection of any kind of organic theory of the state which superimposes higher "values" on those individuals. . . . The model of humanity upon which rests the postulate of self-interest ignores the moral issues which necessarily arise from the context of people as social animals. As a result, the analysis fails to take account of the contribution of social decisions to efficiency and welfare. (p. 19)

Supporters of the new policy argue that the "higher values" of the state will be superimposed on individuals through the nationally mandated core curriculum and relative uniformity of financial support levels. Such a position views the act as a compromise, permitting the exercise of both social and individual interests (G. Morris, 1986).

In reference to Figure 2.1, society is strengthening its control over the setting of goals and objectives by mandating a core curriculum, over allocation of resources in terms of expenditure per pupil, and over production of services in terms of prescribing and monitoring the core curriculum. On the other hand, the family voice in decisions about the distribution of services (the selection of schools) is enhanced, indirectly strengthening its influence on all other decisions. The profession, although losing much discretion over curriculum, still maintains a strong influence over the implementation of the curriculum. In fact, the influence of professionals is strengthened by the shifting to the school level of decisions about the allocation of resources to the instructional process.

Australia

Similar tensions are being experienced by several Australian states and territories. Traditionally, Australian schools have been operated as highly centralized state systems (Butts, 1955; Hancock, Kirst, & Grossman, 1983; Partridge, 1968). There are no local education authorities, and teachers and administrators are selected, employed, and assigned by the respective state bureaucracies. The curriculum is also prescribed by the states.

In the 1960s, public funding was extended to private schools, primarily to save the Roman Catholic schools from collapse at a time when public schools were finding it difficult to accommodate their own burgeoning roles. The intent was equalitarian—to upgrade the quality of education in the underfinanced private sector (Hogan, 1984). For the most part, Roman Catholic parochial schools serve a nonelitist working-class constituency, whereas Protestant and independent schools cater to business and professional classes. Today, the publicly subsidized private schools are providing an alternative to the public schools. Overall, about a third of all school-aged children attend private schools. The proportion is over half at the upper secondary grades. Private schools, regardless of affiliation, now provide the standard of excellence (Boyd, 1987).

In essence, Australia has two publicly financed systems of education—one highly centralized, the other highly decentralized. Ironically, nongovernment schools (the decentralized system) have come to serve as models for the reform of government schools (the centralized system). Reformers charge that extreme centralization has resulted in government schools which are impersonal, uncaring, and institutional in character. They claim that teachers and principals in government schools identify with the Teaching Service (the state bureaus for employing teachers) rather than with the schools and communities to which they are assigned. Transfers are frequent and assignment is based on formula and longevity, not on local conditions or merit (Swanson, 1986).

In reference to Figure 2.1, state governments (society) make decisions for public schools concerning the setting of goals and objectives, allocation of resources, and production of services. For private schools, state governments strongly influence the amount spent per pupil (except for the elite private schools), but school trustees in consultation with their professional employees determine the way money is spent. Decisions about production of services are left largely to the discretion of school personnel within the constraints of the school's goals and objectives, which are set by the school's trustees and the school budget. The family has a choice of a public school (in some places, public schools) and of many private schools, most of which charge low tuition, making them affordable to most families.

Many governmental and educational leaders are working to reshape the incentives of public education in Australia by changing the governance structure. Progress in this direction is being made in Victoria (Chapman & Boyd, 1986; Frazer, Dunstan, & Creed, 1985; Harman, 1987; Victoria Ministry of Education, 1986), South Australia (Jones, 1970), Western Australia (Western Australia Ministry of Education, 1987), and Australian Capital Territory (ACT Schools Authority, 1986; Hughes & Mullford, 1978). The goal is to bring to the public schools those characteristics of private schools which are found appealing without jeopardizing the public interest. To do this, the reformers seek to move much of the authority currently vested in state ministries of education to the schools. They seek to vest in the schools power over the budget and personnel.

These reforms have been initiated by Labour governments in Australia in contrast to a Conservative government in England. Australian proposals go beyond the English proposals for devolution by also placing major responsibility for curriculum with the schools (Australian Capital Territory Schools Authority, 1985; Commonwealth Schools Commission, 1985). But not unexpectedly, the opposition is very strong in Australia, especially from the bureaucrats who do not wish to share their power and from teachers' unions, who find it strategically preferable to bargain with one agency rather than hundreds (Baron, 1981; Blackmore & Spaull, 1987).

JUXTAPOSITION

The issue of allocating authority to make decisions about education is not solely a matter of centralization or decentralization. Nor is it solely a matter of state power, teacher power, or people power. There are legitimate concerns about education at all levels of the sociopolitical hierarchy; the critical issue is achieving the best balance among legitimate interests. The best balance will vary from society to society and over time within a society as contexts, value definitions, and priorities change (Wirt, 1986). The model (Figure 2.1) provides a useful lens through which to observe and evaluate events within a society and across societies. In this section, the experiences of the United States, England, and Australia are discussed in juxtaposition according to the elements and relationships suggested by the model.

The United States developed a highly decentralized system of public schooling a century and a half ago to further the objectives of equality and fraternity in a sparsely populated agrarian society. As the nation grew in population and became more industrialized and urbanized, a relatively equitable rural system evolved into a highly inequitable and divisive urban system. Efforts to restore equality and fraternity through broader state and national policies brought oppressiveness, impersonality, and inefficiency; that is, the schools were "institutionalized" and "bureaucratized." The rising demands for high levels of human competence in the work force and the increasing competitiveness of international markets have raised concern over the ability of the American school system to educate the nation's youths to a level sufficient to enable them to meet the challenges.

In many respects, Australia and the United States are moving in opposite directions (Murphy, 1983); but having started at opposite ends of the spectrum, they are moving toward one another (Hughes, 1987). In the search for equality and efficiency, Australia developed a highly centralized system of public schooling. Also in the name of equality, Australia made extensive financial assistance available to private schools, most of which had been poorly financed. The unintended consequence of this policy enhanced aspects of liberty. Although the government and nonelite private schools now operate at about the same expenditure levels per pupil, the nongovernment schools are setting the standards of excellence (and efficiency). In seeking to bring efficiency to government schools, some states have moved to trim the central educational bureaucracies and to divest authority to the schools. To restore some of the social control over the equality lost in the public financing of private schools, there is a movement toward greater public regulation of private schools. Public schools are becoming more like private schools and private schools are becoming more like public schools.

The pattern in England is the clearest, perhaps because it is a single, though highly devolved, system. The reallocation of power is apparent. As McGinn and Street (1986) suggest, it is not government versus citizens but a redressing of the balance of power between government and citizens to improve efficiency and liberty. The pattern struck by the English Education Reform Act could well be a prototype of the educational structure toward which Australia and the United States are groping. The Committee for Economic Development (1985), for example, recommended that each state in the United States promulgate a core curriculum. Doyle (1988) predicted that the United States will back into a national curriculum.

SUMMARY

The model presented in this chapter highlights five objects of public policy particularly relevant to education: liberty, equality, fraternity, efficiency, and economic growth. Within these objects of policy, the model depicts the decision structure as a grid of decisions (who gets what, when, and how) and decision makers (society/government, the teaching profession, and the family).

The model shifts the focus of the governance debate from a simplistic discussion of the relative virtues of centralized and decentralized power placement to the identification of the optimal distribution of authority among interested parties in the provision and financing of educational services, given certain fundamental values and policy objectives. The model was applied briefly to the historical development of educational governance in the United States and to the current situations in England and Australia. Chapter 3 presents the structure of school governance and finance in the United States more fully.

ACTIVITIES

1. Examine the decision matrix in the center of Figure 2.1. Fill in each blank cell with the decisions which can best be made by each classification of decision maker for each decision type, for example, allocation of resource decisions which can best be made by society, by the teaching profession, by the family.
2. Numerous proposals have been put forth for reforming education. Discuss each proposal listed below in reference to Figure 2.1. For each, describe the change from the status quo in the allocation of decision-making authority and in the relative priorities of the five values.
   a. family choice of public schools
   b. unconstrained educational vouchers
   c. tax credits for private school tuition
   d. professional control over admission to the profession
   e. career ladders for teachers
   f. school-based decision making
   g. full state funding of schooling
   h. state achievement testing to determine successful completion of high school
3. McGinn and Street (cited on page 27) wrote,

> Competition and markets can contribute to social justice in circumstances where there is a relatively equitable balance of powers among the participants in the competition or market. . . . A strong state must first achieve some minimal degree of social equity so that decentralization can lead to genuine participation.

a. Describe policies which might be pursued by a strong state to "achieve some minimal degree of social equity so that decentralization can lead to genuine participation."

b. McGinn and Street used the term "state" in a generic sense. With respect to the United States, at what level can the "minimal degree of social equity" be guaranteed most effectively: federal, state, or local? What is the rationale for your answer?

REFERENCES

Alexander, L. (1986). Time for results: An overview. *Phi Delta Kappan, 68,* 202–204.

Alexander, L., & Kean, T. H. (1986). *Time for results: The governors' 1991 report on education.* Washington, DC: National Governors' Association, Center for Policy Research and Analysis.

Australian Capital Territory Schools Authority. (1985). *Choice of schools in the ACT: Parents have their say.* Canberra: Author.

Australian Capital Territory Schools Authority. (1986). *School boards: Partnership and participation.* Canberra: Author.

Baron, G. (1981). *The politics of school government.* Oxford, England: Pergamon Press.

Benson, C. E. (1978). *The economics of public education* (3rd ed.). Boston: Houghton Mifflin.

Berne, R., & Steifel, L. (1983). Changes in school finance equity: A national perspective. *Journal of Education Finance, 8,* 419–435.

Blackmore, J., & Spaull, A. (1987). Australian teacher unionism: New directions. In W. L. Boyd & D. Smart (Eds.), *Educational policy in Australia and America: Comparative perspectives* (pp. 195–232). New York: Falmer Press.

Boyd, W. L. (1987). Balancing public and private schools: The Australian experience and American implications. In W. L. Boyd & D. Smart (Eds.), *Educational policy in Australia and America: Comparative perspectives* (pp. 163–183). New York: Falmer Press.

Bridge, R. G. (1976). Parent participation in school innovations. *Teachers College Record, 77,* 366–384.

Butts, R. F. (1955). *Assumptions underlying Australian education.* Melbourne: Australian Council for Educational Research.

Callahan, R. E. (1962). *Education and the cult of efficiency: A study of the forces that have shaped the administration of the public schools.* Chicago: University of Chicago Press.

Carnegie Forum on Education and the Economy, Task Force on Teaching as a Profession. (1986). *A nation prepared: Teachers for the 21st century.* New York: Author.

Center for the Study of Public Policy. (1970). *Education vouchers: A report on financing elementary education by grants to parents.* Cambridge, MA: Author.

Chapman, J., & Boyd, W. L. (1986). Decentralization, devolution and the school principal: Australian lessons on statewide educational reform. *Educational Administration Quarterly, 22,* 4, 28–58.

Coleman, J. S., & Hoffer, T. (1987). *Public and private high schools: The impact of communities.* New York: Basic Books.

Committee for Economic Development. (1985). *Investing in our children: Business and the public schools.* New York: Author.

Commonwealth Schools Commission. (1985). *Choice and diversity in government schooling.* Canberra, Australia: Author.

Coons, J. E., & Sugarman, S. D. (1978). *Education by choice: The case for family control.* Berkeley: University of California Press.

Cremin, L. A. (1976). *Public education.* New York: Basic Books.

Department of Education and Science. (1978). *The Department of Education and Science—A brief guide.* London: Author.

Dewey, J. (1916). *Democracy and education.* New York: Macmillan.

Downs, A. (1957). *An economic theory of democracy.* New York: Harper & Row.

Doyle, D. P. (1988). The excellence movement, academic standards, a core curriculum and choice: How do they connect? In W. L. Boyd & C. T. Kerchner (Eds.), *The politics of excellence and choice in education* (pp. 13–23). New York: Falmer Press.

Eckstein, O. (1979). *Public finance* (4th ed.). Englewood Cliffs, NJ: Prentice Hall.

Education Commission of the States. (1987). *The next wave: A synopsis of recent educational reform reports.* Denver: Author.

The education reform act. (1988). London: Her Majesty's Stationery Office.

Frazer, M., Dunstan, J., & Creed, P. (Eds.). (1985). *Perspectives on organizational change: Lessons from education.* Melbourne, Australia: Longman Cheshire.

Friedman, M. (1962). *Capitalism and freedom.* Chicago: University of Chicago Press.

Guthrie, J. W. (Ed.). (1980). *School finance policies and practices: The 1980s, a decade of conflict.* Cambridge, MA: Ballinger.

Guthrie, J. W., Garms, W. I., & Pierce, L. C. (1988). *School finance and education policy: Enhancing educational efficiency, equality and choice.* Englewood Cliffs, NJ: Prentice Hall.

Hancock, G., Kirst, M. W., & Grossman, D. L. (Eds.). (1983). *Contemporary issues in educational policy: Perspectives from Australia and USA.* Canberra: Australian Capital Territory Schools Authority.

Hanson, E. M. (1986). *Educational reform and administrative development: The cases of Colombia and Venezuela.* Stanford, CA: Hoover Institution Press.

Harman, G. (1987). State-wide arrangements for organizing Australian education. In W. L. Boyd & D. Smart (Eds.), *Educational policy in Australia and America: Comparative perspectives* (pp. 283–294). New York: Falmer Press.

Hess, G. Alfred, Jr. (1990). *Chicago school reform: What it is and how it came to be.* Chicago: Chicago Panel on Public School Policy and Finance.

Hogan, M. (1984). *Public vs. private schools: Fundings and direction in Australia.* Ringwood, Victoria, Australia: Penguin Books.

Hughes, P. (1987). Reorganization in education in a climate of changing social expectations: A commentary. In W. L. Boyd & D. Smart (Eds.), *Educational policy in Australia and America: Comparative perspectives* (pp. 295–309). New York: Falmer Press.

Hughes, P., & Mullford, W. (Eds.). (1978). *The development of an independent education authority: Retrospect and prospect in the Australian Capital Territory.* Melbourne, Australia: Council for Educational Research.

Iannaccone, L. (1985). Excellence: An emergent educational issue. *Politics of Education Bulletin, 12,* 1, 3–8.

Iannaccone, L. (1988). From equity to excellence: Political context and dynamics. In W. L. Boyd & C. T. Kerchner (Eds.), *The politics of excellence and choice in education* (pp. 49–65). New York: Falmer Press.

Jones, A. W. (1970). *The freedom and authority memorandum.* Adelaide: Education Department of South Australia.

Kirst, M. W. (1988). Recent educational reform in the United States: Looking backward and forward. *Educational Administration Quarterly, 24,* 319–328.

Levin, B. (1987). The courts as educational policy-makers in the USA. In W. L. Boyd & D. Smart (Eds.), *Educational policy in Australia and America: Comparative perspectives* (pp. 100–128). New York: Falmer Press.

Locke, J. (1956). *The second treatise of government.* Oxford, England: Basil Blackwell.

McGinn, N., & Street, S. (1986). Educational decentralization: Weak state or strong state? *Comparative Education Review, 30,* 471–490.

McNeil, L. M. (1986). *Contradictions of control: School structure and school knowledge.* New York: Routledge, Chapman and Hall.

Morris, G. (1986). The county LEA. In S. Ransom & J. Tomlinson (Eds.), *The changing government of education.* London: Allen & Unwin.

Morris, W. (Ed.). (1969). *The American heritage dictionary of the English language.* New York: American Heritage.

Murphy, J. T. (1983). School administrators besieged: A look at Australian and American education. In G. Hancock, M. W. Kirst, & D. L. Grossman (Eds.), *Contemporary issues in educational policy: Perspectives from Australia and USA* (pp. 77–96). Canberra: Australian Capital Territory Schools Authority and Curriculum Development Centre.

National Commission on Excellence in Education. (1983). *A nation at risk: The imperative for educational reform.* Washington, DC: U.S. Government Printing Office.

Nyberg, D. (1977). Education as community expression. *Teachers College Record, 79,* 205–223.

Nyberg, D. (1981). *Power over power: What power means in ordinary life, how it is related to acting freely, and what it can contribute to a renovated ethics of education.* Ithaca, NY: Cornell University Press.

Partridge, P. H. (1968). *Society, schools and progress in Australia.* Oxford, England: Pergamon Press.

Ravitch, D. (1983). *The troubled crusade: American education 1945–1980.* New York: Basic Books.

Ravitch, D. (1985). *The schools we deserve: Reflections on the educational crises of our times.* New York: Basic Books.

Raywid, M. A. (1985). Family choice arrangements in public schools: A review of the literature. *Review of Educational Research, 55,* 435–467.

Snider, W. (1989a). Boston board takes first step toward total restructuring. *Education Week,* January 11, p. 7.

Snider, W. (1989b). Iowa, Arkansas enact "choice"; Proposals gain in other states. *Education Week,* March 15, p. 1.

Snider, W. (1989c). Parley on "choice," final budget mark transition. *Education Week,* January 18, p. 1.

Swanson, A. D. (1986). Centralization and decentralization of school governance: An American views the conflict in Australia. Unpublished manuscript. State University of New York at Buffalo, Department of Educational Organization, Administration and Policy.

Thomas, H., & Ranson, S. (1988, April). *Education reform: The national initiative in Britain.* Paper presented at the Annual Meeting of the American Educational Research Association, New Orleans, LA.

Tyack, D. B. (1974). *The one best system: A history of American urban education.* Cambridge, MA: Harvard University Press.

Victoria Ministry of Education, Ministry Structures Team. (1986). *Taking the schools into the 1990s*. Melbourne, Australia: Victoria Ministry of Education.

Western Australia Ministry of Education. (1987). *Better schools in Western Australia: A programme for improvement*. Perth: Author.

Wirt, F. M. (1986). *Multiple paths for understanding the role of values in state policy*. (ERIC Document Reproduction Service No. ED278086.) Paper presented at the Annual Meeting of the American Education Research Association, San Francisco, CA.

Wise, A. E. (1979) *Legislated learning: The bureaucratization of the American classroom*. Berekeley: University of California Press.

Wise, A. E. (1988). Two conflicting trends in school reform: Legislated learning revisited. *Phi Delta Kappan, 69,* 328–332.

Wise, A. E., & Darling-Hammond, L. (1984). Education by vouchers: Private choice and public interest. *Educational Theory, 34,* 29–47.

CHAPTER 3

The Structure of School Governance and Finance in the United States

In Chapter 2, a model was presented to array the decisions a society makes about the education of its members by potential decision makers. The matrix was set within the context of enduring social values. It was suggested that the ideal balance in the distribution of authority varies from time to time and from culture to culture according to the relative priority placed on each value.

The distribution pattern of authority can be referred to as the governance structure, and its nature directly influences the nature of decisions made. The governance structure must change to accommodate changes in social expectations or unrest develops and governments fall, either through orderly elections or through revolution. In Western democratic societies, change is usually an evolutionary or incremental process. In this chapter, we address the evolution of the current structure of educational governance and finance in the United States.

HISTORICAL DEVELOPMENT

In a critical analysis of public education in the United States in 1943, Henry C. Morrison referred to its structure disdainfully as "late New England colonial" (p. 258) and described the school district as "a little republic at every crossroads" (p. 75). Morrison was focusing on a characteristic of the system of American public education which made it unique among the systems of the world—its extreme decentralization. Herein lay both its strengths and its weaknesses.

Decentralized systems seem to be more adept than highly centralized and bureaucratic ones at mobilizing the energies of their constituents and adapting curricula and instructional systems to the diversity of their constituents. Yet decentralized systems have a tendency to become inequitable, providing uneven levels of quality of services. The good schools in a decentralized system tend to be very, very good; but such a system also generates—and tolerates—very poor schools. To bring about a greater degree of equity and to set minimally acceptable social standards require intervention of higher levels of government, that is, state or federal. This has been happening with increasing frequency over the fifty years since Morrison made his analysis and especially during the 1960s and 1970s as noted in Chapter 2.

Collective concern over formal education of the young dates to the beginning of European settlement of the continental United States. Massachusetts was particularly influential in setting the parameters for public education. It was the Massachusetts colony that first required parents to train their children in reading and writing, first required towns to establish schools, first appropriated colonial funds to encourage the establishment of schools, and first permitted towns to use revenue from property taxation to support schooling. All of this was accomplished before 1650. These events, however, must be interpreted in the light of the interrelationships between the government of the Massachusetts colony and the Congregational (Puritan) church. Suffrage and office holding were limited to church members, a minority of the total population. The property tax which supported the school also supported the church and its clergy. The "meeting house" served as the school as well as the church and the town hall (Johnson, 1904). This early pattern of community control of schools left its press upon the organization of public education in the United States today although the connection between church and state is no longer permitted.

Several of the authors of the U.S. Constitution in 1787 had firm beliefs about the importance of an educated citizenry to the success of the new republic. But the Constitution, itself, is silent on the subject of education; and the Tenth Amendment of the Bill of Rights assured that the powers not specifically delegated to the federal government were "reserved to the States respectively, or to the people." Founders such as Thomas Jefferson pursued the provision of public education at the state level. In his *Notes on the State of Virginia,* written in 1781–1782, Jefferson (1968) argued, "Every government degenerates when trusted to the rulers of the people alone. The people themselves therefore are its only safe depositories. And to render even them safe, their minds must be improved . . . (p. 390).

In seeking additional funds for education from the New York State legislature, Governor DeWitt Clinton (1826) noted the importance of state sponsorship of education in a democracy:

> The first duty of government, and the surest evidence of good government, is the encouragement of education. A general diffusion of knowledge is the precursor and protector of republican institutions; and in it we must confide as the conservative power that will watch over our liberties, and guard against fraud, intrigue, corruption and violence. (p. 114)

In a desperate effort in 1834 to save Pennsylvania's newly enacted common school legislation from the repeal of tax cutters, Thaddeus Stevens (1900) stated plainly the common benefit to be realized from those tax dollars.

> Many complain of this tax, not so much on account of its amount, as because it is for the benefit of others and not themselves. This is a great mistake; it is for their own benefit,

> inasmuch as it perpetuates the government and insures the due administration of the laws under which they live, and by which their lives and property are protected. (p. 520)

Stevens went on to draw the connection between education and the prevention of crime and argued that it is wiser, less expensive, and more humane to aid "that which goes to support his fellow-being from becoming a criminal, and to obviate the necessity of those humiliating [penal] institutions."

Thus, from the beginning of this country, the social importance of education has been recognized and its provision made a function of the states, not the federal government. Centralized control at the state level was not feasible in the eighteenth and nineteenth centuries, however, because of the dispersion of the population, the primitive means of communication, and the general lack of resources. Thus, the school district was invented to create and oversee schools. Cubberley (1947) commented on the spread of the school district nationwide.

> As an administrative and taxing unit it was well suited to the primitive needs and conditions of our early national life. Among a sparse and hard-working rural population, between whom intercourse was limited and intercommunication difficult, and with whom the support of schools was as yet an unsettled question, local control answered a very real need. The simplicity and democracy of the system was one of its chief merits. Communities or neighborhoods which wanted schools and were willing to pay for them could easily meet and organize a school district, vote to levy a school tax on their own property, employ a teacher, and organize and maintain a school. . . . On the other hand, communities which did not desire schools or were unwilling to tax themselves for them could do without them, and let the free-school idea alone. (pp. 212–213)

Cubberley's description points to one of the difficulties of the district system once universal education became the policy of a state. The district system worked well for the willing and able, but for those who were unwilling, there was not the leadership to organize a district, and for those who were not able, there were not the resources. Inequities within the district system became apparent even during the colonial period, but with the increasing concentration of capital through industrialization and urbanization, inequities became much more severe in the nineteenth and twentieth centuries. Districts which voluntarily came into existence very rapidly attached loyalty to their achievements and took great pride in them. They were not responsive to criticism of their endeavors from the state and resented any and all constraints placed upon them. Those areas which had chosen not to operate a common school were equally resistant to external compulsion to do so, especially when it involved compulsory taxation.

In an effort to establish order out of chaos, state boards of education were formed and provided with an executive officer. The first state to take such action was New York in 1812. As testimony to the sensitive nature of the position, New York's first Superintendent of Instruction, Gideon Hawley, served only until 1821, when the office was eliminated. A similar office was not created until 1854. Horace Mann, the first Secretary to the Board of Education of Massachusetts, ran into similar difficulty; however, attempts to dissolve his office and the board were unsuccessful.

The first school districts to go through the process of consolidation were in cities. Whereas New England cities were coterminous with their school districts from the beginning, this was not typically true of more western cities. Buffalo, the first city to employ a superintendent of schools, serves as a good illustration. Although it had previously had private schools, the first school supported by taxes was established in 1818. By 1837, the city had 15,000 inhabitants and seven one-teacher school districts. That year, a superintendent of schools was appointed to supervise and to coordinate those seven schools, to establish schools in wards of the city which were without schools, and to provide for a central high school. Detroit, Chicago, and Cleveland followed similar patterns. A few cities in the Far West have yet to consolidate into a single school district.

CURRENT ORGANIZATION OF SCHOOL GOVERNANCE

Extensive consolidation of rural school districts had to wait until improved means of transportation were available—well into the twentieth century. The number of school districts did not show a marked decrease until after World War II. In 1930, the number exceeded 127,000 nationwide (U.S. Department of Education, 1980); today there are approximately 14,700 districts (U.S. Department of Commerce, 1989). Hawaii is the only state to function as a single unit, and with 165,000 students, it is smaller than a number of large city districts. Texas leads the states in numbers of school districts with 1,087. Of these, 1,061 are fiscally independent; that is, they have the power to levy taxes. Another 26 are fiscally dependent, in that another unit of local government provides for their financial support. California has 1,028 school districts including 271 which are unified (provide for pupils in all grades K–12), 645 operating elementary schools only, and 112 operating high schools only (Salmon, Dawson, Lawton, & Johns, 1988, p. 44). Over half of California's school districts enroll fewer than 500 pupils. The number and selected characteristics of school districts by state and Canadian province are reported in Table 3.1.

Small school districts are not only a phenomenon of remote rural areas; there are literally thousands in the metropolitan counties surrounding major cities. In fragmenting metropolitan communities, great diversity is found among school districts and municipalities in their ethnic and racial composition and in their ability to support public services. Table 3.2 illustrates this diversity for selected units among the 97 subdivisions of Los Angeles County, California (U.S. Department of Commerce, 1983). These municipalities are not necessarily coterminous with school districts, but a similar disparity exists among school districts. Median family income ranged from $9,624 in Florence-Graham to $48,750 in Palos Verdes Estates. The population of Florence-Graham had a median age of 21.8 years; 28 percent were white, 37 percent African-American, and 35 percent other racial and ethnic groups. Over half of the adult population and 30 percent of the school-age population spoke English poorly or not at all. Only 28 percent were high school graduates. The fertility rate of women aged 35 through 44 was 4.5. Median value of owner-occupied housing was $35,700, and the median contract rent was $152 per month in 1980.

In contrast, the median age of those living in Palos Verdes Estates was 38.9, and 93.5 percent were white. Fewer than 1 percent were African-American. Only 3 percent of the school-age population and 9 percent of the adult population spoke English poorly or not at all. Nearly all of the population had graduated from high school, and the fertility rate

TABLE 3.1. Number of School Districts and Fiscal Authority by State and Province for the United States and Canada

State	Number of Districts			Comments
	Fiscally Dependent	Fiscally Independent	Total	
Alabama	129	0	129	
Alaska	55	0	55	Thirty-two districts are dependent on local governments and 23 Regional Education Attendance Areas are dependent on the state legislature.
Arizona	5	219	224	The fiscally dependent districts serve native American reservations that have no tax base.
Arkansas	0	333	333	
California	1,025	0	1,025	There are 271 unified, 645 elementary, and 112 high school districts.
Colorado	0	176	176	
Connecticut	165	0	165	
Delaware	0	19	19	
Florida	0	67	67	
Georgia	27	159	186	
Hawaii	1	0	1	There is a single, completely state-funded system. Hawaii has no local tax revenue for schools and no local boards of education responsible for their operations.
Idaho	0	116	116	
Illinois	0	994	994	There are unit districts (grades K–12), elementary districts (K–8), and high school districts (9–12).
Indiana	1	304	305	There are 302 fiscally independent school districts (entitled school corporations in Indiana), 2 nonoperating and 1 special department district.
Iowa	0	436	436	
Kansas	0	304	304	
Kentucky	0	178	178	
Louisiana	0	66	66	
Maine	283	0	283	
Maryland	24	0	24	
Massachusetts	437	0	437	
Michigan	0	565	565	The state has 525 K–12 school districts, plus 40 school districts with other grade configurations.
Minnesota	0	434	434	
Mississippi	154	0	154	
Missouri	0	546	546	
Montana	0	554	554	

(Continued)

TABLE 3.1. *(Continued)*

State	Number of Districts			Comments
	Fiscally Dependent	Fiscally Independent	Total	
Nebraska	0	955	955	There are several classifications of districts providing grades K–6, K–8, K–12, and secondary grades only.
Nevada	0	17	17	
New Hampshire	9	159	168	
New Jersey	4	582	586	The fiscally dependent districts are county special services units. There are also 20 county vocational schools and 10 Educational Services Commissions in the state.
New Mexico	88	0	88	
New York	5	724	729	Fiscally dependent districts are the 5 largest urban districts.
North Carolina	141	0	141	
North Dakota	0	309	309	Of the 309 districts, 275 are "high school districts," 48 "graded elementary districts," and 11 one-room "rural districts"; also there are 25 "nonoperating districts" many of which are located on a state line and which participate in schools in a neighboring state.
Ohio	0	615	615	Also there are 87 county offices and 49 joint vocational school boards.
Oklahoma	0	611	611	
Oregon	0	304	304	Two school districts are nonoperating. Out of 36 counties, 30 operate Educational Service Districts, 4 of which levy a property tax.
Pennsylvania	0	501	501	One school district is nonoperating.
Rhode Island	0	40	40	
South Carolina	52	40	92	
South Dakota	0	193	193	
Tennessee	141	0	141	
Texas	26	1,061	1,087	
Utah	0	40	40	
Vermont	0	246	246	
Virginia	139	0	139	
Washington	0	298	298	
West Virginia	0	55	55	
Wisconsin	0	432	432	Districts have several organizational forms: 373 have grades PK–12; 10 have grades 9–12; and 49 have grades PK–8.
Wyoming	0	49	49	Wyoming has K–12 unified districts and districts providing grades K–8.

(Continued)

TABLE 3.1. *(Continued)*

| State | Number of Districts | | | Comments |
	Fiscally Dependent	Fiscally Independent	Total	
Canadian Provinces				
Alberta	149	0	149	There are 99 public school boards, 48 Roman Catholic separate school boards, and 2 Protestant separate school boards; public funds are also available to private schools.
British Columbia	0	75	75	All districts are nondenominational; public funds are available to private schools.
Manitoba	0	54	54	All districts are nondenominational; public funds are available to private schools.
New Brunswick	42	0	42	There are 15 Francophone and 27 Anglophone school boards; public funds are not available to private schools.
Newfoundland	35	0	35	Twenty-one school boards are integrated, 12 are Roman Catholic, 1 is Pentecostal, and 1 is Seventh Day Adventist. School taxes are levied by Local School Tax Authorities made up of members appointed by school boards and municipal representatives; public funds are not available to private schools.
Nova Scotia	22	0	22	All school boards are nondenominational; public funds are not available to private schools.
Ontario	176	0	176	There are 122 public school boards, 59 Roman Catholic separate school boards, and 1 Protestant separate school board; public funds are not available to private schools.
Prince Edward Island	5	0	5	All school boards are nondenominational; public funds are not available to private schools.
Quebec	0	217	217	There are 211 school boards for Roman Catholics, 31 school boards for Protestants, and 4 integrated school boards; public funds are available to private schools.
Saskatchewan	0	116	116	There are 99 public school boards and 22 Roman Catholic separate school boards; public funds are available to private schools.

(Data are abstracted from R. Salmon, C. Dawson, S. Lawton, & T. Johns [Eds]. [1988]. *Public School Finance Programs of the United States and Canada, 1986–87*. Blacksburg, VA: American Education Finance Association.)

TABLE 3.2. Demographic Statistics for Selected Municipalities in Los Angeles County, California, 1979

	Total	Baldwin Park	Beverly Hills	East Los Angeles	Florence-Graham	La Canada Flintridge	Los Angeles	Palos Verdes Estates	Westmont	Willowbrook
Income										
Household median ($000)	17.6	16.4	25.0	12.3	9.6	37.8	15.7	48.8	11.6	11.5
Household mean ($000)	22.5	17.6	52.8	14.6	12.2	48.1	21.7	58.8	14.6	15.1
Per capita ($000)	8.3	5.0	24.4	3.9	3.2	16.1	8.4	19.5	4.9	4.2
Percentage below poverty level	13.4	15.2	8.9	23.3	34.1	2.6	16.4	1.9	26.0	27.5
Percentage unemployed	6.0	7.8	4.0	9.9	12.9	2.6	6.8	2.6	11.6	13.5
Median age	29.8	24.1	43.9	23.9	21.8	37.1	30.2	38.9	23.2	24.0
Percentage white	67.9	70.2	94.1	53.1	28.1	95.7	61.2	93.5	7.5	5.9
Percentage black	12.6	1.3	1.5	.4	37.1	.1	17.0	.9	86.1	70.8
Percentage other	19.5	28.5	4.4	46.5	34.8	4.2	21.8	5.6	6.4	23.3
Percentage 5–17 who speak English poorly	21.0	14.4	7.9	20.4	30.3	2.7	23.9	3.0	33.1	26.5
Percentage 18+ who speak English poorly	32.6	30.5	11.9	45.2	58.3	3.9	37.0	8.9	50.8	49.8
Percentage high school graduates (persons 25+)	69.8	50.1	86.6	26.8	28.3	94.0	68.6	97.0	66.1	49.3
Fertility rate of women 35–44	2.5	3.2	1.6	3.6	4.5	2.4	2.3	2.1	2.8	3.8
Median value of owner occupied housing ($000)	84.4	61.5	200.0+	54.0	35.7	172.5	96.1	200.0+	55.8	42.1
Median contract rent ($)	244.0	245.0	431.0	171.0	152.0	397.0	229.0	499.0	182.0	161.0
Total population (000)	7477.5	50.6	32.4	110.0	48.7	20.2	2966.9	14.4	27.9	30.8

(*Source:* U.S. Department of Commerce, Bureau of Census. [1983]. *1980 Census of Population and Housing: Census Tracts* [Los Angeles-Long Beach, Area] PHC 80-2-226. Washington, DC: U.S. Government Printing Office.)

of women between the ages of 35 and 44 was 2.1. Median value of owner-occupied housing was over $200,000, and the median contract rent was $499 per month in 1980.

In examining the table further, we can easily find other examples of socioeconomic and ethnic segregation. For example, Westmont was 86 percent African-American and Willowbrook was 70.8 percent. The percentages of white residents were 7.5 and 5.9, respectively. La Canada Flintridge was 95.7 percent white and 0.1 percent African-American. East Los Angeles was nearly evenly divided between white and groups other than African-American; African-Americans represented less than 1 percent of the population. With the public schools of the county divided in a similar fashion, the ideal of common schooling is difficult to realize.

Returning to Table 3.1, we see a much different, but less common, policy of school district organization typified by Maryland. Maryland's school districts are organized by county and the City of Baltimore. Maryland has 24 school districts, all of which are fiscally dependent. The county organization prevails in the southeast region of the country; Florida, for example, has 67 fiscally independent school districts and Alabama has 129 fiscally dependent school districts. Some western states also follow a county pattern. Nevada has 17 fiscally independent school districts, and Wyoming has 49 districts of which 10 are fiscally independent. Nebraska, on the other hand, has 955, all of which are fiscally independent (Salmon, Dawson, Lawton, & Johns, 1988). It is apparent that there is a rich diversity in school district organizations among the states and even within some states.

States exercise their authority over public education through general statements in their constitutions which give state legislatures authority to establish a system of public schools. For example, the New Jersey Constitution provides that the state legislature shall provide a "thorough and efficient" system of education. For the most part, the details of school governance, that is, procedures for establishing, financing, and governing school districts, teacher certification, and so on, are established by statutes enacted by state legislatures or regulations established by state boards of education. This system gives states a great deal of flexibility in reforming school governance structures without going through the cumbersome process of constitutional amendment.

Although the U.S. Constitution is silent on education per se, it addresses several issues which affect schools directly. For example, Article I, Section 8 gives Congress the power to "provide for the common Defence and general Welfare." Both areas of responsibility have been cited as justification for the passage of specific federal legislation affecting the conduct and finance of elementary and secondary schools.

Litigation concerning school desegregation (*Brown* v. *Board,* 1954; *Brown* v. *Board,* 1955; *Swann* v. *Charlotte-Mecklenburg,* 1971; *Keyes* v. *School District,* 1973; *Dayton* v. *Brinkman,* 1979) and school finance inequities (*Serrano* v. *Priest,* 1971; *San Antonio* v. *Rodriguez,* 1973; *Hobson* v. *Hansen,* 1971) have invoked provisions of the Fifth and Fourteenth Amendments to the U.S. Constitution. The Fifth Amendment restrains the federal government from depriving any person of "life, liberty or property without due process of law." In the wake of the Civil War, the Fourteenth Amendment was adopted to extend this restraint to the states. The amendment also restrains states and their agents, including school officials, from denying any person "the equal protection of the laws."

Unlike many countries in the world, religiously affiliated elementary and secondary schools are not permitted to receive public monies in the United States, although children attending such schools may have access to publicly provided services. In Canada, for example, five of the ten provinces fund religiously oriented school boards (see Table 3.1.). Five provinces make public funds available to private schools, and two, British Columbia and Manitoba, have only nondenominational public schools. New Brunswick has separate school boards for anglophones and francophones.

The basis for exclusion of public funds for religiously oriented schools in the United States is a narrow interpretation by the federal courts of the First Amendment (*Wolman* v. *Walter,* 1977; *Lemon* v. *Kurtzman,* 1971; *Levitt* v. *Committee,* 1973), which states that "Congress shall make no law respecting an establishment of religion, or prohibiting the free exercise thereof." This provision was made applicable to the states by the Fourteenth Amendment, but many state constitutions have provisions of their own that are less ambiguous, clearly stating the prohibition of the use of public funds or credit in support of any activity, including operation of schools, sponsored by religious groups.

Although the particulars vary from state to state, the dominant pattern of educational governance which has evolved in the United States provides five levels, with authority for making policy concentrated at two of these levels. The primary level of authority is the state, as represented by the legislatures, governors, state boards of education and superintendents, and state education departments. This level is charged with establishing basic policy for the system, including its financing, and overseeing and coordinating its components. The second level of authority is the local school district, which is charged with implementing state policy. The school is the basic operating unit; but this third level is usually permitted little discretion, as it is constrained by policies formulated at higher levels. The range of discretion at the school level may increase in the future if school site management and governance reforms are implemented as discussed in Chapter 16. The fourth level is the most recent school governance invention, the intermediate unit or district, created to provide services to school districts of a region.

The fifth level of governance is the federal government. Congress occasionally passes legislation affecting schools in the interest of "the general Welfare," national defense, or the protection of civil rights. The Office of Education, more recently upgraded to the Department of Education, was created in the executive branch to administer federal laws and to keep statistics. The federal courts are arbitrators of the U.S. Constitution.

Governance patterns constitute a network of educational resources available to highly diverse communities with highly diverse sets of interests. Assignment of authority and responsibility for various functions should be a dynamic process, permitting flexibility, because optimum allocation will vary among regions according to demographic and geographic characteristics and over time according to changing definitions of standards and new technological developments. It is perfectly reasonable for states to delegate or decentralize those functions which can be more effectively and more efficiently handled at the regional, district, or school level. By the same token, it is also reasonable for schools and school districts to do cooperatively that which they cannot do well independently.

THE SCOPE OF SCHOOL FINANCE

Today, education represents major economic, social, and cultural commitments in the United States. Over 4 percent of the gross national product is spent for elementary and secondary schools enrolling 45 million pupils and employing more than 4.5 million persons

TABLE 3.3. Growth in Population, Wealth, and Government Spending, 1902–1986

	Population (millions)	Gross National Product (GNP, billions)	All Government Spending	
			Billions of Dollars	Percentage of GNP
1902	79.2	21.6	1.7	7.7
1922	110.1	74.0	9.3	12.5
1932	124.9	58.5	12.4	21.3
1940	132.5	100.4	20.4	20.3
1950	152.3	288.3	70.3	24.4
1960	180.7	515.3	151.3	29.4
1970	205.1	1015.5	333.0	32.8
1980	227.8	2732.0	959.0	35.1
1986	241.6	4240.3	1696.2	40.0

(*Source:* U.S. Department of Commerce, Bureau of the Census. [1967]. *Historical Statistics on Governmental Finances and Employment.* Washington, DC: U.S. Government Printing Office. Updating from U.S. Bureau of the Census. [1989]. *Statistical Abstract of the United States 1989.* Washington, DC: U.S. Government Printing Office.)

(U.S. Department of Education, 1988). About one in five persons in the United States is involved directly in formal elementary and secondary education.

Table 3.3 reports the national growth in population, GNP, and all government spending during the twentieth century. Total expenditures for all levels of government grew from 7.7 percent of the GNP in 1902 to 40.0 percent in 1986.

Table 3.4 shows the size of federal tax revenues, direct expenditures, and number of employees since 1950 relative to the corresponding categories of state and local governments. In 1950, 65% of all taxes were collected by the federal government. By 1986, the

TABLE 3.4. Federal, State, and Local Revenues, Expenditures and Employment, 1950–86

	Percentage of Total				
	1950	1960	1970	1980	1986
Revenue from Own Sources					
Federal	65	65	62	58	52
State	17	17	20	24	27
Local	18	18	18	18	21
Total Direct Expenditures					
Federal	60	59	55	55	58
State	15	15	17	18	17
Local	24	26	28	27	25
Public Employment					
Federal	33	27	22	18	18
State	16	17	21	23	24
Local	52	55	57	59	58

(*Source:* U.S. Department of Commerce, Bureau of the Census. [1975]. *Historical Statistics of the United States, Colonial Times to 1970.* Washington, DC: U.S. Government Printing Office. Updated from: U.S. Department of Commerce, Bureau of the Census. [1989]. *Statistical Abstract of the United States 1989.* Washington, DC: U.S. Government Printing Office.)

percentage had dropped to 52%. The percentage of taxes collected by states has shown a steady growth over the period, from 17% to 27%, whereas local tax collections have remained stable, at about 18% from 1950 through 1980 but rising to 21% in 1986. Although local governments raised only 21% of total revenue in 1986, they made 25% of all direct governmental expenditures and employed 58% of all civilian public workers.

State and local governments are able to spend relatively more than they collect in revenue from their own sources because of intergovernmental transfers, more commonly known as state and federal aid. Local governments employ the same proportion of public workers today as they did at the turn of the century, when they collected more taxes than state and federal governments combined (Dye, 1987, p. 293). The proportion of public workers employed by the federal government has actually declined from 33% in 1950 to 18% in 1986; the state proportion has increased from 16% to 24%. In 1985, school districts employed 26.5% of all public workers—more than either state or federal governments (U.S. Department of Commerce, Bureau of the Census, 1989).

Table 3.5 compares revenues, expenditures, and outstanding debt by level of government for the period 1970 through 1986. In 1970, the federal budget was "only" $2 billion in deficit. By 1986, the deficit had reached $248 billion. The pattern for state and local government is quite different. Revenue for state governments exceeded expenditures for every year, reaching a surplus of $57 billion in 1986. Local governments ran small deficits in 1970 and 1980 but had surpluses in 1985 and 1986. State and local governments are typically required to have balanced budgets by their constitutions or statutes.

Outstanding debt has increased for all levels of government but at a particularly alarming rate at the federal level. In 1970, the ratio of outstanding debt to revenues for the federal government was 1.8 to 1.0. By 1986, the ratio had reached 2.5 to 1.0. At the state level, the ratio of debt to revenues grew modestly from 0.47 in 1970 to 0.52 to 1.0. In other words, the debt of states is about half of their annual revenues whereas the federal debt is two and a half times annual revenues. In 1970, the debt-to-revenue ratio for local governments was 1.15 to 1.0. By 1986, it had dropped to 0.94 to 1.0. Total debt of local governments is now slightly less than their annual revenues.

Figure 3.1 shows the national trends in revenue sources for public elementary and secondary education for the period 1920–1987. In 1920, 83.2 percent of revenues for public schools was derived from local sources, primarily the property tax. The states provided 16.5 percent and the federal government 0.3 percent. By 1987, half of public school revenues were provided by states; 43.8 percent came from local sources, and 6.2 percent from the federal government. The peak years for federal participation in the financing of public schools were 1979 and 1980, when the federal government provided 9.8 percent of their revenue (National Center for Education Statistics, 1988, p. 94).

In analyzing financial data over time, it is important to keep in mind the impact of inflation on the purchasing power of the dollar. This fact is illustrated in Table 3.6, where the average per capita income in the United States is reported in current dollars and in constant dollars based on the purchasing power of the dollar in 1958, 1967, and 1982. Although average per capita income increased nearly 25 times in current dollars from 1930 to 1987, the increase was less than four times when current dollars are converted to equivalent purchasing power of the 1982 dollar.

Figure 3.2 shows the trends in operating expenditures per pupil for public schools since 1950 in current and in constant dollars expressed in terms of 1985–1986 purchasing

TABLE 3.5. Revenue, Expenditures, and Outstanding Debt by Level of Government, 1970–1986 (in billions of dollars)

	Federal				State				Local			
Year	Revenue	Expenditures	Surplus (deficit)	Debt Outstanding	Revenue	Expenditures	Surplus (deficit)	Debt Outstanding	Revenue	Expenditures	Surplus (deficit)	Debt Outstanding
1970	206	208	(2)	371	89	85	4	42	89	93	(4)	102
1980	565	617	(52)	914	277	258	19	122	258	261	(3)	214
1985	807	1,032	(225)	1,827	439	391	48	212	402	391	11	357
1986	848	1,096	(248)	2,130	481	424	57	248	435	428	7	411

(*Source:* U.S. Department of Commerce, Bureau of the Census. [1989]. *Statistical Abstract of the United States 1989.* Washington, DC: U.S. Government Printing Office, Table 446.)

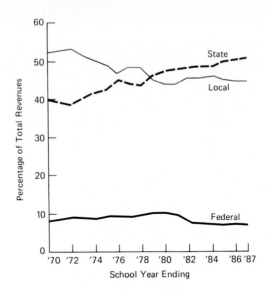

Figure 3.1. National Trends in Revenue Sources for Public Elementary and Secondary Education for Selected School Years Ending 1970–1987. (*Source:* National Center for Education Statistics. [1989]. *The Condition of Education* [Vol. 1]. Washington, DC: U.S. Government Printing Office, p. 35; data from National Center for Education Statistics [1988]. *Digest of Education Statistics.*)

power. In current dollars, per pupil expenditures have increased over eighteenfold from $209 in 1950 to $3,752 in 1986. Taking into account the effects of inflation, expenditures have increased nearly four times, from $960 to $3,752 (National Center for Education Statistics, 1988, p. 92). Expenditure increases between 1950 and the late 1970s enabled educational spending to keep pace with inflation and to allow for significant program

TABLE 3.6. **Personal Income per Capita in Current and Constant Dollars and Purchasing Power of the Dollar, 1930–1987**

	Per Capita Income				Purchasing Power of the Dollar		
Year	Current Dollars	1958 Dollars	1967 Dollars	1982 Dollars	1958 = 100	1967 = 100	1982 = 100
1930	625	1,167	1,250	3,294*	53.6	50.0	—
1940	593	1,303	1,412	3,721*	45.5	42.0	—
1950	1,501	1,810	2,082	5,486*	82.9	72.1	—
1960	2,219	2,157	2,502	6,593*	102.9	88.7	29.6
1970	4,000*	3,050	3,439	9,063	131.1	116.3	38.8
1980	9,919	3,881*	4,337*	11,427	—	—	82.4
1985	13,895	4,229*	4,725*	12,451	—	—	111.6
1987	15,481	4,401*	4,917*	12,955	—	—	113.6

*Interpolated between scales. (*Sources:* U.S. Department of Commerce, Bureau of the Census. [1975]. *Historical Statistics of the United States, Colonial Times to 1970.* Washington, DC: U.S. Government Printing Office. Updated from U.S. Department of Commerce, Bureau of the Census. [1989]. *Statistical Abstract of the United States 1989.* Washington, DC: U.S. Government Printing Office.)

expansions and improvements. The slight decline in constant dollars in the late 1970s (see Figure 3.2) indicates lower spending for schools relative to increases in the cost of living; expenditure growth for public education once again kept pace with inflation during the 1980s.

Data on public and private school enrollments are reported in Table 3.7 for the period 1970–1986. Public school enrollments at the elementary level (K–8) were at their peak in 1970 with nearly 33 million pupils; secondary level (9–12) enrollments peaked in 1976 at 14.5 million. The subsequent decline in elementary enrollments reversed in 1983, and they have been increasing since. Secondary enrollments are projected to increase again beginning in 1990. The projections for public school enrollments to 1997 are shown in Figure 3.3.

Enrollment in the elementary grades peaked earlier for private schools at 4.5 million, but enrollment at the secondary level has remained relatively constant at about 1.2 million. The percentage of pupils enrolled in private schools has remained between 10 and 11 percent for the period 1970–1986 (National Center for Education Statistics, 1988, pp. 106–107).

Although the proportion of pupils enrolled in private schools has remained relatively constant, the composition has not (Cooper, 1988). In 1966, 87.5 percent of the 6,369,807 pupils in private schools were enrolled in Catholic schools; by 1983, only 57.1 percent of the 5,305,041 private school pupils were in Catholic schools. Enrollment in Catholic schools has dropped 46 percent while increasing 186 percent in non-Catholic schools. Enrollment in evangelical schools approached 1 million in 1983, an increase since 1966 of 627 percent. Over half of the private schools and 28 percent of their enrollments were related to Protestant churches in 1983. Table 3.8 reports data showing the nature of private school enrollment as of 1983.

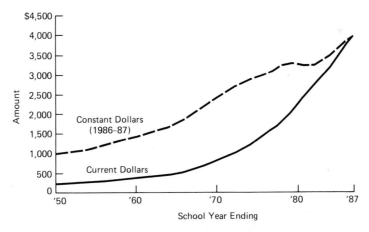

Figure 3.2. Trends in current expenditure per pupil in average daily attendance in current and constant dollars in public schools for selected school years ending 1950–1987. (*Source:* National Center for Education Statistics. [1989]. *The Condition of Education* [Vol. 1]. Washington, DC: U.S. Government Printing Office, p. 37; data from National Center for Education Statistics, *Statistics of State School Systems and Revenues and Expenditures for Public Elementary and Secondary Education,* Common Core of Data Survey.)

TABLE 3.7. Public and Private School Enrollments in Grades K–12, 1970–1986

Fall of Year	Public School			Private School			Private School Enrollment as a Percentage of Total Enrollment		
	Total, K–12	K–8	9–12	Total, K–12	K–8	9–12	Total, K–12	K–8	9–12
	Enrollment (in thousands)						Percentage		
1970	46,193	32,648	13,545	5,655	4,485	1,170	10.9	12.1	8.0
1971	46,575	32,518	14,057	5,378	4,252	1,126	10.4	11.6	7.4
1972	45,344	31,329	14,015	5,203	4,048	1,155	10.3	11.4	7.6
1973	44,945	30,783	14,162	4,945	3,761	1,184	9.9	10.9	7.7
1974	44,957	30,682	14,275	4,867	3,695	1,172	9.8	10.7	7.6
1975	44,520	30,017	14,503	5,001	3,821	1,180	10.1	11.3	7.5
1976	44,201	29,660	14,541	4,804	3,603	1,201	9.8	10.8	7.6
1977	43,153	28,648	14,505	5,025	3,777	1,248	10.4	11.6	7.9
1978	41,976	27,745	14,231	4,978	3,734	1,244	10.6	11.9	8.0
1979	41,343	27,349	13,994	4,663	3,541	1,122	10.1	11.5	7.4
1980	—	27,088	—	—	3,537	—	—	11.5	—
1981	40,897	27,374	13,523	4,701	3,582	1,119	10.3	11.6	7.6
1982	40,131	27,127	13,004	4,702	3,584	1,118	10.5	11.7	7.9
1983	39,701	26,909	12,792	4,868	3,650	1,218	10.9	11.9	8.7
1984*	39,794	27,073	12,721	4,306	3,249	1,057	9.8	10.7	7.7
1985	39,788	27,024	12,764	4,872	3,657	1,215	10.9	11.9	8.7
1986	40,237	27,491	12,746	4,757	3,591	1,166	10.6	11.6	8.4

Note: Blank = not available.
*An unexplained drop occurred in the number and proportion of private school students in 1984, according to the Bureau of the Census. However, the data appear to be an anomaly since the 1985 and 1986 figures for private school students are very similar to those for 1983 and are consistent with the trend from 1979 to 1983. (Source: National Center for Education Statistics. [1989]. The Condition of Education [Vol. 1]. Washington, DC: U.S. Government Printing Office, p. 109; data from U.S. Department of Commerce, Bureau of the Census. School Enrollment—Social and Economic Characteristics of Students: October 1984 [advance report] and October 1985 [advance report]. Current Population Reports, Series P–20, Nos. 404 and 409.)

To serve the 45 million pupils in public schools, local school districts employ the full-time equivalent (FTE) of 4.2 million persons, of which 2.25 million are classroom teachers. There are 450,000 instructional support personnel, including aides, guidance counselors, and librarians, and 540,000 administrators and associated clerical staff. Media personnel, bus drivers, security officers, cafeteria workers, and so on number over 1 million. The percentage of total staff who are classroom teachers dropped from 65 percent in 1960 to 53 percent in 1987. The proportion of administrators and clerks in 1987 was 13 percent; instructional support staff, just under 11 percent; and other support staff, 24 percent. The proportion of professional employees, teachers and administrators, has decreased in recent years, whereas the proportion of noncertified support personnel has increased (National Center for Education Statistics, 1988, pp. 38, 99).

Despite declining enrollments in public schools since 1971, the total number of professional educators has actually increased. This increase has produced a continual decline in the pupil-professional ratio, from 22.3 pupils to 1.0 professional to 17.4 pupils to 1.0 in 1988. There was a corresponding change in median class size (National Center

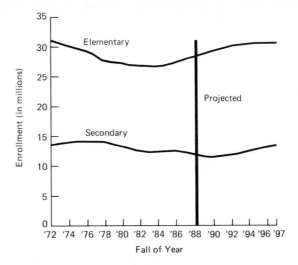

Figure 3.3. Actual and Projected Public School Enrollment, 1969–1997. (*Source:* National Center for Education Statistics. [1989]. *The Condition of Education* [Vol. 1.] Washington, DC: U.S. Government Printing Office, p. 53; data from National Center for Education Statistics. [1988]. *Projections of Education Statistics to 1997–98.*)

for Education Statistics, 1988, pp. 102–103). These statistics are reported in Table 3.9.

Declining pupil enrollments ushered in a period of teacher surplus and weakening support for growth in teacher salaries. Statistics on average teacher salaries, 1960–1987, are reported in Table 3.10. Although average teacher salaries continued to rise, from

TABLE 3.8. Enrollment in U.S. Private Schools by Type, 1965–1983

Type	Enrollment				Percentage growth/decline
	1965–1966	1970–1971	1975–1976	1982–1983	1965–1983
Roman Catholic	5,574,354	4,361,007	3,363,979	3,027,317	−46
Lutheran	208,209	202,362	212,908	280,539	35
Jewish	73,112	83,106	91,533	100,202	66
Evangelical*	110,300	254,211	344,200	912,985	627
Other religions	204,378	230,371	257,363	276,823	35
NAIS[†]	199,329	221,216	277,406	336,797	69
Others	NA	NA	44,960	370,383	NA
Total				5,305,046	

Note: NA = not available.

*Evangelical is a category of self-confessed, "born again" Christian schools which have indicated a fundamentalist ideal.

†National Association of Independent Schools. (*Source:* The table is adapted from B. S. Cooper. [1988]. The Changing Universe of U.S. Private Schools. In T. James & H. M. Levin [Eds], *Comparing Public and Private Schools,* Vol. 1, *Institutions and Organizations.* Sussex, England: Falmer Press, 1988, p. 33. Reprinted by permission.)

TABLE 3.9. Trends in Pupil-Teacher Ratios and Median
Class Size in Public Elementary and Secondary
Schools for Selected Years

Year	(1) Pupil-Teacher Ratio	(2) Median Class Size	
		Elementary	Secondary
1961	25.6	30	27
1966	24.1	29	27
1971	22.3	27	26
1976	20.4	26	25
1981	18.8	25	24
1986	17.9	24	22
1988	17.4	NA	NA

(*Sources:* Data in column 1: U.S. Department of Education [1988]. *Digest of Education Statistics, 1988.* Washington, DC: Department of Education; data in column 2 from National Center for Education Statistics [1988]. *The Condition of Education* [Vol. 1]. Washington, DC: U.S. Government Printing Office, p. 103; National Education Association. [1987]. *Status of the American Public School Teacher 1985–86.* Reprinted by permission.)

$10,174 in 1973 during peak enrollments to $28,044 in 1988, their purchasing power did not keep pace with inflation for much of the period. Stated in terms of the purchasing power of the dollar in 1988, the 1973 salary was equivalent to $28,433. From that high point, the purchasing power of the average teacher salary declined to a low of $24,261 in 1981, when the trend was reversed (National Center for Education Statistics, 1988, p. 100). With increasing enrollments and with increasing numbers of retirements of teachers in service, the demand for new teachers will continue to be strong for the rest of the century and teacher salaries should continue to increase at an above-average rate.

Diversity among political subdivisions at the local level and its impact upon equity in the provision of educational opportunities for children have already been discussed. The inequities are compounded by a similar pattern among states, illustrated by 1987 statistics reported in Table 3.11 (pp. 58–59) for the 50 states. Variation is on every dimension: size, wealth, expenditure, and effort. Enrollments in state school systems range from over 4 million in California to 92,000 in Vermont. Per capita personal income, a measure of wealth or ability to support public services, ranges from $19,599 in Connecticut to $9,716 in Mississippi. The state with the lowest per pupil expenditure is Utah at $2,486. Excluding Alaska, whose figures are distorted by an unusually high cost of living, the highest spending state is Wyoming at $6,253—nearly $4,000 per pupil more than Utah. Again excluding Alaska, average teacher salaries range from $32,800 in Michigan, New York, and Wisconsin to $19,518 in South Dakota. The pupil-teacher ratio is most favorable in Connecticut at 13.7 to 1; the least favorable is in Utah, at 23.4 to 1 followed closely by California, at 23.0 to 1.

The National Center for Education Statistics (1988, pp. 36–37) measures state effort to support public education by the ratio of public school revenues per pupil in relation to per capita income. This ratio, presented in the right-hand column of Table 3.11, "reflects what the average student receives relative to the typical taxpayer's ability to pay" (p. 36).

TABLE 3.10. Estimated Average Annual Salary of Teachers in Public Elementary and Secondary Schools in Current and Constant Dollars for Selected School Years, 1960–1988

School Year Ending	Current Dollars			Constant Dollars (1987–1988)*		
	All Teachers	Elementary Teachers	Secondary Teachers	All Teachers	Elementary Teachers	Secondary Teachers
1960	$ 4,995	$ 4,815	$ 5,276	$19,693	$18,983	$20,801
1962	5,515	5,340	5,775	21,255	20,580	22,257
1964	5,995	5,805	6,266	22,517	21,803	23,535
1966	6,485	6,279	6,761	23,544	22,796	24,546
1968	7,423	7,208	7,692	25,285	24,553	26,201
1970	8,626	8,412	8,891	26,453	25,797	27,265
1971	9,268	9,021	9,568	27,026	26,306	27,901
1972	9,705	9,424	10,031	27,321	26,530	28,238
1973	10,174	9,893	10,507	27,532	26,771	28,433
1974	10,770	10,507	11,077	26,759	26,105	27,521
1975	11,641	11,334	12,000	26,037	25,351	26,840
1976	12,600	12,280	12,937	26,319	25,651	27,023
1977	13,354	12,989	13,776	26,357	25,637	27,190
1978	14,198	13,845	14,602	26,260	25,607	27,007
1979	15,032	14,681	15,450	25,421	24,827	26,128
1980	15,970	15,569	16,459	23,830	23,232	24,560
1981	17,644	17,230	18,142	23,595	23,041	24,261
1982	19,274	18,853	19,805	23,725	23,207	24,379
1983	20,695	20,227	21,291	24,425	23,873	25,129
1984	21,921	21,460	22,557	24,949	24,424	25,673
1985	23,593	23,182	24,193	25,840	25,390	26,498
1986	25,198	24,666	25,866	26,825	26,258	27,536
1987	26,556	25,978	27,262	27,656	27,054	28,392
1988	28,044	27,423	28,895	28,044	27,423	28,895

Note: Data for some recent years have been revised from previously published figures.
*Based on the Consumer Price Index, prepared by the Bureau of Labor Statistics, U.S. Department of Labor, and adjusted to a school-year basis. (*Source:* National Center for Education Statistics. [1989]. *The Condition of Education* [Vol. 1]. Washington, DC: U.S. Government Printing Office, p. 106.; data from National Education Association. *Estimates of School Statistics,* various years [latest edition 1987–88, copyright 1988 by the National Education Association, all rights reserved]; and unpublished data. Reprinted by permission.)

According to the index, Wyoming puts forth the greatest effort, at 54.4, and Alabama makes the least effort, at 19.1. Wyoming's effort may be inflated by a high proportion of oil-producing property, the taxes on which can be exported to oil consumers in other states.

SUMMARY

In this chapter, we have described the legal basis for school governance and finance in the United States. Through statistical tables and charts, the growth of the fiscal power of the federal government was shown as well as the decline of the fiscal strength of local

TABLE 3.11. Selected Public School Statistics Related to Enrollment, Wealth, Expenditure, Staffing, and Effort of State Systems, 1986–1987

State	(1) Enrollment	(2) Per Capita Personal Income 1986	(3) Current Expenditure per Pupil in ADA	(4) Average Salary Instructional Staff	(5) Pupil-Teacher Ratio	(6) Index of Effort
United States	39,837,459	NA	$3,977	$27,722	17.8	NA
Alabama	733,735	$11,337	2,699	24,090	19.8	19.1
Alaska	107,973	17,781	7,242	40,748	16.7	44.9
Arizona	534,538	13,474	3,080	25,298	18.4	19.3
Arkansas	437,438	11,074	2,202	20,538	17.5	23.4
California	4,377,989	17,472	3,840	32,301	23.0	22.2
Colorado	558,415	15,234	3,569	28,400	18.2	28.6
Connecticut	468,847	19,599	5,479	30,193	13.7	27.6
Delaware	94,410	15,005	4,823	28,440	16.0	29.3
District of Columbia	85,612	19,396	5,306	36,413	14.3	23.1
Florida	1,607,320	14,645	4,062	25,552	17.5	26.3
Georgia	1,096,425	13,447	3,167	25,600	18.9	20.9
Hawaii	164,640	14,891	3,840	27,646	22.6	26.5
Idaho	208,391	11,228	2,647	22,315	20.4	22.3
Illinois	1,825,185	15,586	3,904	29,169	17.4	24.1
Indiana	966,780	13,135	4,006	26,421	18.3	27.4
Iowa	481,286	13,347	3,708	23,368	15.5	26.0
Kansas	416,091	14,651	4,068	25,297	15.4	26.4
Kentucky	642,778	11,237	3,105	23,446	18.6	24.0
Louisiana	795,188	11,194	3,008	20,592	18.5	26.2
Maine	211,752	12,794	3,871	21,943	15.5	25.9
Maryland	675,747	16,866	4,675	29,895	17.1	26.3
Massachusetts	833,918	17,722	4,902	30,810	14.4	24.5
Michigan	1,681,880	14,775	3,974	32,800	20.2	25.5
Minnesota	711,134	14,994	4,265	29,350	17.4	27.8
Mississippi	498,639	9,716	2,526	20,036	19.0	22.0
Missouri	800,606	13,789	3,338	24,672	16.4	23.6
Montana	153,327	11,802	4,058	24,260	15.6	34.6
Nebraska	267,139	13,740	3,423	24,138	15.1	23.4
Nevada	161,239	15,441	3,567	28,250	20.4	21.7
New Hampshire	163,717	15,909	3,682	22,625	15.9	22.3
New Jersey	1,107,467	18,627	6,172	30,102	14.7	31.9
New Mexico	281,943	11,423	3,466	27,709	19.0	27.3
New York	2,607,719	17,111	6,375	32,800	15.4	32.3
North Carolina	1,085,248	12,437	3,470	24,791	18.7	24.6
North Dakota	118,703	12,474	3,358	21,960	15.3	24.7
Ohio	1,793,508	13,933	3,756	27,869	18.1	25.4
Oklahoma	593,183	12,283	2,979	22,208	16.9	21.6
Oregon	449,307	13,327	4,382	27,810	18.3	29.0
Pennsylvania	1,674,161	14,249	4,748	28,111	16.3	33.3
Rhode Island	134,126	14,577	5,078	32,026	15.0	28.2

(Continued)

TABLE 3.11. *(Continued)*

State	(1) Enrollment	(2) Per Capita Personal Income 1986	(3) Current Expenditure per Pupil in ADA	(4) Average Salary Insructional Staff	(5) Pupil-Teacher Ratio	(6) Index of Effort
South Carolina	611,629	11,298	3,038	24,212	17.3	25.4
South Dakota	125,458	11,814	3,050	19,518	15.6	25.1
Tennessee	818,073	12,002	2,869	23,323	19.9	21.2
Texas	3,209,515	13,478	3,448	25,329	17.3	26.9
Utah	415,994	10,984	2,486	26,394	23.4	23.8
Vermont	92,112	13,346	4,572	23,293	NA	28.9
Virginia	975,135	15,409	3,809	25,671	16.8	24.4
Washington	761,428	15,011	3,845	28,202	20.5	25.8
West Virginia	351,837	10,578	3,656	22,425	15.3	29.6
Wisconsin	767,819	13,908	4,642	32,800	16.3	30.7
Wyoming	100,955	12,791	6,253	28,230	14.0	54.5

(*Sources:* Data in columns 3 and 4: National Education Association [1988]. *Estimates of School Statistics.* Washington, DC: National Education Association; data in column 5: U.S. Department of Education. [1988]. *Digest of Educational Statistics.* Washington, DC: U.S. Government Printing Office; data in column 6: National Center for Education Statistics. [1988]. *The Condition of Education* [Vol. 1]. Washington, DC: U.S. Government Printing Office. Reprinted by permission.)

governments. Nevertheless, local governments remain the primary provider of social services and the principal employer of public workers. Local governments are able to do this, despite their limited tax bases, because of financial assistance from state and federal governments.

Financed by all three levels of governments, schools have been provided with revenues sufficient to permit expenditures to increase several times the rate of inflation— allowing substantial program expansion. After dramatic growth in the post-World War II period, school enrollments began to decline during the 1970s and 1980s. As we enter the 1990s, however, enrollments are rising, demand for teachers is very strong, and teacher salaries are increasing. Despite greater involvement by state and federal governments, the system remains decentralized in operation and, to a degree, in finance, perpetuating inequities among school districts. In Part Two, we examine the revenue sources which finance public school operations.

ACTIVITIES

1. To what extent should public schools receive financial support from federal, state, and local governments, respectively?
   a. What criteria did you use in arriving at your answer?
   b. Might the optimal distribution of financial support vary from state to state and community to community? What criteria could be used to justify variation?
2. What is the basis for school district organization in your state, for example, special district, function of municipal government, fiscally dependent or independent?

    a. What are the advantages and disadvantages of this arrangement?

    b. What, in your opinion, would be an "optimal" pattern of school governance? What criteria did you use in defining "optimal"?

3. Table 3.9 reports national statistics on the continuing decline in pupil-teacher ratios and average class size.

    a. Does this represent a decline in the efficiency of public schools, an increase in quality of educational services, or some combination of these?

    b. What is the rationale for your response?

4. Table 3.10 reports the purchasing power of teacher salaries in constant dollars from 1960 through 1987. Discuss the rise and fall of teacher salaries in the light of the supply and demand curves depicted in Figure 1.2. What are the implications for federal, state, and school district policies related to teacher salaries?

5. What are the implications, if any, for federal educational policy in the differences among the states in financial ability and in provision of educational services as shown in Table 3.11?

REFERENCES

Brown v. *Board of Education of Topeka,* 347 U.S. 483, 74 Sup. Ct. 686 (1954).

Brown v. *Board of Education of Topeka,* 349 U.S. 294, 75 Sup. Ct. 753 (1955).

Clinton, D. (1826). Annual message to the legislature. In C. Z. Lincoln (Ed.), *State of New York—Messages from the governors* (Vol. III, p. 114). Albany, NY: Lyon Co., 1909.

Cooper, B. S. (1988). The changing universe of U.S. private schools. In T. James & H. M. Levin (Eds.), *Comparing public and private schools* (Vol. 1). Philadelphia: Falmer Press.

Cubberley, E. P. (1947). *Public education in the United States.* Cambridge, MA: Riverside Press.

Dayton Board of Education v. *Brinkman,* 443 U.S. 526, 99 Sup. Ct. 2971 (1979).

Dye, T. R. (1987). *Understanding public policy.* Englewood Cliffs, NJ: Prentice-Hall.

Hobson v. *Hansen,* 269 F. Supp. 401 (1967); *Hobson* v. *Hansen,* 327 F. Supp. 844 (1971).

Jefferson, T. (1968). Notes on the State of Virginia. In *The annals of America* (Vol. 2, pp. 563–573). Chicago: Encyclopedia Britannica.

Johnson, C. (1904). *Old-time schools and school books.* New York: Macmillan.

Keyes v. *School District No. 1, Denver Colorado,* 413 U.S. 198, 93 Sup. Ct. 2686 (1973).

Lemon v. *Kurtzman,* 403 U.S. 602, 1971.

Levitt v. *Committee for Public Education and Religious Liberty,* 413 U.S. 472, 1973.

Morrison, H. C. (1943). *American schools: A critical study of our school system.* Chicago: University of Chicago Press.

National Center for Education Statistics. (1988). *The condition of education* (Vol. 1). Washington, DC: U.S. Government Printing Office.

Salmon, R., Dawson, C., Lawton, S., & Johns, T. (Eds.). (1988). *Public school finance programs of the United States and Canada, 1986–87.* Blacksburg, VA: American Education Finance Association.

San Antonio Independent School District v. *Rodriguez,* 411 U.S. 1, 1973.

Serrano v. *Priest,* 96 Cal. Rptr. 601, 487 P. 2d 124 (1971).

Stevens, T. (1900). Speech on the common school law repeal to the Pennsylvania House of

Representatives, 1834. In *Reports of the Department of the Interior for the fiscal year ended June 30, 1899* (Vol. I, p. 520). Washington, DC: U.S. Government Printing Office.

Swann v. *Charlotte-Mecklenburg Board of Education,* 402 U.S. 1, 91 Sup. Ct. 1267 (1971).

U.S. Department of Commerce, Bureau of the Census. (1967). *Historical statistics on governmental finances and employment.* Washington, DC: U.S. Government Printing Office.

U.S. Department of Commerce, Bureau of the Census. (1975). *Historical statistics of the United States, Colonial times to 1970.* Washington, DC: U.S. Government Printing Office.

U.S. Department of Commerce, Bureau of the Census. (1983). *1980 census of population and housing: Census tracts for Los Angeles-Long Beach, Calif. Standard Metropolitan Statistical Area* (PHC80-2-226). Washington, DC: U.S. Government Printing Office.

U.S. Department of Commerce, Bureau of the Census. (1989). *Statistical abstract of the United States 1989.* Washington, DC: U.S. Government Printing Office.

U.S. Department of Education, National Center for Education Statistics. (1980). *Digest of educational statistics.* Washington, DC: U.S. Government Printing Office.

U.S. Department of Education, National Center for Education Statistics. (1988). *Digest of educational statistics.* Washington, DC: U.S. Government Printing Office.

Wolman v. *Walter,* 433 U.S. 229, 1977.

PART II

Resources for Education

CHAPTER 4

Principles of Taxation

Part I placed educational decision-making processes within the context of the broader political-economic system. We noted that changes in public policy are responses to shifts in circumstances and in priorities given to different values. The structure of school governance and finance in the United States was examined and, now, in Part II we refer to that structure in a discussion of public revenue sources. Attention is given to basic principles of taxation and to the characteristics of the primary revenue sources of federal, state, and local governments. Tax policies define the means by which funds are drawn from private sector households and businesses for use in the public sector. The effectiveness of the tax system depends to a large extent upon fairness of treatment of all taxpayers.

To establish a context for examining revenue sources, we begin with an overview of the federated tax structure. Federal, state, and local levels of government rely to varying degrees on tax bases of wealth, income, consumption, and privilege. Intents and consequences of different taxes can be analyzed in relation to several criteria: yield, equity, neutrality, elasticity, and cost of administration and compliance. These criteria are introduced in this chapter and are used to evaluate strategies for raising revenue at the federal and state levels of government, in Chapter 5, and at the local level, including school districts, in Chapter 6.

OVERVIEW OF THE FEDERATED TAX STRUCTURE

Public finance in the United States is influenced greatly by the separation of powers among federal, state, and local levels of government. Multiple layers, it is believed, can more efficiently and effectively finance public services. The division is not a strict one, however, since there is considerable sharing of tax sources and substantial flow of money from federal and state governments to local subdivisions such as counties, townships, municipalities, and school districts.

A highly decentralized system ties costs to the jurisdiction which provides services. A loose federation among levels of government is believed to stimulate a stronger economy, with goods and factors of production moving freely in response to differing levels of taxes and benefits (Musgrave & Musgrave, 1984, p. 519). On the other hand, a highly decentralized tax structure tolerates inequities in the nature and extent of services provided among tax jurisdictions. Two counties with differing property wealth or personal income, for example, have very different capacities to raise desired revenue from these tax bases. For this reason, higher levels of government may intervene to equalize tax capacity in order to ensure the provision of adequate public services among all jurisdictions at lower levels.

Fiscal federalism in the twentieth century has been characterized by a trend toward greater centralization. In Chapter 3, it was shown that more revenue is now being raised at federal and state levels than in the past, accompanied by an increase in grants-in-aid to states and localities. Despite these two trends—the centralization of revenue sources and the growth in revenue sharing from federal and state to local governments—the provision of services remains largely the responsibility of localities. This service mission continues to justify the property tax as a primary means of financial support for local schools, whereas the broader-based tax systems of the federal and state governments are better suited to their mission of redistributing wealth. The federated system of governance and taxation recognizes advantages of both centralized and decentralized units and promotes interactions among all levels.

Because local governments have no tax authority other than that granted by the state, the state is in a position to coordinate tax policy. For example, many states permit income taxpayers to deduct the value of local property taxes before computing taxes owed, and several others grant income tax rebates for a portion of property taxes paid by low-income and elderly persons (see Chapter 6). Although the federal government has no constitutional responsibility to coordinate tax systems, federal provisions may also influence tax structures at lower levels. States that have income taxes rely to a large extent upon federal income tax policy to reduce administrative costs and ease the burden on taxpayers as they compute taxes and file returns. Similarly, reform of the federal income tax in 1986 eliminated deductions of state and local sales taxes, affecting state tax collections and policy development.

Thus, interdependence characterizes the loosely federated structure of governance and finance in the United States. It is within this framework that we present, in some detail, tax bases and criteria for assessing the appropriateness of various revenue sources.

The Different Tax Bases

Governments collect revenue on four distinct bases: wealth, income, consumption, and privilege. Taxes on real estate, personal belongings, or accumulations at the time of death are based on different forms of wealth at given times. Income-based levies depend upon a different form of wealth, the amount of money earned by an individual or business during a specific tax cycle.

Taxes based on consumption apply to commodities purchased without measuring taxpayers' actual wealth or income. Excise taxes are levied on particular items such as gasoline and alcoholic beverages, whereas general sales and gross receipts taxes are less selective in their application.

Privilege-based taxes permit individuals and businesses to engage in certain activities or make use of public properties. For example, pet owners secure licenses, teachers and other professionals pay certificate fees, and highway users pay tolls.

Revenue sources and specific objects of taxation are related to these tax bases. A decision to tax an individual's economic well-being is accompanied by policy deliberations about such tax objects as wages, income from investments, purchases, or other indicators of money "flow." Similarly, the merits of taxing property, accumulated capital, inventory, net worth, estates, and other measures of the "stock" of wealth are addressed in the policy arena (MacPhail-Wilcox, 1984, p. 325).

Primary Revenue Sources

Federal, state, and local levels of government rely on specific sources of revenue to very different degrees. Proportions of revenue collected from intergovernmental transfers and from each level of government's own tax sources are presented in Table 4.1. Grants-in-aid flow from federal to state governments to provide about one-fifth of states' collections. Transfers from federal and state to local levels make up about one-third of total collections of school districts, municipalities, and special districts. For school districts alone, state and federal aid represents about 56 percent of their total receipts (see Figure 3.1).

Property taxation provides no federal and negligible state funds and is declining in relative importance at local levels. In the 15-year span from 1970 to 1985, the importance of property taxes diminished from 37 percent to about a quarter of total revenue for all local government units. However, the property tax remains the primary revenue source readily available to school districts.

The federal government derives the bulk of its revenue from individual income taxation. States' reliance on this source has grown from 10 percent to 15 percent of their total tax collections, whereas the proportion from taxes on sales and gross receipts has

TABLE 4.1. Revenue for Federal, State, and Local Government (percentage of total* revenue)

	Federal		State		Local	
Source	1970	1985	1970	1985	1970	1985
Intergovernmental	0.0	1.0	22.5	20.5	33.7	34.3
General, own sources	79.6	69.3	65.2	62.6	57.3	53.7
Taxes						
Property	0.0	0.0	1.1	0.9	37.1	24.9
Personal income	43.7	41.0	10.1	14.6	2.2	1.5
Corporate income	16.0	7.6	4.5	4.1	0.0	0.5
Sales and gross receipts	8.7	6.1	30.3	23.9	3.4	5.2
Charges and	8.3	12.9	10.1	13.9	14.6	20.4
miscellaneous						

*Includes other revenue not shown separately. (*Source:* U.S. Department of Commerce, Bureau of the Census. [1987]. *Statistical Abstract of the United States, 1988.* Washington, DC: U.S. Government Printing Office, Table 430, p. 257.)

fallen from 30 percent to 24 percent. These taxes, however, remain the single most important source of state revenue. The corporate income tax is declining relative to other sources at both federal and state levels. User charges and miscellaneous other revenues are growing in importance at all levels of government. At the local level, user fees and sales taxes grew proportionally as the share raised by property taxes diminished.

Trends in revenue collections of the federal government are evident in Table 4.2. Individual income taxation increased from $90 billion to $393 billion between 1970 and 1988. However, its relative importance declined somewhat between 1980 and 1988, contributing 47 percent and 43 percent of total receipts in those years. Reliance on corporate income taxation also diminished relative to other sources, particularly between 1970 and 1980.

Payroll tax collections, including Social Security and unemployment insurance, grew dramatically during this period. The proportion of total federal revenue gained from payroll taxes rose from 23 percent to 36.5 percent. Whereas federal tariffs once provided the bulk of revenue, excise and custom duties together raised only 5.7 percent of total funds in 1988. With reforms in estate and gift taxes in the 1980s, these revenue sources declined even further in importance.

The degree to which the United States relies upon many of these tax sources in comparison with eight other nations is presented in Table 4.3. Canada and Sweden tax personal income more heavily than does the United States. Japan and the United Kingdom place relatively heavier burdens upon corporate income taxes. Four of these eight countries collect a higher percentage of their tax receipts from Social Security than does the United States. All nations but the Netherlands place a heavier burden on employers for these benefits; only Sweden places the total burden for social security on employers. The United States makes relatively lighter use of consumption-based taxes than do all countries but Japan. European nations place a value-added tax on goods in all stages of production, in contrast to Japan's collection of consumption taxes on specific goods and services only.

State Revenue Sources

Because public schools depend heavily upon states' general funds for their support, sources of revenue available to state legislatures is of particular interest to educators. The 50 states vary greatly in the extent to which they use the primary revenue sources.

TABLE 4.2. Federal Government Receipts

Source	Amount (in billions)			Percentage of Total		
	1970	1980	1988*	1970	1980	1988*
Individual income	$ 90.4	$244.1	$393.4	46.9	47.2	43.3
Corporation income	32.8	64.6	105.6	17.0	12.5	11.6
Social Security and unemployment	44.4	157.8	331.5	23.0	30.5	36.5
Excise	15.7	24.3	35.3	8.1	4.7	3.9
Estate and gift	3.6	6.4	7.6	1.9	1.2	0.8
Customs duties	2.4	7.2	16.4	1.2	1.4	1.8
Miscellaneous receipts	3.4	12.7	19.4	1.8	2.5	2.1
Total	$192.8	$517.1	$909.2	100.0	100.0	100.0

*Estimated. (*Source:* U.S. Department of Commerce, Bureau of the Census. [1989]. *Statistical Abstract of the United States, 1989.* Washington, DC: U.S. Government Printing Office, Table 490, p. 305.)

TABLE 4.3. Percent Distribution of Tax Receipts for Selected Countries, 1986 (Percentage of Total*)

Country	Personal Income	Corporate Income	Social Security	General Consumption	Specific Goods and Services
United States	35.4	7.0	29.8	7.6	7.5
Canada	37.0	8.1	13.7	14.6	11.4
France	13.0	5.1	42.7	19.5	8.9
Italy	NA†	NA†	34.3	14.6	8.6
Japan	25.1	20.7	29.8	0.0	11.4
Netherlands	20.3	7.3	42.5	16.5	7.3
Sweden	38.0	4.7	25.0	13.4	10.2
United Kingdom	27.9	10.3	17.9	15.5	13.7
West Germany	28.6	6.0	37.2	15.3	8.6

*Includes property taxes, other payroll taxes, and miscellaneous taxes not shown separately.
†Total individual and corporate income taxes in Italy was 37.9% of total tax receipts.
(*Source:* U.S. Department of Commerce, Bureau of the Census. [1987]. *Statistical Abstract of the United States: 1989.* Washington, DC: U.S. Government Printing Office, Table 1422, p. 827.)

Table 4.4 shows that the total collected by states from consumption-based taxes is larger than that from income-based taxes. The combined revenue from general sales taxes and specific excise taxes on motor fuels, alcohol, and tobacco products in 1987 was $103.2 billion. This amount is larger than the total, $96.8 billion, collected from individual and corporate income taxes in that year. However, the faster rate of growth in individual income taxes (728 percent) than in general sales taxes (463 percent) between 1970 and 1987 suggests that income taxation may become as important in state revenue collections in the future.

All states collect excise taxes on specific goods and services; all but five derive revenue from general sales taxation (U.S. Department of Commerce, 1987, p. 270). The District of Columbia and 44 states support public services through personal income taxes,

TABLE 4.4. State Government Tax Collections, 1970 to 1986 (in Millions)

	1970	1975	1980	1987	Percentage of Increase (1970–1987)
General sales and gross receipts	$14,177	$24,780	$43,168	$79,819	463
Motor fuels	6,283	8,255	9,722	15,661	149
Alcohol and tobacco products	3,728	5,249	6,216	7,696	106
Personal income	9,183	18,819	37,089	76,038	728
Corporate income	3,738	6,642	13,321	20,740	455
Motor vehicle and operators' licenses	2,728	3,941	5,325	9,037	231
Total*	47,962	80,155	137,075	247,149	415

*Includes amounts for types of taxes not shown separately. (*Source:* U.S. Department of Commerce, Bureau of the Census. [1989]. *Statistical Abstract of the United States, 1989.* Washington, DC: U.S. Government Printing Office, Table 461, p. 280.)

and all but 4 states collect corporate taxes. In addition to the primary taxes presented in Table 4.4, states collect revenue from other sources, including estate and inheritance taxes, severance taxes, lotteries, and various user fees.

The Advisory Commission on Intergovernmental Relations (ACIR, 1987a) was created by Congress to monitor and recommend improvements in tax practices and policies. It examines the degree to which states make use of available tax capacity. The ACIR's Representative Tax System (RTS) provides an index of each state's tax base, using the national average rate for each of 26 commonly used levies. Tax effort, measured as a state's actual revenue relative to its hypothetical fiscal capacity, indicates the overall tax burden placed on that base.

Indices of states' tax capacity and effort in 1986 are presented in Table 4.5 (pp. 71–72). They provide information about individual states and reveal regional differences. For example, Rhode Island's capacity is 8 percent below the national average, but the effort index of 111 shows that its capacity is taxed well above average. In general, states in the Mideast, Great Lakes, and Rocky Mountain regions have higher than average effort relative to capacity.

Delaware, Florida, and Nevada exhibit low effort despite their large tax capacities; these three states do not make use of income taxation. In contrast, Wisconsin and Utah have relatively low capacity but exert above-average effort. Many states in the Southeast, Arkansas and Alabama in particular, exhibit low capacity and low relative effort.

ASSESSING THE MERITS OF REVENUE SOURCES

We now look at criteria that are useful in evaluating the merits of a tax under varying circumstances. The primary purpose of taxation is to raise revenues for governmental programs. But merely providing an adequate yield is not a sufficient reason to adopt a revenue plan. Other considerations, such as who is to be affected and in what ways by the tax, must be examined. Taxes serve a number of secondary goals, including redistributing wealth and power, creating an economic climate that supports the growth of domestic business, discouraging the consumption of certain products, and encouraging various social and economic policies. Closely related to these goals are five criteria for evaluating taxes: yield, equity, neutrality, elasticity, and cost of administration and compliance.

Yield

The adequacy of yield, or flow of revenue from a tax, affects the financial health of governments. Without an adequate yield, governments are unable to provide services, balance budgets, and avoid unnecessary debt. Among governments, only the federal government can legally run deficits in its operating budget; but because this practice contributes to inflation, it is desirable to keep revenue flows larger than anticipated expenses. State and local governments must balance their budgets, and thus they require sufficient revenue from other levels of government and their own tax sources to maintain services. A tax with a large yield is preferred to a tax with little expected yield.

TABLE 4.5. Regional Variation in Tax Capacity and Effort, 1986

	Capacity		Effort	
States by Region	**Score**	**Rank**	**Index**	**Rank**
New England				
Connecticut	135	4	94	29
Maine	95	26	99	19
Massachusetts	124	5	103	13
New Hampshire	119	9	62	51
Rhode Island	92	31	111	8
Vermont	99	19	91	33
Mideast				
Delaware	121	7	81	47
District of Columbia	122	6	143	3
Maryland	108	13	99	19
New Jersey	121	7	103	13
New York	107	14	152	1
Pennsylvania	90	35	101	18
Great Lakes				
Illinois	96	23	106	11
Indiana	87	39	94	29
Michigan	96	23	118	5
Ohio	91	32	103	13
Wisconsin	86	40	134	4
Plains				
Iowa	84	41	113	7
Kansas	96	23	96	25
Minnesota	102	17	108	9
Missouri	93	29	82	46
Nebraska	91	32	96	25
North Dakota	94	27	89	37
South Dakota	78	45	95	27
Southeast				
Alabama	74	50	86	41
Arkansas	78	45	91	33
Florida	105	15	77	49
Georgia	94	27	89	37
Kentucky	76	48	89	37
Louisiana	90	35	91	33
Mississippi	65	51	97	24
North Carolina	88	37	92	32
South Carolina	79	44	94	29
Tennessee	84	41	84	44
Virginia	101	18	85	42
West Virginia	76	48	98	22
Southwest				
Arizona	99	20	99	19
New Mexico	91	32	88	40
Oklahoma	98	21	85	42
Texas	104	16	79	48

(Continued)

71

TABLE 4.5. *(Continued)*

States by Region	Capacity		Effort	
	Score	Rank	Index	Rank
Rocky Mountain				
Colorado	117	11	83	45
Idaho	77	47	90	36
Montana	88	37	103	13
Utah	80	43	107	10
Wyoming	151	2	117	6
Far West				
Alaska	177	1	168	2
California	118	10	95	27
Hawaii	113	12	105	12
Nevada	147	3	65	50
Oregon	93	29	98	22
Washington	98	21	103	13
U.S. average	100		100	

(*Source:* ACIR [Advisory Commission on Intergovernmental Relations]. [1989]. *Significant Features of Fiscal Federalism, 1989 Edition, Volume II.* Tables 70–71, pp. 118–119. Washington, DC: ACIR, 1989.)

Elasticity

A tax's elasticity determines the stability or flexibility of its yield in relation to movements of the economy (usually measured by changes in gross national product [GNP] or personal income). An elastic tax is one in which yields increase at a faster rate than the rate of economic growth. Conversely, an inelastic tax is one in which the rate of revenue growth is slower than the rate of economic growth. If growth rates for taxes and the economy are the same, the revenue source has an elasticity of unity.

To obtain a coefficient of elasticity, one divides the percentage change in tax *yield* between two points in time (t_1 and t_2) by the percentage change in personal or national *income* during the same period.

$$\text{Elasticity} = \frac{\dfrac{\text{Yield } t_2 - \text{Yield } t_1}{\text{Yield } t_1}}{\dfrac{\text{Income } t_2 - \text{Income } t_1}{\text{Income } t_1}}$$

For example, assume that income in a given region has grown from $80 million to $100 million during the past five years, and the amount of individual income tax collections increased from $5 million to $7 million. In this case, the income tax is highly elastic, given the resulting coefficient of 1.6. If sales tax revenue had grown from $1.20 million to $1.44 million during this time, the resulting coefficient of 0.8 would indicate an inelastic sales tax.

The yield from a stable tax (with an elasticity of less than 1) does not keep up with a growing economy without increasing tax rates. On the other hand, yield does not decline as rapidly during periods of recession. This provides a degree of dependability essential for planning and budgeting government functions. The large and predictable yields of the relatively inelastic property tax make it a particularly suitable revenue source for local governments.

Revenue growth associated with elastic taxes during periods of economic expansion enables governments to expand programs and services and to balance budgets without the frequent adjustments in rates required by stable or inelastic taxes such as the property tax. But during recession, a time when governmental assistance is more likely to be needed by the general population, tax yields from elastic taxes drop at a rate faster than that of the general economic decline. A tax with a relatively high coefficient of elasticity, such as the income tax, produces revenues that fluctuate with economic conditions. This flexibility, or responsiveness, may be advantageous if the economy is expanding, but it may constrain governmental services during a recession. A more stable tax offers predictable revenue yields—even in an uncertain economy.

Equity

It is generally believed that all individuals in society should contribute to the public good and be treated in uniform ways. The determination of actual tax payments invokes conflicts between the principles of benefits received and ability to pay. Equity is the most complex of the five criteria and the most difficult to measure. In dealing with its complexity, this section considers types of equity, sacrifice theory, and incidence theory.

Benefits Received Principle.   The principle of benefits received states that taxpayers should contribute to government in accordance with benefits derived from public services, just as they do when they make purchases in the private sector. For example, user fees charged for toll roads and national parks collect the same amount from all who benefit without regard to users' income or wealth. To some degree, it might be argued that all tax and expenditure policies within democracies approximate an application of the benefit rule: "People, or some majority thereof, would not be willing to sustain a fiscal program if, on balance, they did not benefit therefrom" (Musgrave & Musgrave, 1984, p. 229).

However, the relationship between benefits received and taxes paid is not always clear. It is difficult to determine who benefits and to what degree from such public services as libraries and parks that are shared generally by residents (and many nonresidents) of a tax jurisdiction. Thus, for general services, ability to pay is considered a more appropriate principle in evaluating tax policy than is a benefits standard.

Ability to Pay Principle.   The ability to pay principle states that taxpayers should contribute in accordance with their economic capacity to support public services. Rather than demanding absolute equality in tax payments, the principle calls for an examination of individuals' abilities to contribute. The ability to pay principle was advanced by Adam Smith as early as 1776:

> The subjects of every state ought to contribute towards the support of the government, as nearly as possible, in proportion to their respective abilities: that is, in proportion to the revenue which they respectively enjoy under the protection of the state. . . . In the observation or neglect of this maxim consists what is called the equality or inequality of taxation. (Smith, 1904, p. 472)

The "revenue" that Smith refers to might include any return from property or investments. Income has become the best measure of ability to pay taxes ". . . for it determines a person's total command over resources during a stated period, to consume, or to add to his wealth" (Eckstein, 1967, p. 60).

Sacrifice Theory.   In the interest of maintaining relative equity in the distribution of the tax burden, people at higher income levels are expected to pay not merely higher dollar amounts but also higher proportions of their income in taxes. This requirement is justified under sacrifice theory, which ties differing abilities to pay with the economic view of diminishing marginal utility. Under this theory, consumers seek to maximize their total satisfaction, or utility, from their income through the acquisition of various goods and services. For example, an initial purchase of an automobile provides a large degree of utility (U_1 in Figure 4.1) in the form of basic transportation. Benefits come from successive purchases of automobiles, but the addition to overall utility is smaller with each new sacrifice of personal resources for transportation. Additional vehicles may give added independence of movement to other family members or serve a specialized function such as recreation. At some point, however, the value of the additional vehicle diminishes in terms of utility. Buying a fifth automobile brings a smaller addition to total utility than did prior purchases (from U_4 to U_5).

Conversely, if an automobile is taken away from an individual owning five, there is less sacrifice, or reduction in utility, than if one is taken from an individual who only owns a single vehicle. A similar reduction of income through taxation represents a greater sacrifice for individuals with less income. An "equal" sacrifice rule then implies that individuals with different income levels should contribute different amounts to the government, in such a way that each forgoes similar amounts of utility.

Horizontal and Vertical Equity.   Equality under the law is reflected in the concept of horizontal equity. Very simply, individuals with equal abilities to pay should contribute the same amount of taxes (i.e., equal treatment of equals). Vertical equity, the unequal

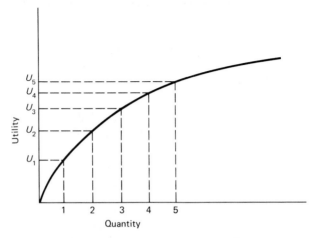

Figure 4.1. Diminishing Marginal Utility

treatment of unequals, calls for differing amounts of taxes from individuals with different abilities to pay. Equity, and its demand for fairness in the treatment of tax burdens, is thus satisfied by unequal tax payments. Those having greater ability to pay contribute more than people with less ability to pay, but all make equal sacrifices.

Tax Incidence. The nature of classifications and the definitions of economic ability are critical to the application of these standards (Johns, Morphet, & Alexander, 1983, p. 88). A narrowly defined group, for example, on the basis of race or sex, would offend the concept of equity even though all members of a given class might be taxed equally. The more appropriate classification for examining tax treatment is income.

Tax incidence is concerned with relative tax burdens for different income groups. Taxpayers are often able to shift their tax burdens. The point of initial impact in these cases is different from that of ultimate incidence, the "settling, or coming to rest, of the tax" (Seligman, 1927, p. 2). An increased tax on a corporation, for example, may be shifted forward to consumers, who pay higher prices for goods, or backward to investors, who receive smaller dividends, or to employees, who receive smaller salary increases. Thus, in estimating the equity of a tax, it is first necessary to know who ultimately pays the tax.

An indirect tax is one in which the burden is easily transferred. Excise taxes on tobacco products, initially imposed on manufacturers who pay the government, are shifted wholly or in part to consumers (depending on market conditions). It is more difficult to shift a direct tax that is imposed on individuals who are meant to bear the burden (e.g., the property tax on a single family, owner-occupied residence or a tax on personal income). But even an income tax can be shifted, as may occur when an individual is transferred to a high income tax jurisdiction and a higher salary is granted to offset the increased tax burden. The employer then attempts to shift this tax burden to consumers through higher prices; the alternative is lower profits and dividends to investors.

Since taxes are ultimately paid from income, tax burdens are compared in relation to personal income. A progressive tax is one in which the proportion of income paid to the government increases as income rises. A tax system that collects $240 and $500 from two individuals with incomes of $30,000 and $50,000 is progressive. A larger percentage of income (8 percent and 10 percent, respectively) is collected from the higher-income earner. If the proportion collected decreases as income levels rise, the tax is regressive. For example, with respect to the property tax, one household may pay 9 percent of its income in taxes whereas another with twice the income pays only 4 percent of its income. A proportional tax demands the same percentage of income from all income groups.

The conclusions drawn from comparisons of revenue sources and the distribution of tax burdens depend in part on the assumptions made about tax incidence. In his analyses of incidence, Pechman (1985) contrasts combined federal, state, and local tax burdens under eight sets of assumptions. All variants assign individual income taxes to taxpayers and general sales and excise taxes to consumers; differences in incidence come through the treatment of corporate income, property, and payroll taxes (pp. 34–37). His least progressive variant, 3b, is reported in Table 4.6. Under this variant, property taxes are divided in such a way that taxes on land fall on landowners, whereas taxes on improvements fall on consumers. This variant also allocates to consumers half the corporation income tax and half the payroll tax on employers. Under Pechman's most progressive set of

TABLE 4.6. Percentage of Income Paid in Federal, State, and Local Taxes under Two Incidence Assumptions, 1966–1988

Group (income decile)	Variant 3b (least progressive)		Variant 1c (most progressive)		
	1966	1985	1966	1985	1988*
First††	27.5	24.0	16.8	17.0	16.4
Second	24.8	20.1	18.9	15.9	15.8
Third	26.0	20.7	21.7	18.1	18.0
Fourth	25.9	23.2	22.6	21.2	21.5
Fifth	25.8	24.4	22.8	23.4	23.9
Sixth	25.6	25.0	22.7	23.8	24.3
Seventh	25.5	25.5	22.7	24.7	25.2
Eighth	25.5	26.2	23.1	25.4	25.6
Ninth	25.1	26.7	23.3	26.2	26.8
Tenth	25.9	27.4	30.1	26.4	27.7
All deciles	25.9	25.3	25.2	24.5	25.4

*Projected from 1985 on the basis of estimates of changes in effective federal tax rates.
†Includes only the sixth to tenth percentiles. (*Source:* Pechman, J. A. [1985]. *Who Paid the Taxes, 1966–85.* Washington, DC: The Brookings Institution, Table 5–2, p. 68, with revisions obtained from author; Pechman, J. A. [1989]. The Case against the Value Added Tax. Statement before the U.S. Senate Finance Committee, p. 7. Reprinted by permission.)

assumptions, variant 1c in Table 4.6, all property taxes are assigned to owners of capital and corporate income taxes are divided between stockholders and owners of capital.

Effective tax rates, the tax paid as a proportion of income, are compared in Table 4.6 for 1966 and 1985 under these two sets of incidence assumptions and for the most progressive variant through 1988. With the exception of the lowest-income earners, who bear a relatively heavy burden, the overall tax system is somewhat progressive. The burden was nearly proportional through the middle range of income (fourth to seventh deciles) in 1966 under each variant. By 1985, there was greater progression for the second through ninth deciles.

Under the most progressive set of assumptions, which Pechman (1989) accepts as the most realistic, there has been a substantial decline in the burden of the highest income decile. In 1985, effective rates were 17.0 percent for individuals earning less than $7,300 and 26.4 percent for those earning over $60,000. The burden was similar in 1966 for the lowest income group (16.8 percent), but there was a much higher burden (30.1 percent) for the highest income decile. Changes in effective rates between 1966 and 1985 favored wealthy taxpayers. The rate for the top 5 percent of income earners declined from 32.7 percent to 26.0 percent, and the rate for the top 1 percent of income earners declined even more dramatically from 39.6 percent to 25.3 percent. Pechman attributes this decline to reductions in personal income tax rates (from a cap of 70 percent to 50 percent in this time period) and in effective corporate rates from 32.8 percent to 16 percent.

Estimates of effective tax rates in 1988 under the most progressive assumptions, reported in Table 4.6, reveal effects of increases in Social Security tax rates since 1985 and revisions in income taxation brought by the Tax Reform Act of 1986. These latter changes in the personal income tax eliminated the tax advantages of some tax shelters and raised personal exemptions and the standard deduction. Despite lower rates, collections from the corporate income tax were increased through the Tax Reform Act by redefining the tax base and removing loopholes (Pechman, 1989).

Overall, tax burdens declined somewhat in the first three income deciles and increased in the top seven, making the tax system more progressive between 1985 and 1988. However, despite restoration of some of the progressivity in effective rates which was lost between 1966 and 1985, the highest income decile continues to benefit from lower effective rates than those paid in 1966.

The incidence of taxes may influence behavior, as when individuals and businesses intentionally shift tax burdens to other groups, many of whom have less ability to pay. Other effects of taxation on human behavior are explored next. Equity issues are discussed further in Chapter 12.

Neutrality

Taxes should be neutral so that there are no undesirable side effects on the operation of the economic system:

> A tax system that introduces distortions into the functioning of the economy typically imposes a loss of welfare on consumers over and above that resulting from the tax payments themselves; this extra welfare loss is the excess burden of the tax. (Oates, 1972, p. 121)

A neutral tax does not distort consumer spending patterns, and it has neither positive nor negative effects on work incentives or choices of alternative means of production.

Taxes may alter methods of production and uses of resources, reducing the potential efficiency of both. For example, an excise tax that raises the price of products may cause a shift in consumer preferences, encouraging manufacturers to divert resources to the production of other commodities. Consumption-based taxes frequently result in reallocations of human and capital resources; the income tax is one of the most neutral of taxes (Webb, McCarthy, & Thomas, 1988, p. 80).

Similarly, businesses consider tax burdens when making location and investment decisions. Differentials in sales or property taxes among states, counties, or municipalities may encourage locations that are less than optimal in terms of production efficiency. Investment incentives in tax policy affect decisions firms make to expand into new markets.

Decisions of individual taxpayers about work and investments are often reactions to actual or perceived tax burdens. Society suffers a loss if taxes diminish the willingness of people to work, to accept more responsible positions, to gain education necessary for professional work, or to take risks (Due, 1976, p. 258). Owners of low-rent housing in urban areas may decide to abandon the property or to allow it to deteriorate if reassessments for property improvements translate into higher tax burdens. Not only do taxes alter behavior, but distortions also reduce revenue and require higher overall tax rates.

In contrast to these negative effects of taxation, some taxes are justified on the basis of desired economic or social effects. Sumptuary taxes deter the consumption of such products as cigarettes and liquor. Duties on imported goods protect domestic producers by making foreign products relatively more expensive. At the same time, however, consumers may pay higher prices and product quality may fall because domestic producers need not introduce the most efficient techniques of production.

Cost of Tax Administration and Compliance

Processes for government to collect a tax are necessary but costly in monetary and other ways. A good tax system should be certain, with no hidden taxes; it must ensure nonarbitrary administration; and its costs must be low enough to enable sufficient relative yield while also discouraging tax evasion. Similarly, processes imposed on taxpayers to determine what they owe should be understandable and not cause a nuisance. Since compliance and administrative costs detract from yield and taxpayer acceptance, they should be minimized.

Taxation should have clearly stated obligations for individuals and businesses:

> The time of payment, the manner of payment, the quantity to be paid, ought all to be clear and plain to the contributor, and to every other person. Where it is otherwise, every person subject to the tax is put more or less in the power of the tax-gatherer. . . . (Smith, 1904, p. 472)

Stability in government and in the private sector depends in part upon a tax system in which payments are predictable. Businesses must be certain about taxes when they make investments, and individuals must be secure against unpredictable taxes to be levied on their incomes (Eckstein, 1967, p. 58).

Fairness in property taxation might be called into question because of exemptions granted to charitable institutions, government-owned property, and Native American reservations. Others might find fault with different assessment ratios applied to businesses, farmland, and vacant property. Political pressure and outright corruption sometimes interfere with the application of uniform procedures called for in tax codes.

Taxpayer acceptance of tax burdens depends to a large extent on ease of compliance. Such methods as payroll deductions for income taxes, inclusion of property tax collections with mortgage payments, and sales tax collections on goods at the time of purchase reduce compliance costs. In contrast, the time and expense of income tax preparation place a costly burden upon taxpayers.

Enforceability is important in the structure of a good tax system. Tax avoidance is a legal activity to maximize after-tax income. Individuals and businesses consider tax provisions as they plan expenditures or decide upon the most advantageous investments. Tax evasion is illegal noncompliance with provisions of the tax code. All tax systems require the government to find and value tax objects. Evasion or avoidance may result if it is easy to hide certain forms of property or income, if it is difficult for assessors to appraise them, or if it is easy to overestimate particular income tax deductions.

Audits that help ensure accurate reporting of property values or taxable income are costly to government agencies, individuals, and businesses. If overly intrusive, they may invoke more dissatisfaction with the tax system than the revenue gained is worth. On the other hand, otherwise honest taxpayers may begin to take advantage of relaxed audit procedures.

TRADEOFFS AMONG TAXATION GOALS

Weighing the advantages and disadvantages of various proposals for tax reform involves value judgments to be resolved in the political arena. The values of equality, liberty, fraternity, efficiency, and economic growth discussed in Chapter 2 are affected by modifications in tax systems. The development of tax policy, continually balancing these often-conflicting values, is an evolutionary process: "Taxation is an art and a technique as well as a science, and it always needs to be judged against the conditions of time and place" (Groves, 1974, p. 24).

Conflicting goals of taxation demand tradeoffs among these values; criteria presented in this chapter help in determining the appropriateness of reform proposals. The goal of maximizing revenue yield, for example, must be balanced with that of minimizing social and economic disruptions. Similarly, a reform proposal designed to improve equity must consider impacts on administrative and compliance costs. Increased import duties, which may be justified by the goal of protecting domestic producers, may be criticized for interfering with the goal of improved efficiency in production methods.

In reality, legislative bodies operate somewhere between a deliberate consideration of just and equitable taxation in relation to these goals and what Johns, Morphet, and Alexander (1983, p. 94) present as the eclectic principle. This approach, referred to as a "social expediency theory" of taxation, recognizes that taxes are obtained most easily when they affect groups least likely to object: "Pluck the goose that squawks the least."

Diverse interest groups, including public school personnel, place pressure on policymakers when a tax bill is being considered. Governmental agencies and special interest groups such as teacher unions and school board associations seek revenue to sponsor new programs, whereas industry, business, and other interest groups desire favorable tax treatment to stimulate investments and productivity. Despite (or perhaps because of) diverse forces, revenue systems of state and federal governments change very slowly. The same groups that argue for reform in tax policy are likely to resist changes that would negatively affect their social or economic positions. The politics of public policy-making are played out to their fullest when processes used to obtain revenue are questioned.

SUMMARY

Just as different policy decisions are made more appropriately at one level than at others, some tax bases are better suited to federal, state, or local governments. Personal and corporate income taxes are primary sources of federal revenue, but the federal government also collects excise taxes on many products. States rely heavily upon sales and income taxes, but a number of other sources like severance taxes and user fees are also tapped. Localities depend to a large extent upon property tax revenue, but some also collect sales and income taxes. The mix in tax bases and sources of revenue results from governments'

continuing need for revenue and from variations in the economic and demographic characteristics of jurisdictions. Division of authority over tax policy is not distinct among levels
of government, and changes in tax structure and administration at one level affect policy
and yield at other levels.

Policymakers must continually assess the potential of various tax bases for raising
necessary revenue to deliver public services while also maintaining a fair system of
taxation. School personnel interact with other public officials, legislators, and private
sector lobbyists in a political arena to make demands for programs that must be financed
from federal, state, and local revenue bases. Criteria presented in this chapter—yield,
elasticity, equity, neutrality, and costs of administration and compliance—are useful
constructs in understanding policy intents and consequences.

Taxes are designed to raise revenue, while also serving various economic and social
goals that affect individuals and businesses. Tax policy development is extremely complex
because of underlying real and perceived threats to equality, liberty, fraternity, efficiency,
and economic growth: "Relief for one class of citizens may mean overburden for another,
and how these tensions are balanced by tax policies affects the social and economic
progress of individuals and the nation" (MacPhail-Wilcox, 1984, pp. 318–319).

There is no ideal tax system which is fully capable of meeting the needs of government
without causing disruption in the marketplace. The federated system of governance and
finance in the United States illustrates that some forms of taxation are better suited to some
jurisdictions than to others. Variations among states in proportions of revenue gained from
the primary tax sources, and differences in their efforts relative to capacities, indicate that
tax policies are shaped through interactions within state political arenas.

We turn next to the merits of various tax sources in relation to the goals of taxation
and criteria presented in this chapter. Chapter 5 devotes primary attention to federal and
state tax policy. The property tax and other revenue sources for local school districts
provide the focus for Chapter 6.

ACTIVITIES

1. What are the justifications, if any, for permitting each level of government to draw
   upon any available tax base for obtaining necessary revenue? For what reasons might
   each level be limited to one or several particular taxes? What is the best mechanism for
   coordinating tax structures and policies among federal, state, and local governments?
2. Record per capita income and tax receipts from selected sources in a given state over
   the past ten years and calculate the elasticity of these taxes relative to income growth.
   Using an electronic spreadsheet will greatly expedite the calculations.
3. Debate the advantages and disadvantages of using tax policy to influence economic
   and social behavior of individuals, private sector businesses, and public agencies.

REFERENCES

ACIR (Advisory Commission on Intergovernmental Relations). (1987a). *Measuring state fiscal
    capacity*. Washington, DC: Author.
ACIR. (1987b). *Significant features of fiscal federalism, 1988 Edition, Volume I*. Washington, DC:
    Author.

ACIR. (1989). *Significant features of fiscal federalism, 1989 Edition, Volume II*. Washington, DC: Author.

Due, J. F. (1976). Alternative state and local tax sources for education. In K. Alexander & K. F. Jordan (Eds.), *Educational need in the public economy* (pp. 257–298). Gainesville: University Presses of Florida.

Eckstein, O. (1967). *Public finance* (2nd ed.). Englewood Cliffs, NJ: Prentice Hall.

Groves, H. (1974). *Two hundred years of thought in Great Britain and the United States*. Madison: University of Wisconsin Press.

Johns, R. L., Morphet, E. L., & Alexander, K. (1983). *The economics and financing of education* (4th ed.). Englewood Cliffs, NJ: Prentice Hall.

MacPhail-Wilcox, B. (1984). Tax policy analysis and education finance: A conceptual framework for issues and analysis. *Journal of Education Finance, 9,* 312–331.

Musgrave, R. A., & Musgrave, P. B. (1984). *Public finance: Its background, structure, and operation* (4th ed.). New York: McGraw-Hill.

Oates, W. E. (1972). *Fiscal federalism*. New York: Harcourt Brace Jovanovich.

Pechman, J. A. (1985). *Who paid the taxes, 1966–85*. Washington, DC: The Brookings Institution.

Pechman, J. A. (1989). The case against the value added tax. Statement before the U.S. Senate Finance Committee.

Seligman, E. R. A. (1927). *The shifting and incidence of taxation*. New York: Columbia University Press.

Smith, A. (1904). *An inquiry into the nature and causes of the wealth of nations* (Vol. II, Book V). London: Oxford University Press.

U.S. Department of Commerce, Bureau of the Census. (1987). *Statistical abstract of the United States, 1988*. Washington, DC: U.S. Government Printing Office.

U.S. Department of Commerce, Bureau of the Census. (1989). *Statistical abstract of the United States, 1989*. Washington, DC: U.S. Government Printing Office.

Webb, L. D., McCarthy, M. M., & Thomas, S. B. (1988). *Financing elementary and secondary education*. Columbus, OH: Merrill.

CHAPTER 5

Federal and State Revenue Sources

This chapter continues our discussion of taxation. The focus shifts from general principles of taxation to a presentation of the primary revenue sources through which federal and state governments support schools and other public services: personal and corporate income taxes, excise and sales taxes, lotteries, severance taxes, estate and gift taxes, and payroll taxes. There is limited treatment of local governments; their primary reliance on property taxation is the subject of Chapter 6.

PERSONAL INCOME TAXATION

All taxes are ultimately paid from personal income. Income is the most widely accepted measure of ability to pay, and taxes on earnings are generally considered the most equitable of the major tax sources. A progressive personal income tax moderates disparities in welfare, opportunity, and economic power arising from unequal distributions of income (Simons, 1938, pp. 18–19).

In colonial America, a faculty tax was collected in varying amounts depending on individual skills and occupations. Although this tax countered effects of duties that imposed higher relative burdens on lower-income consumers, income-based taxes were discontinued. The new nation relied upon tariffs to finance activities of the federal government, until revenue demands of the Civil War necessitated a temporary income tax.

Industrialization and various social movements in the late 1800s revived interest in progressive taxes. An amendment to an 1894 tariff bill would have imposed a federal income tax, but the U.S. Supreme Court declared it unconstitutional (*Pollock* v. *Farmers' Loan and Trust Co.,* 1895). The Court's concern, one of unequal distribution of revenue among states, was clearly addressed in the Sixteenth Amendment to the U.S. Constitution. Ratified in 1913, this amendment empowered Congress to collect taxes on "incomes, from whatever source, without apportionment among the several states, and without regard to any census of enumeration."

The first federal income tax was "born of a partisan movement to achieve social justice" (Waltman, 1985, p. 6). It was a response to regressive tariffs and included a sufficiently large personal exemption to relieve low-income earners. A flat 1 percent tax applied to incomes above $4,000, and a graduated tax was levied on earnings above $20,000. Through the 1900s, a more progressive rate structure and higher overall burdens financed military expenses of two world wars, several "police" actions in Southeast Asia, and an expanding federal government.

Public demands for tax relief in the 1980s initially reduced federal tax rates from 14 percent to 11 percent at the bottom, and from 70 percent to 50 percent at the top, of the income scale. The Tax Reform Act of 1986 reduced the 14 income brackets to 2 income divisions, with taxes of 15 percent and 28 percent, and removed the distinction between ordinary income and capital gains.

Table 5.1 presents proportions of total revenue that states derive from income- and consumption-based taxes. The personal income tax is a graduated tax, collecting a higher percentage from higher-income earners, in the District of Columbia and 33 of the 44 states taxing income. Five other states apply a flat rate to all incomes; 3 states levy a tax that is a percentage of the amount owed in federal income tax; and 3 states have a very limited tax that applies to earnings from interest and dividends. Florida, Nevada, South Dakota, Texas, Washington, and Wyoming do not have any form of personal income taxation. Two of the income tax states, Oregon and New York, rely upon this source for over half of their tax receipts.

Over 3,500 localities levy an income tax in 11 states (ACIR, 1987, pp. 46–49). In addition to many large cities, income taxation is permitted in counties in Indiana, Kentucky, and Maryland and in school districts in Iowa, Ohio, and Pennsylvania.

Merits of Personal Income Taxation

A substantial amount of money is raised by federal and state governments through the income tax (see Tables 4.1 and 4.2). This yield has been highly elastic until recent indexation, which linked growth in revenue produced to the rate of inflation. The coefficient of elasticity of the federal income tax, estimated in the 1970s to be about 1.5, indicated the power of this tax to grow at a rate much greater than that of increases in national income. The rampant inflation of the 1970s inflated family incomes in current dollars, pushing them into higher tax brackets and higher taxes, while their actual purchasing power declined. Termed "bracket creep," these increases in tax liability were not based on real income gains and added substantially to tax coffers without enabling legislation (MacPhail-Wilcox, 1984, p. 327).

Beginning in 1985, tax rates and personal exemptions were indexed to tie their growth to changes in the general level of prices. Slower growth in federal revenue resulted from the restructured and indexed tax brackets. At the same time, Social Security and military retirement benefits were raised to keep pace with the growing cost of living. Diminished yields, but larger commitments, contributed to the growing federal deficit.

Equity goals are more fully realized through income taxation than through consumption- or wealth-based taxes. Exemptions, deductions, and a progressive rate structure

TABLE 5.1. Primary Sources of State Government Tax Collections, 1986 (percentage of total* collections)

State	General Sales or Gross Receipts	Motor Fuels	Alcoholic Beverages and Tobacco Products	Personal Income	Corporate Income
Alabama	28.0	8.5	5.6	25.3	5.2
Alaska	NA	1.2	1.1	0.1	9.6
Arizona	45.7	8.0	2.9	22.0	5.4
Arkansas	38.1	10.8	4.8	27.9	6.2
California	33.7	3.9	1.3	36.8	12.4
Colorado	31.4	8.3	3.2	40.8	5.0
Connecticut	42.4	6.3	3.1	7.8	16.1
Delaware	NA	3.7	1.9	44.6	10.1
District of Columbia	21.0	1.4	0.9	25.9	8.8
Florida	55.1	8.1	7.9	NA	5.3
Georgia	33.4	8.0	4.2	39.6	8.5
Hawaii	50.1	3.0	3.4	31.4	3.0
Idaho	33.6	10.5	2.6	34.4	5.8
Illinois	34.3	6.3	2.7	27.0	8.8
Indiana	48.5	8.3	2.5	29.8	4.1
Iowa	31.3	9.4	3.5	35.1	5.7
Kansas	29.3	7.9	5.4	30.4	8.2
Kentucky	27.4	6.1	2.1	25.5	7.3
Louisiana	31.3	9.3	3.9	12.6	7.3
Maine	34.8	8.3	6.3	30.6	4.7
Maryland	25.5	6.6	2.0	41.3	5.4
Massachusetts	22.4	3.8	3.2	47.2	13.9
Michigan	28.8	6.4	3.4	34.9	15.6
Minnesota	27.7	6.9	3.1	39.8	7.5
Mississippi	53.8	6.5	4.7	14.2	5.1
Missouri	42.4	6.0	3.0	30.9	4.8
Montana	NA	12.8	4.4	27.9	9.6
Nebraska	31.3	13.1	4.0	31.5	4.9
Nevada	49.6	7.6	3.8	NA	NA
New Hampshire	NA	14.5	9.1	5.2	20.5
New Jersey	31.3	4.1	3.3	24.6	11.4
New Mexico	42.8	7.2	2.3	7.0	4.9
New York	20.9	2.1	2.6	50.9	8.4
North Carolina	24.8	7.6	2.6	39.6	9.2
North Dakota	28.7	8.1	2.9	11.9	9.1
Ohio	34.9	7.3	2.8	30.6	5.3
Oklahoma	22.2	7.0	4.3	23.2	3.6
Oregon	NA	6.9	4.4	61.8	8.4
Pennsylvania	30.3	6.0	3.5	24.9	9.0
Rhode Island	32.8	5.3	4.2	32.4	7.7
South Carolina	38.5	8.8	4.6	31.4	5.2

(Continued)

TABLE 5.1. *(Continued)*

State	General Sales or Gross Receipts	Motor Fuels	Alcoholic Beverages and Tobacco Products	Personal Income	Corporate Income
South Dakota	49.3	14.1	5.9	NA	5.9
Tennessee	57.0	11.3	4.4	2.0	8.2
Texas	38.9	9.1	6.5	NA	NA
Utah	41.0	8.6	2.2	33.1	4.8
Vermont	19.8	7.6	5.4	32.3	6.2
Virginia	21.0	6.4	2.4	44.9	5.8
Washington	59.6	7.5	3.9	NA	NA
West Virginia	43.9	8.2	2.3	25.9	4.8
Wisconsin	28.1	7.1	3.0	40.8	7.4
Wyoming	23.1	4.7	0.8	NA	NA
Total	32.7	6.1	3.3	29.6	8.1

*Includes amounts for taxes and license fees not shown separately.
NA = Not applicable. (*Source:* U.S. Department of Commerce, Bureau of the Census. [1987]. *Statistical Abstract of the United States.* Washington, DC: U.S. Government Printing Office, p. 270.)

recognize that taxpayers have differing abilities to pay. The personal exemption, a flat dollar amount that applies to all taxpayers and their dependents, removes low-income earners entirely from tax obligations. Other exemptions adjust the tax base to reflect family size, blindness, and senior citizen status.

Deductions encourage charitable donations and reflect such financial obligations as medical expenses, state income taxes, interest payments, and casualty losses. Adjusted gross income takes into account these exemptions and deductions prior to the determination of an individual's tax bracket. Finally, tax credits reduce the amount owed by low-income earners, encourage various investments, and offset costs of energy conservation. Because of these adjustments, the personal income tax has been progressive over the income scale, with only slight regressivity at the very top (Pechman, 1985, p. 53). Many states' income tax policies further relieve the burden on the poor through more liberal exemptions and additional deductions. Income taxes are also the mechanism for property tax relief in 31 states and the federal government (see Chapter 6).

These provisions help achieve the goal of vertical equity. However, adjustments to income erode the tax base and raise concerns about preferential treatment for some groups of taxpayers. What is designed to be a legitimate recognition of an individual's economic well-being or tax capacity is often termed a "loophole." Despite these limitations that may influence the behavior of taxpayers who desire to avoid excessive tax obligations, income-based taxes are capable of being more neutral in their social and economic effects than are taxes on consumption or property. Income taxation does not involve direct intervention in market activities.

The absolute cost of income tax administration and compliance is high for taxpayers and governments alike. This is the only major tax in which the burden is placed on taxpayers to assess their own tax liability. Regulations and interpretations of the tax code by the Internal Revenue Service (IRS) guide taxpayers. The cost of tax consultation services provided by private vendors is high, as are the expenses of audits and dispute resolution by the IRS and tax courts. Nevertheless, the relative cost of administration is estimated to be only about 0.5 percent of revenue (Pechman, 1983, p. 61).

The elaborate system of deductions and credits complicates this tax and often motivates creative tax avoidance on the part of taxpayers. Taxpayers must keep detailed records and often must turn to accountants and tax consultants to prepare returns. On the other hand, the practice of withholding estimated tax payments through payroll deductions distributes the burden of tax payment throughout the year. Costs of administration and compliance are minimized for state income taxation because state policies generally follow those of the federal government.

There are many advantages of federal and state income taxation, but its use at the local level has been criticized on a number of grounds (Due, 1970, p. 320). Multiple taxation by communities, resulting because income is often earned in one locality by residents of another, creates problems and raises costs of administration and audits. If there is strong incentive for individuals and businesses to migrate to localities with no income tax, economic distortions result.

Reform of Income Taxation

Ever-present calls for reform in income taxation center on tax simplification to reduce its complexity and high compliance costs. The many preferences expressed through deductions and tax credits interfere with horizontal equity, perhaps damaging taxpayer morale when other people with the same income pay lower taxes.

Analyses of effective rates, the percentage of income paid in taxes after exemptions and deductions, reveal that revenue was lost under the federal tax system prior to reform in 1986 because of its many tax preferences. In 1985, effective rates ranged from 0.7 percent on incomes below $5,000 to 26.4 percent for incomes between $500,000 and $1 million (Pechman, 1984a, pp. 16–17). In comparison, incomes over $1 million were taxed at an effective rate of only 23.1 percent, far below the 50 percent rate then called for in the tax code. Eliminating all personal deductions, exclusions, and investment incentives broadens the tax base, permitting the same revenue to be raised with lower rates and a higher personal exemption: "A personal income tax conforming strictly with the 'equal treatment' principle would apply to all income from whatever source derived, making allowances only for the taxpayer and his dependents" (Pechman, 1986, p. 45). The 1986 reforms were only partially successful in meeting this goal.

Musgrave and Musgrave (1984) define income to include all accretion, with no consideration for whether it is saved or consumed. They call for a meaningful and consistent criterion of equity: "In the absence of such a norm, technical issues of taxable income definition applicable to particular cases cannot be settled in a consistent and equitable fashion and the ever-present pressures for loophole snatching cannot be resisted" (p. 351).

Capital gains taxation was a major source of complication and economic distortion until recent reforms. In principle, each year's appreciation in value should be taxed as it accrues. In practice, gains were taxed for many years only when sales of properties or stocks occurred and at substantially reduced rates to promote investment and risk taking. Most gains escaped taxation, and ordinary income was often converted into capital gains to take advantage of reduced rates. With changes in the code in 1986, capital gains are treated the same as ordinary income for tax purposes. The end of this special treatment of long-term capital gains meant an increase from 9 percent to 21 percent in the average tax rate paid (Lindsey, 1987). Pressure to restore the preferential treatment of income from capital gains remains strong.

Many changes have occurred in income taxation since ratification of the Sixteenth Amendment. The process of reform is a political one, however, and those individuals and businesses that are treated favorably resist dramatic change. Goals of equity and economic efficiency are often set aside to accommodate other social and economic objectives. For example, wealthy taxpayers benefit greatly from the exclusion of municipal bond interest from ordinary income. At the same time, however, construction of schools and other public facilities would be more costly without tax incentives for these investments.

CORPORATE INCOME TAXATION

Taxation of corporate income once contributed a quarter of federal revenue but now accounts for under 8 percent of the total. All states except Nevada, Texas, Washington, and Wyoming employ the tax, and this revenue source accounts for over 10 percent of collections in seven states (see Table 5.1). Michigan repealed its corporate income tax in 1976, replacing it with a single business tax which is a modified value-added tax (ACIR, 1990, p. 61).

Benefits received by businesses have been tied to costs of public services for many years. When the constitutionality of personal income taxation was in question in the late 1880s, Congress levied an excise tax on the privilege of engaging in business. The initial 1 percent rate became a graduated tax to meet growing revenue needs. Since 1987, corporate incomes below $50,000 have been taxed at 15 percent and those between $50,000 and $75,000 at 25 percent. Corporations earning over $75,000 pay a 34 percent tax to the government (ACIR, 1990, p. 19).

Rates apply to a corporation's taxable income, defined as sales revenue less costs of production, interest and rent payments, depreciation on capital equipment and facilities, and state and local taxes. Credits and incentives reduce tax owed and serve economic and social goals. For example, investment and energy credits encourage businesses to acquire new equipment to raise productive efficiency and to install energy-saving devices. Tax incentives help businesses contribute to employees' pension plans, hire disadvantaged persons, and participate in public-private partnerships.

Similar problems are posed for tax policy development as were identified for personal income taxation. It is difficult to secure agreement on which costs of business should be deductible expenses and which incentives are important enough to be included as credits to reduce taxes paid.

Each deduction and credit reduces the tax base. The effective rate, the tax as a percentage of profits before deductions and other tax preferences, has fallen. When the corporate income tax rate was 48 percent and profits were $80.4 billion in 1965, the effective tax rate was 34.5 percent. By 1982 it had declined to 13.1 percent, but the nominal rate was 46 percent and profits were $238.3 billion (Pechman, 1984b, p. 144).

Merits of Corporate Income Taxation

Corporate income tax yield is relatively high and very elastic, offering advantages of potential growth for federal and state governments. Because it has few direct effects upon voters, and because of the widely held perception that it is a tax on the rich, corporate income taxation is politically popular. However, not all shareholders are wealthy, particularly in the case of workers whose retirement plans are invested heavily in corporations. If it is assumed that the incidence of corporate taxes falls on consumers who pay higher prices or on employees who receive reduced wages, the basis for an assumption of progressivity disappears (Pechman, 1985, p. 57). Tax burden is further compounded when individuals pay a number of times on the same income—first through individual income taxes on earnings, then through corporate and sales taxes on their purchases.

Costs of administration are minimal relative to yield, but interstate commerce brings problems with allocations of corporate income among states. Multiple taxation of this income is minimized among states that have adopted uniform systems for reporting income and allocating collections to respective states. Compliance costs are high for corporations that plan expenditures carefully and maintain complete records to minimize tax liability.

EXCISE AND SALES TAXATION

Federal and state excise taxes are charged either on a per unit basis (e.g., gallon of motor fuel and distilled spirits) or on an ad valorem basis (e.g., percentage of airline ticket cost or telephone charges). These taxes on selected goods are often defended as substitutes for service charges. Gasoline and vehicle taxes, for example, are viewed by many governments as user charges to support highway maintenance, and they dedicate this revenue for that purpose.

State sales taxes are more general in their application to the retail value of goods and services. Falling property and income tax receipts during the Depression of the 1930s led many states to adopt emergency sales taxes. These taxes became more entrenched during World War II, and since that time sales tax rates have risen steadily (ACIR, 1990, p. 74; Due, 1982, p. 273). Only 5 of the 36 states with a sales tax in 1962 levied a rate of 4 percent, then the highest rate. The most common rate in 1989 was 5 percent (14 states). Nineteen states levied between 3 percent and 5 percent, and 12 states and the District of Columbia had a rate higher than 5 percent. Connecticut had the highest rate (8 percent) in 1989. Alaska, Delaware, Montana, New Hampshire, and Oregon do not rely upon general sales taxes (see Table 5.1).

Thirty states permit localities to levy a sales tax (ACIR, 1990, pp. 78–81). For example, the addition of city and county sales taxes to statewide rates results in total rates of over 9 percent in Chicago, Mobile, and New Orleans.

Merits of Excise and Sales Taxes

The yield of consumption-based taxes is substantial. Sales and gross receipts taxes account for more than 50 percent of tax revenue in Washington, Tennessee, Florida, Mississippi, and Hawaii (see Table 5.1). All states levy an excise tax on motor vehicle fuel; in fact,

27 states raise more than 10 percent of their total revenue from this source. No state grosses more than 10 percent of total revenue from excise taxes on alcoholic beverages and tobacco products. Taken together, these consumption-based taxes account for over 40 percent of the total collected by states.

Growth in the amount of revenue collected by states from sales and excise taxes between 1970 and 1987 was presented in Table 4.4. Collections from selective excise taxes on motor fuels, tobacco, and alcohol more than doubled, and there was a 463 percent increase in general sales taxes. There has also been an increase in local dependence on sales taxes (see Table 4.1). Sales and gross receipts taxes accounted for 3.4 percent and 5.2 percent of local government tax revenue in 1970 and 1985, respectively.

In comparison to this growth in states' collections of consumption taxes, their revenue from personal income taxes increased 728 percent, from $9.2 billion to $76.0 billion, during this time frame. Differences in growth rates reflect the elasticity of these taxes. Because consumption-based taxes are less elastic than income taxes, the 463 percent growth in general sales taxes is due in large measure to rate increases. With an elasticity of unity, sales tax revenue grows only as the income base rises. Rates must be changed to stimulate substantial revenue growth.

Consumption-based taxes are less sensitive to equity goals than are income taxes because they are levied *in rem* (on things) rather than *in personam* (on the person). The amount of tax owed does not account for conditions of individual taxpayers other than their patterns of purchases. Manufacturers and retailers may bear the initial impact of excise and sales taxes, but the ultimate incidence is clearly upon consumers. Rates applied to the value of purchases are the same for all consumers regardless of income level, and there are no deductions or progressive rate schedules. It is only the exemption of basic necessities, including food and medicine, in many state plans that make general sales taxes less regressive because these items represent a higher proportion of the budgets of the poor.

Individuals with the same income but with different consumption habits pay varying amounts of excise and sales taxes; thus horizontal equity is not satisfied. People with different incomes also have dissimilar spending and saving patterns. As incomes rise, consumption declines as a percentage of income. Because excise and sales taxes place a heavier burden upon lower income groups, vertical equity is not satisfied. Pechman's (1985, pp. 55–56) analysis, discussed in Chapter 4, indicates that the lowest income decile paid an effective rate of 18 percent of income in sales tax, whereas the highest income group paid only 1 percent.

Sales tax policy has been sensitive to this regressivity by exempting necessities or providing a credit on the amount of income tax owed in the form of a "circuit breaker." In 1989, the District of Columbia and all but 1 of the 45 sales tax states exempted prescription drugs, and 27 of these jurisdictions also exempted food but not restaurant meals. Sales tax is not charged on a portion of electric and gas utilities in 26 states, and clothing is partially exempt in 6 states (ACIR, 1990, pp. 70–72). Rent is universally excluded from the sales tax.

Despite their political appeal and reduced tax burdens, exemptions cause substantial revenue loss (estimated between 20 percent and 25 percent of potential tax yield), complicate retailers' collection and states' enforcement of the tax, and exclude many expenditures of middle- and upper-income groups (Due, 1982, p. 273). For example, a ceiling on the amount of tax or on the rate for purchases of automobiles and other vehicles makes the tax more regressive and reduces revenue.

The elimination of all exemptions, even for food and prescription drugs, would simplify administration and raise greater revenue. A preferred approach for reducing regressivity may be through a circuit breaker, the mechanism that seven states use to relieve sales tax burdens. Some income tax credits provide a flat dollar amount per family member regardless of income, and others apply a declining rate as income rises. A cash refund is often available for individuals whose income is sufficiently low to exclude them from tax liability. However, these low-income earners may neglect to submit the tax forms required to receive the refund.

Consumption-based taxes are not neutral and often cause severe economic and social effects. Shopping habits of consumers may be affected, particularly if sales tax rates differ within a relatively small geographic area. Decisions about the location of shopping plazas and automobile dealerships may be influenced by rate differences among municipalities, among counties, or even across state lines. Eliminating geographic rate differentials would make the tax more neutral. In particular, better control over interstate transactions would recapture lost revenue from exemptions made for goods shipped across state lines.

Higher rates on "demerit" goods may discourage consumption of alcohol and tobacco. These excise taxes are often justified on the basis of the costs to society that can result from excessive use of the products and on sumptuary grounds because their consumption is considered immoral and unhealthy. If these taxes were effective, however, both consumption and tax revenue would decline (Musgrave & Musgrave, 1984, p. 438).

The relatively simple tax structure of sales and excise taxes minimizes administration and compliance costs. Manufacturers pay excise taxes according to the quantity produced, and retailers charge consumers general sales taxes at the time sales are made. Computerized cash registers simplify sales tax procedures, reducing clerks' errors that once were a problem, particularly in states with exemptions of certain goods. Costs of auditing retailers' accounts are minimal, estimated to be about 1 percent of the revenue collected (Due, 1970, p. 305).

Personal Expenditure and Value-Added Taxes

Very different approaches to consumption-based taxation are offered in proposals for personal expenditure and value-added taxes. A personal expenditure tax (PET) is based upon an individual's aggregate consumption (Courant & Gramlich, 1984; Musgrave & Musgrave, 1984). Income from all sources would be added to assets at the beginning of the tax year. Increasing this amount by net borrowing and decreasing it by net investments during the year would give an indication of funds available for personal expenditures.

At the end of the year, assets would be subtracted from this total, yielding the annual amount of consumption. Tax liability would then be determined from a progressive tax rate structure. Replacing income and general sales taxes, the PET would offer advantages of both. By including high personal exemptions and progressive rates, it would protect low-income groups, who consume higher proportions of their income. For most taxpayers, it would encourage saving and discourage consumption.

A value-added tax (VAT) has also been suggested as an alternative to retail sales taxation. Used successfully in many countries, the VAT is the basic instrument of tax coordination among nations in the European Common Market. Large deficits in the United States during the 1980s brought attention to this tax to stimulate investments and improve the balance of payments in international trade.

An "invoice method" of tax calculation recognizes that goods increase in value at various production stages, with final prices reflecting the sum of increments in value. The base of a VAT is the gross receipts of a business minus the value of intermediate materials and other production costs. Tax liability results from (1) applying the VAT rate to this base and (2) crediting against the gross tax the amount of VAT already paid by suppliers of intermediate and capital goods.

Opponents view the value-added tax as a hidden and regressive tax (Aaron, 1981; McLure, 1984, p. 185). The initial impact is upon producers, but by shifting the tax forward as the price increases, the incidence falls ultimately upon consumers. As with the general sales tax, regressivity might be reduced through exemptions for necessities or income tax credits. Such measures would moderate the VAT's regressivity, making it proportional to income for the lower half of the income distribution, but it would continue to be regressive for upper-income levels (Pechman, 1986, p. 8). Costs of administration for the government and businesses would be much greater under a VAT than under general sales taxes.

The division of revenue among government levels would need to be considered in the development of a VAT policy. If the federal government's VAT replaced states' general sales taxes such that industrial states benefited from taxes imposed at the production stage, many other states would lose tax revenue currently collected at retail levels. Similarly, states could forfeit revenue currently gained from imported automobiles and other products.

For the VAT to be justified, it must be argued that the tax system is too progressive or that substantial revenue is needed to fund a major new federal direction or to close an intolerable deficit. The political environment, with as many businesses being helped as would be hurt, will not support a VAT (Aaron, 1984, p. 217). Because of its disadvantages and potential complications for the current tax structure, it is not likely that a value-added tax will be adopted in the United States.

LOTTERY AS TAXATION

A governmentally sponsored lottery is a voluntary tax (Thomas & Webb, 1984, p. 297). The portion paid in prizes is a product sold by the state, and the remaining revenue, less operating expenses, is an excise tax on that product (Guthrie, Garms, & Pierce, 1988, p. 95). As with other privilege taxes, the government collects a fee for permitting people to participate in games of chance.

Lotteries have been used throughout history to resolve disputes objectively and to raise funds for churches and governments. Their revenue potential has been overshadowed by political corruption and claims that this form of gambling encourages immoral behavior. Abuses in the late 1800s brought legislation against using postal services for transporting lottery materials.

The lottery was revived in the mid-1960s in New Hampshire and New York. By

1988, 28 states and the District of Columbia had operating lotteries. In 1987, 7 states reported yield in excess of $1 billion: California, Illinois, Massachusetts, New Jersey, New York, Ohio, and Pennsylvania (ACIR, 1989, p. 80). Of the $11.5 billion collected nationwide, $6 billion was paid in prizes, leaving $5.6 billion in tax revenue.

Proponents argue that the revenue gained outweighs the lottery's disadvantages. Unlike many unpopular taxes, voluntary games provide some degree of enjoyment for participants. This public entertainment raises state revenue without raising other taxes. Prize money itself becomes a revenue source for the federal government since winnings are subject to income taxation.

The ease of compliance is an advantage, with readily accessible and low-cost tickets; however, the cost of administration is high relative to its yield. This revenue source accounts for less than 7 percent of state revenues, and costs of marketing, printing tickets, and paying off winners are high. From 10 percent to 40 percent of sales is spent in operating costs, as compared to less than 5 percent of other taxes (Thomas & Webb, 1984, p. 303). As a result, only about 40 percent of lottery receipts supports government programs, and the remainder finances prizes.

This 40 percent excise tax rate is higher than those charged for liquor and tobacco. As with other consumption-based taxes, the price of the ticket is the same for all. The burden is upon the poor, who spend a higher proportion of their income for tickets, and it is argued that the lottery is more regressive than general sales or excise taxes. If the lottery tax were lower to be more comparable with other such taxes, prizes could be higher, but the government's share would decline.

The moral dilemma raised by lotteries can be cast within the criterion of neutrality. Opponents contend that the government should not lead the citizenry into immoral behavior and that legalized gambling encourages organized crime, political corruption, and fraud. In response, advocates argue that governmentally sponsored games compete with and thus deter organized crime.

More than half the lottery states earmark proceeds for public education, senior citizen programs, or other specific purposes. These designations encourage ticket sales and enhance political appeal, but earmarking this revenue may make little difference in overall financial support. Previously allocated money from states' general funds may be siphoned off to support other programs (Curry, 1984).

States have turned to this voluntary tax despite its regressivity, low yield, high administrative costs, and opposition from groups concerned about its social effects. The success and current popularity of lotteries suggest that they will continue as an alternative to traditional revenue sources.

SEVERANCE TAXES

Thirty-three states collect severance taxes for the privilege of extracting natural resources from land or water. Production, license, and conservation taxes are levied on such resources as coal, natural gas, minerals, forest products, and fish. Oil and gas production accounts for over 80 percent of these taxes. Energy-related industries also bring revenue to states and localities through rents and royalties on mineral leases for energy production on public land, corporate income taxes, and local property taxes.

Severance taxes are either specific rate, based on the quantity of resources removed (e.g., per ton of coal), or ad valorem, based on gross receipts from sales. Differing extraction processes complicate the task of valuation for tax purposes. In some cases, a very large investment must be made to extract very little mineral; in others, a low-cost extraction process yields much return.

Collections from severance taxes grew rapidly following the 1973 oil embargo and subsequent deregulation of the oil and gas industries but fell during the 1980s. States realized an increase in severance taxes from $800 million in 1972 to $7.4 billion in 1983. By 1986 revenues had declined to $6.1 billion (U.S. Department of Commerce, 1987, p. 272). Severance taxes accounted for over 20 percent of total state revenues in 1986 in Texas, Alaska, Louisiana, Oklahoma, New Mexico, Wyoming, and Montana. With its small population and large production, Alaska collects about $1,270 per capita. Montana, the state with the highest severance tax rate, collects only $200 per capita annually (McLure & Mieszkowski, 1983, p. 2).

States, counties, and school districts with energy revenues are better able to finance public services, and they can export a large share of the tax burden to nonresidents (Cuciti, Galper, & Lucke, 1983, p. 17). Several reforms have been suggested to limit severance taxation to a given percentage of production value or to a certain level of total revenue per capita. Producing states and counties might share some portion of tax revenue with energy-consuming regions, but a counterargument can be made that severance taxes are fair compensation for the environmental damage associated with many extraction processes.

ESTATE AND GIFT TAXATION

The base of gift, estate, and inheritance taxes is wealth. Federal and state governments tax estates for the privilege of transferring an individual's wealth to heirs, and many states collect an inheritance tax on the privilege of receiving a bequest. These taxes reallocate a portion of very large wealth accumulations in concert with beliefs that a wealthy and politically powerful aristocracy might otherwise disrupt free enterprise and that large inheritances might cause heirs to lead less than productive lives.

Tax reform in 1976 joined estate and gift taxes to reduce the incentive to give away the individual's wealth to avoid taxation at death. Estates below $600,000 are exempt from taxation at the federal level, and a gift tax exclusion permits annual transfers of up to $10,000 for each qualified recipient.

Revenue from these sources has been quite small, accounting for less than 1 percent of total federal revenue (see Table 4.2). All states benefit from a portion of the federal tax. Nine states levy an additional tax on estates, 18 states place a tax on inheritance, and 7 states have an additional gift tax (ACIR, 1990, p. 131).

PAYROLL TAXATION

Unlike the foregoing revenue sources that yield money for general government expenses, payroll deductions are earmarked specifically to finance two federal insurance programs, Social Security and unemployment compensation. Initiated by the Social Security Act of

1935, these programs reduce the financial burdens of old age, premature death of family providers, and long-term unemployment. These required payroll taxes supplement other retirement and insurance programs available to educators.

The Old-Age, Survivors, Disability, and Health Insurance (OASDHI) program, as it has been called since the addition of health benefits in 1965, is the largest program sponsored by the federal government. The original intent of Congress was to establish a fully funded insurance program. Payroll taxes would be invested in a trust fund to guarantee future benefits. The inclusion of unemployment benefits in 1939 altered the investment approach, creating a "pay as you go" system of financing (Davies, 1986, p. 169). For many years the trust fund could not keep pace with demands placed on the system. Collections from these taxes increased rapidly between 1970 and 1987 (see Table 4.2), and with recent rate increases, collections have outpaced benefit payments.

Social Security began in 1937 as a 1 percent tax, collecting a maximum of $30 on the covered earnings base of $3,000. Since 1972, the earnings base has been raised annually to keep pace with average wages. The 7.51 percent tax collected on earnings below $45,000 in 1988 increased to 7.65 percent for 1990 and thereafter (ACIR, 1987, p. 21). The total tax is over 15 percent, including the matching contributions of employers. In addition, employers pay 6.2 percent of the first $7,000 of each employee's income for the unemployment compensation tax. These taxes represent a sizable annual expense for school districts, as for all employers.

Payroll taxes, which are nearly proportional for income levels to the covered earnings base, are regressive for upper income groups because they do not contribute beyond this point. The benefit schedule is more progressive. Low-income earners receive relatively higher proportions of the taxes they pay into the system (Davies, 1986, p. 171).

Increased rates and a raised ceiling in the 1980s eased concerns that earlier retirement ages, longer life expectancies, and unpredictable rates of unemployment would jeopardize future benefits. It has been estimated that only two workers will support each retiree after the year 2000, in comparison with a three-to-one ratio in the mid-1980s. To maintain solvency and reduce regressivity, more drastic reforms may be necessary: removing ceilings on contributions, graduating tax rates, supporting health insurance (Medicare and Medicaid) programs with income taxes, or reducing the cost of living allowance to reflect the lower cost of housing for retirees.

SUMMARY

Revenue sources detailed in this chapter provide money for federal, state, and to some degree, local governments. Personal income taxation provides high revenue yield that responds well to the economy, contributes to vertical equity, causes minimal social and economic disruption, and has a relatively low cost of administration. However, its complexity, high compliance costs, and perceptions that loopholes unfairly give an advantage to some taxpayers continue to call for tax simplification. Excise and sales taxes have simplified structures, with no deductions or exemptions based on taxpayers' incomes, and thus minimize administrative and compliance costs. However, these consumption taxes result in economic distortions, and unless provisions are made for exemptions of necessities or for income tax credits, they work against equity goals. These two primary sources of tax revenue offer federal and state governments different advantages that argue for augmenting their role in tax policy. Their weaknesses offer opportunities for reform.

Lotteries, severance taxes, estate and gift taxes, and payroll taxes also contribute to governments' resources. Because they rely upon very different tax bases, these taxes offer ways to diversify tax policy. States rely to very different degrees upon income, consumption, wealth, and privilege taxes because of particular conditions of population, geography, natural resources, economy, and tradition. Finding the appropriate mix of tax revenue in relation to these conditions and to criteria for evaluating the merits of taxes continues to challenge policymakers.

The next chapter identifies the structure and administration of property taxation. Unlike the taxes examined in this chapter, the property tax has been the principal revenue producer of local governments in the United States.

ACTIVITIES

1. Trace the history of one revenue source, identifying the initial rationale, changes in its provisions that may have altered the original purpose, and trends in rates and collections over time.
2. Debate the advantages of income- versus consumption-based taxes in relation to criteria of yield, equity, neutrality, and costs of administration and compliance.
3. Investigate the primary state-level taxes that support schools in a selected state. What proportion is derived from personal income, corporate income, excise, sales, lottery, severance, inheritance, and other taxes? What modifications might you suggest to make this state's revenue system more responsive to tax criteria of yield, equity, neutrality, and costs of administration and compliance?
4. Design an instrument to survey residents of your community or state to determine their preferences for reform in tax policy in the coming decade.

REFERENCES

Aaron, H. J. (Ed.). (1981). *The value-added tax: Lessons from Europe, Studies of government finance*. Washington, DC: The Brookings Institution.

Aaron, H. J. (1984). The value-added tax: A triumph of form over substance. In C. E. Walker & M. A. Bloomfield (Eds.), *New directions in federal tax policy for the 1980s* (pp. 217–240). Cambridge, MA: Ballinger.

ACIR (Advisory Commission on Intergovernmental Relations). (1987). *Significant features of fiscal federalism, 1988 edition, Volume I*. Washington, DC: Author.

ACIR. (1989). *Significant features of fiscal federalism, 1989 edition, Volume II*. Washington, DC: Author.

ACIR. (1990). *Significant features of fiscal federalism, 1990 edition, Volume I*. Washington, DC: Author.

Courant, P., & Gramlich, E. (1984). The expenditure tax: Has the idea's time come? In J. A. Pechman, (Ed.) *Tax policy: New directions and possibilities* (pp. 27–36). Washington, DC: Center for National Policy.

Cuciti, P., Galper, H., & Lucke, R. (1983). State energy revenues. In C. E. McLure & P. Mieszkowski (Eds.), *Fiscal federalism and the taxation of natural resources* (pp. 11–60). Lexington, MA: Lexington Books.

Curry, B. (1984). State lotteries: Roses and thorns. *State Legislatures, 10,* 161–168.

Davies, D. G. (1986). *United States taxes and tax policy.* Cambridge, England: Cambridge University Press.

Due, J. F. (1970). Alternative tax sources for education. In R. L. Johns, I. J. Goffman, K. Alexander, & D. H. Stollar (Eds.), *Economic factors affecting the financing of education* (pp. 291–328). Gainesville, FL: National Education Finance Project.

Due, J. F. (1982). Shifting sources of financing education and the taxpayer revolt. In W. W. McMahon & T. G. Geske (Eds.), *Financing education: Overcoming inefficiency and inequity* (pp. 267–289). Urbana: University of Illinois Press.

Guthrie, J. W., Garms, W. I., & Pierce, L. C. (1988). *School finance and education policy: Enhancing educational efficiency, equality, and choice.* Englewood Cliffs, NJ: Prentice-Hall.

Lindsey, L. B. (1987). Capital gains taxes under the Tax Reform Act of 1986: Revenue estimates under various assumptions. *National Tax Journal, 40,* 489–504.

McLure, C. E. (1984). Value added tax: Has the time come? In C. E. Walker & M. A. Bloomfield (Eds.), *New directions in federal tax policy for the 1980s* (pp. 185–213). Cambridge, MA: Ballinger.

McLure, C. E., & Mieszkowski, P. (1983). *Fiscal federalism and the taxation of natural resources.* Lexington, MA: Lexington Books.

MacPhail-Wilcox, B. (1984). Tax policy analysis and education finance: A conceptual framework for issues and analysis. *Journal of Education Finance, 9,* 312–331.

Musgrave, R. A., & Musgrave, P. B. (1984). *Public finance: Its background, structure, and operation* (4th ed.). New York: McGraw-Hill.

Pechman, J. A. (1983). *Federal tax policy.* Washington, DC: The Brookings Institution.

Pechman, J. A. (1984a). Comprehensive income tax reform. In J. A. Pechman (Ed.), *Tax policy: New directions and possibilities* (pp. 13–18). Washington, DC: Center for National Policy.

Pechman, J. A. (1984b). *Federal tax policy* (4th ed.) Washington, DC: The Brookings Institution.

Pechman, J. A. (1985). *Who paid the taxes, 1966–85.* Washington, DC: The Brookings Institution.

Pechman, J. A. (1986). *The rich, the poor, and the taxes they pay.* Brighton, England: Wheatsheaf Books, Harvester Press.

Simons, H. C. (1938). *Personal income taxation: The definition of income as a problem of fiscal policy.* Chicago: University of Chicago Press.

Thomas, S. B., & Webb, L. D. (1984). The use and abuse of lotteries as a revenue source. *Journal of Education Finance, 9,* 289–311.

U.S. Department of Commerce, Bureau of the Census. (1987). *Statistical abstract of the United States, 1988.* Washington, DC: U.S. Government Printing Office.

U.S. Department of Commerce, Bureau of the Census. (1989). *Statistical abstract of the United States, 1989.* Washington, DC: U.S. Government Printing Office.

Waltman, J. L. (1985). *Political origins of the U.S. income tax.* Jackson: University Press of Mississippi.

CHAPTER 6

The Property Tax in Support of Education

The financial mainstay of local government is the property tax. In 1985, this tax produced over $100 billion in revenue, of which $43.5 billion was used for public schools. This substantial yield is nearly equal to states' revenue from sales and gross receipts taxes combined, $105 billion. It exceeds states' receipts from personal and corporate income taxes, $64 billion and $18 billion, respectively (U.S. Bureau of the Census, 1987, pp. 132, 157).

The property tax is the only significant tax that is well suited to local jurisdictions. Its stability permits school officials to predict accurately annual revenue flow as they plan school programs and hire personnel. The property tax is also defended vigorously because of its close tie with local governmental autonomy and because of the visible link it provides between public services and their costs to individuals and businesses. With county and state administrative mechanisms in place for many years, the cost of tax collection is relatively low.

Despite these advantages, property taxation is also severely criticized. Described as the "most wretchedly administered tax" (Shannon, 1973, p. 27), it has acquired a poor public image because of perceptions of unfair and differentially applied assessment policies. It is often the most painful tax for businesses and homeowners to pay. Challenges to continued reliance on property taxation cite the regressive burden placed on the poor, its contribution to the deterioration of urban housing, its inability to capture the real fiscal capacity of communities, and the inequities it creates in educational opportunities for children in different school districts.

Because of the significance of the property tax to the financing of public schools, an understanding of its structure and administration is important to school administrators and policymakers. This tax is also a concern of states as they increasingly take local property wealth into account in determining the amount of assistance they provide to school districts. Following a discussion of the property tax base, this chapter describes procedures for valuing property and calculating the tax. The merits of property taxation are discussed relative to criteria presented in Chapter 4, and the conflict between local autonomy and statewide control of this revenue source is explored. We also examine revenue and spending limitations and relative tax capacity and effort among states.

THE PROPERTY TAX BASE

Property taxes are imposed on wealth in the form of tangible personal property, intangible personal property, and tangible real property. Tangible personal property consists of such objects as machines, inventories, livestock, and equipment owned by businesses as well as individually owned jewelry, furniture, vehicles, and personal computers. Intangible personal property in the form of stocks, bonds, savings, and other investments has no physical existence beyond the accounts or certificates that represent its value.

Tangibles are a more common tax base in states because they are more readily identifiable, often through licensing processes, than are intangibles. Only 13 states include intangibles within local tax bases, whereas 20 states tax business inventories, 17 tax household personal property, and 19 include motor vehicles (U.S. Department of Commerce, 1989, pp. XI, XII). Thus, the majority of states exempt tangible and intangible personal property.

The bulk of property taxation today falls on tangible real property, which includes land and improvements in the form of houses, commercial buildings, swimming pools, and so on. Table 6.1 shows that locally assessed real property amounted to over $3.9 trillion in 1986, whereas personal property was assessed at $466 billion. With an additional $243 billion assessed by states, the total net assessed value available to localities was nearly $5 trillion. The growth in the real property portion of this tax base, over 1,800 percent from 1956 to 1986, has been substantial. The term "property," as used in this chapter, refers to real property.

For many years, the rationale for property taxation to support local government evolved from the principle of benefits received (see Chapter 4). The extent of police and

TABLE 6.1. Assessed Values of Real and Personal Property, 1956–1986 (in Billions of Dollars)

	1956	1966	1976	1986	Percentage Change 1966–1986
Total assessed value (net locally taxable)	$272.2	$484.1	$1,189.4	$4,619.7	1,597
State-assessed property	22.5	41.6	84.7	242.9	980
Locally assessed property	249.7	442.5	1,104.7	4,376.9	1,653
Real property	202.8	378.9	959.1	3,910.7	1,828
Personal property	46.9	63.6	145.6	466.3	894

(*Source:* U.S. Department of Commerce, Bureau of the Census. [1989]. *1987 Census of Governments, Vol. 2: Taxable Property Values,* Table A, p. VII. Washington, DC: U.S. Government Printing Office.)

fire protection, as well as public libraries and schools, within a community increases the value of properties. Individuals who receive the benefits of such services should pay associated costs. It had been assumed that "the benefits which result are roughly proportional to property values" (Musgrave & Musgrave, 1984, p. 231).

In accordance with benefit theory, property owners and tenants should be willing to pay higher taxes directly, or indirectly through rent, in communities with more extensive and better-quality public services than would residents of other communities. However, relationships among benefits, property values, and levels of taxation do not hold as tightly as they once did. Owners of real estate do not necessarily benefit from local services in proportion to property values. And individuals who do not reside in a given tax jurisdiction may benefit from city parks, libraries, and museums financed by the local property tax base.

Property taxation is a general tax in that there is an assumption of a general distribution of benefits. Tax liability continues to be based on the value of property owned, rather than being tied to taxpayers' income, total wealth, or other measures of ability to pay. In some countries, for example, England, the tax is levied on rent paid, or rental value in the case of owner occupancy.

PROPERTY VALUATION AND TAX DETERMINATION

An understanding of processes used to assess real property and calculate taxes owed is essential before discussing this revenue source in relation to specific criteria.

Assessing Real Property

Counties, municipalities, special purpose districts, and fiscally independent school districts levy ad valorem property taxes according to the value of land and improvements. The amount of equity, the portion of the property that represents the owner's wealth, is not of concern. A bank or other holding company may have title to the larger share of the property's value, but an individual or business is liable for the full tax upon its total value.

Statutes that authorize local governments to levy taxes call for an assessment of property to determine its value. An appointed or elected official, usually at the county, city, or town level of government, is responsible for discovering, listing, and valuing each taxable property in the jurisdiction. Other local jurisdictions use this official tax roll. Statutes may specify an assessment cycle. Some states specify a period of time (e.g., 8 years) during which the assessor must review the value of each parcel. Others indicate a fraction (e.g., one-quarter) of the jurisdiction to be reappraised each year.

The ideal appraisal is a recent sales price. Fair market valuation, often stated as true or full value, is defined as the amount that a willing seller of property would receive from a willing buyer in an open market. Residential property and vacant land are generally appraised according to sales of comparable properties, but because business and industrial properties do not change hands frequently, current market values are not readily available. Their appraisals are more often based on their income-earning capacity or on the cost of replacing the property (Oldman & Schoettle, 1974, Chap. 3).

A primary limitation of the three commonly used appraisal methods is their subjectivity. Market data assume that the value of a given property can be estimated from sales of other properties of somewhat similar age, condition, location, and style. A cost approach relies on estimates of land value, current costs of replacing buildings and other improvements, and depreciation. The income method depends on estimates of the remaining life of the property and of an appropriate capitalization rate to calculate the present value of future income to be derived from the property. Limitations of each method are offset by advantages of others, and the fairest valuations depend on appraisers who can objectively apply several methods.

Advances in technology offer opportunities for greater objectivity and more frequent valuations. So-called "scientific" appraisals rely on statistical techniques to relate actual selling prices of homes or businesses with a large array of characteristics including location, land acreage, square footage, type of heating and ventilation system, and number of fireplaces. It is then possible to maintain assessments that are closer to full value and to reappraise all properties annually without actual inspections. Increased costs of technology and model development may be offset by revenue from more current and accurate appraisals, particularly during periods of rapidly changing real estate markets.

Assessed valuation is generally a percentage of fair market value even in states that call for full valuation. Assessment ratios, which express the relationship between assessed and full values, often differ among classifications of property. Several states adopted classification systems in the early 1970s in response to judicial concerns about additional burdens placed on businesses. Local assessors often used their own "extralegal" (Shannon, 1973, p. 29) system of classifications to deviate from uniformity mandates. Because the same tax rate is later applied to all properties in a jurisdiction, the effect of classification schemes is to shift legally the tax burden from some groups of taxpayers to others.

Assessment ratios are illustrated in Table 6.2. Full valuation is called for in 21 states, including New York. Another 15 states, like Connecticut and Indiana, specify a single percentage of full valuation to be applied to all taxable property. The remaining 14 states, including Arizona and Tennessee, assign different ratios to various classes. Higher ratios are common for assessments of industrial and commercial property relative to those for agricultural and residential property. Minnesota, with its 23 divisions that range from 5 percent to 43 percent, has the largest number of classifications.

Property is valued on the basis of its "highest and best" use, in accordance with the application naturally suited to the site and likely to maximize its potential monetary return.

TABLE 6.2. Assessment Ratios and Classifications of Real Property in Selected States

Arizona	Nine classes: mines and timber, 25%; telephones, gas, and utilities, 25%; commercial and industrial, 25%; agricultural and vacant, 16%; residential, 10%; residential rental, 10%; railroads, 22%; historic, 5%; producing oil and gas companies, 100%
Connecticut	All property at 70% of market value
Indiana	All property at 33-1/3% of market value
New York	All property at 100% of market value
Tennessee	Three classes: public utilities, 55%; industrial and commercial, 40%; farm and residential, 25%

(*Source:* U.S. Department of Commerce, Bureau of the Census. [1989]. *1987 Census of Governments, Vol. 2: Taxable Property Values,* Appendix A. Washington, DC: U.S. Government Printing Office.)

Several assessment methods provide incentives to hold agricultural, recreational, open space, and historic land from development. A preferential assessment approach, employed by 26 states in 1986, gives a low assessment based on current income or use rather than on the true market value of the land and continues until the qualified use ends without any later penalty.

A deferred taxation approach, used by 30 states, also offers a preferential use assessment, but it requires a penalty or recoupment of back taxes when land use changes. Another method, used by 14 states, is the restrictive agreement whereby a contract is made between the landowner and the local government to hold land in qualified use for a specified period of time in exchange for lower assessment or deferred taxation. For example, agricultural reserves and nonprofit conservation trusts maintain farm and open land in exchange for lower or forgiven taxes.

Maximizing taxpayer satisfaction with tax schemes often justifies residential assessments that are below fair market values. The public is less likely to complain about these lower assessments or to vote for a change in local politicians. Similar practices reduce business assessments to attract manufacturing or commercial activity or to discourage industry from leaving the locality. On the other hand, residential and business properties which do not receive preferential assessments must absorb tax burdens deferred or exempted from properties receiving preferential treatment, causing them to pay higher taxes than they would if all properties were subject to the same standards. Deviation of assessments from policy or standards, especially when there is evidence of favoritism or political "cronyism," conflicts with goals of sound fiscal policy and tax equity.

States that base allocations of aid to localities or school districts in relation to local property wealth often account for varied assessment practices among jurisdictions through equalization ratios, the ratio of assessed value to market value. Dividing the assessed value by the equalization ratio yields an estimate of market value, thereby bringing all assessments to a common basis. The school district depicted in Table 6.3 overlaps four assessing jurisdictions, such as towns or villages. Jurisdiction A has the highest equalization ratio, not because it is the wealthiest town, which it is, but because of its practice of assessing properties above market value. Jurisdiction D has the lowest assessed value, but its equalized value is higher than either B or C. The reason for this is that jurisdiction D assesses its property at only 15 percent of market value whereas jurisdictions B and C assess theirs at 85 percent and 50 percent, respectively.

Once the state determines equalized values for each jurisdiction, allocations of state

TABLE 6.3. Illustration of Equalization Ratios for Several Tax Jurisdictions within a School District

Jurisdiction	Assessed Value	Equalization Ratio	Equalized Value
A	$324,000,000	1.20	$270,000,000
B	85,000,000	0.85	100,000,000
C	45,000,000	0.50	90,000,000
D	21,000,000	0.15	140,000,000
Total	$475,000,000		$600,000,000

funds can be based more accurately on local tax capacity. Without a system of equalized assessment ratios, there is an incentive for tax jurisdictions to underassess properties to understate their wealth.

Exemptions and Tax Relief

Localities give up a portion of their tax base in the form of total exclusion or partial exemptions for (1) schools, universities, and governments; (2) religious and welfare organizations, including churches, chambers of commerce, fraternal organizations, and labor unions; (3) heads of households, the elderly, veterans, volunteer fire fighters, and handicapped persons; and (4) incentives to rehabilitate housing or to attract industry. Another form of tax relief is to grant a credit against income tax payments to individuals whose property taxes exceed a given percentage of their income.

Exemptions are defended by the promotion of desired social values. It is assumed that the benefits nonprofit organizations provide to the community are sufficient to offset the cost of public services that are in effect given to them without payment of taxes. When the Supreme Court examined claims of unconstitutional aid to religion, tax exemptions for churches were not found to violate the First Amendment: "Elimination of exemption would tend to expand the involvement of government by giving rise to tax valuation of church property, tax liens, tax foreclosures, and the direct confrontations and conflicts that follow in the train of those legal processes" (*Walz* v. *Tax Commission of the City of New York,* 1970).

On the other hand, exemptions are criticized because of the diseconomies they create. For example, there may be income-producing office buildings, hotels, and medical centers located on exempt church and university land. Manufacturing plants that are leased by counties to private corporations may be constructed on exempt public land. Although constructed on private land, enterprise zones receive tax breaks to encourage economic development. Industries located in these tax enclaves benefit in the short run (generally not over 10 years) from no taxation or favorable tax rates. Moreover, they gain long-term benefits from the enlarged tax base that reduces future tax burdens.

Many exemptions and tax breaks provide governmental subsidies for diverse interest groups, with other residents and businesses paying higher taxes. The loss of tax bases to support local governments can be substantial. For example, $8.4 billion (over 9 percent) of the total locally assessed value is tax exempt in Illinois. For many large cities, the loss can be even greater. In New York City, nearly 11 percent ($6.3 billion) of locally assessed property is exempt (U.S. Department of Commerce, 1989, pp. 49, 67).

Cities with reduced tax bases would benefit from state reimbursement of lost revenue, in a similar manner to the financial payments that the federal government provides to school districts affected by military installations and Native American reservations (see discussion of P.L. 874 in Chapter 10). In this way, individuals who do not reside in the community but who use public libraries, parks, universities, and other facilities would share the cost of exemptions. A second method to spread the tax burden requires exempt organizations to pay user charges for selected governmental services. For example, many universities make payments to municipalities to offset large public service costs and to maintain community goodwill.

Nearly all states give some individual taxpayers relief from property taxes. Known as homestead exemptions, they came into being during the Depression of the 1930s and were granted to homeowners regardless of income. Since then, exemptions have been granted to most elderly homeowners, veterans, and volunteer fire fighters. These exemptions are criticized because they reduce the tax base, complicate tax administration, and may provide a subsidy for individuals who are otherwise able to pay taxes (Shannon, 1973, pp. 35–37).

Circuit breakers in 32 states permit a credit against state income taxes for property tax payments that exceed a specified proportion of income for elderly and low-income homeowners and, in some cases, renters. For example, Pennsylvania offers rebates ($10 minimum, $500 maximum) of taxes due from people over 65. These credits range from 100 percent for incomes under $5,000 down to 10 percent for incomes greater than $9,000 (U.S. Department of Commerce, 1989, p. XXI).

Maintaining the local tax base and having income redistribution at the state level through circuit breakers are preferable to general homestead exemptions. However, circuit breakers may not help all low-income earners. Property owners and renters who have little or no taxable income for the year still qualify for rebates of property taxes paid. As in the case of income tax credits to offset sales taxes on food and necessities, these low-income families may not file for property tax relief. Renters do not qualify for circuit breakers in all states, but they should be eligible if it is assumed that tenants bear the full property tax burden.

Because circuit breakers do not always address these concerns, Aaron (1973) contends that singling out this one household expenditure for relief may be due to its political acceptability. A housing allowance may be more appropriate, if property taxes affect housing costs. On the other hand, relief granted for all taxes paid over a given fraction of income would recognize that property and other taxes excessively burden certain households.

Calculating the Property Tax

In addition to the technical function of assessment to determine the value of property in a jurisdiction, there is a political decision that sets the tax rate. The former process determines the capacity of the tax base, and the latter identifies the level of tax effort the community is willing to exert to support public services.

The difference between projected costs of desired programs for a given fiscal year and the amount of revenue anticipated from federal, state, and other local sources is the local tax amount (*levy*) to be collected. This levy is divided by the aggregate assessed, or in some states equalized, value (*AV*) of property in the tax jurisdiction to yield a tax rate (*rate*):

$$\text{Rate} = \text{levy}/AV$$

A mill is defined as one-tenth of a cent (0.001). A rate of 10 mills places a 1 percent tax on the assessed value of property. For example, the school district depicted in Table 6.3 has a total equalized valuation of $600 million. If a levy of $15 million is necessary for local support of its schools' operations, the required tax rate is 0.025 (calculated as $15 million/$600 million). This 25-mill tax is equivalent to a rate of $25 per thousand, or $2.50 per hundred, of valuation.

TABLE 6.4. Illustration of Tax Rates and Levies for Tax Jurisdictions within a School District

Juris-diction	Tax Rate on Equalized Value	Equali-zation Ratio*	Tax Rate on Assessed Value[†]	Assessed Value*	Tax Levy[†]
A	25.00	1.20	20.83	$324,000,000	$6,750,000
B	25.00	0.85	29.41	85,000,000	2,500,000
C	25.00	0.50	50.00	45,000,000	2,250,000
D	25.00	0.15	166.67	21,000,000	3,500,000

*See Table 6.3.
[†]Rounded.

Calculations of tax levies in Table 6.4 apply this 25-mill tax rate to the four tax jurisdictions (initially presented in Table 6.3). The rate for the total district divided by the four respective equalization ratios yields tax rates that can be applied to the initial assessed values. Resulting tax levies for the four jurisdictions total the required $15 million for district operations.

Once tax rates have been established for jurisdictions, a tax bill is prepared for each property. The tax rate is multiplied by the appraised value (AV_i), where i ranges from the first to the last parcel on the tax roll:

$$\text{tax}_i = (\text{rate})\,(AV_i)$$

Calculations of property taxes for four parcels in Table 6.5 illustrate the application of this formula and the effect of exemptions for homesteads, senior citizens, and others. The properties have the same market value, $80,000; however, because the equalization ratios are different for the two jurisdictions, the assessed values for parcels 1 and 2 are different from parcels 3 and 4. Even though parcels 1 and 3 have different assessed values and tax rates, their owners pay the same amount of taxes and have the same "effective"

TABLE 6.5. Determining Net Tax and Effective Tax Rate

	Jurisdiction B		Jurisdiction C	
	Parcel 1	Parcel 2	Parcel 3	Parcel 4
Net Tax				
Market value	$80,000	$80,000	$80,000	$80,000
Equalization ratio	.85	.85	.50	.50
Assessed value	$68,000	$68,000	$40,000	$40,000
less exemption	− 0	− 5,000	− 0	− 5,000
Taxable value	$68,000	$63,000	$40,000	$35,000
by tax rate*	× 0.02941	× 0.02941	× 0.05000	× 0.05000
Net tax owed	$2,000	$1,853	$2,000	$1,750
Effective tax rate (per $1,000 market value)	$25.00	$23.16	$25.00	$21.88

*From Table 6.4. In Table 6.4, the tax rates are expressed in dollars per $1,000 of assessed value. For computation purposes, they are expressed here as a ratio.

tax rates. Parcels 2 and 4 benefit from exemptions and pay less tax than parcels 1 and 3. Because exemptions are applied to assessed values, and because parcel 4 is assessed at a smaller ratio than is parcel 2, the effect of the exemption is greater for parcel 4, which pays the lowest taxes and has the lowest effective tax rate.

Property may be taxed by several overlapping branches of local governments independently or in combination. In addition to school districts, property taxes may be levied, for example, in support of counties, towns, cities, villages, fire districts, lighting districts, sewer districts, water districts, or road districts. A given piece of property is usually assessed by only one authority such as a town or county; however, an authority such as a school district may encompass several assessing authorities, as in the preceding example, necessitating the use of equalization ratios. Taxes may be collected by an authority other than that levying the tax.

MERITS OF THE PROPERTY TAX

Property taxation as a revenue source is examined next in relation to criteria presented in Chapter 4: yield, equity, neutrality, and cost of administration and compliance.

Yield

State and local revenue from property taxation totaled $121 billion in 1986–1987 (U.S. Department of Commerce, 1989, p. XIV). Trends evident from data presented in Table 6.6 indicate that local tax revenue grew from $12.6 billion to $116.6 billion between 1956–1957 and 1986–1987. However, its contribution to local revenue declined both in relation to total revenue received (from 43 percent to 25 percent) and in relation to total local tax revenue (87 percent to 74 percent). Property taxes also add to state revenue ($4.6 billion in 1986–1987), and their proportionate contributions also declined relative to other funds received by states.

Elasticity of this tax is best determined by change in its yield in relation to change

TABLE 6.6. Revenue from Property Taxes, 1956–1957 to 1986–1987 (dollar amounts in millions)

	State Governments			Local Governments		
Year	Property Tax Revenue	Percentage of Revenue from All Sources	Percentage of Tax Revenue	Property Tax Revenue	Percentage of Revenue from All Sources	Percentage of Tax Revenue
1956–1957	$479	1.9	3.3	$12,618	43.4	87.0
1961–1962	640	1.7	3.1	18,416	42.6	87.9
1966–1967	862	1.4	2.7	25,186	39.0	86.6
1971–1972	1,257	1.1	2.1	40,876	36.1	83.5
1976–1977	2,260	1.1	2.2	60,267	30.7	80.5
1981–1982	3,113	1.0	1.9	78,805	25.2	76.0
1986–1987	4,609	0.9	1.9	116,618	24.8	73.7

(Source: U.S. Department of Commerce, Bureau of the Census. [1989]. 1987 Census of Governments. Vol. 2, Taxable Property Values, Table F, p. XIV. Washington, DC: U.S. Government Printing Office.)

in the underlying tax base, the market value of properties, rather than in terms of personal income (Netzer, 1966, pp. 184–190). Assessed valuations, the legal base of the tax, do not necessarily reflect market values, and coefficients of elasticity appear to be below unity. The inclusion of business properties in particular reduces its elasticity, whereas residential property assessments more closely respond to changes in the economy. Netzer discusses studies that examined elasticity in relation to market values or to state-equalized tax bases. They often revealed an elastic tax, with coefficients between 1.0 and 1.2.

The slower response of assessments to changes in the general economy account for property tax stability, which is both a strength and a weakness of property taxation. On the one hand, stability is important to local officials who must plan budgets and balance expenditures with available revenue. On the other hand, assessments are slow to respond to fluctuations in prices and incomes. Unlike income and sales taxes that are adjusted less frequently, property tax rates must be reexamined each year.

Without an expanding tax base between the Great Depression and World War II, school expenditures lagged behind the growth rate of the general economy. Growth in assessments and strong public support for education permitted increases in property tax rates during the 1950s and 1960s, which helped to finance the rapid expansion of public schooling during that period. In contrast, the general economic recession during the 1970s brought restricted governmental growth, regardless of the tax source. Federal and state governments, with their heavier reliance on more elastic taxes, faced potentially large shortfalls. School districts that relied heavily on property taxation were in many cases relatively advantaged because of the stability of the tax and the dependability of its yield.

Assessment practices have improved in recent years and properties are now typically valued more frequently. When this happens, rising assessments reflect larger market values during periods of inflation; but, still, there is a tendency for growth in property tax assessments to lag behind growth in home values (Musgrave & Musgrave, 1984, p. 475). With more frequent appraisals in the future, assessments should more closely reflect market values. Property tax elasticity will enable the yield to grow more in relation to the economy, and tax rates will need to be adjusted less frequently.

Equity

In an agrarian society, where land ownership was closely tied to wealth, income, and power and to benefits received from the government, real property was a good indicator of an individual's ability to pay taxes. But in information and industrial societies, land ownership is only one form of wealth, and equal treatment under tax codes is generally measured in terms of income.

There is little relationship between the income of an individual taxpayer and the amount of property tax paid. Horizontal equity is violated because individuals with the same income do not necessarily pay the same amount of tax. To determine the degree to which this revenue source satisfies vertical equity, the unequal treatment of unequals, it is necessary first to consider who bears the burden of the tax and then to identify its relationship with taxpayers' income.

Taxes on housing are borne by occupants. The property tax is a direct tax on homeowners, who may be able to recoup a portion of taxes paid when houses are later sold for appreciated values. Under favorable circumstances, owners of rental property are able to raise rents and shift tax increases to tenants, who cannot later recoup any portion of taxes paid. Assuming lower relative valuations of higher-priced houses and a higher proportion of income spent on housing by low-income families, tax on residential property has been thought to be regressive (Netzer, 1966, p. 131). Under this traditional view of incidence, tax burdens are assumed to be higher for low-income earners. Residential taxes fall on tenants rather than landowners, and property taxes on businesses fall on consumers rather than owners or stockholders.

A second approach to incidence considers the property tax to be a tax on capital such that its incidence is upon owners. Thus, taxes on commercial and industrial property are distributed in line with income from capital rather than on the basis of consumption expenditures (Aaron, 1975). If property owners are assumed to bear the burden, the tax is more progressive. This conclusion rests upon the presumed close relationship between ownership of capital and the distribution of income.

Overall tax burdens under these two sets of assumptions were discussed in Chapter 4 (see Table 4.6). Except for the lowest income level, which bears a relatively heavy burden, the proportion of income paid in all taxes in 1985 rose slowly with income under either set of assumptions. Even assuming the property tax burden itself to be regressive, it does not appear to make overall tax burdens regressive. Homestead exemptions and circuit breakers based on income serve to reduce property tax regressivity in many states.

Neutrality

A neutral tax has little or no effect on the mix of resources (land, labor, and capital) in production processes. A tax on land itself, without a tax on improvements, does not hinder production: "the whole value of land may be taken into taxation, and the only effect will be to stimulate industry, to open new opportunities to capital, and to increase the production of wealth" (George, 1879, p. 412). Proposals for site-value taxation would simplify property valuation by reducing the property tax base to include only land without buildings and other improvements. This approach would stimulate the development of real estate to its full potential, particularly in deteriorating central cities, because it is in owners' interests to maximize the use of land (Peterson, 1973). However, site-value taxes might discourage investors from keeping older buildings, single-story structures, parking lots, and other improvements that do not maximize land use.

The effects of taxing improvements within the taxation of real property, as it is presently structured and administered by localities, are not neutral. Property taxes influence choices of geographic location for residences and businesses, contribute to the deterioration of urban areas, and cause disparities in educational programs.

Communities engage in "fiscal mercantilism" (Netzer, 1966, pp. 45–59) to maximize tax bases in relation to the demand for public services. Lower tax rates become incentives for individuals and businesses to migrate from cities to suburbs and from northern to southern and western states. Tax benefits and restrictive zoning regulations that define land use encourage formation of industrial enclaves. High-income families are attracted to communities with very different residential wealth, whereas low-income families, who do not contribute to the tax base but who increase public service costs, are discouraged from residing there.

Because land values are underassessed and improvements are overassessed, land is withheld from its most productive use in deteriorating sections of cities. Upgraded properties in generally blighted neighborhoods do not necessarily bring larger rents; but improving property will certainly result in higher taxes generated by the higher assessments which accompany improvements. The overassessment of poor neighborhoods creates tax delinquency, and many cities are slow in enforcing tax collections (Peterson, 1973, p. 10).

Yinger, Bloom, Borsch-Supan, and Ladd (1988) found strong evidence that differences in effective property tax rates are, to some extent, capitalized into the price of housing. This is the case because, all else being equal, a household is willing to pay more for a house with low taxes than a comparable house with high taxes. They conclude,

> Because households compete with each other for access to housing in jurisdictions with low tax rates, jurisdictions with relatively low tax rates will have relatively high house values, and vice versa. In equilibrium, households must be exactly compensated for higher property tax rates by lower housing prices. (p. 56)

Full capitalization of the property tax would impose the same burden on each unit of housing regardless of the actual tax levied; however, effective tax rates are not fully capitalized. The studies by Yinger and colleagues found the degree of capitalization to range between 16 percent and 33 percent. These differing treatments of property taxes may influence the selection of homes and communities.

Property taxes contribute to disparities in spending levels among school districts. In most states, the level of resources available for each pupil depends to some degree on the wealth of local communities and on the level of effort taxpayers exert to support schools. The more local school districts depend on the property tax for their financial support, the greater will be the disparity in funding levels among school districts.

The property tax itself, however, does not cause many of these economic distortions. The problem lies with the fragmentation of the local governance structure. If another revenue source, say the income or sales tax, had been tied traditionally to local governments, similar disparities would be evident: "large differentials in the rates of any major local tax among neighboring and competitive jurisdictions are likely to be bad rather than good" (Netzer, 1966, p. 172).

Administration and Compliance Costs

Criticism of the property tax is centered on its administration. Revenue is maximized, as are taxpayer acceptance and support, if valuation and collection procedures are administered efficiently and fairly.

Unlike income taxes, liability for property taxes is not determined by individual taxpayers. Property assessment and tax calculation are the responsibility of local public officials, nearly eliminating compliance costs. However, many assessors are poorly trained in appraisal procedures, serve only part time, and are often concerned about their reelection or advancement in the local or state political arena. Problems of tax administration are epitomized by the conflict faced by assessors who must raise assessments to keep pace with inflation and property improvements while maintaining favor in the local power structure. Removing these individuals from the elective process, and appointing them on the basis of demonstrated abilities to assess properties, would contribute to the professionalization of the assessment function (ACIR, 1973, p. 69).

The cost of administration is low, relative to its yield and in comparison with costs of other major revenue sources. However, the low cost is indicative of deficiencies in assessment practices, predominantly related to inefficiencies of small units of government. Making full disclosure of local assessment practices and improving appeals procedures offer advantages of reducing inequities and political interference with the system while increasing public confidence. It would be possible to have good property tax administration at a cost of about 1.5 percent of tax collections, an acceptable amount when compared with administrative costs for income and sales taxes (Netzer, 1966, p. 175).

Summary

Property taxation brings a stable and productive revenue source to local governments. As assessments and yield more closely reflect market values in the future, its greater elasticity will enable growth with the general economy without continual rate adjustments. Property taxation is not as regressive as once believed, and economic distortions are not caused by property taxation per se but rather by the governance structure. A crucial policy question concerns the degree to which local autonomy and resulting disparities in expenditure levels are to be tolerated.

LOCAL AUTONOMY AND STATE-LEVEL PROPERTY TAXATION

Having access to a substantial revenue source is important to the autonomy of local governments, and the property tax is the revenue source best suited to local governments. Although decisions about school programs could be made locally even if all funds were allocated from higher levels, access to this revenue source enables local officials to determine the total level of resources and services to be provided, at least at the margin.

When the property tax is weighed against criteria of yield, equity, neutrality, and costs of administration and compliance, there is no overriding concern that argues for its elimination and replacement by another tax source. It would be difficult, particularly for those states that have relied heavily on property taxation, to replace local with state revenue. However, where the case is strong against fiscal disparities among communities, state or regional property taxation might be considered as a part of a more equitable school finance policy.

Continuing to place a large burden on small local governmental units to finance schools is inconsistent with goals of equity and efficiency in resource allocation (Netzer, 1973, pp. 13–24). A larger state role in school finance equalizes educational opportunities at a time when increased mobility of labor among localities distributes the positive and negative consequences of school quality to many other communities through "geographic spillovers." Similarly, efficiency in tax administration is better served through state or regional, rather than school district, control of tax policy.

In response to judicial decisions, tax study commissions, and other pressures to meet equity goals, many states deemphasized local property taxation during the finance reform movement of the 1970s. Assumption by state and federal governments of increased responsibilities for the finance of elementary and secondary education eased the burden on local revenue (see Figure 3.1). Greater "fiscal federation" promised a broader base of support, equalization of local districts' capacities to finance schools, and improved assessment practices (ACIR, 1973, p. 77).

Rather than eliminate property taxation, larger state involvement in school finance often means that states take into account funds raised locally as they distribute financial aid to school districts (see Chapter 8). In effect, larger tax bases, including utilities and industrial property, are spread among more localities. Tax-based disparities, and service disparities, are thus greatly reduced. Even in states which have assumed a large financial involvement, property tax administration remains, for the most part, a local government responsibility, but states use equalization ratios and exercise more control over assessment practices.

For many individuals, the defense of property taxation is deeper than its historical significance, high yield, or stability. It is symbolic of the autonomy of local government, and any move to have the state assume property taxes is resisted. This revenue source "serves as the sheet armor against the forces of centralization" (Shannon, 1973, p. 28).

The educational reform movement of the 1980s directed attention once again to the advantages of maintaining control over many decisions at the district or school level. Control over fiscal affairs is an important part of program control. The policy dilemma concerns the most appropriate level or combination of levels of government to finance schools and develop policy, rather than a debate about the merits of the property tax as a revenue source.

LIMITATIONS ON TAXATION AND EXPENDITURES

Tax and spending limitations restrict government's capacity to deliver public services with the intention of encouraging fiscal responsibility. Officials who are overzealous in their desire to meet demands of constituents may raise taxation and indebtedness to a dangerous level. The Revolutionary War was fought to ensure that the citizenry would have a voice in decisions about governmental taxation. Two subsequent movements addressed the large debt incurred by local governments in the late 1800s and the growth in government and taxes in the 1970s.

Debt and Tax Limits

State constitutions and statutes that define the structure of local governments also limit their fiscal powers. Localities are typically restricted with regard to the type of taxes or the maximum tax rates they may levy. Limits on indebtedness define the maximum percentage of the local government's property tax base that can be obligated for future payments.

Table 6.7 illustrates provisions for limiting tax rates, assessments, revenues, and expenditures of school districts in several states. Limits on tax rates, often referred to as millage limits, are the most common form of tax limitation. Limiting assessment increases also imposes controls, particularly when used in combination with rate increases to contain governmental growth. Levy limits slow the increase in revenue from year to year either

TABLE 6.7. Limitations on Property Taxation for Current Expenses in Selected States

State	Type of Limitation	Provisions
Illinois	Tax rate limit	Without referendum, 9.2 mills for K–8 and 9–12 districts, and 17.5 mills for K–12 districts; with voter approval, 35 mills for K–8 and 9–12 districts and 40 mills for K–12 districts
Wyoming	Tax rate limit	Without voter approval, 26 mills; referendum required for assessing 2 mills beyond 26 mills
Oregon	Assessment limit	Assessed values reduced by a ratio for each property classification so that no class can increase more than 5% annually
Kentucky	Revenue limit	Revenues may not exceed 1986–1987 tax rate times 1986–1987 assessment; exception for new property and tax increase that does not yield revenue in excess of 4% of prior year
Michigan	Revenue limit	Tax rates rolled back if revenue increase exceeds inflation rate (consumer price index)
Iowa	Expenditure limit	Maximum per pupil increase in budget, $87 in districts above state-established base cost; maximum growth in local costs, $96 per pupil
Kansas	Expenditure limit	Increase limited to 103.5% of per pupil budget in prior year or 102% of median budget per pupil for districts in same enrollment category; 2% increase allowed in any case

(*Source:* D. Verstegen. [1988]. *School Finance at a Glance* [SF-88-1], pp. 63–81. Denver, CO: Education Commission of the States. Reprinted by permission.)

by a specified percentage amount or in concert with some measure of inflation or income growth. Expenditure limitations influence increases in spending per pupil for schools.

Similar limitations in many states restrict long-term borrowing for capital outlay for constructing buildings and purchasing school buses. Open-disclosure laws require hearings and referenda prior to creating debt or raising indebtedness above a given level. Additionally, school boards of fiscally dependent districts cannot themselves incur debt.

Limitation Movements

With the growth of municipalities during an inflationary period following the Civil War, current expenses were paid by "floating debt" carried forward each year rather than through increased taxes. Many jurisdictions overextended their tax bases prior to the recession of the 1870s, and states responded with measures to limit debt and public services in relation to local revenue. By 1880, a total of 10 states had limitations on taxes and one-half of the states imposed limits on debt incurred by cities (Wright, 1981, p. 42).

Public perceptions of uncontained growth and inefficiency in government stimulated a similar movement a century later to contain taxes and expenditures. Confidence and trust in government waned in the 1970s, and it was claimed that reducing taxes would force efficiency in the delivery of essential services. Due (1982, p. 281) concluded that this tax revolt was a response to the growth of federal, state, and local governments during the

1950s and 1960s: "The votes are votes against inflation and irritating regulations and government actions, not just against taxes." Taxation became the focal point, however, and public referenda called for tax and expenditure limitations of two forms: (1) reducing the existing size of government, premised on beliefs that tax burdens are too heavy and that government is not a good investment; and (2) containing the growth of government, premised on the belief that government is as large as it should be relative to the rest of the economy (Palaich, Kloss, & Williams, 1980, pp. 1–2).

Typical of the first of these groups, California's 1978 Proposition 13 satisfied the broader goal of cutting overall governmental expenditures. This constitutional change limited local property tax rates to 1 percent of 1975–1976 fair market value, restricted annual increases in assessments to a maximum of 2 percent, and brought assessments to current levels only when property changed ownership or was newly constructed. Proposition 4, passed one year later by a wider margin of California voters, illustrates the containment attitude of the tax revolt. Growth in state and local appropriations from tax revenue was limited to increases in the cost of living and to changes in population. This referendum also made it possible for a simple majority of voters to adjust the spending limit of any government unit and called for full state reimbursement of the costs of mandates associated with any new or upgraded program.

The 1980 Massachusetts Proposition 2-1/2 served both to reduce taxes and to contain the growth of government. It limited property tax rates to 2-1/2 percent of "full and fair cash value," required jurisdictions that were previously taxing above that level to reduce levies, and held revenue from real estate to a 2-1/2 percent annual growth rate. In the course of the movement, 19 states adopted revenue limits. Most of these actions tied increases in collections to changes in the cost of living, to a fixed percentage increase over prior years, or to a fixed percentage of property value (Wright, 1981, pp. 29–30).

During the period of tax limitations, 1966 through 1986, trends in effective tax rates evidenced a slower growth in taxation relative to the value of homes in nearly all states. Effective tax rates reported in Table 6.8 represent tax liability as a percentage of the market value of houses financed through the Federal Housing Authority. The average rate in the nation grew from 1.34 percent in 1958 to 1.70 percent in 1966; but with the tax revolt and concomitant shift in revenue burdens to states, this trend was reversed and effective rates diminished to 1.16 percent in 1986. In all but eight states, there was a higher rate in 1966 or 1977 and a lower rate evident by 1986. Effective rates in California, for example, increased from 1.50 percent in 1958 to 2.21 percent in 1977, the year prior to Proposition 13, then declined to 1.06 percent in 1986.

This reversal in effective rates does not necessarily mean a decline in actual millage rates levied on appraised value or tax amounts collected. Rapidly rising market values bring increases in tax payments (assuming similar increased assessments) even if millage rates remain the same or decline somewhat. For example, taxes on a house appraised in 1966 for $22,000 would be $374, applying the average effective rate of 1.70 percent. If this same house were appraised in 1986 at $45,000, it would be taxed $522, given the national average rate of 1.16 percent. The increased tax owed reflects growth in the appraisal, despite the substantial decline in the effective rate.

Much has been written about the aftermath of Proposition 13 in California. The feared reductions in government spending and services did not materialize, and in the long run, the state's economy may have been strengthened because of tax cuts (Adams, 1984, pp.

TABLE 6.8. Average Effective Property Tax Rates*

State	1958	1966	1977	1986	Rank[†]
Alabama	0.56%	0.66%	0.74%	0.39%	49
Alaska	1.12	1.42	NA	0.82	41
Arizona	2.14	2.41	1.72	0.68	45
Arkansas	0.86	1.09	1.49	1.09	25
California	1.50	2.03	2.21	1.06	28
Colorado	1.72	2.20	1.80	1.09	24
Connecticut	1.44	2.01	2.17	1.46	12
Delaware	0.71	1.14	0.88	0.73	43
District of Columbia	1.08	1.37	NA	1.17	21
Florida	0.76	1.09	1.13	0.89	39
Georgia	0.84	1.30	1.27	0.90	36
Hawaii	0.62	0.81	NA	0.51	48
Idaho	1.14	1.23	1.46	0.91	35
Illinois	1.35	1.96	1.90	1.59	9
Indiana	0.84	1.64	1.66	1.28	19
Iowa	1.34	2.12	1.76	1.96	8
Kansas	1.65	1.96	1.37	1.06	29
Kentucky	0.93	1.03	1.25	1.10	22
Louisiana	0.52	0.43	0.61	0.25	50
Maine	1.50	2.17	1.65	1.21	20
Maryland	1.47	2.05	1.69	1.30	18
Massachusetts	2.21	2.76	3.50	1.08	27
Michigan	1.45	1.81	2.63	2.26	5
Minnesota	1.57	2.14	1.39	1.03	31
Mississippi	0.66	0.93	1.10	0.77	42
Missouri	1.12	1.64	1.59	0.89	38
Montana	1.32	1.70	1.31	1.32	17
Nebraska	1.90	2.67	2.48	2.21	7
Nevada	1.06	1.47	1.71	0.61	46
New Hampshire	1.81	2.38	NA	1.55	10
New Jersey	1.77	2.57	3.31	2.33	1
New Mexico	0.93	1.30	1.65	1.01	32
New York	2.09	2.40	2.89	2.22	6
North Carolina	0.90	1.31	1.35	NA	33
North Dakota	1.54	1.81	1.26	1.37	15
Ohio	1.07	1.44	1.26	1.08	26
Oklahoma	0.86	1.11	0.95	0.90	37
Oregon	1.55	1.98	2.25	2.26	4
Pennsylvania	1.50	1.88	1.85	1.37	16
Rhode Island	1.67	1.96	NA	1.49	11
South Carolina	0.48	0.60	0.82	0.70	44
South Dakota	2.01	2.64	1.79	2.31	2
Tennessee	0.97	1.37	1.40	1.04	30
Texas	1.36	1.62	1.84	1.44	13
Utah	1.05	1.52	1.03	0.93	34

(Continued)

TABLE 6.8. *(Continued)*

State	1958	1966	1977	1986	Rank[†]
Vermont	1.63	2.27	NA	NA	NA
Virginia	0.90	1.13	1.21	1.42	14
Washington	0.92	1.14	1.75	1.10	23
West Virginia	0.56	0.71	NA	0.88	40
Wisconsin	1.82	2.31	2.22	2.27	3
Wyoming	1.17	1.34	0.87	0.57	47
U.S. Total	1.34%	1.70%	1.67%	1.16%	NA

*Effective rates are for existing FHA-insured mortgages only, which represent varying percentages (by state) of total single-family homes.
†In cases where 1986 data were not available, rank was based on data for most recent year. (*Source:* ACIR [Advisory Commission on Intergovernmental Relations]. [1987]. *Significant Features of Fiscal Federalism, 1988 edition,* Table 30, p. 70. Washington, DC: ACIR, 1987.)

171–174). Increased user fees for public swimming pools, golf courses, marina docking, and so on placed the burden for services directly on beneficiaries. With business property turning over at a faster rate than anticipated, raised assessments shifted the burden for property taxation from residences to businesses. With respect to schools, Proposition 13 resulted in the replacement of property tax revenue with state financial aid; this narrowed disparities in expenditures per pupil among school districts.

On the other hand, greatly increased dependency upon state revenue resulted in a loss of local autonomy and a weakening of citizen participation in decision making. Reductions in property taxes were not always passed on to consumers and renters; and beneficiaries of the revolt included businesses, large oil companies and property owners (Due, 1982, pp. 281–283). Newly constructed or newly purchased property was taxed differently from property that had not changed hands, creating inequities in effective rates for properties within neighborhoods. Californians paid higher federal income taxes because of the lower deductions they could claim for property taxes paid. With the shift to user fees, homeowners still had to pay for services but lost the federal income tax deductions for which they could qualify if the services were paid through property tax revenue. Even with the state paying proportionately more for public education, there was a large drop in total revenue for schools. California dropped in per pupil spending for schools from among the top 10 in the nation prior to Proposition 13 to a low of thirty-fifth; by the end of the 1980s its rank had stabilized at twenty-fifth (Verstegen, 1988, p. 85).

The movement to limit taxes and expenditures slowed in the early 1980s. Proposition 9, defeated by California voters in June 1980, proposed a constitutional amendment to halve state income tax rates, index rates to stem bracket creep, and abolish the state's inventory tax. In the same year that the Massachusetts proposition passed, initiatives failed in another five states. In 1988, tax or expenditure limitation measures placed before voters in three states failed.

Property tax revenue, which had fallen nationally from $66.4 billion in fiscal 1978 to $64.9 billion a year later, grew substantially each year since and reached $121.2 billion in fiscal 1987 (U.S. Department of Commerce, 1989, p. V). In the late 1980s, public opinion shifted once again in support of public services, especially those related to expenditures for education. Quality and excellence were desired, and the public voiced its willingness to raise state and local taxes to finance improved schools. The drive to ensure adequate funds for public education brought another California initiative. Proposition 98, approved by voters in 1988, amended the state constitution so that public education would receive the larger of either 40 percent of any new state revenue or the previous year's allocation increased by the rate of inflation and enrollment growth. State money that could not otherwise be spent because of spending limits imposed by Proposition 4 was also diverted to support education.

PROPERTY TAX CAPACITY AND EFFORT IN THE STATES

Disparities in property tax bases and tax rates among states and local tax jurisdictions reveal differences in abilities and willingness to tax real property. Tax capacity, effort, and revenue collected are presented for states in Table 6.9.

The Advisory Commission on Intergovernmental Relations (ACIR, 1987a) defines capacity to include (1) estimated market values of residential and farm properties and (2) net book values of commercial/industrial and public utility properties. Many of the states with low per capita tax bases are in the South, including Arkansas, Kentucky, Mississippi, and South Carolina. Low residential and commercial/industrial capacities in Montana and the Dakotas are offset by higher farm capacities. States with higher residential tax bases, like Hawaii, California, and Connecticut, have relatively low farm capacity. The states with the highest commercial/industrial tax capacities are Delaware, New Jersey, and Texas. Energy-rich states of Wyoming, West Virginia, and New Mexico have high public utility tax bases in contrast to New England states, in which utilities account for little of their capacities.

Per capita tax capacities reveal the revenue potential that is possible from property taxed at a national average rate. Not all states, however, tax their capacities at that level, and others exceed the national average by a considerable amount. Property tax revenue raised per capita and an index of relative tax effort, which expresses the relationship between actual revenue and tax capacity, are also indicated in Table 6.9. Alaska and Wyoming are ranked high in effort but are able to export much of their energy-related property taxes to other states; New York and Michigan are not in that enviable position. Connecticut exerts somewhat less effort but collects a similarly high revenue per capita because of its high tax capacity. With relatively low tax capacities and very low efforts, Alabama, Louisiana, and New Mexico collect lower revenue per capita from property taxes.

New England has traditionally relied more heavily on property taxes than have other sections (Gold, 1979, pp. 298–303). There has been a strong commitment to local control, a high degree of fiscal decentralization, low levels of state-financed relief, and few state-imposed limitations on local taxes and spending. States in the Plains and Great Lakes area, once near the top of the nation in terms of tax burdens, have led other states in adopting circuit breakers, local income taxation, and property tax limitations.

Southeastern states have traditionally had low property taxes because their fiscal centralization brings more state grants-in-aid. Localities in the Southeast rely more heavily

TABLE 6.9. Property Tax Capacity and Revenue per Capita, 1985

State	Capacity per Capita				Revenue per Capita	Tax Effort	
	Residential	Farm	Commercial/ Industrial	Public Utility		Index	Rank
Alabama	$161.27	$ 14.04	$ 82.40	$ 49.99	$115.91	37.7	50
Alaska	300.99	2.64	146.71	32.46	1071.61	222.0	1
Arizona	367.45	19.91	86.96	42.85	366.31	70.8	38
Arkansas	133.12	36.77	81.64	48.21	173.46	57.9	45
California	440.94	13.71	131.33	27.46	420.79	68.6	40
Colorado	432.51	29.57	114.63	38.82	495.50	80.5	31
Connecticut	425.11	2.91	146.38	27.42	702.93	116.8	19
Delaware	370.96	10.95	189.03	37.29	203.74	33.5	51
District of Columbia	331.11	0.00	122.37	39.43	726.99	147.5	7
Florida	309.75	11.15	79.45	33.76	378.39	87.2	29
Georgia	214.41	12.48	104.45	37.49	294.40	79.8	32
Hawaii	570.42	17.64	76.88	20.53	293.21	42.8	48
Idaho	203.83	69.95	78.76	29.13	278.34	72.9	35
Illinois	214.61	20.88	126.41	37.24	528.40	132.4	13
Indiana	161.86	23.98	118.03	42.25	376.81	108.9	22
Iowa	183.94	79.15	83.74	39.37	528.77	136.9	11
Kansas	176.02	58.30	109.59	60.93	498.24	123.1	15
Kentucky	141.21	22.51	100.16	46.22	182.35	58.8	44
Louisiana	191.30	18.08	137.77	48.44	176.56	44.6	47
Maine	296.27	7.14	87.26	24.10	471.59	113.7	20
Maryland	298.82	8.08	89.63	30.66	406.54	95.2	26
Massachusetts	329.97	1.77	122.09	26.99	567.62	118.1	18
Michigan	203.06	8.43	120.23	35.27	619.72	168.9	3
Minnesota	268.64	38.10	117.24	30.87	505.04	111.0	21
Mississippi	156.65	28.97	75.83	36.85	209.25	70.1	39
Missouri	163.13	25.77	107.93	38.93	240.88	71.7	37
Montana	145.49	104.52	66.63	58.64	629.06	167.6	4
Nebraska	222.51	83.32	85.23	48.88	549.17	124.8	14
Nevada	290.15	13.75	83.04	52.60	315.94	71.9	36
New Hampshire	354.60	4.90	109.84	22.76	692.72	140.8	8
New Jersey	332.61	2.83	149.40	29.07	717.22	139.6	9
New Mexico	189.66	32.30	77.32	60.82	150.00	41.7	49
New York	242.28	2.67	133.89	27.48	688.20	169.4	2
North Carolina	226.89	13.69	107.54	34.18	246.45	64.5	42
North Dakota	120.86	137.25	65.74	59.96	339.82	88.5	28
Ohio	217.03	10.57	124.36	34.35	374.72	97.0	24
Oklahoma	191.51	36.13	123.63	55.14	225.65	55.5	46
Oregon	300.48	24.77	93.73	42.75	618.43	133.9	12
Pennsylvania	229.11	7.08	117.46	37.15	366.66	93.8	27
Rhode Island	242.31	1.60	100.09	15.20	587.90	163.7	6

(Continued)

116

TABLE 6.9. *(Continued)*

State	Capacity per Capita				Revenue per Capita	Tax Effort	
	Residential	Farm	Commercial/ Industrial	Public Utility		Index	Rank
South Carolina	180.88	9.43	86.27	44.32	239.51	74.6	34
South Dakota	175.24	100.34	62.79	37.57	458.20	121.9	16
Tennessee	182.62	17.64	95.49	41.34	218.04	64.7	41
Texas	208.29	34.66	150.94	46.37	465.69	105.8	23
Utah	223.88	23.14	84.71	28.96	345.81	95.9	25
Vermont	307.84	19.42	87.55	24.29	529.71	120.6	17
Virginia	288.60	11.72	98.54	28.55	366.10	85.7	30
Washington	365.49	21.79	99.83	51.50	410.87	76.3	33
West Virginia	150.56	6.40	82.10	78.26	198.86	62.7	43
Wisconsin	252.72	20.05	103.14	33.74	568.36	138.7	10
Wyoming	335.04	77.28	132.55	116.85	1101.87	166.5	5
U.S. Total	$264.28	$18.46	$115.47	$36.91	$435.11	100.0	

(*Source:* ACIR [Advisory Commission on Intergovernmental Relations]. [1987]. *Measuring State Fiscal Capacity*, Tables 3–25 to 3–27, pp. 94–96. Washington, DC: ACIR, 1987.)

on user charges and sales taxes, and their property classification schemes and homestead exemptions reduce tax collections. There are fewer commonalities about states in the Rocky Mountain, Southwest, or Far West regions.

SUMMARY

Taxation of real property has ably served municipalities and school districts for many generations. Its productive yield and stability have effectively countered arguments against it. Stability offers predictability, enabling local officials to plan programs within a balanced budget. The property tax is inelastic relative to income- and consumption-based taxes because assessed values used in determining tax yield respond slowly to changes in the economy. As valuation practices improve, so that the tax base more closely reflects market values, the yield will grow, with fewer annual adjustments in tax rates.

Property tax structure and administration vary considerably from state to state. Assessment ratios, exemptions, revenue and expenditure limitations, and tax relief mechanisms affect tax bases and yields. These policies and arbitrary assessments also interfere with equity and neutrality goals. Some provisions shift tax burdens from one group to another, resulting in misallocations of economic resources and to inequities among taxpayers of different incomes. Careful policy development, including circuit breakers to ease tax burdens on low-income families, can reduce the regressivity of this tax. Other provisions affect housing purchase and rehabilitation, location of businesses and industry, and development of vacant and farm land. Urban redevelopment is discouraged, and businesses and upper-income families are encouraged to migrate to localities with lower tax rates but better services.

Property taxation in most states enables localities to expand educational programs beyond minimal offerings financed by state aid programs. However, disparities in tax bases (capacity) and in tax rates (effort) among communities often result in program inequities. State or regional responsibilities for valuing properties might ease inequities in taxation and reduce disparities in programs. If properties such as utilities and industrial plants that serve broad regions were removed from the local tax base and taxed only by the state, tax capacity of localities would be more evenly distributed and many negative social and economic effects of property taxation would be reduced.

However, these reforms must be balanced against the strong historical precedent for preserving local autonomy. Assessment practices can be improved while local governments are exercising some degree of independence by continuing to place the responsibility for setting tax rates at the local or regional level. A primary goal for states and localities in the 1990s should be to strengthen the integrity of property taxation through continued improvements in its structure and administration.

In the next chapter, we explore several other strategies for tapping local resources in support of school district operations. Investments bring new money and volunteers supply new talent at minimal cost while borrowing and other cash flow procedures ensure continuous school operations.

ACTIVITIES

1. During a public meeting at which you are presenting a proposal to raise the tax rate to finance program expansion in your school district, you are asked why the property tax is an appropriate revenue source for this purpose. How might you respond?
2. Contact your tax assessor, and inquire about the current tax rates for school districts, municipalities, and other special districts served by this tax jurisdiction. When were properties last assessed and when will they next be appraised? Which of the three methods—market data, cost, or income—are most likely to be used to appraise residential, business, and agricultural property? What proportion of appraised value is exempt from taxation?
3. Develop a rationale for tax incentives in the form of lower assessments to attract new industry or commercial development. Keep in mind that taxes will increase for currently operating businesses in order to expand municipal and educational services.
4. Prepare a chart which contrasts the strengths and weaknesses of property taxation with those of income- and consumption-based taxes, referring to yield, equity, neutrality, and costs of administration and compliance. List the four tax criteria along the left margin. Label three columns across the top for the primary tax bases: wealth, income, and consumption. In each cell, place the names of the primary revenue sources discussed in Chapters 5 and 6 which most closely correlate with the designated base and criterion.
5. Describe provisions in one state's constitution or statutes that limit local governments' power to tax or that contain growth in revenue or spending. Design a study to determine legislators' and superintendents' perceptions about the value of such limitations.
6. Express a tax rate of 23.2 mills in terms of dollars per thousand and dollars per hundred of assessed valuation. Given this rate, what is the tax on a house that is assessed at $64,000?

7. A school district having total market valuation of $510 million and 5,000 pupils levies a tax of 28 mills.

   a. How much would the district raise per pupil, given a statewide assessment ratio of 33-1/3 percent?

   b. How much more or less is raised at the same tax rate if the state assessment ratio is increased to 40 percent?

   c. What tax rate in mills is needed to raise $1,428 per pupil, given the assessment ratio of 40 percent?

REFERENCES

Aaron, H. J. (1973). What do circuit-breaker laws accomplish? In G. E. Peterson (Ed.), *Property tax reform* (pp. 53–64). Washington, DC: The Urban Institute.

Aaron, H. J. (1975). *Who pays the property tax: A new view*. Washington, DC: The Brookings Institution.

ACIR [Advisory Commission on Intergovernmental Relations]. (1973). *Financing schools and property tax relief—A state responsibility* (Report A-40). Washington, DC: Author.

ACIR. (1987a). *Measuring state fiscal capacity*. Washington, DC: Author.

ACIR. (1987b). *Significant features of fiscal federalism, 1988 Edition*. Washington, DC: Author.

Adams, J. R. (1984). *Secrets of the tax revolt*. New York: Harcourt Brace Jovanovich.

Due, J. F. (1982) Shifting sources of financing education and the taxpayer revolt. In W. W. McMahon & T. G. Geske (Eds.), *Financing education: Overcoming inefficiency and inequity* (pp. 267–289). Urbana: University of Illinois Press.

George, H. (1879). *Progress and poverty*. Garden City, NY: Doubleday.

Gold, S. D. (1979). *Property tax relief*. Lexington, MA: Lexington Books.

Musgrave, R. A., & Musgrave, P. B. (1984). *Public finance in theory and practice* (4th ed.). New York: McGraw-Hill.

Netzer, D. (1966). *Economics of the property tax*. Washington, DC: The Brookings Institution.

Netzer, D. (1973). Is there too much reliance on the local property tax? In G. E. Peterson (Ed.), *Property tax reform*. Washington, DC: The Urban Institute.

Oldman, O., & Schoettle, F. P. (1974). *State and local taxes and finance: Text, problems and cases*. Mineola, NY: Foundation Press.

Palaich, R., Kloss, J., & Williams, M. F. (1980). *Tax and expenditure limitation referenda* (Report F80-2). Denver: Education Commission of the States.

Peterson, G. E. (Ed.). (1973). *Property tax reform*. Washington, DC: The Urban Institute.

Shannon, J. (1973). The property tax: Reform or relief? In G. E. Peterson (Ed.), *Property tax reform* (pp. 25–52). Washington, DC: The Urban Institute.

U.S. Department of Commerce, Bureau of the Census. (1987). *Statistical abstract of the United States, 1988* (108th ed.). Washington, DC: U.S. Government Printing Office.

U.S. Department of Commerce, Bureau of the Census. (1989). *1987 census of governments, Vol. 2: Taxable property values*. Washington, DC: U.S. Government Printing Office.

Verstegen, D. (1988). *School finance at a glance*. Denver: Education Commission of the States.

Walz v. *Tax Commission of the City of New York*. (1970). 397 U.S. 664.

Wright, J. W. (1981). *Tax and expenditure limitation: A policy perspective*. Lexington, KY: The Council of State Governments.

Yinger, J., Borsch-Supan, A., Bloom, H. S., and Ladd, H. F. (1988). *Property taxes and house values: The theory and estimation of intra-jurisdictional property tax capitalization*. San Diego, CA: Academic Press.

CHAPTER 7

Expanding Local Resources

The traditional view of resources immediately available to school districts centers on property taxation because it provides the largest amount of funds within control of localities. Schools are not limited to this revenue, and their resource bases can be expanded by careful cash flow management, including timely decisions to borrow and invest, and through creative uses of partnerships.

This chapter examines opportunities for enriching resources available at the local level. Because federal, state, and local revenues flow into school system accounts when financial obligations are not due, school districts meet short-term shortages through loans. Long-term capital projects are financed through the issuance of bonds. At other times, there may be a larger flow of revenue than is immediately needed, producing excess or idle funds. These monies are invested to gain interest earnings until payroll and other payments are due. Other resources—both monetary and human—are becoming more available through partnerships, educational foundations, and volunteerism. This private sector involvement in public schools expands resources and political support for school improvement efforts.

BORROWING

Short-Term Borrowing

School district revenue includes such receipts as taxes, federal and state aid payments, gifts, investment earnings, and tuition and fees. Short-term loans and long-term bond issues are classified as nonrevenue money because they are ultimately repaid from anticipated revenue. These nonrevenue monies enable finance officers to maintain an even flow of district funds to meet payrolls and payments to vendors on schedule.

If finance officers could not borrow against district assets, school operations would be disrupted, future purchases of needed materials would be more expensive as suppliers' faith in prompt payment declines, and employee morale would be negatively affected. If school systems could not issue bonds with payment over a long period, it would be difficult to construct facilities or purchase expensive equipment. Sound financial management depends on district abilities to borrow needed funds; but at the same time, states regulate borrowing to ensure responsible use of short- and long-term debt.

Short-term loans allow districts to meet current obligations prior to receipt of anticipated funds. This borrowing is limited to the amount of revenue that will be forthcoming, and repayment is generally scheduled to occur within the fiscal year during which aid payments or local taxes will be received. Several mechanisms are available to ease an interim cash deficit.

Revenue anticipation notes allow districts to borrow against anticipated revenues other than property taxes (e.g., intergovernmental transfers), and tax anticipation notes allow districts to borrow against anticipated receipts from property or other taxes. Such borrowing provides money to meet general operating expenses. Once the issuance of bonds has been approved (see the following discussion), districts may obtain advance funds through bond anticipation notes, but these funds are usually restricted to the same purpose as the bond authorization. Funds to assist with an unforeseeable emergency may be forthcoming through a budget note to be repaid during the following fiscal year (Dembowski & Davey, 1986).

Long-Term Borrowing

Long-term debt enables school systems to construct new school facilities and renovate older buildings to meet changing enrollment patterns and program demands. These capital projects require more funds than districts typically have at ready disposal from state and local sources for school operations. Capital outlay funds are allocated for school buildings and equipment whose useful lives extend beyond a single school year. Local tax bases have traditionally been burdened with the repayment of funds borrowed for these purposes. Despite the increased reliance upon state revenue for financing, only a few states have assumed primary responsibility for constructing facilities within which programs are delivered.

Without borrowing, few districts would have sufficient revenue to finance capital projects. Drawing from current revenue would be possible in only the wealthiest and largest school districts. For other districts, borrowing helps maintain somewhat consistent tax rates from year to year. In some states, districts can save property tax revenue in so-called "sinking" or "construction" funds over a lengthy period of time in anticipation of a construction project. However, these accumulated reserves may not be adequate for financing needed facilities in times of extraordinary population growth or school aging. Furthermore, school boards and taxpayers are reluctant to pledge funds for uncertain future projects, particularly when subsequent elections may alter priorities. Rather than delay construction until savings accrue, borrowing makes funds available for specific projects at the time they are needed. Several advantages of borrowing offset additions to a project's cost due to interest to be repaid. First, the debt created is paid by future users, consistent with benefit theory discussed in Chapter 4. Second, facilities that are constructed at today's costs may actually bring savings to the district because they will be paid with future tax revenue that is generally worth less, given inflation.

The issuance of bonds is the vehicle most commonly used for raising money for capital improvements at the local level. Salmon and Thomas (1981) define a bond as a "written financial instrument issued by a corporate body to borrow money with the time and rate of interest, method of principal repayment, and the term of debt clearly expressed" (p. 91). Payments are made through either future receipts (as may be the case for sports facilities) or property tax revenue. Governing boards, in the case of fiscally dependent school districts, or school district voters, in the case of fiscally independent districts (see Chapter 3 for definition), decide whether or not to issue bonds and to levy property taxes for a fixed term to pay the principal (capital outlay) and interest (debt service). Unlike home mortgages and other forms of long-term debt that rely upon the property itself as collateral, general obligation bonds are secured by a public entity's pledge of its "full faith and credit." They obligate the district to raise taxes for repayment.

Bonds are marketed through a competitive bid process to bond underwriters, who in turn make them available to investors. Because interest paid to investors is exempt from federal and state income taxation, municipal and school district bonds can be marketed at substantially reduced interest rates, thus lowering the cost of capital projects. School district credit ratings further affect the rate of interest paid. National bond-rating companies, such as Moody's Investor Service and Standard and Poor's, consider such factors as local property valuation, outstanding debt, current tax rates, and enrollment trends in informing potential investors about the relative security of a bond issue. A prospectus (Wood, 1986, pp. 568–583) communicates to the financial community the purpose of the bond issue; its type and denomination; and full disclosure of the financial condition of the district, including outstanding debt, pending litigation that may affect the bond sale, and other information. This information prepared by the bond underwriter, as well as the current national economy, influences the actual interest rates paid to investors.

The type of bond most often issued for school construction is serial bonds, which structure repayment so that a portion of the debt is retired on periodic (e.g., annual) maturity dates and the total debt is paid over a period of time (e.g., 10, 20, or 30 years). Interest rates are lower for short amortization periods than for long periods. Investors and school districts alike are cautious about defining interest rates over a long period, given fluctuations in the economy that may mean either sharply lowered returns for investors or excessive interest payments for districts.

Callable bonds include provisions under which bonds can be reissued after a specified number of years. Noncallable bonds carry more favorable rates but limit districts' abilities to control the amount of interest paid in the future. Even when a school district appears to be saddled with a high interest rate on a noncallable bond issue, advanced refunding may offer the potential of lowering the total net cost of borrowing. In this mechanism, which is not legal in some states, new bonds are issued at a lower interest rate and funds are invested with maturity just prior to the original bond issue's payment date.

Table 7.1 presents trends in expenditures over a twenty-year period for capital outlay projects of elementary/secondary and higher education. State and local expenditures for capital improvements grew in the majority of states. However, a pattern of decline in spending reflected tighter resources and declining enrollments during the decade from 1966–1967 to 1976–1977 in many states. A growth trend between 1976–1977 and 1986–

TABLE 7.1. State and Local Government Expenditure for Capital Outlay (millions of dollars)

State	Elementary/Secondary			Higher Education		
	1966–1967	1976–1977	1986–1987	1966–1967	1976–1977	1986–1987
Alabama	$ 67.6	$ 82.9	$ 106.8	$ 119.3	$ 77.9	$ 127.1
Alaska	16.6	59.7	203.5	1.6	22.2	16.7
Arizona	22.3	131.1	472.2	42.1	44.7	132.9
Arkansas	23.4	44.4	229.8	21.1	31.8	33.3
California	455.3	560.7	972.9	223.2	390.0	802.3
Colorado	27.1	131.7	313.6	41.1	63.0	80.8
Connecticut	66.0	49.9	94.5	20.0	9.6	42.3
Delaware	17.8	10.6	13.0	13.7	18.6	33.8
District of Columbia	17.3	32.9	53.1	—	0.1	4.9
Florida	94.8	280.0	765.1	58.9	133.7	241.0
Georgia	66.3	123.4	408.1	45.2	48.2	124.7
Hawaii	21.1	38.2	70.9	5.3	31.4	32.3
Idaho	11.7	30.5	37.0	11.2	19.0	38.5
Illinois	195.2	292.7	455.7	111.7	148.7	299.7
Indiana	96.6	193.2	246.8	65.3	47.3	128.8
Iowa	41.1	49.4	84.5	28.7	27.5	128.8
Kansas	26.4	60.2	96.9	15.5	33.4	57.8
Kentucky	42.9	106.9	99.9	58.7	57.7	71.7
Louisiana	90.2	98.5	181.1	59.3	37.2	83.8
Maine	13.6	19.5	69.1	11.0	2.5	31.1
Maryland	116.4	219.6	171.9	30.1	49.1	134.7
Massachusetts	86.4	113.4	107.1	39.4	46.3	108.8
Michigan	220.5	287.8	289.9	153.0	93.6	283.5
Minnesota	134.3	116.1	214.7	46.9	61.8	132.2
Mississippi	25.6	40.8	93.9	12.9	42.5	40.9
Missouri	90.4	88.4	188.5	66.2	34.9	169.6
Montana	12.0	25.9	31.1	10.5	6.2	24.4
Nebraska	16.7	43.6	58.6	17.7	20.8	63.8
Nevada	12.2	20.8	52.9	7.2	11.9	16.6
New Hampshire	16.6	14.2	71.7	10.9	21.7	33.4
New Jersey	100.1	118.8	259.4	23.9	41.6	135.3
New Mexico	28.8	50.6	128.5	20.2	20.7	46.2

New York	391.7	249.3	767.9	250.0	195.0	451.8
North Carolina	80.5	158.5	302.3	53.6	75.5	239.3
North Dakota	30.7	13.0	41.6	9.4	13.3	18.9
Ohio	220.7	221.5	326.6	129.1	130.0	306.0
Oklahoma	34.4	93.8	231.5	38.7	36.6	54.1
Oregon	40.6	103.6	97.3	28.2	60.3	84.9
Pennsylvania	245.8	344.6	475.2	79.4	58.2	162.2
Rhode Island	16.4	15.6	13.5	7.5	4.4	5.4
South Carolina	30.7	74.7	213.6	15.4	33.6	89.5
South Dakota	16.3	20.5	22.4	7.1	14.1	11.3
Tennessee	70.9	121.9	161.1	66.6	45.2	83.7
Texas	267.9	478.3	1,364.9	132.5	258.2	442.7
Utah	37.0	85.4	93.3	23.7	31.8	80.3
Vermont	3.6	4.0	10.3	8.9	3.6	10.6
Virginia	103.3	153.7	257.9	40.6	27.6	141.0
Washington	72.7	120.3	338.4	42.1	86.4	137.3
West Virginia	21.6	66.9	83.0	17.9	7.0	17.3
Wisconsin	121.8	89.4	117.0	126.6	74.7	115.3
Wyoming	5.8	30.2	72.5	9.2	9.1	15.8
Total	$4,085.8	$5,981.6	$11,632.8	$2,405.7	$2,860.6	$6,168.6

Source of funds

Local	$3,972	$5,772	$11,127	$341	$548	$705
State	114	209	198	2,065	2,313	5,464
Local as percentage of total	97.2	96.5	98.3	14.2	19.1	11.4

Note: — Zero or rounds to zero. (*Source:* U.S. Department of Commerce, Bureau of the Census. [1968]. *Governmental Finances in 1966–67* [Series GF67, No. 3], pp. 25, 43. Washington, DC: U.S. Government Printing Office; [1978]. *Government Finances in 1976–77* [Series GF77, No. 5], pp. 36–37; [1988]. *Government Finances in 1988–87* [Series GF87, No. 5], pp. 15, 34.)

1987 followed this period of decline as resources became more available and as renovation of buildings built during the 1950s and 1960s became necessary. This pattern is more apparent for higher education than for elementary/secondary education, with 22 states declining over the first decade in actual dollars spent but growing during the second. Spending for elementary/secondary schools followed this pattern in only 8 states, including Connecticut, Delaware, Minnesota, Missouri, New Hampshire, New York, North Dakota, and Wisconsin. Oregon followed the reverse trend, having larger expenditures in 1976–1977 but declining by 1986–1987. Spending in Rhode Island declined throughout the period. The most dramatic growth in capital outlay during these twenty years occurred in Alaska, Arizona, Arkansas, Colorado, and Wyoming; spending grew by a factor of at least 10 in each of these states.

The burden fell most heavily on local governments for elementary and secondary school construction. Of the total amount spent throughout the country, localities funded nearly all of the $4.1 billion spent in 1966–1967, the $6.0 billion expended in 1976–1977, and the $11.6 billion spent in 1986–1987 (see Table 7.1). A large state role is evident in the support of higher education facilities. For example, only 11 percent of the $6.2 billion spent on higher education in 1986–1987 was raised locally, with the remainder financed primarily from state revenue. A limited amount of federal capital outlay funds for elementary and secondary education (only $13 million in 1986–1987) is allocated primarily to support school construction for areas affected by military installations and Native American reservations (see Chapter 10). Federal support of higher education construction is devoted primarily to service academies.

Outstanding debt for elementary and secondary schools amounted to $37.7 billion in 1985–1986. This was only a small increase over the $34.3 billion in unpaid debt a decade earlier. However, school systems incurred long-term debt of $8.3 billion in 1985–1986, nearly three times the amount issued ($3 billion) in 1977–1978. The amount of debt retired doubled between these years, from $3.1 billion to $6.1 billion (U.S. Department of Commerce, 1980, p. 12; 1988a, p. 10). This growth in debt assumed by districts reflects the increase in numbers of construction projects referred to previously as well as the increased construction costs and higher interest rates charged in the 1980s.

Despite increases in amounts spent and in debt incurred, the proportion of all educational expenses devoted to capital outlay declined from 7.2 percent in 1977–1978 to 6.8 percent in 1985–1986 (U.S. Department of Commerce, 1980, p. 10; 1988a, p. 6). Of the total state and local expenditures for all capital outlays in this time period, the proportion spent on elementary/secondary and higher education also declined. In 1966–1967, the $6.5 billion spent for both elementary/secondary and higher education capital outlay amounted to 28.9 percent of overall capital outlay expenses of state and local governments. By 1976–1977, this proportion had dropped to 22.8 percent, and by 1985–1986 to 21.5 percent (U.S. Department of Commerce, 1968, p. 43; 1978, p. 37; 1988b, p. 34).

Funds borrowed can be used to acquire land and construct new facilities, make additions to or remodel existing buildings, and purchase equipment, but these funds may not be diverted to school operations. States specify how projects are to be approved and bonds are to be issued. Once a school board has approved plans for construction and received clearance from the state, a public notice about the project is issued and an open hearing is held. In some fiscally independent school districts, a referendum is required to authorize the borrowing of money. The nature of bonds to be issued is also regulated, with specification of acceptable types of bonds, lengths of time to maturity, and maximum interest rates.

States may limit districts' use of long-term debt, and they may specify the maximum amount of debt to be incurred. A debt ceiling is often imposed to prohibit districts from overcommitting their tax bases and to ensure favorable credit ratings in the future. The ceiling may take the form of a maximum tax rate to raise capital outlay funds or a given proportion (e.g., 6 percent) of property valuation (see Chapter 6). Many poor districts are unable to meet capital outlay needs because their limited bonding capacity restricts the amount to be raised for facility construction and remodeling. Debt ceilings allow wealthier districts to raise more funds through bond issues than less wealthy districts, even though these restrictions bear no relationship to facility needs (Augenblick, 1977, p. 12).

This concern with inequities among districts' abilities to meet facility needs is also raised in relation to defeats of bond issue referenda. However, studies of voters' rejection of school construction projects reveal no relationship between election outcomes and either school district size or per pupil assessed valuation (Hack, 1976; Piele & Hall, 1973). Given these findings, states have been encouraged to reform capital outlay financing, not merely to ensure funds for poor districts but also to enhance access to adequate facilities in all districts.

Many states have eased inequities in facilities among districts or relieved pressure on local tax bases by creating funds from which loans can be made for approved projects or by making direct allocations for capital outlays. Loans of money derived from retirement programs, direct appropriations, permanent funds established for this purpose, and borrowing by the state make money available without the necessity of marketing bonds and without exceeding debt ceilings (Wilkerson, 1981, p. 204). In 1986–1987, seven states earmarked funds for low-interest loans to districts (Salmon, Dawson, Lawton, & Johns, 1988, p. 9).

In contrast to loans that require repayment, the majority of states grant capital outlay funds that are conditioned on such measures of need as the cost of approved projects, number of students or instructional units, fiscal capacity, and/or tax effort (see models presented in Chapter 8). Three states (Alaska, California, and Hawaii) assume complete support of capital outlay. Even in these states, project approval and funding restrictions constrain complete state assumption of facility construction, and a large burden continues to fall upon localities (Augenblick, 1977, pp. 7–8; Salmon & Thomas, 1981, p. 96).

Several states permit the formation of public corporations for financing capital improvements. Building authorities, first created in the early 1900s to circumvent debt restrictions of municipalities and school districts, are subject to their own taxing and debt limitations. Camp and Salmon (1985) report that as many as 19 states have experimented with building authorities, but they continue to operate at either state or local levels in only 8 states. For example, New York City's Educational Construction Fund represents an innovative local approach to financing school facilities for large cities. This authority constructs buildings on school-owned land, but schools occupy only portions of the facilities and rental of remaining space pays the debt. Five states operate bond banks to consolidate bond issues, thus taking advantage of lower interest rates than would be available for individual district projects. Camp and Salmon suggest that multicounty public authorities and regional bond banks may offer financial advantages and economies of scale that are similar to those gained by cooperatives for delivering educational services.

There are a number of advantages to state assumption of a larger role in financing capital outlay. When poorer districts can access broader-based tax revenue for expanding and improving facilities, there is greater equalization of educational opportunities. School districts realize savings in debt service costs, whether bonds are issued by using states' higher credit ratings or direct grants are received without borrowing. Furthermore, guidelines and standards for approval of projects to receive state funding often outline cost-effective construction practices, influence the design and location of school buildings, and contribute to energy conservation (Johns, Morphet, & Alexander, 1983, p. 286; King & MacPhail-Wilcox, 1988).

On the other hand, a larger state role has disadvantages, including the alienation of local citizens from public schools when power and control become more centralized. Resulting uniformity in facility design and function across a state may inhibit innovation and the recognition of unique local needs. There may be delays in addressing locally expressed needs, given intense competition for resources at the state level (Salmon & Thomas, 1981, p. 96).

The future will bring increased need for capital outlay funds and many localities will respond with increased taxes to repay debt. Because of population shifts among communities and states, some school systems will construct new facilities and others will close or convert underused buildings for other purposes. There will be continued experimentation with joint occupancy arrangements with other public entities to maximize facility use and to reduce construction costs. Public school facilities will house prekindergarten activities during the week and continuing education and community college classes for adults during evenings and weekends. Recreation facilities including swimming pools and tennis courts will be constructed in concert with municipalities and senior citizen organizations. New elementary, middle grades, and secondary organizational patterns and uses of technologies (see Chapter 15) will also create pressures for remodeled buildings.

INVESTMENT OF DISTRICT FUNDS

School districts, particularly fiscally independent districts, expand their resources by investing revenue and nonrevenue money. Large revenue payments, especially proceeds from the property tax, are concentrated at one time of the year, whereas operating expenditures are more evenly distributed. For example, most districts' fiscal years are from July 1 to June 30, giving benefits from property tax collections during the summer and early fall (Candoli, Hack, Ray, & Stollar, 1984, pp. 389–390). Borrowing is minimized since money is collected early in the budget year, and a large amount of idle cash can be invested for a long period. The windfalls created by tax collections, state and federal aid payments, and proceeds from bond issues or bond anticipation notes create large cash balances and opportunities to generate additional revenue through investment in short-term bank deposits or in long-term government notes and other securities.

Table 7.2 presents investments by state for 1977–1978 and 1985–1986. The amount invested by school districts throughout the nation had doubled in this eight-year period, from $14.9 billion to $29.6 billion. Many states shifted investment priorities between short-term cash and deposits and long-term securities, but the total amount invested nationally in each of these categories also doubled. Cash and deposits grew from $10.8

billion to $21.4 billion, and there was a similar rate of increase in the amount invested in securities, from $4.0 billion to $8.2 billion. School systems invested fewer funds in 1985–1986 than in 1987–1988 in only three states. Although overall investments and the amount saved in cash and deposits declined in Connecticut, Montana, and Ohio, school districts in these states increased the amount invested in securities.

Dembowski and Davey (1986) define cash management as "the process of managing the moneys of a school district to ensure maximum cash availability and maximum yield on investments" (p. 237). Goals of monitoring cash flow include (1) liquidity, the ability to convert investments to cash without such penalties as the loss of interest so that there is sufficient money available to meet daily needs; (2) yield, earning the maximum return on investments; and (3) safety, protecting the school district's assets against loss. These goals may conflict, such as when some degree of risk may yield higher interest but the safety of the public's money is jeopardized. Similarly, longer terms to maturity may gain higher interest, but the lost liquidity may necessitate short-term loans to cover expenses.

Several important nonfinancial goals are served by the way districts manage their cash flow. Sound financial management builds trust and goodwill within the taxpaying and business community, promotes favorable business relationships with vendors and banks, and ensures the orderly conduct of financial aspects of district operations (Dembowski, 1986). Careful cash flow strategies also prevent charges of embezzlement and graft. The public visibility of spending and investment decisions compels personnel to follow procedures in law including any limitations placed on investments (Candoli, Hack, Ray, & Stollar, 1984, p. 48). For example, many states require collateral (e.g., FDIC insurance on first $100,000 deposits) for school investments, but banks pay lower interest rates when they must maintain assets as collateral rather than diverting them to more lucrative purposes (Dembowski & Davey, 1986). Finance officers exercise caution when proposed interest rates are higher than anticipated, perhaps signaling that a bidder may be on brink of insolvency and needs to attract investors.

Several short- and long-term investment strategies are available to school districts. Savings accounts offer the advantage of immediate liquidity. Withdrawals are possible without prior notification and interest is earned on a daily basis. However, interest earnings are lower from savings than from other investments. Interest on money market accounts fluctuates with economic conditions, offering opportunities to improve yield during periods when interest rates are rising. There may, however, be limits on the number of withdrawals each month, reducing flexibility from ordinary savings accounts. Certificates of deposit also offer security but with higher interest earnings. Interest rates increase as the term lengthens for deposits, and districts gain investment flexibility when they coordinate investment terms (between one week and one year) with projected dates for expenditures. Early withdrawals bring a penalty of lost interest, reducing their liquidity.

U.S. government securities are among the safest long-term investments. Treasury bills offer districts high security and liquidity. The government guarantees these investments, which are sold at a discount from stated face values. The full value of bills is paid at maturity; the difference represents the interest earned by the investor. An advantage of Treasury bills is their liquidity because of the presence of a strong and receptive secondary market. Other investors will purchase them on the open market prior to their maturity, allowing a school district to liquidate when necessary.

Investments in federal agency securities offer similar safety, even though they are

TABLE 7.2. Cash and Security Holdings in Public School Systems* (millions of dollars)

State	Cash and Deposits		Securities		Total Investments	
	1977–1978	1985–1986	1977–1978	1985–1986	1977–1978	1985–1986
Alabama	$ 46.2	$ 101.4	$ 52.4	$ 119.5	$ 98.7	$ 220.9
Alaska	†	†	†	†	†	†
Arizona	336.0	732.8	17.6	9.1	353.7	741.9
Arkansas	120.5	238.1	—	—	120.5	238.1
California	1,604.2	3,200.6	120.8	23.1	1,725.0	3,223.6
Colorado	279.1	461.9	63.7	154.0	342.8	615.9
Connecticut	8.0	3.1	—	0.6	8.0	3.8
Delaware	3.5	12.6	—	0.4	3.5	13.0
District of Columbia	†	†	†	†	†	†
Florida	507.6	788.4	219.2	973.1	726.9	1,761.5
Georgia	326.3	145.1	—	511.7	326.3	656.2
Hawaii	†	†	†	†	†	†
Idaho	40.4	107.0	4.0	0.3	44.4	107.3
Illinois	344.3	691.1	994.0	1,758.5	1,338.4	2,449.5
Indiana	458.6	595.9	—	—	458.6	559.9
Iowa	37.5	235.7	168.2	45.7	205.7	281.4
Kansas	286.1	549.8	6.9	11.3	293.0	561.1
Kentucky	80.6	181.8	1.5	—	82.1	181.8
Louisiana	280.3	146.8	35.6	704.4	315.9	851.2
Maine	7.2	55.2	—	—	7.2	55.2
Maryland	†	†	†	†	†	†
Massachusetts	58.2	63.6	—	4.1	58.2	67.7
Michigan	365.8	367.1	581.6	1,008.5	947.4	1,375.6
Minnesota	137.7	830.4	353.2	—	490.9	830.4
Mississippi	86.4	215.7	6.5	10.1	92.9	225.8
Missouri	346.6	550.3	6.6	13.3	353.3	563.6
Montana	100.1	149.3	70.9	—	171.0	149.3
Nebraska	164.2	316.2	—	1.8	164.2	318.0
Nevada	15.9	106.2	—	30.8	15.9	137.0
New Hampshire	11.7	24.4	—	12.0	11.7	36.5
New Jersey	346.2	610.7	—	—	346.2	610.7
New Mexico	60.8	189.1	—	—	60.8	189.1
New York	504.0	1,358.0	46.0	182.1	550.1	1,540.1

North Carolina	†	†	†	†	†	†
North Dakota	47.7	180.2	—	—	47.7	180.2
Ohio	997.9	986.2	15.4	20.0	1,013.3	1,006.2
Oklahoma	216.3	698.5	28.7	—	245.0	698.5
Oregon	309.8	360.0	15.9	—	325.7	360.0
Pennsylvania	228.0	855.4	493.9	634.2	721.9	1,489.7
Rhode Island	0.1	0.8	—	—	0.1	0.8
South Carolina	128.3	160.5	17.1	119.6	145.4	280.1
South Dakota	75.7	120.8	—	—	75.7	120.8
Tennessee	7.8	8.5	—	—	7.8	8.5
Texas	1,317.7	4,079.7	41.6	163.9	1,356.3	4,243.6
Utah	50.2	71.1	133.3	231.1	183.5	302.1
Vermont	18.4	67.4	—	0.4	18.4	67.8
Virginia	†	†	†	†	†	†
Washington	55.1	34.9	337.4	840.5	392.4	875.4
West Virginia	157.0	235.1	29.0	87.9	186.1	322.9
Wisconsin	160.0	260.7	177.0	515.8	337.0	776.5
Wyoming	79.3	275.8	1.2	3.3	80.5	279.1
Total	$10,810.8	$21,423.9	$4,039.5	$8,191.1	$14,850.2	$29,614.9

*Holdings of employee retirement funds are excluded.

†Holdings of dependent school systems are not reported.

Note: — Zero or rounds to zero. (Source: U.S. Department of Commerce, Bureau of the Census. [1980]. *Finances of Public School Systems, 1977–78* [Series GF78, No. 10], p. 12. Washington, DC: U.S. Government Printing Office; [1988]. *Finances of Public School Systems in 1985–86* [Series GF86, No. 10], p. 10. Washington, DC: U.S. Government Printing Office.)

not legal obligations of the government. For example, the Federal Land Bank, the Federal Home Loan Bank, the Banks for Cooperatives, the Federal Intermediate Credit Bank, and the Federal National Mortgage Association offer higher yield than Treasury securities because of their low marketability.

Districts may enter into repurchase agreements, referred to as "repos," to earn relatively large returns in a short period. They purchase Treasury bills or other government securities under an agreement to sell them back to the issuing bank in the future. This strategy gives districts the opportunity to invest idle funds in a safe, high-yield investment for as short a period as one day.

A cash flow schedule (Dembowski & Davey, 1986, p. 240) tracks incoming revenue and outgoing expenditures to help finance officers plan the most productive cash management strategy. Deposits are invested as soon as they are received. Today's electronic transfers of funds speed transactions, especially for the deposit of large state and federal aid payments. Disbursements are timed to remove cash from district accounts as close as possible to when payments are owed to vendors. When checking and savings accounts are maintained with as small a balance as possible to meet current expenses, cash resources of separate funds can be pooled to yield potentially higher earnings from longer-term investments that require large deposits. Interest gained by pooled investments are dispersed to individual accounts in the same proportion as the original contributions. Small school districts may gain similar advantages from pooling investment funds to maximize yield and minimize paperwork for finance officers.

PARTNERSHIPS, FOUNDATIONS, AND VOLUNTEERISM

Schools have historically relied upon private resources to supplement public monies. Citizens, students' parents in particular, once contributed substantial time, talent, and money through tuition and special fees, fund-raising social activities, direct donations, and volunteer time. There was less involvement of individuals and the private sector in building the resource base, other than through property taxation, during the past few decades for several reasons. Changes in family structures and priorities for the use of time meant fewer hours to devote to schools. The growth of communities and schools altered the relationship between parents and school personnel. States assumed a greater share of the responsibility for financing public education, and a larger and more specialized profession displaced volunteers.

The 1980s brought new attitudes toward greater privitization within public education. Tax limitation efforts of the late 1970s reduced local revenue in many states, stimulating schools to turn once again to private sources of human and monetary inputs. The private sector, concerned about economic growth and international competition, encouraged school districts to involve businesses and communities in planning future educational structures and acquiring resources. Formalized partnerships with private sector businesses, community organizations, universities, and other groups emerged.

The private sector and public schools forged new relations through formal "adopt-a-school" programs. Corporations loaned executives to improve school leadership and management skills, hired teachers during the summer to acquaint them with the needs of business, and financed advertising campaigns to raise consciousness about the need for school improvement and to discourage students from dropping out. Adult and continuing education programs shared school space, and municipalities jointly financed the construction of special-use facilities. Educational foundations stimulated individuals and corporations to donate funds, and senior citizens and parents volunteered in classrooms. We examine private sector support for schools within the categories of partnerships, educational foundations, and volunteerism.

Partnerships

Formal and informal relationships between school districts or individual schools and businesses accomplish a number of purposes. The private sector desires a better educated work force to improve its productivity and to reduce on-the-job training costs. Interest in school improvement derives in part from the realization that tomorrow's labor market is in the schools today (Justiz & Kameen, 1987). Investments in human capital development, explored more fully in Chapter 13, yield returns to business and society alike. Changing demographics, including fewer students of high school age and a high proportion of dropouts, mean declines in the number of entry-level employees and more alternatives for well-educated individuals.

Schools represent a large market for the sale or donation of goods and services. Businesses profit from direct sales and schools benefit from research and development undertaken to provide more efficient products. Private sector involvement is also motivated by tax benefits that derive from donations of money and products to public schools (Wood, 1990).

On a very different level, economic competition motivates business involvement in school improvement. Wynne (1986) discusses partnerships in relation to broader national concerns: "They are necessities, prerequisites for a literate public capable of competing in a world where the United States is no longer the sole leader in world politics and commerce" (p. 94). He concludes that the private sector realizes that there will never be strong businesses if there are not strong schools.

In return for private sector collaboration, there are expectations for schools to improve their performance. In contrast to school systems' desires for more resources to produce better results, Doyle (1989) states that the premise often underlying business involvement is that results will produce more resources:

> Business should expect of the schools precisely what it expects of itself and what its customers expect of it: performance. Schools must be able to describe and defend what they do in terms of value added. What difference does going to school make? In what measurable ways is a student better off having gone to school? (p. E100)

School-business collaborations that yield improved schooling offer returns in the form of resources *and* results for both parties.

Meno (1984) categorizes partnership activities as donor, shared, and enterprise activities. Donor activities, the primary focus of our discussion, are directed to soliciting goods, services, and money. Shared or cooperative activities permit schools to pool resources with community organizations, colleges and universities, or government agencies to reduce costs. Enterprise activities involve school districts in many revenue-producing services:

providing food preparation, data processing, and transportation services for other organizations; leasing surplus buildings for alternative community uses, athletic fields to professional athletic teams, or facility space to profit-making enterprises such as credit unions; providing driver education and swimming instruction, which generate user fees and service charges; and selling access to school markets such as food-service rights, vending machines, and advertising space on calendars and educational television.

McLaughlin (1988) describes a somewhat different school-business relationship that emerged from the educational reform movement. In this approach, third-party intermediaries work in a manner similar to the United Way to secure and allocate funds and other contributions. These groups broaden the base of political support for public schools in the private sector, in communities and legislatures. For example, local education funds (LEFs) sponsored by the Ford-supported Public Education Fund view contributions as part of a political strategy of coalition building, rather than as ends themselves:

> LEFs adopt a highly leveraged view of cash and noncash resources. The LEF convenes representatives from business, the community, and the schools, brokers private-sector resources (both cash and noncash), and takes responsibility for overseeing the use of these resources. The LEF thus reduces the transaction costs for both contributors and beneficiaries by assuming the information-search costs as well as the administrative overhead associated with private sector philanthropy. (p. 69)

The political support engendered through this approach offers public education a different kind of resource. Private sector advocacy assists efforts to obtain additional revenue and public support for school programs. Each of these types of partnership activities offers school districts opportunities for expanding their resources. We devote primary attention to those efforts from which schools secure additional capital and human resources because of the incentives they offer for school improvement.

Table 7.3 indicates that the number of partnerships with public schools grew from 42,200 in 1983–1984 to 140,800 in 1987–1988 (National Center for Education Statistics, 1989). This growth is reflected in the increase in the average number of partnerships (from 3.3 to 4.6) present in schools that reported such activities. Partnerships were most prevalent in the Southeast (54 percent of schools in 1987–1988), in urban and suburban schools (51 percent and 44 percent of schools, respectively), in secondary schools (46 percent), in larger schools (57 percent of schools with over 1,000 students), and in schools having high proportions of students who qualify for free or reduced-price lunches. These rankings shift somewhat when the mean number of partnerships present in schools is considered. The highest average number of active partnerships were reported in rural schools (5.2 in 1987–1988), secondary schools (5.5), schools with over 1,000 pupils (6.4), and schools serving between 10 percent and 41 percent of pupils from low-income families (5.0).

Inman (1984) and Mann (1987b) discuss why school-business partnerships are less likely to form in rural areas than in larger, more urbanized districts. Strong preexisting connections, dispersed economies, a local culture of thrift, and the unintended consequences of competition in rural communities either remove the need for alliances or make creating them undesirable. Rural school districts do not have as large an economic base, and thus contacting businesses for donations of funds or supplies may be unwise when they are also asked to raise taxes to support an increased school system budget. Smaller

TABLE 7.3. Public Schools Participating in Partnerships

School Characteristic	Number of Partnerships		Percentage of Schools		Mean Number of Partnerships	
	1983–1984	1987–1988	1983–1984	1987–1988	1983–1984	1987–1988
Region						
Northeast	6,000	24,700	16	37	2.8	4.6
Central	9,800	33,800	15	32	2.9	4.4
Southeast	12,700	39,100	22	54	3.7	4.4
West	13,700	43,100	17	39	3.5	4.8
Metropolitan status						
Urban	9,000	38,100	23	51	2.2	3.9
Suburban	11,400	44,200	18	44	2.9	4.5
Rural	21,800	58,500	14	31	4.5	5.2
Instructional level*						
Elementary	20,900	71,600	15	36	2.9	3.9
Secondary	20,100	66,500	22	46	3.7	5.5
School enrollment						
Less than 300	6,900	26,400	12	28	2.8	4.4
300–999	26,900	89,500	18	42	3.1	4.3
1,000 or more	8,400	24,900	30	57	4.4	6.4
Percentage of students eligible for free or reduced-price lunches						
10 or less	10,600	27,200	15	34	3.7	4.4
11–40	17,200	71,100	17	40	3.0	5.0
41 or more	14,500	41,400	20	45	3.3	4.1
Total	42,200	140,800	17	40	3.3	4.6

*Elementary schools include those in which the lowest grade is less than 6 and the highest grade is less than 9; secondary schools include schools in which the lowest grade is greater than 5 and the highest grade is greater than 6; data for schools in which the lowest grade is less than 6 and the highest grade is greater than 8 are not reported for this category, because there were only 19 in the sample, but are included in the totals and in analyses by other school characteristics. (*Source:* National Center for Education Statistics. [1989]. *Education Partnerships in Public Elementary and Secondary Schools* [Survey Report No. CS89-060], pp. 18–19. Washington, DC: Office of Educational Research and Improvement.)

districts enjoy better communications among schools, businesses, and community agencies; the lack of these linkages is often a motivation for partnerships in cities. Urban school districts are the largest beneficiaries of partnership activities in part because businesses tend to support schools located within the same community.

Numerous partnerships were formed during the 1980s to improve schools. Among the highly visible initiatives serving large cities were the New York Alliance for the Public Schools, the California Business Roundtable in San Francisco, the Atlanta Partnership, and the Minnesota Business Partnership in Minneapolis. The Boston COMPACT was formed in 1982 as a joint venture in which the public schools would teach according to jointly specified standards and businesses would provide job opportunities. Seattle's Partners in Public Education (PIPE), a nonprofit brokerage agency, paired interested businesses with individual schools. The Chicago Adopt-a-School Program joined many corporations and universities with public schools.

Countless schools have been beneficiaries of private sponsorship of programs. The RJR Nabisco Corporation's Next Century Schools Program funded challenge grants, or venture capital, to stimulate school-based innovations. The Thomas Jefferson High School for Science and Technology in Alexandria, Virginia, received donations of high-tech equipment worth over $4 million from local businesses. The High School for Creative and Performing Arts, an inner-city magnet school in Cincinnati, supplemented school resources with community contributions (over $400,000 in one year) to finance performances (Wilson & Rossman, 1986). Direct sponsorship of academies through The Corporate/Community Schools of America encouraged reform based on sound research, successful teaching methods, and "market-driven" innovations. Its flagship elementary school opened in 1988 in Chicago with several goals: to involve parents actively in the school's learning community; to create programs for connecting families with social service agencies; to develop better measures of students' physical, emotional, social, and academic development; to link with universities to develop cooperative programs and conduct educational research; and to initiate working partnerships with public schools to share information and encourage adoption of successful methods (Doyle, 1989).

Students who have dropped out or who are at risk of not completing schooling were the target of many partnership activities (Justiz & Kameen, 1987). The Cooperative Federation for Education Experiences, a collaborative effort of the Digital Corporation and schools in Oxford, Massachusetts, sponsored academic study, counseling, training, and preemployment experience in high-tech industries for school dropouts. The Stanford Mid-Peninsula Urban Coalition linked one school district with area businesses. It sponsored academies within high schools to reduce the high rate of minorities not completing school, to increase their employability, and to reduce the number of unfilled entry-level jobs in Silicon Valley industries. A number of schools and high-risk students benefited from coordinated services and resources of entire communities through the Washington-based Cities in Schools program. The Cleveland Initiative for Education established a college scholarship fund in which students were credited payments based on higher grades earned.

Higher education has also formed partnership agreements with elementary and secondary schools. The Chelsea, Massachusetts, public schools turned to Boston University for assistance in implementing educational reforms. State legislation in 1989 enabled the university to manage the school system for 10 years. The State University of New York

College at Purchase and Westchester County public schools collaborated to increase the pool of qualified college students, foster vitality in the teaching profession, raise standards, strengthen career counseling, develop leadership, and improve teaching and learning in secondary schools (Gross, 1988).

Even with the rapid growth in partnership activities in the 1980s, and despite McLaughlin's (1988) report that 64 percent of 130 major corporations list elementary and secondary education as their number one community affairs concern, corporate contributions are estimated to be only between $15 million and $50 million. Timpane (1984) reports that only about 3 percent of corporate contributions to education are directed to precollegiate public education. Hess (1987) surveyed 62 Chicago-based funding organizations and found that they made 446 grants that totaled $7.7 million. However, this represented just 4.6 percent of their total giving. Mann (1987a, 1987b) contends that businesses are permitted only limited roles. His studies of 108 school systems, including 23 large cities, found that only 17 percent of the schools visited had developed relationships with all four features of "new style" business involvement: a coordinating structure, multiple purposes, multiple players, and stability. Mann (1987a) states that the modest role of businesses in addressing school improvement is understandable:

> After having designed a system of limited government in order to minimize the abuse of power, after having vested most control in professionals, and after having inserted boards between the schools and their communities, why should we be surprised that no one— least of all the business community—has much power to solve problems? (p. 126)

Many partnerships avoid areas of conflict and help schools acquire funds and materials. Business reluctance to become involved in schools, according to Timpane (1984), stems from feelings that the sponsorship of isolated projects is not likely "to improve the performance of school systems caught in webs of programmatic, managerial, and financial control created by years of governmental inaction at local, state and federal levels" (p. 391). However, their limited partnership roles do not enable schools to take advantage of business expertise, leadership, and political clout as reform directions are forged.

In contrast to these reports of limited roles for business is a study of effective schools in which collaborative efforts are shown to make a large difference in school programs. Wilson and Rossman's (1986) investigation of programs and policies of 571 exemplary secondary schools revealed several common themes. These schools actively recruited human resources from the community and used aggressive public relations campaigns that relied on parent volunteers who served as promoters, communicators, and decision makers. The schools successfully attracted financial resources from individuals and businesses. There was mutual benefit in having communities make extensive use of school facilities and in jointly forming positive identities with their communities. What set these schools apart from other schools were the frequency of cooperation between schools and communities, the high level of participation, and the degree to which these activities were considered central to the schools' missions and programs.

Partnership activities that offer more than cosmetic changes in school programs hold much potential for school improvement. The nature and extent of the partner's involvement may be an important distinguishing feature of effective restructured schools.

Educational Foundations

The creation of privately financed, nonprofit school foundations expands the capacity of a school's fund-raising efforts. An outgrowth of partnership activities, educational foundations in many districts coordinate and encourage gifts from individuals and businesses through a variety of strategies. Special purpose funds attract donations for facility construction or particular school programs. Foundations often target specific groups such as alumni or industries that employ graduates. Long-term development activities encourage estate planning to establish endowments from which future income will be derived to support teaching positions or student scholarships. Funds from foundations finance an array of special projects including science and computer laboratories, field trips locally and abroad, grants for teachers to improve instruction, endowed teaching chairs, athletic facilities, and incentives for students to complete high school.

Foundations may benefit schools throughout a state (e.g., the Kentucky Educational Foundation) or within specific school systems (e.g., the Baltimore City Foundations and the Los Angeles Educational Partnership). The "I Have a Dream" Foundation seeks sponsors for at-risk students in 32 cities to provide incentives for students to complete school by ensuring later support of their higher education expenses. The Minneapolis Five Percent Club, the first of several such foundations, relies upon peer pressure among businesses to stimulate giving (McLaughlin, 1988). Many smaller school districts (Ballew, 1987; Neill, 1983; Nesbit, 1987) have also created foundations to solicit and manage donations. The Public Education Fund Network of Pittsburgh stimulated the formation of foundations that differed in scope and budget, from $3,000 in a rural North Carolina county to $2 million in Los Angeles (White & Morgan, 1990).

Federal and state statutes define the legal structures of foundations, either as charitable trusts or nonprofit corporations (Wood, 1990). Because they generally operate as self-governed entities, foundations may limit school boards and personnel to advisory roles. School personnel should help external groups decide priorities for uses of resources and the appropriateness of gifts of equipment and teaching materials. They should also monitor cash flow to avoid claims of fund misuse. Wood (1990) discusses this latter concern in relation to the financial mismanagement and fraud that forced the Dallas, Texas, public schools to bring legal action against the Foundation for Quality Education in the late 1970s.

Foundation activities offer businesses and individuals an opportunity to support public education without devoting large amounts of time. On the other hand, this banking or "checkwriting" mode of philanthropy (McLaughlin, 1988) falls short of broader partnership goals because it does not foster direct involvement of donors. Rather than increasing the distance between donors and recipient schools, such intermediary organizations as local education funds can involve donors in specific educational programs. For example, when the John Hancock Insurance Company donated $1 million through the Boston COMPACT, company executives served on a committee to review teachers' proposals for the use of grants. McLaughlin (1988) concludes, "These intermediary organizations thus foster knowledge, understanding, and identification, rather than alienation or distancing from the public schools" (p. 69). This observation suggests that the nature and extent of donors' involvement is as important to school improvement as is the amount of the donation.

Volunteerism

Parents, community residents, and other individuals directly support schools when volunteering their time and ideas. Nonpublic schools, like other organizations in the independent sector, have benefited greatly over the years from volunteerism. The total number of hours donated to these tax-exempt organizations during 1984 was equivalent to 4.7 million employees; the value of their volunteer time was $74.4 billion (Hodgkinson, 1986, p. 3). It is estimated that volunteers contributed 20 percent of total employment in nonpublic schools.

To a lesser degree, public schools involve volunteers, primarily in support of extracurricular activities and fund-raising efforts. Booster clubs provide assistance to school personnel in support of athletic, band, choral, debate, and drama activities. Parent-teacher organizations sponsor carnivals and save grocery receipts and coupons to acquire instructional and playground equipment. The Dedicated Older Volunteers in Educational Service (DOVES) represents a more formal arrangement in which Springfield, Massachusetts, residents serve as tutors, mentors, guest speakers, and library assistants in the public schools (Gray, 1984). In an innovative approach, the Chapel Hill–Carrboro, North Carolina, school district benefits from substantial proceeds of two thrift shops that sell donated clothing and furniture. Each school receives a portion of funds for discretionary purposes; allocations among schools consider both the number of students enrolled and the number of volunteer hours posted by parents and students from respective buildings.

School management and instruction can benefit from services of volunteers. Community leaders serve on advisory committees and participate in strategic planning activities, residents share their expertise in in-service staff development programs, and corporations lend executives to give advice on management practices. Parents and senior citizens become involved in classrooms and field trips, reducing the pupil–adult ratio so that greater individual attention can be given to students. Brown (1990) observes that additional local resources strengthen school site management: ". . . voluntarism may be regarded as a variation on the theme of decentralization since it permits discretionary decision making with private resources in a similar way that school-based management permits flexibility with public dollars" (p. 1).

Gray (1984) discusses the characteristics of successful, institutionalized volunteer programs. The superintendent, school board, and business leaders give strong and visible support, including formal adoption of a policy of support which then helps school staff overcome traditional barriers to volunteerism. A systemwide manager coordinates volunteer services and facilitates information sharing, and building-level coordinators conduct needs assessments and identify potential resource people. The emphasis is on people who bring personal talents and commitments, rather than on procuring money. There are many options for volunteers to assist in instruction, pupil counseling, and school management. Collaborative, long-range planning involves volunteers in seeking ways to improve schools. Sandfort (1987) urges schools to give greater responsibility to parents and other volunteers to close the growing distance between schools and homes.

Benefits and Costs of Partnership Activities

The monetary and human benefits derived from greater involvement of the private sector in schools need to be weighed with the potential costs to public education in appraising these activities fairly. The forgoing presentation of foundations and volunteerism stresses such returns as enriched programs and stronger political support. Concerns have been expressed that these gains will be substantial only in wealthy school districts and that partnerships may have negative effects on current revenue sources and on decisions about public education.

It is difficult to determine the monetary value of many partnership and volunteer activities. Wilson and Rossman (1986) suggest that involving the community, opening schools to other organizations, and building political support across constituencies are more important than financial supplements to school budgets:

> It builds commitment and loyalty. It creates a special identity for the school that includes the surrounding community. The ethic of mutual caring that is created multiplies the effectiveness of the school and integrates the school into its community. (p. 708)

Opening schools to the community improves relationships and contributes to "social capital" (Coleman & Hoffer, 1987). Similar to gains in productivity derived from greater investments in human capital development, schools and communities benefit from investments in social capital. Coleman and Hoffer discuss this concept as it enriches private school capabilities:

> The social capital that has value for a young person's development does not reside merely in the set of common values held by parents who choose to send their children to the same private school. It resides in the functional community, the actual social relationships that exist among parents, in the closure exhibited by this structure of relations and in the parents' relations with the institutions of the community. (pp. 225–226)

In a similar manner in which nonpublic schools have nurtured and benefit from close ties with their clientele, partnerships and volunteerism in public schools may pay large dividends. As the public's feelings of responsibility and ownership for their schools grow, the local resource base expands and schools have greater opportunities for improvement.

On the other hand, substantially increased reliance on partnerships, foundations, and volunteerism in public schools may have negative effects on current revenue sources, governance, and equity goals. If the public and businesses view requests for additional monetary donations from the private sector to be another tax, albeit voluntary, to support schools, one consequence may be opposition to various forms of public support (Brown, 1989). If increased volunteerism means that fewer certified professionals or paid assistants are required for program delivery, teacher unions may express concerns about possible displacements by unpaid workers.

There is also concern that increased privitization of public schooling may bring undue influence over educational decisions to the detriment of traditional school board governance. Meno (1984) warned that as nontraditional finance activities grow, educators and policymakers would have to decide whether or not fiscal benefits are worth potential modifications in present practices. In contrast, McLaughlin (1988) observes that corporations respect educators' expertise and that the primary donors are small businesses which are unable to influence school decisions. It might be argued that direct and indirect pressure to alter educational policy to receive partnership assistance is not necessarily negative. Educators need to be comfortable in deciding whether it is advantageous to form partnerships or receive gifts, especially when they have concerns about impacts on school policy and curricula.

Equity concerns relate to fund-raising abilities and allocation decisions. Just as varying tax bases enable school districts to raise different levels of revenue, socioeconomic statuses of communities give school districts and schools within them unequal settings for obtaining private resources. To the degree that partnerships become a potent force for raising funds in the future, disparities in educational programs and extracurricular activities are perpetuated. Wood (1990) discusses privitization in relation to the goal of equalizing educational opportunities:

> To allow public school districts to pursue outside sources of fiscal support, however noble in the intent to support public education, is to allow the districts to engage in *laissez-faire* self interest. . . . This agenda is indifferent to local resources or lack thereof, the educational or fiscal needs, and the allocation of resources to this goal. Within this system, every school district is capable of seeking to maximize its present assets in a manner competitive with all other school districts. (p. 60)

Privatization within public education is appealing in that schools take advantage of the entrepreneurial skills of individuals and groups in the larger society. However, these activities are not available in many small and rural school districts. Timpane (1984) observes that equity concerns have taken second place to concerns for educational excellence:

> Educational equity is a hollow goal if it does not promise and expect excellence, but excellence will also echo falsely if it does not apply to all students—including the poor, minorities, and the handicapped, whose education has been less than excellent so far. Will corporations help education maintain the difficult but necessary balance between excellence and equity? (p. 392)

McLaughlin (1988) comments that dollars made available through these activities are small in comparison with total school district budgets and do not underwrite inequalities of the scale that result in judicial challenges (see Chapter 11). Many partnerships and foundations operate at the district level to ensure that all schools benefit from donations. For example, the Los Angeles Educational Partnership gives bonus points to applications for grants from teachers in inner-city schools and supports programs that benefit the district as a whole through workshops, incentive programs for students, and math/science collaboratives.

Despite these limitations, partnerships, foundations, and volunteerism represent a potentially large resource base for schools. The success of school improvement efforts depends in part upon the active involvement of communities and businesses.

SUMMARY

The focus of this chapter is on the opportunities school districts have to expand their resources from the traditional reliance on property taxation. Careful planning and management of the flow of money through school district accounts at times require borrowing to increase available cash and at other times free idle cash to be invested. In addition to cash flow management, wise use of partnerships, foundations, and volunteers can enhance monetary and human resources.

Nonrevenue money obtained through short- and long-term borrowing is important to maintain an even flow of funds. Short-term borrowing through tax and revenue anticipation notes enables districts to pay employees and outside vendors on schedule when there is a revenue deficit. Facility construction and remodeling are enabled by the issuance of general obligation bonds when pay-as-you-go financing is not feasible. However, the dependence on local valuations for repayment of bonds results in large disparities in the nature of school buildings among communities. State-sponsored loan programs, direct grants of state funds, and public bonding authorities ease burdens on local tax bases and help districts reach goals of providing adequate, if not equal, educational opportunities.

Investment strategies are selected according to their potential yield; the safety, or amount of risk entailed; and the liquidity, or ease to which funds can be accessed without loss of interest. Districts can add considerably to their revenue when short- or long-term investments are planned around the flow of revenue and nonrevenue money into the district in relation to future expenditures, and when checking and saving account balances are minimized and small accounts are pooled to maximize investments.

One benefit from tax limitation and educational reform movements has been expanded opportunities to garner private resources through partnerships, educational foundations, and volunteers. In addition to discretionary money and other goods and services gained for schools, these activities enrich linkages among schools, businesses, community agencies, and parents. The potential for enlarging the local resource base is substantial, and meaningful involvement of individuals and groups can improve instruction and school leadership. However beneficial these activities may be in many predominantly urban and suburban districts, there is concern that supplements to school resources may not reach relatively poor and small school systems.

The chapters in Part III examine state and federal sources of revenue for public education and forms of financial assistance provided for school districts.

ACTIVITIES

1. Discuss the management of cash flow, including the timing of borrowing and investing decisions, with a school district finance officer. What opportunities exist for school-level administrators to borrow and invest funds? In what ways do state-imposed limits on borrowing and investments strengthen financial management practices? In what ways do these limitations impede the flexibility required to maximize the benefits of these cash flow strategies?
2. Debate the appropriateness of the state or federal government assuming a larger role in capital outlay financing.

3. Investigate to what extent private resources supplement schools and school districts in a given locality or state. What demographic or organizational conditions present within schools appear to be related to the amount of resources gained from partnerships, foundations, and volunteerism?
4. Determine the nature of business partnership involvement in a given school district. To what extent do partnerships show the four characteristics of "new style" involvement identified by Mann (1987a): a coordinating structure, multiple purposes, multiple players, and stability?

REFERENCES

Augenblick, J. (1977). *Systems of state support for school district capital expenditure* (Report No. F76-8). Denver: Education Commission of the States.

Ballew, P. (1987, November). How to start a school foundation. *Executive Educator, 9,* 26–28.

Brown, D. J. (1989). *Private resources for public education.* Interim Report for the Social Sciences and Humanities Research Council of Canada. Vancouver, Canada: University of British Columbia.

Brown, D. J. (1990). *Voluntarism for public schools.* Paper presented at the annual conference of the American Education Finance Association, Las Vegas.

Camp, W. E., & Salmon, R. G. (1985, Spring). Public school bonding corporations financing public elementary and secondary school facilities. *Journal of Education Finance, 10,* 495–503.

Candoli, I. C., Hack, W. G., Ray, J. R., & Stollar, D. H. (1984). *School business administration: A planning approach* (3rd ed.). Boston: Allyn & Bacon.

Coleman, J. S., & Hoffer, T. (1987). *Public and private high schools: The impact of communities.* New York: Basic Books.

Dembowski, F. L. (1986). Cash management. In G. C. Hentschke, *School business management: A comparative perspective* (pp. 214–245). Berkeley, CA: McCutchan.

Dembowski, F. L., & Davey, R. D. (1986). School district financial management and banking. In R. C. Wood (Ed.), *Principles of school business management* (pp. 237–260). Reston, VA: ASBO International.

Doyle, D. P. (1989, November). Endangered species: Children of promise. *Business Week,* Special Supplement, E4–E135.

Gray, S. T. (1984, February). How to create a successful school/community partnership. *Phi Delta Kappan, 65,* 405–409.

Gross, T. L. (1988). *Partners in education: How colleges can work with schools to improve teaching and learning.* San Francisco: Jossey-Bass.

Hack, W. G. (1976, Fall). School district bond issues: Implications for reform in financing capital outlay. *Journal of Education Finance, 2,* 156–172.

Hess, G. A. (1987). *1985 education survey.* Chicago: Donors Forum of Chicago.

Hodgkinson, V. A. (1986). *Dimensions of the independent sector: A statistical profile* (2nd ed., ERIC Document ED301131). Washington, DC: Independent Sector.

Inman, D. (1984, Fall). Bridging education to industry: Implications for financing education. *Journal of Education Finance, 10,* 271–277.

Johns, R. L., Morphet, E. L., & Alexander, K. (1983). *The economics & financing of education* (4th ed.). Englewood Cliffs, NJ: Prentice Hall.

Justiz, M. J., & Kameen, M. C. (1987, January). Business offers a hand to education. *Phi Delta Kappan, 68,* 379–383.

King, R. A., & MacPhail-Wilcox, B. (1988, Spring). Bricks-and-mortar reform in North Carolina: The state assumes a larger role in financing school construction. *Journal of Education Finance, 13,* 374–381.

McLaughlin, M. L. (1988). Business and the public schools: New patterns of support. In D. H. Monk & J. Underwood (Eds.), *Microlevel school finance: Issues and implications for policy* (pp. 63–80). Cambridge, MA: Ballinger.

Mann, D. (1987a, October). Business involvement and public school improvement, Part 1. *Phi Delta Kappan, 69,* 123–128.

Mann, D. (1987b, November). Business involvement and public school improvement, Part 2. *Phi Delta Kappan, 69,* 228–232.

Meno, L. (1984). Sources of alternative revenue. In L. D. Webb & V. D. Mueller (Eds.), *Managing limited resources: New demands on public school management* (pp. 129–146). Cambridge, MA: Ballinger.

National Center for Education Statistics. (1989). *Education partnerships in public elementary and secondary schools* (Survey Report No. CS89-060). Washington, DC: Office of Educational Research and Improvement.

Neill, G. (1983). *The local education foundation: A new way to raise money for schools* (NASSP Special Report). Reston, VA: National Association of Secondary School Principals.

Nesbit, W. B. (1987, February). The local education foundation: What is it, how is it established? *NASSP Bulletin, 71,* 85–89.

Piele, P. K., & Hall, J. S. (1973). *Budgets, bonds and ballots: Voting behavior in school financial issues.* Lexington, MA: Heath.

Salmon, R., Dawson, C., Lawton, S., & Johns, T. (Eds.). (1988). *Public school finance programs of the United States and Canada, 1986–87.* Blacksburg, VA: American Education Finance Association.

Salmon, R., & Thomas, S. (1981, Summer). Financing public school facilities in the 80s. *Journal of Education Finance, 7,* 88–109.

Sandfort, J. A. (1987, February). Putting parents in their place in public schools. *NASSP Bulletin, 71,* 99–103.

Timpane, M. (1984, February). Business has rediscovered the public schools. *Phi Delta Kappan, 65,* 389–392.

U.S. Department of Commerce, Bureau of the Census. (1968). *Governmental finances in 1966–67* (Series GF67, No. 3). Washington, DC: U.S. Government Printing Office.

U.S. Department of Commerce, Bureau of the Census. (1978). *Governmental finances in 1976–77* (Series GF77, No. 5). Washington, DC: U.S. Government Printing Office.

U.S. Department of Commerce, Bureau of the Census. (1980). *Finances of public school systems in 1977–78* (Series GF78, No. 10). Washington, DC: U.S. Government Printing Office.

U.S. Department of Commerce, Bureau of the Census. (1988a). *Finances of public school systems in 1985–86.* (Series GF86, No. 10). Washington, DC: U.S. Government Printing Office.

U.S. Department of Commerce, Bureau of the Census. (1988b). *Governmental finances in 1986–87* (Series GF87, No. 5). Washington, DC.: U.S. Government Printing Office.

White, G.P., & Morgan, N.H. (1990, April). Education foundations: The catalyst that mixes corporation and community to support schools. *The School Administrator, 47,* 22–24.

Wilkerson, W. R. (1981). State participation in financing school facilities. In K. F. Jordan &

N. H. Cambron-McCabe (Eds.), *Perspectives in state school support programs* (pp. 191–213). Cambridge, MA: Ballinger.

Wilson B. L., & Rossman, G. B. (1986, June). Collaborative links with the community: Lessons from exemplary secondary schools. *Phi Delta Kappan, 67,* 708–711.

Wood, R. C. (1986). Capital outlay and bonding. In R. C. Wood (Ed.), *Principles of school business management* (pp. 559–587). Reston, VA: ASBO International.

Wood, R. C. (1990). New revenues for education at the local level. In J. E. Underwood & D. A. Verstegen (Eds.), *The impacts of litigation and legislation on public school finance: Adequacy, equity, and excellence* (pp. 59–74). New York: Harper & Row.

Wynne, G. E. (1986, September). School business partnerships—A shortcut to effectiveness. *NASSP Bulletin, 70,* 94–98.

PART III

Local, State, and Federal Interrelationships in School Funding

CHAPTER 8

Intergovernmental Transfer Payments

Parts I and II of this text examined the extent to which society should become involved in the provision of education and the means by which federal, state, and local governments support public services. Part III explores the flow of funds from state and federal governments to finance schools at the local level.

In this chapter, we discuss the rationale for intergovernmental transfer payments; distinguish general, block grant, and categorical funds; and present alternative ways of structuring aid formulas. Measurement and administrative considerations in state aid programs provide the focus of Chapter 9, and the federal role in educational policy and finance is examined in Chapter 10.

JUSTIFICATION FOR TRANSFER PAYMENTS

Channeling money raised at federal and state levels for use by localities serves a number of purposes. First, state governments are constitutionally responsible for providing systems of public education and have a parallel responsibility for their financial support. State aid for education and granting school districts the authority to tax real property are two primary mechanisms used by states for meeting this latter responsibility.

Second, higher levels of government are better able to ensure the availability of adequate public services, including public education, throughout the nation or state. If local governments were dependent solely upon their own revenue-generating sources, they would base decisions about the level and quality of services to be provided on expected returns to the locality rather than to the larger society. State and federal financial assistance encourages and enables localities to meet goals defined by these higher levels of government in addition to those defined locally.

Third, a central government (state or federal) can take advantage of broader tax bases and economies of scale to improve schools in all localities. Allocations enable a higher basic level of education, expand educational opportunities, and broaden course offerings in communities that may have little tax base or that are unwilling to raise sufficient revenue.

In many ways, the general quality of education can be improved through state and federal leadership and financial resources. On the other hand, the regulations which may accompany such financial aid programs are often considered to be unwarranted interventions into the affairs of local government. Rather than promoting efficiency and economies of scale, mandates may stifle educators' abilities to address particular needs of pupils and communities. The different types of aid programs reflect the struggle to identify an appropriate degree to which higher levels of government can shape educational programs and services without weakening the ability of school boards and personnel to respond to priorities set by communities.

TYPES OF AID PROGRAMS

There are three basic types of aid programs: general, categorical, and block grant. General financial aid flows from federal and state governments to municipalities and school districts to finance educational programs as determined by local authorities within established guidelines. General aid from states provides the largest proportion of support for the operation of schools. Categorical aids link grants to specific objectives of the government providing the aid, and thereby constrain program design and delivery. To qualify for such aid, a school district must comply with program requirements. Thus, unlike general aid, categorical grants can be used only for a certain group of students (e.g., physically handicapped), a specific purpose (e.g., pupil transportation), or a particular project (e.g., construction of a school building).

State categorical aid, once the predominant form of financial assistance, communicates legislative priorities through appropriations that restrict local control over the use of funds. Similarly, most federal funds are designated for specified program priorities, most notably for vocational education and for broadening educational opportunities for disadvantaged and handicapped pupils. Entitlement programs direct funds to school districts according to the number of qualifying pupils, whereas other categorical grants flow in accordance with specific program proposals initiated by school districts and approved by the granting agency.

Program control through categorical aid means greater centralization of decision making and more complex administration. Legislatures decide priorities, and federal- or state-level decision making replaces local discretion. State and federal bureaucracies oversee programs and ensure that funds are used for intended purposes. They develop guidelines for entitlement programs, request and review proposals for competitive grants, monitor the use of money, and evaluate results.

The administration of categorical aid is also far more involved for local officials than that required for general operating aid. Once a grant is received, a separate account is maintained to restrict expenditures to designated programs. A large burden may be placed on project coordinators to show that grants are spent to supplement rather than to supplant, or replace, state and local revenue. Whereas general aid flows to school units each year with little administrative attention, many categorical aids call for annual applications, frequent program evaluations, and documentation of expenditures. The paperwork involved in administering categorical aids places small and rural districts at a disadvantage in competing for funds.

General aid and categorical grants occupy the ends of a continuum of funding types; block grants define a middle-ground approach. State and federal block grants allow a range of services within a broad set of governmental purposes. Requirements for planning, implementing, and assessing programs are also less distinct than for categorical aid.

The block grant label was popularized when the federal government combined a number of former categorical programs within Chapter 2 of the Education Consolidation and Improvement Act of 1981. States receive funds according to the total number of pupils rather than in relation to specific educational needs or program goals. In turn, state-developed formulas consider enrollments as well as other measures of need in making allocations to school districts. This block grant program outlines several broad purposes and allows school district personnel greater discretion in designing programs than was true under prior categorical aids. Block grants still must be accounted for separately, as do more restrictive categorical aids.

Local school boards, administrators, and teachers generally prefer unrestricted grants that minimize administrative processes and permit latitude to meet local priorities. Special interest groups and many educators, concerned about weakened programs under less restrictive approaches, argue that policy should be defined at broader state and federal levels. The political reality, once favoring equity goals through strict categorical funding, turned in the 1980s to support liberty and efficiency goals through block grants and greater local initiative. Control over fund use differentiates these types of aid approaches.

MODELS FOR FINANCE

State aid mechanisms are designed to make funds available for the provision of educational services to children of the state at some defined level of adequacy. In practice, state legislatures usually leave the definition of quality to state education departments and local school boards. In providing state funds in support of those programs, locally levied taxes, normally the property tax, are an important part of the calculations. Thus, in discussing state aid programs, there are four key concepts which apply to all models: level of support, defined in terms of expenditure per pupil or classroom unit; division of fiscal responsibility between state and local jurisdictions; local ability to raise taxes in support of education, defined as property value or personal income per pupil; and local effort, defined as the tax rate on the value of real property.

Federal aids, with few exceptions, are supplementary to the basic educational program. As such, federal aids are based primarily on the characteristics of target populations and do not usually take into account characteristics of school districts, as do most state aids. The models discussed in this chapter pertain to state aid programs specifically; Chapter 10 focuses on federal aid.

States have followed several general approaches in defining the structure through which public school programs are funded, including matching grants, flat grants, foundation programs, various forms of tax base equalization, and full state funding. Each takes fiscal capacity and effort into account to different degrees.

Typically a combination of these approaches is used by states in formulating their school aid policies. Table 8.1 lists states according to the primary finance approach taken to fund basic school operations as classified by Verstegen (1988) and Salmon, Dawson, Lawton, & Johns (1988). The table also indicates per pupil expenditures and relative proportions of funds derived from federal, state, and local levels. New Hampshire, for example, is heavily reliant on local revenue (89 percent) in its foundation plan. In contrast, Hawaii has a fully state-financed (91 percent) funding plan; the remaining 9 percent comes

TABLE 8.1. State Finance Plans, Proportion of Revenue by Source, and per Pupil Expenditures

State	Finance Program*		Source of Revenue			Expenditure	
	Salmon	Verstegen	State	Local	Federal	Per Pupil	Rank
Alabama	FND	FND	69.3%	17.9%	12.8%	$2,752	47
Alaska	PCT	FND	67.3	25.3	7.3	7,038	1
Arizona	FND	FND	53.5	43.0	3.5	3,265	38
Arkansas	FND	FND	61.3	29.3	9.4	2,410	49
California	FULL	FND	68.1	24.6	7.3	3,994	25
Colorado	GTB/Y	GYLD	37.9	57.5	4.6	4,359	16
Connecticut	GTB/Y	GTB	42.2	53.8	4.1	6,114	5
Delaware	FLT	FND	68.6	23.8	7.5	4,994	9
Florida	FND	FND	52.5	40.8	6.6	4,389	15
Georgia	FND	F/GTB	56.2	36.8	7.6	2,939	44
Hawaii	FULL	FULL	91.2	0.1	8.7	3,625	32
Idaho	FND	FND	61.2	31.5	7.4	2,814	45
Illinois	FND	FND	38.0	54.6	7.4	4,217	19
Indiana	FND	FND	60.0	36.0	4.0	6,616	33
Iowa	FND	FND	43.2	51.3	5.6	3,846	29
Kansas	PCT	GYLD	43.8	51.5	4.7	4,262	18
Kentucky	FLT	F/DPE	69.5	20.4	10.1	3,355	36
Louisiana	FND	FND	53.3	34.4	12.3	3,211	39
Maine	FND	FND	54.2	40.2	5.5	4,276	17
Maryland	FND	FND	39.8	54.9	5.3	4,871	12
Massachusetts	FND	F/PCT	46.7	47.6	5.7	5,396	7
Michigan	GTB/Y	GYLD	35.2	61.2	3.6	4,122	21
Minnesota	FND	FND	56.9	38.5	4.6	4,513	14
Mississippi	FND	FND	54.5	29.8	15.7	2,760	46
Missouri	FND	F/GTB	40.5	53.7	5.8	3,566	34
Montana	FND	F/GYL	49.2	42.8	7.9	4,061	23
Nebraska	FLT	FND	26.6	68.2	5.3	3,641	31
Nevada	FND	FND	40.1	55.8	4.2	3,829	30
New Hampshire	FND	FND	7.6	89.1	3.3	3,990	26
New Jersey	GTB/Y	GTB	42.7	53.1	4.2	6,910	2
New Mexico	FULL	FND	76.3	11.8	11.9	3,880	28
New York	PCT	PCT	43.4	51.6	5.0	6,864	4
North Carolina	FLT	FND	64.5	29.1	6.4	3,911	27
North Dakota	FND	FND	51.2	41.4	7.4	3,353	37
Ohio	FND	FND	47.4	48.1	4.5	4,019	24

(Continued)

TABLE 8.1. *(Continued)*

State	Finance Program*		Source of Revenue			Expenditure	
	Salmon	Verstegen	State	Local	Federal	Per Pupil	Rank
Oklahoma	FND	F/DPE	64.9	29.5	5.7	3,059	43
Oregon	FND	FND	26.6	67.1	6.3	4,574	13
Pennsylvania	PCT	F/PCT	46.1	49.6	4.3	5,063	8
Rhode Island	PCT	PCT	43.2	52.5	4.3	5,456	6
South Carolina	FND	FND	56.0	35.9	8.2	3,074	42
South Dakota	GTB/Y	FND	27.7	63.3	9.0	3,159	41
Tennessee	FND	FND	50.4	40.0	9.6	3,189	40
Texas	FND	FND	44.6	47.9	7.5	3,462	35
Utah	FND	F/DPE	57.2	37.0	5.7	2,658	48
Vermont	FND	FND	34.4	59.7	5.9	4,949	11
Virginia	FND	FND	34.9	60.3	4.8	4,145	20
Washington	FULL	FND	73.6	20.6	5.8	4,083	22
West Virginia	FND	FND	61.0	26.8	12.1	3,895	27
Wisconsin	GTB/Y	GTB	40.3	55.2	4.5	4,991	10
Wyoming	FND	FND	43.1	53.9	3.0	6,885	3

* DPE—district power equalizing
  FLT—flat grant
  FND—foundation
  FULL—full state funded
  F/DPE—foundation and DPE
  F/GTB—foundation and GTB

F/PCT—foundation and PCT
F/GYL—foundation and GYLD
GTB—guaranteed tax base
GYLD—guaranteed yield
GTB/Y—guaranteed tax base/yield
PCT—percentage equalization

(*Source:* R. Salmon, G. Dawson, S. Lawton, and T. Johns. [1988]. *Public School Finance Programs of the United States and Canada, 1986–87*, p. 4. Blacksburg, VA: American Education Finance Association; D. Verstegen. [1988]. *School Finance at a Glance*, pp. 4, 85–86. Denver, CO: Education Commission of the States.)

from the federal government. Ohio, Pennsylvania, and Texas divide the support of public schools nearly equally between state and local revenue sources.

Figure 8.1 shows the distribution of states by the percentage of state funding and average state expenditure per pupil. The relationship between the two variables, represented by lines of "best fit," appears to be curvilinear (an inverted **U**) with the curve peaking between 40 percent and 50 percent. The average expenditure per pupil for states that have a percentage of state funding between 40 percent and 50 percent is $4,982. This average compares with $4,203 for states providing less than 40 percent, and $3,762 for states providing more than 50 percent, of total school funding. Those states that fully utilize both local and state tax bases, in general, finance education at a higher level than states relying primarily on either the state or local tax base.

The models presented in this section describe a number of options for taking school districts' fiscal capacity and tax effort into account in determining state aid allocations. They range in scope from no state financial assistance to full state funding of education.

No State Involvement

Even though states had assumed responsibility for education through their constitutions, they did not assume a large role in financing schools until the twentieth century. States created school districts in the eighteenth and nineteenth centuries to encourage the spread

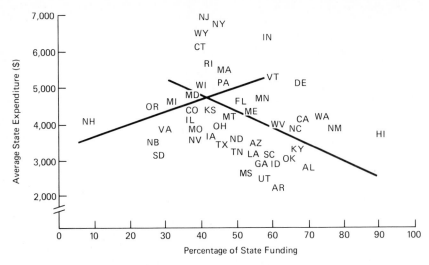

Figure 8.1. Distribution of States by Average Expenditure per Pupil and Percentage State Funding. (*Note:* Regression lines represent distributions of states with over 40% state funding and under 60% state funding.)

of schooling at a time when attendance was voluntary. The schools were financed through school district property taxes (authorized by state government), minimal state aid, and private contributions. Equalization of opportunities (in terms of financial inputs) was only within, and not among, school districts.

Under this arrangement, per pupil expenditures varied greatly among communities, depending on the wealth of individuals, the capacity of tax bases, and the willingness of individuals and taxpayers to divert funds to schooling. Spending for school programs closely reflected property assessments and tax rates (see Chapter 6). Districts with large capacity (i.e., per pupil valuations) could raise needed revenue even with low effort (i.e., tax rates); districts with low capacity could not finance an adequate program even with high tax effort.

These conditions were present at the turn of the century when Cubberley (1906) advocated a state role in school finance:

> while it may be possible to maintain schools entirely or almost entirely by local taxation, the doing so involves very slight efforts on the part of some communities, and very excessive burdens for other communities. . . . These excessive burdens, borne in large part for the common good, should be in part equalized by the state. To do this some form of general aid is necessary. (p. 250)

Matching Grants

One of the first forms of state aid was matching grants. These payments stimulate local taxation by requiring localities to match state contributions. Although matching grants may be effective in motivating voters to raise taxes, the amount of funds received depends on both fiscal capacity and effort. In a direct dollar-for-dollar matching, these grants work against the goal of equalizing capacity because they favor wealthy districts, which are most able to raise required local revenue with little tax effort. Further amplifying disparities in expenditure levels among districts, they promote "inequalities in educational opportunities or burdensome local school taxes" (Burke, 1957, p. 395).

Matching grants are no longer used to provide general state aid for school districts and this model is not listed in Table 8.1. Nevertheless, some states call for matching funds to construct school facilities and the federal government aids vocational and technical education through matching grants.

Flat Grants

Matching grants were abandoned as general aid in favor of strategies that could better extend educational opportunities to districts that were unwilling to exert tax effort and/or had little assessed valuation. Per capita flat grants allocate money according to a count of students or teachers, without regard to either local fiscal capacity or effort. School census, the count of school-aged children, was the basis for apportioning funds in 38 states early in the century (Cubberley, 1906, p. 100). Pupil measures, whether census, actual enrollment, or attendance, work to the disadvantage of smaller schools in rural areas because of diseconomies of scale, discussed at length in Chapter 13. For this reason, many states later allocated flat grants according to the number of teachers or instructional units. States continue to allocate categorical flat grants.

This finance approach presumes that an appropriate state role is to guarantee each student a minimum level of schooling. Responding to the complete reliance on local property tax bases early in the century, Cubberley (1906) argued that the state should "equalize the advantages to all as nearly as can be done with the resources at hand" (p. 17). Although it was the state's duty to secure for all pupils as high a minimum of education as possible, he cautioned against reducing all to this level. Thus, local control of schools remained a priority, with states providing only "the central support necessary to the health of the program without detriment to the local operating unit" (Mort & Reusser, 1941, p. 375).

A flat grant approach leaves to local school boards decisions about providing desired programs beyond the minimum provided through the basic finance package. Through permissive property taxation, this model recognizes the importance of local support and control of schools and allows communities to rise above the presumed adequate base as far as possible. If equality is defined in terms of minimum program standards, variations in total expenditures because of local optional taxes are not viewed as being inequitable.

Figure 8.2 illustrates the flat grant plan, showing uniform per pupil allocations of state aid and unequal total revenue because of amounts raised by optional local taxes. This general model assumes that all districts of the state tax themselves at the same rate; thus, a relatively wealthy District B supplements the uniform state grant with more local funds than does its poorer neighbor, District A. In actual practice, the choice of millage rate (effort) is left to localities, and even larger disparities in expenditures result when variations in tax rates come into play.

Uniform grants allocate the same amount for each pupil or teacher. Local capacity and effort are not considered in the base; the total amount of state funds available is simply divided by the number of pupils or instructional units. Variable flat grants permit different

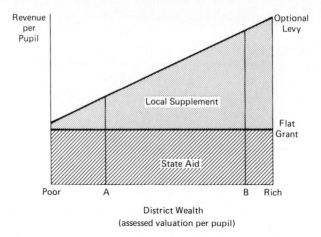

Figure 8.2. Flat Grant Model (assuming an optional levy applied at a uniform rate). (*Note:* In actual practice, the choice of millage rate is a local option and varies widely.)

funding levels according to particular needs of pupils or classes. Weighted pupil or instructional unit techniques, discussed fully in Chapter 9, account for varying costs of educational programs and services.

Salmon, Dawson, Lawton, and Johns (1988) name four states as having flat grant programs: Delaware, Kentucky, Nebraska, and North Carolina. North Carolina allocates state aid through personnel allotments that specify positions to be filled (see the overview presented in Table 8.2, State Finance Plan 1). These allotments vary, reflecting characteristics of teachers and class size for particular programs, but are not distributed in relation to any measure of local financial wealth or tax effort. Local resources, primarily from property taxation, supplement state allocations. Disparities in total spending among districts have traditionally been small because of the high proportion of state funds (64 percent in 1988–1989).

Even when the basic operations of a school district are financed through one of the other models to be presented, categorical programs are often financed through flat grants (Verstegen, 1988, pp. 41–55). For example, special education in Illinois is partially financed by the state through a flat grant of $8,000 per certified, and $2,800 per approved noncertified, employee. Per capita grants also finance many federal programs, including the Chapter 2 block grant of the Education Consolidation and Improvement Act.

Foundation Programs

In a foundation plan, as in the flat grant model, the state legislature defines a funding level associated with basic education, and localities are free to fund additional programs. The difference between these models appears in the responsibility for financing the base or foundation level. Under a flat grant, the state alone funds the uniform per pupil or per classroom amount. In a foundation plan, the state and each school district form a partnership to finance the required program cost, with the state determining the required level of local participation. Over half of the states use this approach.

Strayer and Haig (1923) devised a plan through which states access local revenue to

TABLE 8.2. State Finance Plan 1 (variable flat grants in North Carolina)

General Description

State funds are distributed according to personnel allotments without regard to local wealth or tax effort. Localities supplement these flat grants through property taxation.

State Funding of Base Program

There is no required local contribution to the basic support program. Allotments of state funds are based on instructional units that are defined by the number of students in average daily membership. The variable grants reflect state-adopted class size ratios that depend on grade level and pupils' education needs.

Allotments also vary according to teacher experience and training through a statewide salary schedule. Between $14,080 and $29,120 per instructional unit was provided in 1987–1988. Additional allotments for administrative and supervisory, teacher assistants, and other personnel are also determined by the number of pupils enrolled.

Local Support beyond the Basic Program

The 140 school districts are fiscally dependent. Counties levy taxes to operate and maintain facilities, hire additional personnel, and supplement state salary levels. An additional tax, up to 50 cents (60 cents in districts with over 100,000 population) on $100 appraised valuation, is permitted with voter approval.

(*Source: North Carolina Public Schools Allotment Policy Manual*. [1987]. Raleigh: State Board of Education. R. Salmon, C. Dawson, S. Lawton, & T. Johns. [1988]. *Public School Finance Program of the United States and Canada, 1986–87*, pp. 238–243. Blacksburg, VA: American Education Finance Association. D. Verstegen. [1988]. *School Finance at a Glance*, pp. 10, 79. Denver, CO: Education Commission of the States.)

share basic educational program costs. According to their plan, a uniform statewide tax rate "sufficient to meet the costs only in the richest district" is levied, and deficiencies in all other districts are made up by state subventions (p. 176). In practice, the uniform statewide tax rate is usually considerably lower. Under foundation programs, effort is controlled and fiscal capacity dictates the division between local and state funds that apply to the foundation.

In the general model presented in Figure 8.3, the foundation amount appears as a horizontal line, often referred to as a "Strayer-Haig line." Below this minimum foundation of spending per pupil or per instructional unit, revenue from a required local effort (RLE) blends with state funds. Districts with greater tax capacity contribute proportionately more; thus, the poorer District A receives more state dollars per unit than does its wealthier counterpart, District B. With a higher fiscal capacity, District B raises a larger share of the foundation level.

The foundation, or guaranteed funding, level corresponds to the state's minimum educational standards or to an educational plan that includes "all the activities the state wishes to assure the communities of least ability to support schools" (Mort & Reusser, 1951, p. 397). Establishing this guarantee is often a political decision dictated by available revenue rather than a rational determination of educational needs and costs. If it is too low, there may not be adequate money in those districts that choose not to levy additional taxes. The state may claim that its responsibility is fulfilled, but the minimum may be insufficient to support a basic educational program.

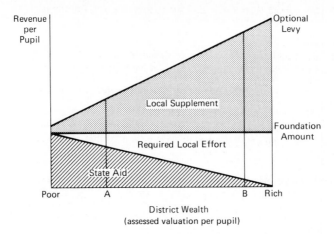

Figure 8.3. Foundation Model (assuming an optional levy applied at a uniform rate). (*Note:* In actual practice, the choice of millage rate is a local option and varies widely.)

Johns, Morphet, and Alexander (1983, p. 249) suggest that the state should provide a relatively large percentage, at least 75 percent, of the guarantee to take advantage of broader-based taxes and to recognize the heavy reliance that localities place on property taxes for capital outlay and program supplements. The extent of state participation in finance plans indicated in Table 8.1 ranges greatly for foundation plans. New Hampshire, with a minimal proportion of revenue from the state (8 percent), contrasts with New Mexico's relatively large (76 percent) state contribution, which nearly equalizes all local resources.

The required local effort is in essence a state-imposed property tax. If the RLE is set so that the foundation level is met by local money in the wealthiest district, as depicted in Figure 8.3, the state effectively leverages property taxes to create a higher funding base than could be obtained under a flat grant program. However, state legislatures are reluctant to deny any district state aid. Actual state implementation of this plan then diminishes the equalizing potential of the foundation plan in several ways.

First, if the foundation guarantee is maintained at a high level while the RLE is reduced, more state dollars flow to all districts, but especially the wealthiest district. Second, some states build a foundation plan upon a flat grant guarantee, so that even the wealthiest districts that would otherwise receive no state funds are assured a minimum grant. This model is depicted in Figure 8.4. District A has benefit of the flat grant as well as equalization aid, whereas the wealthier District B receives only state aid through the flat grant. Both districts expand revenues through the optional levy, and District B retains local money raised by the RLE above the foundation level. Third, in some states the local effort specified in statute or regulations is not required. The amount that should be raised is a "charge back" against the foundation level in districts unwilling to raise the expected local levy. Thus, there are spending disparities within the foundation amount because anticipated local funds that should be raised in accordance with the computational tax rate are deducted from state allocations.

The yield of the optional levy (also referred to as local leeway) builds upon the base

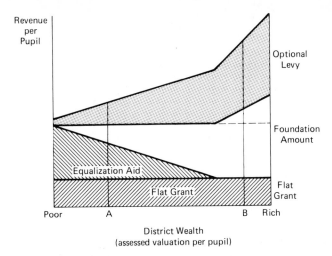

Figure 8.4. Foundation Model with Flat Grant (assuming an optional levy applied at a uniform rate). (*Note:* In actual practice, the choice of millage rate is a local option and varies widely.)

foundation level for school operations. The models in Figures 8.3 and 8.4 assume a constant tax rate. In actual practice, however, millage rates are usually permitted to vary according to local voters' desires to supplement the minimum. Disparities in spending reflect not only differing tax efforts but also tax capacities to which rates are applied. The foundation amount satisfies goals of equalization, and the latitude that districts exercise to tax and spend above the foundation guarantee satisfies liberty goals.

Rather than abandon the stimulation brought by rewards for local effort in early matching grants, finance theorists argue that local voter involvement encourages innovation and efficiency without constraints of state-defined levels of adequacy. This "adaptability," or propensity of districts to change with the times (Mort, 1933), enables lighthouse districts to experiment (*Fleischmann report,* 1973, p. 87; Jones, 1985, pp. 106–107). If adaptations are proven effective and are disseminated to other school systems, a state's foundation level might be adjusted upward so that all localities can take advantage of their benefits.

A large proportion of states employ a foundation plan for basic operating expenses (see Table 8.1), and several states also finance school construction through this mechanism. The Minnesota foundation program equalizes local fiscal capacity in its basic aid and in several tiers of optional local levies (see Table 8.3, State Finance Plan 2). The foundation amount for all districts consists of local taxes raised through a uniform rate (22.7 mills), and state aid is distributed in inverse relation to local assessed valuation. Localities have access to additional state revenue through the five tiers, which differ in their consideration of teacher and district characteristics and in the percentage of funds to be equalized. Voters may also approve tax levies to raise funds in addition to these equalized amounts.

Tax Base Equalizing Programs

A different form of combining state and local revenue is found in several forms of tax base equalization. Unlike the policy of ensuring a minimum education under flat grant and foundation approaches, these plans stress local determination of a desired level of spending

TABLE 8.3. State Finance Plan 2 (foundation program in Minnesota)

General Description

Basic foundation aid for general operating funds considers locally raised taxes under a uniform levy. There are, in addition, five tiers of discretionary aid and levies that differ according to teacher and district characteristics, local board choice of necessary revenue, and equalization at various percentages.

Local/State Shares

The largest component, Basic Aid and Levy, provides uniform revenue per pupil unit. This aid is the difference between the formula allowance ($1,720 in 1987–1988 times the number of pupil units) less property tax yield (22.7 mills times adjusted assessed valuation). Pupil units are weighted to consider grade-level differences and eligibility for Aid to Families with Dependent Children (AFDC).

Tier one cost differential aid is fully equalized to $400 per pupil; it provides additional revenue based on teacher training and experience and district sparsity. Second through fifth tiers call for decreasing allowances (from $150 to $50) and decreasing percentages (from 100% to 50%) for equalization by state revenue.

Local Support beyond the Equalized Program

The 565 school districts are fiscally independent. Voters can approve additional levies (beyond the five tiers) that are not equalized by the state.

(*Source:* R. Salmon, C. Dawson, S. Lawton, & T. Johns. [1988]. *Public School Finance Programs of the United States and Canada, 1986–87,* pp. 169–178. Blacksburg, VA: American Education Finance Association; D. Verstegen. [1988]. *School Finance at a Glance,* pp. 8, 77. Denver, CO: Education Commission of the States.)

or taxation. Once local officials or voters set an expenditure goal, the state equalizes school districts' abilities to raise necessary funds.

Giving localities a dominant role in finance decisions was advanced by Updegraff and King (1922), who wrote:

> Efficiency in the conduct of schools should be promoted by increasing the state grants whenever the true tax-rate is increased and by lowering it whenever the local tax is decreased. (p. 118)

Their view of an appropriate state role was one of helping schools deliver educational programs fashioned by local educators, neutralizing the disparities in local tax bases. No states adopted this policy alternative until the 1960s, after which several mathematically equivalent variations emerged: percentage equalization, guaranteed tax base, and district power equalization. Sixteen states are indicated in Table 8.1 as including one or more of these forms of tax base equalization.

Like the foundation plan, these models contribute to states' goals of financial equalization, but they involve localities in determining the level of state support. Coons, Clune, and Sugarman (1970) were instrumental in articulating the concept of fiscal neutrality, which has been the cornerstone of many of the court challenges to the constitutionality of existing state schemes for financing public schools. This standard of fiscal neutrality demands resources for public education that are a function of the wealth of the state as a whole rather than that of localities. These authors identified two essential characteristics of an acceptable system of state aid:

First, any right of subunits of the state to be relatively wealthy for educational purposes is denied. The total financial resources of the state should be equally available to all public school children. Ultimate responsibility for public schools is placed squarely with the state. Second, on the other hand, *the units should be free, through the taxing mechanism, to choose to share various amounts of the state's wealth* (by deciding how hard they are willing to tax themselves). (pp. 201–202, emphasis added)

Rather than making the total level of resources available in all districts the same, a fiscally neutral system ensures that communities have the financial power to raise funds to support schools at their chosen spending level.

Percentage Equalization.   In percentage equalizing formulas, local and state shares of locally determined expenditures are a function of school district wealth (taxing capacity) relative to the wealth of the state as a whole. State aid in a percentage equalizing plan is calculated by the following formula:

$$\text{State aid ratio} = 1 - c\left(\frac{\text{school district taxing capacity}}{\text{state average taxing capacity}}\right)$$

The constant c represents the portion of expenditures to be financed by a district of average state wealth as determined by legislation. If it is assumed that the state average wealth is $100,000 per pupil and the constant is 0.75, the formula becomes:

$$\text{State aid ratio} = 1 - .75\left(\frac{\text{school district taxing capacity}}{\$100,000}\right)$$

The school district taxing capacity and the state average taxing capacity change automatically every year according to assessment rolls and equalization ratios. The required percentage of local share can be changed only through legislation. Figure 8.5 shows distribution lines for three possible constants: .75, .50 and .25. If the constant specified in legislation is .75, then 75 percent of expenditures is financed from local resources in a district of average wealth and 25 percent is financed through state aid. A higher aid ratio (40 percent) is evident in the poorer-than-average District A, having per pupil valuation of $80,000. In this district, the locality pays 60 percent of any expenditure level chosen by the school board or voters.

Still assuming a constant of .75, all districts with valuations exceeding $133,333 per pupil do not receive any state money at any level of expenditure. District B, with a per pupil valuation of $180,000, falls into this category. The computation of an aid ratio for District B yields a negative number, $-.35$, indicating that it would have to pay to the state 35 percent of its property tax receipts. This practice, known as recapture, has rarely been successfully implemented by states. Not only are states reluctant to take money away from districts, but also political realities ensure that all districts receive some state aid. In implementing percentage equalizing schemes, a minimum amount of state aid that any district can receive is specified in the form of a flat grant, stated either as a dollar amount or a minimum aid ratio.

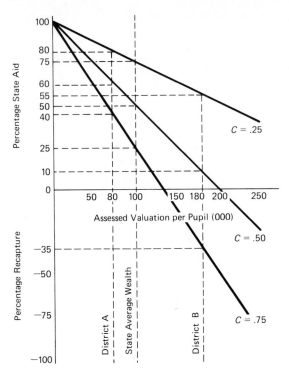

Figure 8.5. Percentage Equalization Model Illustrating Constants of .75, .50, and .25. (*Note:* The constant term defines the percentage of spending to be paid by local taxes in the district of average wealth.)

Figure 8.5 also illustrates the significance of raising and lowering the constant (the proportion of local financing in the district of average wealth). Lowering the constant to .50 from .75 (the state meets half the cost of schooling in the district of average wealth) increases the percentage of state aid (or decreases the amount of recapture) for all districts. When the constant is .50, District A's aid ratio increases to .60 and B's to .10. If the constant is lowered to .25 (the state meets 75 percent of the cost of schooling in the district of average wealth), virtually every district would qualify for some state aid. District A's aid ratio becomes .80, or 80 percent, and District B's ratio becomes .55, or 55 percent. Lowering the constant is beneficial for all districts, but especially for districts of high wealth; of course, lowering the constant is very expensive from the state's perspective. On the other hand, raising the constant lowers aid to all districts, but especially to districts of high wealth; at the same time, it reduces the overall commitment of state funds. Equalization of the poorest districts in a state can be accomplished with a relatively small commitment of state funds if the ratio is kept high. Adjustments in the constant make it possible for any state, regardless of revenue devoted to schools, to afford this plan.

Another common modification to a pure application of tax base equalization theory is placing a *ceiling*, or upper limit, on per pupil expenditures that will be aided by the state. This limits the state's total financial obligation. If the ceiling is set below what most school districts are spending, the formula will be ineffective in meeting pupils' educational needs in all districts and the plan functions similarly to the foundation program.

The greatest negative impact of a ceiling is on poor districts. Raising the portion of the local share by raising the constant shifts the financial burden from broad-based state revenues to the local property tax, and vice versa. The failure to recapture excess revenue and the imposition of floors and ceilings inhibit the potential of power equalizing approaches to neutralize the relationship between wealth and spending (Phelps & Addonizio, 1981).

In the New York percentage equalization plan (see Table 8.4, State Finance Plan 3), each district's aid ratio is a combination of its property and personal income tax bases relative to state averages for those bases. Total operating aid is a function of the number of aidable pupil units, the aid ratio, and the expenditure level. This plan calls for both a

TABLE 8.4. State Finance Plan 3 (percentage equalization in New York)

General Description

An aid ratio compares the wealth of each district to the wealth of the state as a whole to determine local and state shares of spending.

Local/State Shares

The average daily attendance of resident pupils in each district is used in determining its total wealth pupil unit (TWPU).

The 724 fiscally independent and 5 fiscally dependent districts finance their share of locally determined spending according to a combined wealth ratio (CWR). This ratio includes the equalized full valuation (FV) of property and the adjusted gross income (INC) per TWPU. Given a statewide average full value per TWPU of $108,400 and an average adjusted gross income per TWPU of $55,700 in 1987–1988:

$$\text{CWR} = (0.5)\left(\frac{\text{district FV/TWPU}}{\$108,400}\right) + (0.5)\left(\frac{\text{district INC/TWPU}}{\$55,700}\right)$$

The local share is a district's CWR times a constant (0.64). An operating aid ratio determines the state share; a district of average wealth has a CWR of 1.00 and the state pays 36% of its expenditures:

$$\text{Aid ratio} = 1.00 - (\text{CWR})(0.64)$$

A ceiling ($3,576 in 1987–88) limits the state's financial commitment. Thus, if a district is spending at or above the ceiling,

$$\text{Operating aid} = \$3,576\,[1 - (.64)(\text{CWR})](\text{TAPU})$$

where total aidable pupil units (TAPU) considers grade levels and program costs.

A minimum of $360 per TAPU grants aid to all districts regardless of wealth. Districts are also guaranteed no less than the amount of operating aid received in the base year (241 districts were held harmless in 1986–1987). Some districts have been on save-harmless for over 15 years.

Local Support beyond the Equalized Program

Without recapture, many districts raise taxes to expend beyond the ceiling.

(*Source:* R. Salmon, C. Dawson, S. Lawton, & T. Johns. [1988]. *Public School Finance Programs of the United States, 1986–87,* pp. 225–237. Blacksburg, VA: American Education Finance Association; D. Verstegen. [1988]. *School Finance at a Glance,* pp. 10, 79. Denver, CO: Education Commission of the States.)

ceiling on local spending to be equalized within the formula and a floor that ensures that all districts receive at least a minimum in state assistance. In addition, a save-harmless provision guarantees state funding at the level set in prior years. Because of the many modifications to a pure percentage equalizing concept, the amount of aid received by many districts is not determined by the formula and aid is not a function of fiscal capacity, pupils' educational needs, or local effort.

Six states, Alaska, Kansas, Massachusetts, New York, Pennsylvania, and Rhode Island, are classified in Table 8.1 as employing a percentage equalizing formula for determining state aid. This approach may also be used to fund particular programs beyond basic operating aid. New York uses its combined wealth ratio in determining support for special educational programs. State assistance for school construction in Massachusetts, New York, and Washington is based on a percentage equalizing formula (Verstegen, 1988, pp. 29, 30, 31, 43).

Guaranteed Tax Base.   In this variation of tax base equalization, each district is guaranteed a state-defined valuation per pupil. As in percentage equalizing plans, the local district determines its spending level and the state ensures that all districts have a uniform tax base from which to achieve their spending goals. As the school district chooses higher spending levels, the local tax effort grows proportionately along with the state's obligation. The desired budget (spending) per pupil divided by the guaranteed tax base (GTB) yields the tax rate the district must apply to its market valuation:

$$\text{Tax rate} = \text{spending/GTB}$$

The difference between amounts that would be raised under the GTB and that are actually raised under the local assessed valuation (*AV*) is funded by state resources:

$$\text{State aid} = (\text{rate})(\text{GTB}) - (\text{rate})(AV)$$

Given the same parameters as for the illustration of percentage equalization (25 percent state aid to a district of average wealth—$100,000), the guaranteed tax base is $133,333 (computed as .25/.75 × $100,000). If District A in Figure 8.6 desires a spending level of $4,000 per pupil, its tax rate is 30 mills (calculated as $4,000/$133,333). When this rate is applied to its per pupil valuation of $80,000, the local share is $2,400. The difference between this amount and that which would be raised by the GTB at 30 mills ($4,000) represents the state share ($1,600), the same amount as it would have received under the percentage equalizing formula.

Although percentage equalization and guaranteed tax base plans are equivalent mathematically, the GTB focuses on taxation rather than on spending. In essence the GTB plan, as illustrated, guarantees all districts a tax base of $133,333. For the district of average wealth to spend at this same level ($4,000), it, too, must levy a tax of 30 mills. However, its larger tax base ($100,000) demands a local contribution of $3,000, or 75 percent of the total. The state's share is $1,000. The effect of the plan on selected districts is illustrated in Figure 8.6.

In contrast to relatively poor districts that receive more state money because their tax bases are under the guaranteed level, districts whose valuations exceed the GTB are subject

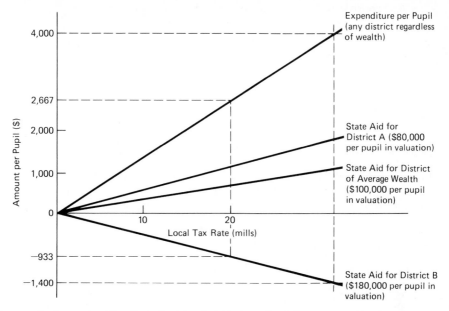

Figure 8.6. Guaranteed Tax Base Model at $133,333 per Pupil (25% state aid in district of average wealth at $100,000 per pupil in full value).

to state recapture of excess funds. For example, if District B desires a spending level of $4,000 per pupil, it would levy a tax of 30 mills ($4,000/$133,333). Because this tax rate applied to its valuation of $180,000 yields $5,400, an amount that is larger than that allowed under the GTB, the excess ($1,400 per pupil) would be paid to the state. This is not actually done in practice.

Like percentage equalizing plans, ceilings are usually applied to limit the amount of state commitment, and floor funding levels ensure that all districts receive some state aid regardless of their wealth. In such cases, the plan equalizes only those districts whose tax bases are less than the state GTB (Reilly, 1982).

The Wisconsin plan includes two guaranteed valuations (see Table 8.5, State Finance Plan 4) but does not recapture excess revenue. Districts spending below the legislatively defined ceiling ($3,860) calculate state funds according to the guaranteed tax base ($283,800) included in "primary" aid. Higher-spending districts also take advantage of "secondary" aid. The lower guaranteed valuation ($172,100) in this formula provides for equalization of poorer districts' tax bases if they set high spending goals. Recapture of amounts generated in districts whose tax bases exceed the GTB was called for in the legislation passed in 1973, but the Wisconsin Supreme Court disallowed negative aid before it could be applied (*Buse* v. *Smith*, 1976).

District Power Equalization.   The same result can also be generated by focusing on local effort or tax rate. Instead of guaranteeing a tax base, the state specifies and guarantees a given revenue yield for each mill of tax levied locally. Continuing with the same parameters, a state could guarantee to school districts a yield of $133.33 per pupil for each mill levied rather than a tax base of $133,333. A tax rate of 30 mills yields revenue per pupil

TABLE 8.5. State Finance Plan 4 (guaranteed tax base in Wisconsin)

General Description

The comparison of a school district's per pupil property valuation with the state's guaranteed tax base (GTB) determines state aid.

Local/State Shares

Equalized property valuation per pupil in average daily attendance determines the fiscal capacity of the 431 fiscally independent school districts.

Two guaranteed valuations are defined by grade-level structure and expenditure level. For K–12 districts in 1987–1988, GTB was $283,800 per pupil for that portion of expenditures up to the "primary cost ceiling," that is, 110% of the prior year's state average shared cost per pupil ($3,860). Districts spending above this ceiling also receive aid based on a lower "secondary" guaranteed valuation, set at the state average equalized valuation per pupil ($172,100). For K–8 and high school districts, guaranteed tax bases are 1.5 and 3.0, respectively, times the values for K–12 districts.

Formulas for primary and secondary aid are

$$\text{Primary aid} = \left(\begin{array}{cc} \text{Primary} & \text{District's} \\ \text{guaranteed} - \text{equalized} \\ \text{valuation} & \text{valuation} \end{array} \right) \left(\begin{array}{c} \text{Primary} \\ \text{shared} \\ \text{cost} \end{array} \middle/ \begin{array}{c} \text{Primary} \\ \text{guaranteed} \\ \text{valuation} \end{array} \right)$$

$$\text{Secondary aid} = \left(\begin{array}{cc} \text{Secondary} & \text{District's} \\ \text{guaranteed} - \text{equalized} \\ \text{valuation} & \text{valuation} \end{array} \right) \left(\begin{array}{c} \text{Secondary} \\ \text{shared} \\ \text{cost} \end{array} \middle/ \begin{array}{c} \text{Secondary} \\ \text{guaranteed} \\ \text{valuation} \end{array} \right)$$

If secondary aid is negative, it is subtracted from any primary aid. If total aid is negative, the district does not receive aid; but it is not required to pay negative aid to the state.

Total aid for shared cost equals per pupil aid calculations for primary and secondary aid times average daily membership. In 1986–1987, 390 districts received primary aid; 88 districts received both primary and secondary aid.

(*Source: Elementary and Secondary School Aid.* [1987]. Madison, WI: Legislative Fiscal Bureau; R. Salmon, C. Dawson, S. Lawton, & T. Johns. [1988]. *Public School Finance Programs of the United States and Canada, 1986–87*, pp. 361–381. Blacksburg, VA: American Education Finance Association; D. Verstegen. [1988]. *School Finance at a Glance*, pp. 13, 81. Denver, CO: Education Commission of the States.)

of $4,000 per pupil, the same as for previous examples. A tax rate of 20 mills would yield revenue per pupil of $2,667. Once the level of desired spending is determined, the associated tax rate is applied locally and the difference between this local contribution and the spending level is financed by the state. Unlike a foundation plan, which also involves a state–local partnership, the choice of effort is a local option and the state's share applies to total spending associated with that level of effort. Figure 8.6 illustrates the effect of district power equalizing as well as guaranteed tax base.

If a wealthy school district generates an amount in excess of the spending guarantee, a fully operational district power equalization (DPE) model, as advocated by Coons, Clune, and Sugarman (1970), would recapture the excess yield. By returning funds to the state, the integrity of a fiscally neutral plan, one in which all districts choosing a given level of tax effort have the same spending level, is maintained. Although recapture (or negative aid) was a part of power equalizing plans in Maine, Utah, and Wisconsin, no state currently has a DPE plan fully implemented in its ideal form.

When recapture is not required, the DPE approach is termed a guaranteed yield plan. In Michigan, for example, a dollar yield is generated for each mill levied locally (see Table 8.6, State Finance Plan 5). It is not a true DPE plan because a flat grant is included so that all districts receive state aid, and there is only partial recapture of funds raised above guaranteed spending levels.

This Michigan plan's schedule is linear in that there is a guaranteed number of dollars per pupil per mill levied. Other states have adopted plans that include a breaking point, or kink (Johns, Morphet, & Alexander, 1983, p. 258), below which a higher yield is guaranteed. Districts with tax rates above this breaking point gain revenues at a lower level per increase in tax levy. In Utah's mixed foundation and guaranteed yield program, for example, the state guarantees $19 per pupil unit for the first 2 mills and $4 per pupil unit for an additional 8 mills beyond the foundation plan's required levy of 21.28 mills. This differentiated approach "levels up" poorer districts' abilities to generate revenue while discouraging districts from increasing property tax rates excessively.

Full State Funding

In contrast to the shared state-local partnership evident in foundation and percentage equalizing plans is the complete state assumption of all costs. To promote uniformity in education across school units, Morrison (1930) proposed state administration and full

---

TABLE 8.6. State Finance Plan 5 (guaranteed yield program in Michigan)

General Description

This modified DPE plan guarantees a dollar yield for each mill of local taxes and includes a partial recapture.

Local/State Shares

The 152 fiscally dependent school districts receive state aid in relation to their wealth and tax effort. In 1987–1988, each pupil in average daily membership was guaranteed a combined state—local yield or gross allowance of $306 plus $75.10 for each mill of local property taxes.

The local district's share of this guarantee is calculated by multiplying the district's equalized valuation per pupil by its chosen operating millage rate. The state provides the difference between the guaranteed yield specified by the gross allowance and the local share.

A "recapture" provision results in a deduction in state categorical funds for districts that exceed the state per pupil guarantees because of high fiscal capacities (approximately 30% of the districts in 1987–1988). The deduction is based on a sliding scale according to local property wealth and cannot exceed 60% of the state categorical funds for which the district is eligible.

Local Support beyond the Equalized Program

With only a partial recapture, many districts have local funds available outside the basic program. Disparities in spending are restrained by a limitation on growth in the local mill levy; yield cannot increase more than the inflation rate as measured by the national consumer price index.

(*Source:* R. Salmon, C. Dawson, S. Lawton, & T. Johns. [1988]. *Public School Finance Programs of the United States and Canada, 1986–87*, p. 163. Blacksburg, VA: American Education Finance Association; D. Verstegen. [1988]. *School Finance at a Glance*, pp. 8, 64, 77. Denver, CO: Education Commission of the States.)

financial support of schools that serve public, or social, goals. He reasoned that local autonomy should yield because education and citizenship training are state concerns.

Proponents of this approach believe that the level of funds available for designing educational programs should not in any way rely upon districts' fiscal capacity or effort. The *Fleischmann Report*'s (1973, Chap. 2) recommendation of full state funding for New York State considered the benefits:

> Full state funding makes possible, though it does not automatically provide, more effective controls over expenditures. It permits the state to invest in improvement in quality at a rate consonant with the growth of the over-all economy of the state. It eliminates the present competition among wealthy districts for the most elaborate school-house and similar luxuries. (p. 56)

The simplified model of full state funding (see Figure 8.7) illustrates that all revenue, whether from state or local sources, is equalized by the state. The poorer District A and its wealthier counterpart, District B, have the same level of funds available for each pupil. Property taxation could continue as a statewide revenue source. But school boards and voters would not set spending levels, and they would have no power to tax to supplement the state-established funding level. Neither local fiscal capacity nor tax effort affects spending for schools under the full state funding model.

Only Hawaii has a fully state-financed educational system. As a result of two movements referred to in earlier chapters—the school finance reform movement, with its goal of equalizing school resources, and the subsequent movement to limit taxes and expenditures—a few state finance plans, including those of California, New Mexico, and Washington, approach full state assumption (see Table 8.1). By placing a cap on local leeway to moderate disparities in total expenditures, the New Mexico foundation program permits districts to spend very little revenue beyond the state guarantee (see Table 8.7, State Finance Plan 6). Only 5 percent of local property taxes, federal impact aid, and forest reserve revenue is retained by local districts; nearly all of these revenues become a part of the state's guaranteed funding level. Despite full state control of revenue in these

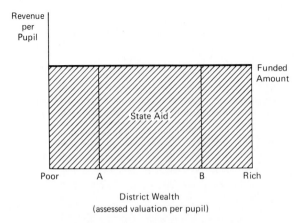

Figure 8.7. Full State Funding Model

TABLE 8.7. State Finance Plan 6 (full state funding in New Mexico)

General Description
The state specifies the property tax rate and takes much of this yield and several other local revenue sources into account in making its allocations. There is nearly full state funding.

Local/State Shares
The 88 fiscally dependent school districts contribute 95% of revenue from a required 0.5 mill property tax, federal impact aid (P.L. 874), and forest reserves as the local contribution to the foundation program.
State allocations bring each district to the equalized level ($1,689 per unit of need in 1987–1988). Foundation aid is the sum of weighted pupil units (including considerations for various program costs) times this program guarantee, less 95% of the designated local revenues.

Local Support beyond the Basic Program
There is minimal local revenue permitted above the equalization guarantee. Localities retain only 5% of the required property tax and other designated revenue.

(*Source:* R. Salmon, C. Dawson, S. Lawton, & T. Johns. [1988]. *Public School Finance Programs of the United States and Canada, 1986–87,* pp. 221–224. Blacksburg, VA: American Education Finance Association; D. Verstegen. [1988]. *School Finance at a Glance,* pp. 10, 78. Denver, CO: Education Commission of the States.)

states, school districts continue to develop budgets and oversee operations. Even with its single school board and strong legislative and executive control of resources for public education, Hawaii has seven administrative districts.

Full state funding illustrates the tension among the goals of equality, liberty, and efficiency presented in Chapter 2. This plan equalizes spending, attains fiscal neutrality, and shifts the burden for educational finance to broader state taxes. On the other hand, more uniform finances and educational policies might bring a regimented education that is inefficient and heavily controlled by an impersonal bureaucracy. Diminished local involvement in policy and finance could inhibit responses to unique needs of communities, and there would be less of the fiscal flexibility that enables districts to finance innovations. Unless there is sufficient revenue to raise all districts to the spending level available in the highest-spending units prior to implementation of full state funding, it would be difficult for any state to satisfy fully demands in all localities. Reallocating currently available state revenue, even including all local property taxes, would result in leveling many districts down, a politically unpopular strategy.

In some states, including those in which general school operations are not fully state-financed, there is state assumption of the full cost of various categorical programs. For example, special education in Pennsylvania and Montana and school construction and pupil transportation in Maryland receive full state support (Verstegen, 1988, pp. 28, 34, 42, 43).

SUMMARY

Transfers of funds from federal and state governments help ensure provision of basic public services in all communities, equalize districts' fiscal capacities through broader tax bases, and extend their capabilities to meet pupils' educational needs adequately. The degree to which these transfers constrain local decision making depends upon their structure as general, block grant, or categorical aids. These three approaches affect the governmental level at which program goals are defined, the degree to which funds are targeted by group or purpose, burdens placed on personnel to develop proposals and monitor programs, and the structure of fund accounting.

Two primary factors define the amount of locally raised revenue: the size of the tax base, or fiscal capacity, and the tax rate, or effort exerted. If local funds alone were considered to finance educational programs, there would be large variations in per pupil spending because both capacity and effort are allowed free rein. State finance plans control these two variables in varying degrees, and in so doing, they moderate spending disparities among school districts.

Matching grants favor wealthier districts, as allocations respond directly to local tax capacity and effort. The state share of a flat grant does not take either local capacity or effort into consideration, whereas state allocations in a foundation plan control local effort and direct funds in inverse relation to fiscal capacity. Optional levies are permitted in each of these plans through which localities can supplement the base amount; their tax capacities and tax rates determine total spending available. In the different forms of tax base equalization, state allocations respond to local effort, but capacity is controlled. Localities determine spending levels and the state equalizes the ability of school districts to reach spending goals. Because full state funding controls both fiscal capacity and effort, there is no variation in per pupil spending among school districts.

The next chapter explores measurement and administrative considerations that give latitude to states as they adapt basic school finance models to address particular needs of pupils and school districts.

ACTIVITIES

1. Compare finance provisions of several state and federal programs. Would you classify them as general, block grant, or categorical assistance? Why?
2. Describe fully the finance plan for a given state, comparing it with the general models presented in this chapter. Notice that any one state may employ a combination of strategies to finance its basic operations and other special programs and services.
3. Write a computer program, or construct an electronic spreadsheet, to simulate the distribution of revenue available to school districts in your state under several of the models.
4. Review reports of professional associations, school finance commissions, or state agencies about the advantages and shortcomings of the finance plan in place in your state. What do these evaluations suggest for strengthening the plan's consideration of fiscal capacity and tax effort?
5. A committee of legislators and educators is considering alternative finance plans that will equalize educational opportunities and encourage districts to experiment with different curricular approaches. Discuss the dilemma presented in the committee's charge in terms of equality and liberty goals, and present a rationale for the committee to advance one of the general finance models presented in this chapter.

EXERCISES

1. Assume that a given state has $4,394,500,000 to allocate for education of its 2,350,000 pupils in average daily membership.
   a. What is the amount of a uniform flat grant distribution?
   b. If two districts supplement this state aid with a tax of 10 and 18 mills on their respective per pupil equalized valuations of $240,000 and $180,000, how much total revenue is available in each district per pupil?
   c. What is the effect of raising the state grant by $600 and placing a cap of 12 mills on local leeway (assume both districts then tax at this rate)?
2. A school district has a total assessed valuation of $300 million and 2,000 pupils.
   a. If the state requires a local levy of 4 mills and guarantees $2,400 per pupil, how much does the state contribute under a foundation plan?
   b. If the district levies a total tax of 10 mills (including the RLE), what total per pupil amount is available including the state transfer payment and local tax?
3. Assume that the district of average wealth ($220,000 per pupil valuation) contributes 48 percent of its spending in a percentage equalizing plan.
   a. Calculate state aid as a percentage of spending in three districts having per pupil valuations of $160,000, $250,000, and $520,000.
   b. If each of these districts spends $4,800 per pupil, how much state aid is owed or how much local revenue is diverted to the state in recapture?

REFERENCES

Burke, A. J. (1957). *Financing public schools in the United States* (rev. ed.). New York: Harper & Row.

Buse v. *Smith*. (1976). 74 Wis. 2d 550, 247 N.W. 2d 141.

Coons, J. E., Clune, W. H., & Sugarman, S. D. (1970). *Private wealth and public education.* Cambridge, MA: Belknap Press of Harvard University Press.

Cubberley, E. P. (1906). *School funds and their apportionment.* New York: Teachers College, Columbia University.

Elementary and secondary school aid. (1987). Madison, WI: Legislative Fiscal Bureau.

The Fleischmann report on the quality, cost, and financing of elementary and secondary education in New York State (Vol. 1). (1973). New York: Viking Press.

Johns, R. L., Morphet, E. L., & Alexander, K. (1983). *The economics and financing of education* (4th ed.). Englewood Cliffs, NJ: Prentice Hall.

Jones, T. H. (1985). *Introduction to school finance: Technique and social policy.* New York: Macmillan.

Morrison, H. C. (1930). *School revenue.* Chicago: University of Chicago Press.

Mort, P. R. (1933). *State support for public education.* Washington, DC: The American Council on Education.

Mort, P. R., & Reusser, W. C. (1941). *Public school finance: Its background, structure, and operation.* New York: McGraw-Hill.

Mort, P. R., & Reusser, W. C. (1951). *Public school finance* (2nd ed.). New York: McGraw-Hill.

North Carolina public schools allotment policy manual. (1987). Raleigh: State Board of Education.

Phelps, J. L., & Addonizio, M. F. (1981, Summer). District power equalizing: Cure-all or prescription? *Journal of Education Finance, 7,* 64–87.

Reilly, G. J. (1982, Winter). Guaranteed tax base formulas in school finance: Why equalization doesn't work. *The Journal of Education Finance, 7,* 336–347.

Salmon, R., Dawson, C., Lawton, S., & Johns, T. (1988). *Public school finance programs of the United States and Canada, 1986–87.* Blacksburg, VA: American Education Finance Association.

Strayer, G. D., & Haig, R. M. (1923). *The financing of education in the State of New York, Report of the Educational Finance Inquiry Commission* (Vol. 1). New York: Macmillan.

Updegraff, H., & King, L. A. (1922). *Survey of the fiscal policies of the state of Pennsylvania in the field of education.* Philadelphia: University of Pennsylvania.

Verstegen, D. (1988). *School finance at a glance.* Denver: Education Commission of the States.

CHAPTER 9

Technical Aspects of State Aid Programs

This chapter continues the discussion of state school finance policy. Consideration is given to measurement and administrative issues related to educational and financial needs of school systems, their taxing capacities, and their tax efforts. The chapter closes with a discussion of activities to monitor whether funds are spent appropriately to satisfy those needs.

Early allocation plans measured educational needs simply in terms of the number of pupils served. Over time, measurement became more sophisticated, taking into consideration causes of variation in costs over which local communities have little or no control (Mort, 1924, p. 6). Formula adjustments in today's financial aid systems recognize that different levels of funds are required to finance programs appropriate to pupils' learning abilities and educational needs, and they recognize that costs of delivering educational programs vary among districts in terms of the sparsity or density of population, cost of living, and characteristics of personnel.

Another concern of aid programs is the blend of state and local funds to meet identified needs. Chapter 8 showed different ways in which state finance plans incorporate contributions from local revenue sources. This chapter explores problems of measuring districts' fiscal capacities and the effort local taxpayers make in financing school operations. This chapter also discusses program and financial audits and other accountability mechanisms which state agencies use to ensure that funds are spent appropriately and to identify impacts of programs and funds on educational outcomes.

MEASURING PUPILS' EDUCATIONAL NEEDS

The scope of public education is crudely expressed in terms of the number of the students served. This measure of school district "need" is closely tied to the size of the teaching force, the extent of programs and facilities, and ultimately the amount of money required.

But state aid programs are also concerned with the nature and cost of programs necessary to meet the educational needs of students with a variety of characteristics which require special attention. The "need" measure can be weighted to reflect the presence of high-cost programs.

Pupil Count

The number of students served continues to be the primary determinant of the amount of money necessary to finance education. Allocations early in the century relied upon a full census of school-aged children or a count of all school-attending pupils whether enrolled in public or private schools. The first technique offered little incentive for keeping children enrolled in schools, and the second one overfunded many communities having large proportions of pupils attending private schools.

Average daily membership (ADM) and average daily attendance (ADA) in today's state aid plans provide better estimates of costs associated with numbers of pupils actually enrolled or in attendance. Specific dates (e.g., 10th-day enrollment) or periods of time (e.g., average attendance in October) are often established in statute for collection of pupil counts.

The choice between these measures has political, pedagogical, and efficiency implications. ADM recognizes that costs of school operations continue regardless of the actual presence of pupils, but there may be inefficiencies if districts are not held accountable for reducing absenteeism and truancy. The use of ADA parallels the enforcement of compulsory attendance laws and beliefs that pedagogical goals are maximized when absenteeism is reduced. The former approach (ADM) works to the advantage of cities that have higher absence rates, whereas ADA shifts available state aid to suburban and rural school systems. Several states, for example, Missouri, compute state aid by using an average of ADM and ADA to capture the benefits of each approach.

Shifts in enrollments create unanticipated costs that may justify state assistance. Declining enrollment during the 1970s brought revisions in about half of the states' funding formulas to ease the impact of sudden reductions in aid. Some state plans include a hold- (or save-) harmless provision, guaranteeing the same or a percentage of a prior year's pupil count to minimize disruptions. Nevada guarantees payment for 100 percent of the previous year's enrollment; Delaware funds 93 percent of pupil units from the prior year; and Idaho bases aid on the previous year's ADA less 1 percent if the decline is greater than 1 percent (Verstegen, 1988, pp. 21–22). New York guarantees the dollar amount of operating aid in the previous year, a policy which has caused some school districts to be on "save-harmless" for as many as 15 years. Other state policies include a rolling average of several years' pupil enrollment or attendance to cushion the impact of reduction in resources. Ohio school districts receive funding based on the current year's ADM or the average of the current year and the 2 preceding years.

If districts are able to continue prior years' pupil counts for aid purposes, there is a more predictable resource base for planning programs and making personnel commitments. However, even in states without such provisions, fears of greatly diminished program quality from rapid losses of personnel and instructional support funds were overstated (King, 1984). Save-harmless clauses, resulting in no loss of funds, unnecessarily protect districts from confronting critical issues of reduction (Leppert & Routh, 1978, p. 190). They also introduce inequities by channeling funds to some districts with little need for a cushion and inefficiencies by discouraging local economies (Goettel & Firestine, 1975, p. 212). Policies that include percentage reductions in student units, a short term for phasing in reductions, or an average of several years' enrollments more effectively encourage planning and efficiencies than do provisions that continue inflated pupil counts into the future.

Although there may be similar additional costs associated with large enrollment increases, they are considered in very few finance plans. Indiana, Maine, and New York include growth adjustments to reflect unusual increases in enrollment or attendance within funding formulas (Salmon, Dawson, Lawton, & Johns, 1988, pp. 113, 148, 229).

Grade Levels and Special Programs

The simplified models of state finance plans presented in Chapter 8 suggest that the same level of funding is tied to each pupil. In reality, the amount of aid varies considerably depending upon student characteristics that policymakers agree warrant special and more expensive programs. Consistent with the concept of vertical equity (the unequal treatment of unequals), state finance policy calls for funding recognition of higher costs of education at different grade levels and for specified categories of students because of smaller classes and more support personnel, equipment, and instructional materials.

Many states base allocations on weighted-pupil or weighted-classroom units, an approach conceived by Mort (1926) in his refinement of early foundation plans. His "weighted pupil" and "typical teacher" units provided objective measures of educational need to give "extra weight to the actual number of pupils in those situations where the true per pupil cost of a given educational offering is high" (p. 15).

This method uses the cost of an elementary program for a "typical" child, usually in grades 1–6, as a unit of 1.0. Students in higher-cost programs or instructional units are given an additional weighting. Higher weights reflect traditionally larger expenditures in secondary grades and in vocational and special education programs. Weights listed in Table 9.1 for South Carolina's foundation program correspond to anticipated average costs of each grade level and program relative to those of fourth through eighth grades. The weights recognize, for example, that programs for emotionally and orthopedically handicapped children cost twice the amount than those for elementary school students who are not placed in a special program. High school students carry a weighting of 1.25, and vocational pupils are assigned a slightly larger weight (1.29).

Because some children are served for only a portion of a school day, the concept of full-time equivalency (FTE) is often used to express pupil counts. For example, South Carolina's support of only half-day kindergartens means that 148 students would be considered as 74 FTEs with a weight of 1.30, or 0.65 each. In other states, student enrollment for one hour of a day in a compensatory or bilingual program brings 0.6 FTE, and placement of a mainstreamed pupil for a split day justifies 0.5 FTE, in addition to the weights earned for these students' grade-level assignments.

To determine financial need under a weighted-pupil approach, the number of FTE students enrolled or in attendance in each grade level and applicable special program is multiplied by the weight specified in statute. The resulting products for all programs and grade levels are then totaled to obtain a composite measure of educational need. This weighted measure of pupils' needs can be entered into the finance plans presented in Chapter 8. In a foundation plan, for instance, the legislatively established dollar guarantee for a given year is multiplied by the total number of weighted pupil units served.

TABLE 9.1. Weighted Pupil Categories
in South Carolina

Category	Weight
Grade levels	
Kindergarten (half-day program)	0.65
Primary (grades 1–3)	1.24
Elementary (grades 4–8)	1.00
High school (grades 9–12)	1.25
Vocational programs	
Vocational	1.29
Special education	
Learning disabilities	1.74
Educable mentally retarded	1.74
Trainable mentally retarded	2.04
Emotionally handicapped	2.04
Orthopedically handicapped	2.04
Visually handicapped	2.57
Hearing handicapped	2.57
Speech handicapped	1.90
Homebound	2.10

(*Source:* R. Salmon [1988]. *Public School Finance Programs of the United States and Canada, 1986–87*, p. 285. Blacksburg, VA: American Education Finance Association and VPI & SU. Reprinted by permission of the author.)

In a similar manner, states that finance schools according to instructional units calculate grade level and special program needs by specifying varying ratios of pupils to teachers. For example, the 12 categories for special education in the Delaware plan specify class sizes that range from 4 to 15 pupils.

The size of weights generally reflects cost differences prevailing in schools (i.e., what is) rather than being grounded in studies of what funding would most appropriately finance educational programs to meet pupils' needs (i.e., what should be). Mort's (1924) development of recommended weights for high schools, for example, was based on costs associated with the average practice of assigning more teachers per pupil in high school grades than in elementary grades and on the higher salaries paid to them. Accepting the rationality of average practice, that procedure became the benchmark to be applied when assigning state aid. Similarly, indices of average per pupil cost depicted by the National Education Finance Project (Johns, Alexander, & Jordan, 1971, Chap. 6) were based on actual costs of grade levels and special program offerings within selected school districts rather than upon true measures of need. The disadvantage of accepting average practice in aid formulas was addressed by New York's *Fleischmann Report* (1973):

> The pedagogical wisdom of weighting secondary students more heavily than elementary students is questionable; we suspect that in many instances it might be good policy to spend more money per student in the elementary grade than in the secondary, but the present weighting factor has a psychological effect of suggesting that all districts should spend more money on secondary students. (p. 64)

Thus, average costs based on past program experience may tend to drive all programs to that expenditure level.

Although designed to provide additional dollars to meet educational needs determined locally, weighted unit methods may in practice create incentives to misclassify pupils, and possibly remove them unnecessarily from regular classrooms for the additional state aid generated. Furthermore, in the absence of close monitoring, state dollars may not actually be spent on intended programs.

Another approach to accommodating higher costs is through an excess cost reimbursement strategy. According to this procedure, the state repays partially or fully those expenditures that exceed a given level for specified educational programs. By paying these costs, states encourage local districts to expand programs to serve qualifying students, such as those enrolled in vocational or special education offerings. Pupils in special programs are aided twice, first under the basic formula and second under the excess cost formula. The amount of assistance may be variable, depending in some states upon the actual cost of programs and in others upon local wealth and tax effort. This method enables poorer districts to provide special programs they could not otherwise afford. However, in states that finance the same amount of excess cost (e.g., through a flat grant) in all school districts regardless of local wealth, allocations may be disequalizing since wealthy and poor districts receive full payment.

If a state fully assumes costs, there may be little incentive for districts to operate efficient programs. For this reason, states may require local funds to be applied to special programs by only partially reimbursing excess costs. For example, Colorado and Oregon pay 80 and 30 percent, respectively, of special education program expenses (Verstegen, 1988, pp. 41, 43).

The degree to which funding mechanisms create incentives to misclassify pupils concerns policymakers and educators. Hartman's (1980) analyses indicated that weighted pupil and other child-based formulas in which funds depend upon a count of eligible pupils encourage misclassification. Instructional unit and other resource-based formulas in which payments derive from the number and type of personnel have fewer incentives for misclassification because additional funds follow larger numbers of pupils than in the case of weighted pupil plans. Reimbursement plans that partially finance excess costs offer the least incentive to misclassify pupils because they demand local matching funds.

These two approaches—weighted unit and excess cost reimbursement—determine the amount of state aid essential to finance diverse programs to address pupils' educational needs beyond the simple count of pupils in ADM or ADA. Students enrolled in special education programs justify additional resources in all states. The additional costs of classes for pupils with physical, mental, behavioral, emotional, or other interferences to learning are fully or partially reimbursed in 23 states. Another 17 states follow a weighted pupil technique, and 7 states direct additional resources to serve pupils' needs on an instructional unit basis (Verstegen, 1988, pp. 41–44).

Gifted and talented pupils are identified in finance plans in 18 states. Their needs are met through additional pupil weights, flat dollar amounts for eligible students, variable competitive grants for innovative programs, or support for residential high schools for exceptional students. For example, Arkansas provides an additional weight of 0.25 for gifted and talented pupils. Michigan's flat grant provides $79 per pupil, but it is limited to 5 percent of the pupils in a district or consortium of districts and gives a minimum of $5,000 to small units (Verstegen, 1988, pp. 53–55).

There is similar diversity in aid plans for vocational education. Categorical support for approved programs continues to be the predominant funding method, but weighted pupil and instructional unit approaches gained popularity during the 1970s. Delaware's finance plan calls for one classroom unit for each 15 FTE pupils enrolled in vocational programs, whereas Florida's weighted pupil plan allocates additional dollars on the basis of nine categories that range in weight from 1.262 to 1.899. Kansas considers community characteristics, basing its categorical allotments on local ability to pay, the number of pupils, and local poverty and unemployment rates (Salmon, Dawson, Lawton, & Johns, 1988, pp. 71, 77, 128).

Compensatory programs serve low-income or educationally disadvantaged pupils through additional state aid in 28 states, 12 of which allocate flat grants and 11 of which permit additional weighted pupil units for students served by programs (Verstegen, 1988, pp. 45–47). In some states, such as Florida, the number of pupils scoring in the lowest quartile on statewide assessment tests determines eligibility. In others, such as Pennsylvania and Texas, eligibility is tied to family income, following guidelines for defining AFDC or for free and reduced-price lunches under the National School Lunch Program. In still others, such as Maryland, pupils qualify under federal Chapter I criteria, which include measures of family income and educational deficiencies. These different determinants of need have limitations. Some assume a correlation between family income and educational deficiencies, whereas others that are designed to compensate for low academic performance may inadvertently reward schools for their poor performance.

English-language-deficient pupils enrolled in approved programs in 22 states are financed through excess cost reimbursement and weighted pupil approaches. New Jersey, for example, provides an additional weight of 0.23 for each pupil enrolled in approved programs. Wisconsin pays 63 percent of districts' expenditures for salaries, special books and equipment, and other related expenses for approved bilingual-bicultural educational programs (Salmon, Dawson, Lawton, & Johns, 1988, pp. 213, 376).

The following provisions illustrate that state finance plans offset costs while giving incentives for districts to adopt programs to meet a host of other educational needs. New York's "attendance improvement/dropout prevention" aid allocates a flat grant to districts with low attendance ratios. Wisconsin provides integration aid to finance inter- and intradistrict transfers of minority pupils. Programs for four-year-olds are financed in Texas, where half-day prekindergartens serve children who cannot speak and comprehend English or who are from low-income families. Similarly, Minnesota's foundation plan takes local wealth into account in allocating funds for districts' early childhood family education programs. Adult education can also be financed through state assistance, as in Virginia, where school districts are reimbursed for general adult education programs on a fixed cost per pupil or cost per class basis (Salmon, Dawson, Lawton, & Johns, 1988, pp. 173, 233, 309, 343, 374).

The educational reform movement of the late 1980s introduced somewhat different aid provisions to stimulate programmatic changes. For example, California's instructional time incentive provides flat grants to districts that meet conditions for the length of the school year and day. Michigan grants $29 per pupil for high schools that adopt higher graduation standards. Florida's Merit School Incentive Program allocates incentive grants to schools that exceed expected student achievement (Salmon, Dawson, Lawton, & Johns, 1988, pp. 47, 78, 163).

Pupil counts and programs delivered to meet educational needs are important components of state aid mechanisms. These measures of districts' needs are further refined by characteristics of school districts themselves which affect costs. These factors are the focus of the next section.

RECOGNIZING COMMUNITY AND SCHOOL DISTRICT CHARACTERISTICS

State finance policies consider several aspects of communities that affect costs. Research indicates that inequities in programs and finance among districts result from differences in per pupil wealth and from variations in per pupil costs of providing equivalent educational opportunities (Johns, 1975, p. 160). Adjustments are made in state aid plans for the sparsity or density of the population, the cost of personnel hired by the district, and the cost of living in the community.

School and District Size

The size of districts and individual schools varies widely. Some urban districts are large both geographically and in terms of pupil enrollment, whereas some rural districts cover many sparsely populated square miles. Large and densely populated school systems may benefit from economies of scale up to a point (see the discussion of economies of scale in Chapter 13). Because of these conditions, state finance plans often include corrections of need associated with size.

This need is measured more appropriately in terms of the number of students served or by the sparsity or density of the general population rather than by per pupil expenditures. Swanson (1966) observed that sparsely populated rural districts and densely populated cities may each have high expenditures, but their schools are costly for very different reasons. Small class sizes and diseconomies of scale influence costs in small, rural districts, whereas costs may be as high in larger systems because of expanded services to at-risk populations and additional personnel. Large, urban districts and small, rural schools and districts, particularly in geographically isolated areas, tend to have higher per pupil costs for equivalent services than do suburban schools and districts even though suburban districts may spend as much or more, thus yielding a richer level of services.

Aid adjustments for sparsity of population or small size of pupil count for rural areas recognize (1) higher costs of smaller classes; (2) diseconomies resulting from the division of some expenses (e.g., superintendent and principal salaries) among fewer students; and (3) additional salaries needed to attract teachers, particularly in subjects experiencing shortages, to remote areas of states. Indicators of population sparsity and pupil counts within schools or school districts listed in Table 9.2 illustrate that state provisions for size adjustment vary greatly. Aid plans provide additional pupil weights or instructional units, additional flat grants, or proportionately more funds to compensate for costs related to size.

Small, isolated schools, despite being more costly, may be declared "necessary" and

TABLE 9.2. Adjustment in Selected States for Small Size

California	Districts with necessary but small schools may elect to receive a prescribed dollar allocation based on ADA and the number of certified teachers: districts below 2,501 ADA, elementary schools under 101 ADA and 4 or fewer teachers, and secondary schools below 301 ADA and 15 or fewer teachers.
Connecticut	Towns that are members of a K–12 regional school district receive a bonus grant of an additional $25 per pupil.
Montana	Per pupil support is higher on a graduated scale for elementary schools with fewer than 300 pupils and for high schools with fewer than 600 pupils.
Nebraska	Support increases in accordance with population density: by 10% if density is between 3 and 4 persons per square mile, 20% if density is from 2 to 3 persons, 30% if density is from 1 to 2 persons, and by 40% if density is less than 1 person per square mile.
New Mexico	Additional pupil units are granted by formulas for small schools, with a weight of 1.0 for elementary and junior high schools with fewer than 200 pupils and with a weight of 2.0 or 1.6 for senior high schools with fewer than 200 or 400 pupils, respectively; for small districts with a weight of 0.15 for districts below 4,000 pupils; and for rural isolation with consideration of total enrollment and the number of high schools.

(*Source:* R. Salmon [1988]. *Public School Finance Programs of the United States and Canada, 1986–87*, pp. 48, 190, 196. Blacksburg, VA: American Education Finance Association and VPI & SU. Reprinted by permission of the author.)

receive additional cost recognition to serve students close to their residences. Determinants of an essential small school include such factors as distance from another school, terrain and road conditions that create safety problems, and length of bus routes to alternative schools. The island of Ocracoke, located off the North Carolina coast and having 38 students in K–12, receives a special allotment. In Texas, school districts with fewer than 130 pupils that qualify under a formula of necessity receive state aid as if they had that number of students (Salmon, Dawson, Lawton, & Johns, 1988, p. 306).

Adjustments should not encourage the creation or continuation of unnecessary and inefficient districts (Johns, 1975, p. 202). State aid correction factors that ensure adequate educational opportunities in necessary schools should apply only when mergers are not feasible. Otherwise, size adjustments may become "allocative disincentives" (Cohn, 1975, p. 216) for schools and districts to remain small. Explicit penalty and incentive structures within state aid plans provide stimuli for changing school organization when there is considerable waste of resources (Cohn, 1974, pp. 95–103). Penalties reduce state aid by a portion of the cost savings that would be realized had the district operated schools with more optimal enrollments. Under incentive systems, districts that undertake grade-level reorganization and district consolidation receive additional general aid and assistance with capital projects.

Needs and costs in large cities may justify additional state funds through density or large-size adjustments to the degree that weighted unit and excess cost finance plans fail to aid higher urban expenditures. These corrections recognize that demands on local tax bases for competing public services, often referred to as municipal overburden, create fiscal stress in cities (Sjogren, 1981). On the other hand, because individuals live in communities that offer the kinds of public services they desire and are willing to pay for (Tiebout, 1956), it might be argued that state intervention is unwarranted.

Pennsylvania is the only state identified by Verstegen (1988, p. 19) as having a density factor that combines population and enrollment data. The highest percentage of instructional expenses is paid to school units with over 5,950 population per square mile and over 35,000 weighted pupil units. Other states consider higher costs of delivering education in urban areas through corrections based on enrollment. The Colorado finance system provides different levels of funding for eight categories of districts, one of which consists of Denver itself because of its unique characteristics. New York provides special services aid to its five largest city school districts, which are not eligible for state assistance granted to other districts that participate in Board of Cooperative Educational Services (BOCES) programs (Salmon, Dawson, Lawton, & Johns, 1988, pp. 235, 272).

State aid provisions for urban areas need to be sensitive to the extent of participation, encompassing only those communities that warrant additional funds. The amount of aid is also a concern, with states desiring to offset only those costs that are beyond the control of schools: maintenance related to crime and vandalism; larger salaries and benefit packages to attract teachers to difficult situations; land for school construction; desegregation; and disproportionate numbers of language-deficient, handicapped, and disadvantaged students. To the degree that such costs are recognized by other formula adjustments for pupil needs and the cost of personnel, a provision based on population density may not be necessary.

Costs of Personnel

Allocations of additional funds to small schools having lower pupil–teacher ratios, and thus higher personnel costs per pupil, emerged initially as alternate forms of sparsity correction. State aid corrections today recognize costs associated with differing qualifications of certified employees.

Early in the century, Cubberley (1906) argued that ". . . the real unit of cost is the teacher who must be employed to teach the school, and not the children who may or do not attend" (p. 252). Placing teachers in a prominent place in apportionment plans would reflect personnel costs and efforts made by communities to support schools. It was also believed that this focus on teachers, regardless of their level or subject area, would stimulate the development of innovative programs. Updegraff and King (1922) later refined the concept of the "teacher unit" to make adjustment for other characteristics of communities. Like a sparsity or density factor, different ratios of average daily attendance per teacher would compensate for costs in rural and urban communities, in elementary and secondary schools, and for special subjects.

Adjustments for personnel costs now present in state policies rely primarily on the two traditional determinants of salaries. The extent of training and experience of teachers, counselors, administrators, and other certified personnel is reflected in minimum salary schedules as used in some states to fund personnel costs through formulas based on instructional units. Other states recognize personnel costs through additional weighted pupil units. In this form of aid adjustment, a matrix identifies weights associated with personnel characteristics to determine an average level of training and experience present within each district (see, for example, the Utah schedule presented in Table 9.3). School systems having low weights because of a concentration of teachers with bachelor's degrees and few years of experience generate fewer additional weighted pupil units, and thus less enhancement in state aid, than do districts having many highly experienced and trained professionals.

Without state assistance for this aspect of need, districts that have difficulty financing

TABLE 9.3. Professional Staff Cost Formula in Utah

Additional pupil units are derived from a composite index of experience and training of professional staff, calculated as:

(a) Multiply the number of FTE professional staff in the school district at each level of experience by the weighting factor under the appropriate training level:

Years of Experience	Bachelor's Degree	Bachelor's + 30 Quarter Hours	Master's Degree	Master's + 45 Quarter Hours	Doctoral Degree
1	1.00	1.05	1.10	1.15	1.20
2	1.05	1.10	1.15	1.20	1.25
3	1.10	1.15	1.20	1.25	1.30
4	1.15	1.20	1.25	1.30	1.35
5	1.20	1.25	1.30	1.35	1.40
6	1.25	1.30	1.35	1.40	1.45
7	1.30	1.35	1.40	1.45	1.50
8	1.35	1.40	1.45	1.50	1.55
9			1.50	1.55	1.60
10				1.60	1.65
11					1.70

(b) Divide the total obtained in (a) by the number of professional personnel included in (a) and reduce this quotient by 1.00 to obtain an average training and experience factor for the district; and

(c) Multiply the result of (b) by 1/4 of the weighted pupil units derived from prior calculations of pupil needs.

(*Source:* R. Salmon [1988]. *Public School Finance Programs of the United States, 1986–87*, p. 323. Blacksburg, VA: American Education Finance Association and VPI & SU. Reprinted by permission of the author.)

adequate salaries might deny tenure or stimulate turnover as teachers gain experience and graduate degrees. This is less likely as teacher unions gain power and as state legislation guarantees due process in removal procedures. Despite assistance to poorer school systems, the net effect of this aid is often to help wealthy districts maintain their competitive edge in attracting and holding the highest-quality teachers (Cohn, 1974, p. 16). Teachers in high socioeconomic status (SES) communities tend to possess higher levels of formal training and more years of experience, and SES explains much of the variation in salaries among districts (King, 1979). The "disequalizing effect on local school finances" (Leppert, Huxel, Garms, & Kuller, 1976, p. 19) brought about by assisting districts with costs incurred for salaries of personnel should be examined closely by states.

With the education reforms of the 1980s came allocations of state funds to upgrade the teaching profession. Career ladders and performance-based merit pay plans expand traditional considerations of training and experience (see Chapter 14). Many states allocate grants for staff development, and Florida directly finances teachers' participation in intensive subject matter content summer in-service training programs. In contrast to these categorical approaches, Pennsylvania allocates instructional improvement subsidies to all districts according to their "Market Value Personal Income" aid ratios and the number of professional staff (Salmon, Dawson, Lawton, & Johns, 1988, pp. 78, 274).

Cost of Living

Similar to the rationale for density corrections for cities, higher costs of school operations in other expensive regions of states argue for cost of living indices. This adjustment is needed most when finance plans are nearly fully state funded. Florida's highly equalized foundation plan includes a Price Level Index in which cost differentials of county units are based on a three-year average of consumer prices. This index considers many factors (e.g., housing, food, transportation, health, and recreation) that influence salary levels, and thus it is assumed to approximate educational costs because a high proportion of school budgets is personnel related. Wendling (1981) argues that such indices should include a broader set of determinants of salaries: personal characteristics, professional environment, fiscal capacity, student characteristics, school district characteristics, and regional characteristics.

Few states have adopted cost of living corrections. In some cases, aid adjustments for teacher characteristics relieve this need. In other cases, demands for more aid to supplement salaries receives little attention in the political arena. Since high-cost areas tend to be major metropolitan areas, it is believed that the presence of cultural amenities, opportunities for advanced education, and generally higher quality of public services counter demands for additional aid. Moreover, the most fiscally able districts tend to be located in metropolitan areas, putting high-cost aid in opposition to equalization goals.

Cost of living indices might become more common as they take into account differences in actual costs faced by schools to purchase specific instructional supplies and personnel. A resource cost model can be developed which assesses the extent to which differences in the costs of educational services reflect variations in prices paid for comparable resources, pupils' programmatic needs, and scale of school and district operations (Chambers, 1980; Chambers & Parrish, 1986). Educational costs are identified in such models by listing a uniform set of educational programs, determining the specific resource requirements (e.g., personnel time, supplies, and equipment) for each of these programs regardless of location of the school, and attaching prices that prevail within localities to each of these resources. Ideally, state aid based on such a model gives all districts the purchasing power to give pupils access to the same kinds and combinations of resources.

Following the determination of the educational needs of students and the financial needs of districts, state aid plans consider what measures of local capacity and effort will determine the amount of local revenue to be applied to meet those needs.

DEFINING FISCAL CAPACITY AND TAX EFFORT

In previous chapters, much has been made of fiscal inequities caused by the extreme decentralization of the school district pattern of governance. The financial ability of districts and the willingness of elected officials or the voters to deliver more resources to education often dictate the amount of available funds. Chapter 8 discusses a number of approaches for equalizing such inequities. Basic to all except flat grants and full state funding is an accurate measure of the school district's tax base.

Measurement of Fiscal Ability

Fiscal capacity "represents the resources of a government or taxing jurisdiction that are available for taxation" (Sparkman, 1976, p. 302). Fiscal ability, or "wealth," of a jurisdiction is the ratio of fiscal capacity to a measure of the demand for public services:

$$\text{Fiscal ability} = \frac{\text{fiscal capacity}}{\text{demand for public services}}$$

State school finance plans have traditionally considered property valuation as the measure of fiscal capacity because of the historic reliance on this tax base and the number of pupils as the measure of demand for services:

$$\text{School district fiscal ability} = \frac{\text{district property valuation}}{\text{number of pupils}}$$

Over the years, greater sophistication has developed in measuring both the numerator and denominator of the ratio to assess fiscal ability more accurately and inject greater equity into state distribution schemes.

Problems in measuring fiscal capacities of large cities illustrate shortcomings of relying upon property valuation alone. Urban areas such as Atlanta, Denver, New York, and San Francisco have relatively large commercial and industrial tax bases to draw upon for school support. However, this property-based wealth is a poor representation of the local money available for schools, given competing demands for public funds and services. Because state aid flows in inverse proportion to local wealth, and localities are expected to draw upon their property tax base for the remainder, equalization formulas assume that all school districts have equal access to property tax bases. This assumption works to the disadvantage of urban centers.

Other large cities, such as Baltimore, Buffalo, and St. Louis, faced large-scale migration of businesses and higher-income families to suburbs during the past several decades. With deteriorated tax bases and diminished economic activity, there is less financial ability to provide adequate municipal services *and* public education. At the same time, growing concentrations of low-income families increase the proportion of children in need of high-cost educational programs.

Table 9.4 shows that heavily populated counties spent a smaller proportion of tax revenues on schools than did less urbanized counties in 1985–1986. Total revenue per capita in the largest counties ($2,590) was twice that of the smallest counties ($1,283). State aid per capita for education in large counties was only slightly more ($397) than in less populated counties ($317), and the largest counties depended more heavily on property taxes ($583 and $291 per capita, respectively), much of which was devoted to school support. Expenditures were also nearly twice as large per capita in the most urbanized counties ($2,055 and $1,105). Spending for elementary and secondary schools ($670 and $521, respectively) did not vary as greatly as overall expenditures. In comparison, public welfare ($170 and $33); transportation, including highways and airports ($145 and $94); public safety, including support for police, fire, and corrections ($138 and $69); environment and housing ($254 and $77); and utilities, including water, electricity, and gas ($340 and $166) place a heavy demand on the resources of urban areas. Expenditures for

TABLE 9.4. Per Capita Revenue and Expenditures by County Population, 1985–1986

Item	County Population					
	1,000,000 or more	500,000 to 999,999	250,000 to 499,999	150,000 to 249,999	100,000 to 149,999	Less than 100,000
Total revenue*	$2,590	$2,009	$1,769	$1,584	$1,472	$1,283
Federal	111	131	77	67	76	50
State	732	520	496	466	468	429
Education	397	302	337	339	328	317
Public welfare	154	66	45	29	34	17
Health and hospitals	25	17	15	12	12	8
Highways	26	22	20	19	27	33
General local government support	64	67	47	40	41	32
Other	66	46	32	26	27	23
County sources	1,371	1,135	969	886	766	656
Property taxes	583	559	465	437	379	291
Sales and excise	183	102	83	68	53	47
Income taxes	93	45	20	12	21	6
Charges and miscellaneous	511	428	401	368	313	312
Utilities	223	153	196	146	150	142
Total general expenditures*	2,055	1,670	1,535	1,402	1,282	1,105
Education	726	645	674	659	620	542
Elementary and secondary	670	611	634	623	587	521
Higher education	56	34	40	36	33	21
Public welfare	170	94	69	53	55	33
Health and hospitals	160	113	101	90	95	114
Transportation	145	100	98	94	90	94
Public safety	138	199	144	126	106	69
Environment and housing	254	219	188	138	113	77
Government administration	120	109	92	93	80	73
Utilities	340	265	265	168	178	166
Education expenditures as a percentage of total revenue	28	32	38	42	42	42

*Includes amounts not listed separately. (*Source:* U.S. Department of Commerce, Bureau of the Census. [1988]. *Local Government Finances in Major County Areas: 1985–86,* Table 3, pp. 4–5. Washington, DC: U.S. Government Printing Office.)

education vary from 28 percent of the total revenue collected in the most populated counties to 42 percent of the revenue collected in the least populated counties.

Concerns with heavier costs of services and demands on property tax bases in cities call for a broader view of fiscal capacity, and many states have modified their finance plans to

1. expand property wealth measures to include other economic indicators;
2. measure capacity on a per capita rather than a per pupil basis; and
3. adjust the per pupil denominator in wealth measures to reflect educational needs of school districts (Goertz, 1981; Odden, 1977).

Although the majority of states employ either assessed (10 states) or equalized (20 states) valuation, 18 states make use of multiple measures of capacity (Salmon, Dawson, Lawton, & Johns, 1988, p. 7). Including other sources of revenue actually received by the district and/or various indicators of economic health that may not be subject to local taxation creates a more accurate picture of districts' ability and willingness to raise local revenue. Table 9.5 lists several states that determine fiscal capacity from broader measures. For example, county wealth in Alabama and Michigan is determined from indices that consider assessed valuations and a number of other economic indicators. Despite their complexities, such indices offer a more complete measure of capacity according to Ladd (1975) and Gurwitz (1977).

Personal income, a partial determinant of fiscal capacity in 12 state plans, was presented in Chapter 4 as the best indicator of the ability to pay taxes. Personal income is considered by some analysts to be a more valid measure of capacity than is property valuation since

All taxes go back to the individual taxpayer's ability-to-pay, which is basic to both the state's and the district's fiscal capacity, irrespective of whether the tax handle used is

TABLE 9.5. Measures of Fiscal Capacity in Selected States

Alabama	County index of local ability includes assessed valuations; collections from sales tax, auto license, public utilities, and personal income tax; and value of farm income and value added by manufacturing.
Arkansas	Sum of assessments on real property, personal property, utilities, and regulated carriers plus 75% of revenues from federal forest reserves, grazing and mineral rights, and other miscellaneous funds. This is adjusted by a credit allowance for the number of instructional staff holding master's degrees or higher.
Connecticut	Equalized property value per capita modified by a ratio of a town's 1983 per capita income to the wealthiest town's per capita income.
Kansas	An average of adjusted property valuation and resident taxable income in the district plus 75% of the prior year's adjusted property valuation and resident taxable income.
Maryland	The sum of net taxable income, assessed valuation of real property, and 50% of assessed value of personal property.
Michigan	County index, including assessed valuation of public utilities, motor vehicle license receipts, value of farm products, personal income tax, employed workers, and sales tax.
Nevada	Yield from 1-1/2-cent sales tax and 2.5-mills property tax plus per pupil wealth from additional 5 mills, motor vehicle tax, and other sources.
New York	Real property valuation and adjusted gross income per resident pupil are weighted equally.
Oregon	Property valuation per pupil plus statutorily designated nonproperty tax sources of revenue. Property valuation is adjusted upward to reflect monies received through the Western Oregon Timber Severance Tax.
Tennessee	Total assessed valuation and property equivalent of Tennessee Valley Authority payments in lieu of taxes.
Virginia	Composite index including real property valuation, individual income, and taxable sales on both a per pupil and per capita basis.

(*Source:* D. Verstegen. [1988]. *School Finance at a Glance* [SF-88-1], pp. 71–73. Denver, CO: Education Commission of the States. Reprinted by permission.)

consumption (for state sales taxes) or real property (for property taxes). Each school district has access to income through the tax handle of real property. (McMahon, 1978)

Measures that include income strengthen state assessments of fiscal capacity, particularly in districts that receive local income tax revenue. However, even when income taxes are collected, there may be difficulties with accounting applicable revenue, particularly in states where school district boundaries are not coterminous with county or municipal boundaries. For example, a study of income as a partial measure of capacity in New York revealed many limitations because of inaccurate, incomplete, and untimely reporting of income tax revenue to be credited to school districts (Dembowski, Green, & Camerino, 1982). Nevertheless, defining capacity in terms of income per pupil reflects both financial ability and pupils' educational needs (Adams & Odden, 1981, p. 152).

When both property valuation and personal income are taken into account in finance plans, cities appear to be poorer because of their relatively higher per pupil property values and relatively low incomes. Suburban districts with high personal incomes appear to be wealthier. In Connecticut, for example, property wealth is adjusted through a comparison of per capita local income with the state's highest-income district. This adjustment makes the computed fiscal capacity of many cities lower, giving them higher state aid than would be received under a property-tax-based formula (Goertz, 1981, p. 125).

Per capita, rather than per pupil, measures of fiscal capacity increase the denominator of the wealth-size ratio. More state aid is directed to districts with a smaller than average proportion of the population enrolled in public schools. This is often the case for large cities, especially in the Northeast. Including total population is a better measure of the ability of municipalities to raise revenue to support multiple public services. However, per capita factors also direct more aid to districts having large proportions of pupils enrolled in private schools and thus do not account for their increased abilities to support the remaining pupils (Odden, 1977, p. 362). Several states employ per capita measures of capacity: Massachusetts considers property value per capita; Connecticut includes both per capita property valuation and per capita income; and Virginia's composite index includes property valuation, personal income, and taxable sales on both a per pupil and per capita basis (Verstegen, 1988, pp. 71–73).

The importance of correcting pupil counts according to educational needs was addressed in previous sections; several states also modify the definition of local tax bases. Adjusting fiscal capacity to reflect pupil needs is an advantage to cities because of their disproportionate enrollment of students in high-cost programs. New York considers special educational needs and handicapping conditions in the determination of Total Wealth Pupil Units. An alternative method of defining wealth in Illinois permits districts to give additional weight to the number of eligible Chapter I pupils (Salmon, Dawson, Lawton, & Johns, 1988, pp. 103, 227).

Measurement of Effort

Working in concert with fiscal capacity is the amount of effort put forth to determine local contributions toward the support of school programs. Tax effort is defined as the "extent to which government is actually using the resources available to it for tax purposes" (Sparkman, 1976, p. 302). Two school districts may have the same fiscal capacity, but the one that exerts the greatest effort has the higher level of revenue for school operations.

Measures of tax effort involve a ratio of tax revenues or expenditures to some measure of fiscal capacity:

$$\text{Effort} = \frac{\text{tax revenues}}{\text{fiscal capacity}}$$

This ratio often serves as a proxy for the willingness of school boards or voters to support their schools, often reflecting such factors as the public's attitudes toward public schools and taxation to support public services generally.

Expenditure levels are often used to approximate effort, but they are an unsatisfactory measure because spending in wealthier districts is exaggerated. These districts can raise and expend large amounts of local revenue with little actual tax effort, given their larger fiscal capacities. Locally determined tax rates, which express the ratio of revenue to property valuation, are commonly used indicators of voters' sacrifice to support schools. The fairest comparison of this property tax effort among school systems is effective tax rates. By relating tax rates to full market or equalized values, differing assessment practices are taken into account (see Chapter 6).

Similar to the broadening of fiscal capacity measures to include personal income and other indicators of economic status, some analysts consider other aspects of local effort. Revenue is often expressed as a percentage of personal income (per capita or per pupil) to compare effort among states in relation to ability to pay (see Table 3.11). Similarly, the representative tax system discussed in Chapter 4 examines actual tax receipts in relation to available (whether used or not) tax bases to compare effort (see Table 4.5).

Local fiscal capacity and tax effort are important constructs in the reform of finance structures. Even though disparities in educational opportunities are most often a function of differing levels of capacity and effort, local property tax yield is viewed by many as the answer to the desire to increase the total revenue available. It is easy to agree that local fiscal capacity and effort are important components of nearly all state finance plans; it is less clear what measures of each dimension are fair indicators of available wealth and the public's willingness to support education.

The politics of school finance come alive in debates about the most appropriate measures of capacity and effort within state aid formulas. Potentially large shifts in state aid accompany any change in definitions of fiscal capacity and tax effort, and "winning" and "losing" school districts express their positions in the policy arena. Strong rationale for revisions and accurate projections of impacts of alternative measures are essential to counter arguments made solely to protect resources granted under less effective measures of fiscal capacity.

Financial capacity and tax effort define local contributions to state aid plans designed to meet educational needs of pupils and districts. Following receipt of aid to finance schools, the role of the state becomes one of monitoring to ensure that the funds are spent according to policy goals and to assess the degree to which needs are addressed.

FISCAL AND PROGRAM ACCOUNTABILITY

Accountability in school finance policy is defined broadly as responsibility for "the results or outcomes derived from the exercise of discretionary authority by school policy-makers or administrators in fiscal matters including revenue and taxation, budgeting and appropriation, and expenditure and resource management" (Hack, Edlefson, & Ogawa, 1981, p. 252). Implicit in this statement are two aspects of accountability: (1) to assess decisions about the distribution of resources in relation to pupils' needs and (2) to hold the school system responsible for the effectiveness of programs.

The first concern of this accountability encourages policymakers and school personnel to allocate and spend state funds in appropriate ways. Program and financial audits are intended to ensure that monies allocated are directed toward goals defined by legislatures and state boards of education, that instructional programs reflect educational standards and curriculum guides, and that programs serve particular groups of children for whom funds are intended. The structure of state aid to finance special programs, with their inclusion of either categorical (e.g., flat grant and excess cost reimbursements) or general aid (e.g., weighted pupil formulas), directly affects the complexity of the audit process required.

General and categorical aid programs are differentiated in Chapter 8. The well-defined cycle demanded of categorical grants establishes a framework for program planning, budget development, identification of pupils, expenditures for personnel and other resources to deliver services, and program evaluation and fiscal audits. In contrast, processes for monitoring expenditures of local and state money for general school operations are not program-specific. State statutes and regulations that govern fiscal management outline necessary budgeting, accounting, and auditing procedures for local use of general operating aid. Proposals for spending are examined through public budget hearings or state review of expenditure plans; the overall effectiveness of resource use is later assessed, if at all, through internal performance reviews, external accreditation processes, and statewide testing programs.

Many categorical flat grant and excess cost reimbursement provisions target money to groups of pupils with particular educational needs, restrict spending through special accounts, and closely monitor program content and outcomes. Following the flow of money makes it easier to identify spending patterns among schools and classrooms within a district. These financial aids tie funding with the delivery of services more closely than do weighted unit plans and make it more difficult to integrate categorically aided services with other instructional programs. With greater flexibility in planning and budgeting, weighted unit plans permit latitude in instructional program delivery to meet locally identified pupil needs. These plans rarely call for fiscal audits to ensure that monies generated according to pupil placements are actually spent within grade levels or special programs. Nevertheless, schools should be held accountable for program outcomes under either of these funding approaches.

The second aspect of accountability stresses the importance of holding policymakers and school personnel responsible for outcomes. Actual and perceived declines in school performance in the 1970s, including highly visible standardized test scores, raised numerous questions and fueled efforts to improve if not dramatically alter public education. In this reform context emerged a number of accountability mechanisms such as publication of average standardized test scores by school building, district, and state. One such wallchart is prepared annually by the Department of Education (State education performance chart, 1990). States are ranked according to pupils' performance on college entrance exams (ACT and SAT); graduation rates; resource inputs including the percentage of schools with Advanced Placement programs, teachers' salaries, pupil–teacher ratios, and expenditure levels; and demographic characteristics such as per capita income and the proportion of pupils who live in poverty, are minorities, or are handicapped. However, these comparisons present an incomplete picture of schooling outcomes (Department of Education, 1988) since they fail to capture indicators of students' performance in problem solving, creative thinking, writing, and the arts.

Other accountability mechanisms compare gains in performance made during a school year and consider pupil backgrounds. Some states, including South Carolina and California, use "comparison bands" to present the performance of individual schools or districts in relation to those of similar units in terms of student characteristics. These reports more fairly recognize the social context of schools and place attention on the results of good schooling rather than social privilege. Other techniques permit comparisons of schools' expected scores based on prior performance to show the amount and direction of change in various measures.

Once high- and low-performing schools and school districts are identified, recognition or intervention may be called for. Notable improvements in student outcomes should bring public recognition, financial rewards, and incentives to continue successful practices; diffusion of ideas to other settings; and relaxed or waived state regulations that often inhibit local innovation (Department of Education, 1988). Deficiencies in school performance should also trigger local and state responses, including increased technical assistance and possibly funding, changes in personnel and program delivery, or consolidation with more effective units. Despite the need for assessing and improving schools (and the rhetoric of politicians demanding it), efforts of states and localities are often inhibited by budgets, staff expertise, technologies, and internal and external political climates.

The most extreme response to poor performance is to declare local school systems academically "bankrupt." Policies enacted in eight states between 1983 and 1988 authorized state education agencies to assume district operations when pupils are academically deficient (Jennings, 1989). For example, the New Jersey Education Department is empowered to dismiss and replace the school board, superintendent, and district administrators responsible for curriculum, personnel, and finance. Interventions can last up to five years or until the state decides that local control can be restored.

The presumption of state technical assistance and educational bankruptcy is that state-level officials can perform better than local officials. These accountability mechanisms should be most effective if their intent is to guide and assist local districts to improve school operations and resource use consistent with other reform directions that call for placing greater control over curriculum and finance at the lowest level possible (see the discussion of school-based management in Chapter 16).

SUMMARY

State finance policy allocates resources to augment capabilities of school systems to meet the educational needs of their pupils. The measurement of needs has expanded greatly from simply counting students enrolled to a consideration of differential costs of grade levels and special programs. Many states have adopted weighted pupil and instructional unit approaches to finance anticipated costs, whereas others allocate flat grants or reimburse actual costs of such offerings as special education, vocational courses, bilingual programs, and compensatory education.

State aid systems also recognize that the cost of school operations reflects community and school district characteristics. Size adjustments respond to economies and diseconomies of scale related to population sparsity or density and to pupil enrollments. Factors may be designed to raise funding in districts where the general cost of living and other costs of educational resources are unusually high. Personnel training and experience also affect program delivery costs, and state aid assists districts in meeting salary obligations. The many adjustments in finance plans presented in this chapter can offset legitimate costs that would otherwise burden localities or diminish the amount of state funds intended for instruction. Adjustments can also provide incentives for local district policymakers to adopt new directions for program improvement. However, due care must be exercised that each additional recognition of pupil and district "needs" does not create excessive revenue disparities outside otherwise equalized allocation systems.

Measures of fiscal capacity and tax effort are indicators of the ability and willingness of localities to support public education. State aid plans that include local contributions would be strengthened by expanding measures of capacity to include both property valuation and personal income and by examining effort in terms of revenue received in relation to that capacity.

Once aid is received through the mechanisms discussed in Chapters 8 and 9, states monitor the use of funds and their impacts. Finance and program accountability mechanisms inform policymakers and the public about allocation and expenditure decisions in relation to broad educational and financial goals. Program-specific audits and evaluations ensure that intended beneficiaries in special programs receive resource supplements, determine whether programs and services are appropriate for pupils' educational needs, and assess outcomes in relation to resources provided.

State aid, the major source of intergovernmental financial assistance for education, has greatly expanded the capabilities of districts to meet the educational needs of pupils. We turn our attention next to federal legislation and aid programs and their role in defining local district policy and curriculum.

ACTIVITIES

1. Define need, capacity, and effort of school districts and list several measures of each. Discuss the contribution of these concepts to the functioning of state aid plans.

2. If ADM recognizes pupil costs associated with the number of students served, why do some states adopt ADA to count pupils? Describe the school systems that would be most benefited by each approach.

3. Differentiate a weighted pupil strategy from a full or partial excess cost reimbursement approach to compensate districts for the higher costs of instructional programs required to meet special educational needs. What incentives are implicit in each approach and what are the likely consequences of each method for addressing needs effectively?

4. Debate the merit of adjustments in funding formulas: sparsity, density, and cost of living factors; teacher experience and training indices; enrollment decline or growth measures; and so on. How might you research whether these modifications provide

legitimate recognition of needs and costs of school districts or whether they represent "political tampering" with formulas to serve the interests of particular school systems?

5. Why have some states funded schools on an instructional unit basis rather than directly recognizing higher costs associated with highly trained and experienced teachers? Which method better reimburses districts for actual costs of personnel? Which one better controls class size? Which one most limits local flexibility?

6. Examine a state's policy for defining school district wealth in its finance plan. Collect data and compare effects of changing the definition (a) to blend property valuation and income, or (b) to include per capita or per pupil measures of fiscal capacity. Which measures work to the advantage of rural, suburban, or urban school districts?

7. Outline an accountability mechanism that would provide information about the use of state and local funds devoted to educational programs. What specific data are needed for making decisions about program modification, program continuation with increased or decreased funds, or termination? Who should be responsible for program and finance decisions?

8. Given the national press for "excellence," might a state legislature modify finance plans to give more resources to districts that prove themselves to be effective in raising levels of pupil achievement or other performance measures?

REFERENCES

Adams, E. K., & Odden, A. (1981). Alternative wealth measures. In K. F. Jordan & N. H. Cambron-McCabe (Eds.), *Perspectives in state school support programs* (pp. 143–165). Cambridge, MA: Ballinger.

Chambers, J. G. (1980, Winter). The development of a cost of education index. *Journal of Education Finance, 5,* 262–281.

Chambers, J. G., & Parrish, T. B. (1986). *The RCM as a decision making process.* Stanford, CA: Stanford Education Policy Institute.

Cohn, E. (1974). *Economics of state aid to education.* Lexington, MA: Lexington Books.

Cohn, E. (1975, Fall). A proposal for school size incentives in state aid to education. *Journal of Education Finance, 1,* 216–225.

Cubberley, E. P. (1906). *School funds and their apportionment.* New York: Teachers College, Columbia University.

Dembowski, F. L., Green, M., & Camerino, J. (1982, Summer). Methodological issues in the use of income in the allocation of state aid. *Journal of Education Finance, 8,* 73–92.

Department of Education. (1988). *Measuring up: Questions and answers about state roles in educational accountability.* Washington, DC: Office of Educational Research and Improvement.

The Fleischmann report on the quality, cost and financing of elementary and secondary education in New York State, Vol. 1. (1973). New York: Viking Press.

Fox, W. F. (1981, Winter). Reviewing economies of size in education. *Journal of Education Finance, 6,* 273–296.

Goertz, M. (1981). School finance reform and the cities. In K. F. Jordan & N. H. Cambron-McCabe (Eds.), *Perspectives in state school support programs* (pp. 113–142). Cambridge, MA: Ballinger.

Goettel, R. J., & Firestine, R. E. (1975, Fall). Declining enrollments and state aid: Another equity and efficiency problem. *Journal of Education Finance, 1,* 205–215.

Gurwitz, A. (1977). *The financial condition of urban school districts: A federal policy perspective.* Santa Monica, CA: Rand Corporation.

Hack, W. G., Edlefson, C., & Ogawa, R. T. (1981). Fiscal accountability: The challenge of formulating responsive policy. In K. F. Jordan & N. H. Cambron-McCabe (Eds.), *Perspectives in state school support programs* (pp. 251–279). Cambridge, MA: Ballinger.

Hartman, W. T. (1980, Fall). Policy effects of special education funding formulas. *Journal of Education Finance, 6,* 135–159.

Jennings, L. (1989, October 11). Board in New Jersey completes takeover of troubled district. *Education Week, 9,* 1, 21.

Johns, R. L. (1975). An index of extra costs of education due to sparsity of population. *Journal of Education Finance, 1,* 159–204.

Johns, R. L., Alexander, K., & Jordan, K. F. (Eds.). (1971). *Planning to finance education* (Vol. 3). Gainesville, FL: National Education Finance Project.

Johns, R. L., Morphet, E. L., & Alexander, K. (1983). *The economics and financing of education* (4th ed.). Englewood Cliffs, NJ: Prentice Hall.

King, R. A. (1979, Winter). Toward a theory of wage determination for teachers. *Journal of Education Finance, 4,* 358–369.

King, R. A. (1984, November). Enrollment decline: A blessing in disguise? *NASSP Bulletin,68,* 122–126.

Ladd, H. F. (1975, June). Local education expenditures, fiscal capacity and the composition of the property tax base. *National Tax Journal, 28,* 145–158.

Leppert, J., Huxel, L., Garms, W., & Fuller, H. (1976). Pupil weighting programs in school finance reform. In J. J. Callahan & W. H. Wilken (Eds.), *School finance reform: A legislators' handbook.* Washington, DC: The Legislators' Education Action Project, National Conference of State Legislatures.

Leppert, J., & Routh, D. (1978). An analysis of state school finance systems as related to declining enrollments. In S. Abramowitz & S. Rosenfeld (Eds.), *Declining enrollment: The challenge of the coming decade* (pp. 187–208). Washington, DC: National Institute of Education.

McMahon, W. W. (1978). A broader measure of wealth and effort for educational equality and tax equity. *Journal of Education Finance, 4,* 65–88.

Mort, P. R. (1924). *The measurement of educational need: A basis for distributing state aid.* New York: Teachers College, Columbia University.

Mort, P. R. (1926). *State support for public schools.* New York: Teachers College, Columbia University.

National Institute of Education. (1982). *School size: A reassessment of the small school.* Washington, DC: U.S. Department of Education.

Odden, A. (1977, Winter). Alternative measures of school district wealth. *Journal of Education Finance, 2,* 356–379.

Salmon, R., Dawson, C., Lawton, S., & Johns, T. (1988). *Public school finance programs of the United States and Canada, 1986–87.* Blacksburg, VA: American Education Finance Association.

Sjogren, J. (1981). Municipal overburden and state aid for education. In K. F. Jordan & N. H. Cambron-McCabe (Eds.), *Perspectives in state school support programs* (pp. 87–111). Cambridge, MA: Ballinger.

Sparkman, W. E. (1976). Tax effort for education. In K. Alexander & K. F. Jordan (Eds.), *Educational need in the public economy* (pp. 299–336). Gainesville: University Presses of Florida.

State education performance chart, 1982 and 1989. (1990, May 9). *Education Week, 9,* 33, 28–29.

Swanson, A. D. (1966). *The effect of school district size upon school costs: Policy recommendations for the state of New York.* Buffalo, NY: Committee on School Finance and Legislation.

Tiebout, C. M. (1956, October). A pure theory of local expenditures. *Journal of Political Economy, 65,* 416–424.

Updegraff, H., & King, L. A. (1922). *Survey of the fiscal policies of the state of Pennsylvania in the field of education.* Philadelphia: University of Pennsylvania.

U.S. Department of Commerce, Bureau of the Census. (1988). *Local government finances in major county areas: 1985–86.* Washington, DC: U.S. Government Printing Office.

Verstegen, D. (1988). *School finance at a glance.* Denver: Education Commission of the States.

Wendling, W. (1981, Spring). The cost of education index: Measurement of price differences of education personnel among New York State school districts. *Journal of Education Finance, 6,* 485–504.

CHAPTER 10

The Federal Role in School Finance

Like intergovernmental transfers from states to school districts, federal aid to public education expands the capabilities of local and state governments. Some federal funds help school systems address goals established at the local level. Other federal directives and aid shape priorities for the use of educational monies regardless of their source. In this chapter, we discuss principles of intergovernmental transfers presented in Chapter 8 in relation to the federal role in educational policy and finance.

Differing views of federalism shape debates about the degree of the federal government's involvement in educational policy and finance. On the one hand, local school districts are said to be in the best position to determine the educational needs of their students and to conceive innovations in education. Decision making about programs and services should thus be lodged as close as possible to the populations affected (Elazar, 1972). Greater efficiency and responsiveness are believed to come from having local officials accountable to the constituencies who pay for and use public services (Levin, 1982). On the other hand, it is argued that the extent and quality of education provided throughout the nation depend upon the federal government's leadership. Whereas local and state resources are often committed to maintaining existing efforts, the "federal government, free of such constraints, can attempt to pinpoint its resource inputs on the margins of change" (Milstein, 1976, p. 126).

Intergovernmental transfers recognize that local governance does not always serve broader state and national interests. In the same way that state intervention influences local priorities and equalizes fiscal abilities, the early basis for federal aid was "to stimulate the correction of weaknesses in state school systems, particularly in those areas in which national interest had evolved" (Mort & Reusser, 1941, p. 473). The expanding federal role during most of the twentieth century responded to urgent social needs, desires to equalize resources and educational opportunity, and the trend toward centralization as schools and society became more bureaucratic. A different view of federalism in the 1980s launched an era that is characterized by deregulation and decentralized decision making. The nature and intent of federal involvement in public education rest upon policymakers' determinations of the national interest and views of federalism. Themes drawn from federal legislation presented in this chapter illustrate the issues that have defined national interests. Levels of funds allocated for the largest federal programs give evidence of shifts in priorities among national interests. Finally, we examine impacts of changing views of federalism and deficit reduction on prospects for future federal aid to public education.

DEFINING THE NATIONAL INTEREST: A HISTORY OF FEDERAL INVOLVEMENT IN EDUCATION

The U.S. Constitution, which defines the powers and responsibilities of the federal government, is silent on the subject of education. Unlike many other countries, there is no national educational system. The Tenth Amendment within the Bill of Rights leaves such responsibilities as education to the states: "The powers not delegated to the United States by the Constitution, nor prohibited by it to the States, are reserved to the States respectively, or to the people."

Even though the federal government can assume only the duties expressly granted by the Constitution, implied powers and judicial interpretations of constitutional provisions shape its role in education. In Chapter 3, we discussed the national interest in education as it is derived from Article I, Section 8, of the Constitution, a statement that gives Congress the power to collect taxes and to "provide for the common Defence and general Welfare of the United States." Legislative and judicial interpretations of the nation's general welfare permit federal actions in any number of areas, including education, which may not be explicitly defined in the Constitution.

Judicial interpretations of state infringement of guarantees under the equal protection and due process clauses of the Fourteenth Amendment expand federal influence over state and local educational policy. For example, the Supreme Court's unanimous decision that state-sponsored "separate but equal" schools deny equal protection of the laws (*Brown* v. *Board of Education,* 1954) and subsequent federal district and appeals court rulings that stipulate inter- and intradistrict desegregation remedies affect students' educational opportunities and state and local resource allocations. The due process clause protects students' procedural rights to a notice of charges and a hearing prior to the denial of schooling because of constitutional property and liberty interests (*Goss* v. *Lopez,* 1975). This clause also protects substantive due process rights, permitting government action when a legitimate societal interest is served, despite denials of personal freedom. For instance, the government's "police powers" extend to such matters as the vaccination of children, search of students' lockers and personal belongings, and teachers' academic freedom.

Congress, because of its power to make laws and appropriate funds, directly influences national educational policy. A number of themes that characterize federal involvement in elementary, secondary, and higher education emerge from the history of education-related legislation (National Center for Education Statistics, 1988, pp. 291–296). Although any one statute might suggest several rationales for federal action, this categorization places legislative acts within six themes: strengthening national productivity, improving defense and international relations, improving nutrition and health, expanding educational opportunities, strengthening school programs and improving facilities, and advancing research and development.

Strengthening National Productivity

The Constitution itself may not address public education, but even before it was ratified, the Continental Congress communicated the importance of schooling to the nation. Ordinances of 1785 and 1787 reserved one section, about 6 square miles, of each township from which rent and other income would be derived for public schools. Article 3 of the 1787 Northwest Ordinance stated, "Religion, morality and knowledge being necessary to good government and the happiness of mankind, schools and the means of education shall forever be encouraged." There was minimal financial support forthcoming from these land grants, but the federal interest in having a well-educated citizenry had been established.

Direct financial assistance to elementary, secondary, and higher educational institutions is justified by the government's desire to strengthen the economy, a purpose that clearly falls within the general welfare clause. These actions often coincide with economic, political, and social changes such as wars and depressions. It was the Civil War and later industrialization and urbanization that stimulated government programs to improve farm and factory production. The Morrill Acts of 1862 and 1890 allocated public land, in the amount of 30,000 acres for each representative in Congress, from which states and territories would derive income for establishing and maintaining colleges. The initial mission of land grant institutions, to advance instruction and research in agricultural and mechanical arts, broadened over time in the 69 land grant colleges and universities that continue today to receive earnings from land holdings.

World War I coincided with federal actions to improve food production and vocational training programs. As the nation entered the war, the Smith-Lever Act of 1914 financed teacher training in agriculture and home economics and provided extension services by home demonstration agents, 4-H leaders, and county agricultural agents. The Smith-Hughes Act, also referred to as the Vocational Education Act of 1917, granted states funds for trade-related programs in high schools. More than weapons production motivated this first direct federal support of precollege education. Industries required skilled workers and educators wanted to enlarge school curricula to accommodate larger and more diverse secondary school enrollments.

A large lobbying force for vocational education (Grubb & Lazerson, 1974) urged expansions in federal aid to maintain a qualified work force, reduce unemployment, and ensure national preeminence throughout the century. The Vocational Rehabilitation Act of 1918 and the Smith-Bankhead Act of 1920 provided grants for job training for World War I veterans. Unemployment during the Great Depression stimulated legislation to create the Federal Emergency Relief Administration (1933), which sponsored adult education and vocational rehabilitation; the Public Works Administration (1933), which constructed public buildings including schools; and the Civilian Conservation Corps (1933–1943), which provided work and education for youths as they restored depleted natural resources and constructed dams and bridges. World War II continued the federal government's involvement in vocational education. The 1943 Vocational Rehabilitation Act assisted disabled veterans, and the George-Barden Act (Vocational Education Act of 1946) expanded support for vocational education programs.

Congress enacted the 1944 Servicemen's Readjustment Act to compensate veterans for the war effort and to ease their reentry into a changing workplace. More commonly called the GI Bill, this act gave veterans opportunities for higher education in public or private colleges and universities and prevented a crisis of unemployment as factories retooled from weapons production. The 1985 Montgomery GI Bill extended benefits to individuals who had entered service or reserve duty after June 1985. Benefits of the GI Bill strengthened the quality of the work force and ultimately contributed to national productivity. This act demonstrated the potential role of the federal government in extending educational opportunities and served as precedence for public support of nonpublic education (see Chapter 17).

Domestic conditions renewed the federal interest in vocational education between 1960 and 1984. Occupational training funded by the 1961 Area Redevelopment Act and the Manpower Development and Training Act of 1962 was intended to ease unemployment and poverty. An enlarged Vocational Education Act of 1963 created work-study opportunities for students, developed programs for out-of-school youths, and provided funds for the construction of area vocational schools. Grants to states from the 1966 Adult Education Act encouraged adults to continue education or job training, and the 1968 Vocational Education Act increased funds to states for new programs and established the National Advisory Council on Vocational Education.

The 1973 Comprehensive Employment and Training Act (CETA) created employment and training opportunities for the economically disadvantaged and unemployed. In the late 1970s Congress created four "set asides" that allocated 50 percent of basic state grants for programs to serve disadvantaged, handicapped, postsecondary, and bilingual populations. The Perkins Vocational Education Act of 1984 expanded federal financial assistance; it also addressed another national interest by making vocational education more accessible on a nondiscriminatory basis. Vocational education, the first direct federal assistance made to public schools, is described in greater detail in Table 10.1, Federal Program 1.

Increasing awareness of occupational choices and encouraging students to continue formal education relate to future national productivity. The 1974 Juvenile Justice and Delinquency Prevention Act developed programs to prevent students from dropping out and to limit unwarranted expulsions from schools. The Youth Employment and Demonstration Projects Act of 1977 promoted literacy training, vocational exploration and on-the-job skills training. To help elementary and secondary students understand potential careers stimulated the 1978 Career Education Incentive Act.

The goal of strengthening the nation's productivity expanded federal assistance for several other curricular areas in the 1980s. The purpose of the Education for Economic Security Act of 1984 was to improve the quality of mathematics and science instruction and to promote careers in these fields as well as in engineering, computers, and foreign languages. Funds encouraged the formation of partnerships among the business community, institutions of higher education, and elementary and secondary schools. It established Presidential Awards to recognize teaching excellence and competitive Excellence in Education grants to improve educational quality. The 1988 Education and Training for American Competitiveness Act cited challenges to the nation's "preeminence in international commerce" as the rationale for grants to improve elementary and secondary education in mathematics, science, foreign languages, and technologies and to help functionally illiter-

TABLE 10.1. Federal Program 1: Vocational Education

Intent:	To enable states to offer education and training to improve skills of the existing and future work force and to strengthen productivity and promote economic growth.
Enacted:	Originally enacted as the Smith-Hughes Act (1917). A number of legislative actions initiated new programs; the Vocational Education acts of 1946 and 1963 increased financial assistance to secondary schools. The Carl Perkins Vocational Education Act of 1985 was designed to improve programs, assist in applying new technologies, expand access for underserved populations, and reduce sex-role stereotyping in career choices.
Appropriation:	$1,080,614,000 in F.Y. 1989, including $832 million in basic grants to states for vocational education and $162 million for adult education.
Distribution:	Matching grants encourage a high level of state financial participation. Grants flow through State Educational Agencies (SEAs), and state boards for vocational education oversee the development, implementation, and evaluation of states' plans. Local advisory councils assess needs and submit proposals to SEAs. States must allocate at least 80% of federal funds to public schools, vocational institutions, and correctional facilities; the remaining 20% pays administrative costs. The majority (57%) of funds distributed under the Perkins Act serves the Vocational Educational Opportunities Program to expand access to disadvantaged, handicapped individuals entering nontraditional occupations; adults in need of retraining; single parents; individuals with limited English-speaking proficiency; and individuals in correctional institutions. The remaining 43% is for the Vocational Education Improvement, Innovation, and Expansion Program.
Restrictions:	Federal assistance for vocational education is categorical in that funds are targeted by purpose, but states have discretion in developing state plans to meet their vocational training priorities. Funds are targeted by population under the Perkins Act, with percentages of funds specified for programs to serve needy groups identified above.

(*Source:* 20 USC 2301; 34 CFR 400; Final Education Department budget for fiscal 1990. [1989, December 6], *Education Week,* p. 20.)

ate adults and out-of-school youths to obtain skills. One section of this legislation, the Educational Partnerships Act, encouraged schools to apply resources from private and nonprofit sectors to strengthen education and enrich students' career awareness. Like the continuing support for vocational education, federal grants for these areas of the curriculum are intended to improve national productivity.

Improving Defense and International Relations

Closely related to strengthening the economy has been the government's interest in national defense. Although a number of the actions described in the previous section coincided with wars, the relationship between war and change in national educational policy is less than direct. Times of national crisis fostered, rather than caused, expansions in federal support of vocational education: "Wars both threaten and unite a nation, creating reasons for large scale mobilization of talent and resources that tend to outweigh traditional resistance to centralized control of education" (Kaestle & Smith, 1982, p. 391).

Nevertheless, defense interests directly involved the federal government in public education with creation of the U.S. Military Academy (1802), Naval Academy (1845), Coast Guard Academy (1876), and Air Force Academy (1954). These postsecondary institutions are nearly fully funded by the federal government, which also sponsors Reserve Officer Training Corps (ROTC) programs in other educational institutions.

To promote communities' acceptance of defense operations, the government began in the 1940s to help finance the education of military dependents. The Lanham Act of 1941 provided federal assistance for constructing, maintaining, and operating schools in areas affected by military bases and other installations. The expanded School Assistance to Federally Affected Areas, enacted in 1950 as Public Law (P.L.) 81-815 for school construction and as P.L. 81-874 for school operation, increased this "impact aid" at the time of the Korean War. These programs recognize that school districts are affected by the increased number of children to be educated and by the loss of property taxation because the tax-exempt status of federal military bases, government buildings, and Native American reservations. Children of families residing within and/or working for such federal activities bring financial assistance to the public school they attend in accordance with provisions outlined in Table 10.2, Federal Program 2.

Impact aid payments for children of families who do not live on federal land are controversial. Many children of federal employees (e.g., those residing in counties bordering the District of Columbia) attend schools in districts that have lost no property to federal installations. These districts may in fact have been helped economically by their proximity to these activities. Thus, students whose parents work for the government but do not reside on federal land are given a lower priority in fund distribution. Revisions in the Impact

TABLE 10.2. Federal Program 2: Impact Aid

Intent:	To provide financial assistance for public schools in areas affected by federal activities. School districts receive funds for children in families with government-related employment and for children whose parents live on Native American reservations but are not regularly employed on nonfederal property. The primary purpose is to offset lost property tax revenue.
Enacted:	School Assistance to Federally Affected Areas enacted in 1950 for school operations (P.L. 81–874) and school facility construction (P.L. 81–815).
Appropriation:	$733,096,000 in FY 1989, including $558 million in payments to schools for "a" children and $135 million for "b" children, $14.8 million in payments for maintenance and operation of federal property, and $24.7 million for construction projects.
Distribution:	Applications for operational funds are made through State Education Agencies. Aid is provided to school districts that enroll children whose parents live and work on federal property (termed "a" students) and whose parents are employed by the federal government but do not live on federal land (termed "b" students). Differential weights give priority to federally connected children with handicapping conditions, students residing on Native American reservations, children in low-rent housing that is tax-exempt because of federal action, and heavily impacted school systems. The amount of federal assistance depends on the greater of 50% of average per pupil expenditure for the state, the nation, or comparable school districts in the state. Allocations are made first for districts with a high percentage (larger than 20% of total enrollment) of "a" students, including those who are handicapped and on Native American land. Remaining funds are distributed in decreasing priority to districts according to the degree of federal impact and student characteristics.
Restrictions:	Impact aid is general rather than categorical in nature, with the exception of supplemental aid provided to children with handicapping conditions. This aid is to be spent in addition to other state and federal funds designated for qualifying pupils.

(*Source:* 20 USC 242(b); 34 CFR 222; Final Education Department budget for fiscal 1990. [1989, December 6], *Education Week,* p. 20.)

Aid Reauthorization Act of 1988 guaranteed full distribution for federally connected handicapped children and for districts that are heavily impacted with military or Native American students. Allocations of remaining funds follow a schedule that gives decreasing priority to less impacted districts, so that little or no aid flows to school systems with low enrollments of qualifying children whose parents do not reside on federal land.

In most districts, impact aid is spent as general aid to supplement local and state resources, with two primary exceptions. First, supplemental aid received for special education services beyond the basic amount is categorical and regulations ensure that payments are expended for designated pupils. Second, seven states successfully satisfy one of two standards ("wealth neutrality" and "disparity") by which they may apply impact aid receipts, just as they consider local property taxes, in allocating state equalization aid (34 CFR 222). The "wealth neutrality" test demands that at least 85 percent of total current expenditures or revenue are wealth neutral; that is, districts have the same amount of funds per pupil for the same tax effort under the state aid program. The "disparity" standard demands that the disparity in current expenditures or revenue for all districts, or for districts grouped by grade-level structure, is no more than 25 percent. These standards determine the "extent to which a state had removed from the local district one of the primary reasons for the federal aid—the loss of local taxable wealth" (Magers, 1977, p. 126).

Desires to improve international relations by understanding other people and ideas bring federal support of education. The Fulbright Act of 1945 and the Information and Education Exchange Act of 1948 sponsored programs to exchange elementary, secondary, and higher education faculty and to share knowledge and skills between the United States and other countries. The 1966 International Education Act provided grants to stimulate international studies and research in colleges and universities.

Goals of strengthening national defense and preeminence through education became very apparent during the cold war. The National Science Foundation was created in 1950 to "promote the progress of science; to advance the national health, prosperity and welfare; to secure the national defense; and for other purposes." Coincidental with the Soviet Union's launch of its Sputnik satellite, Congress enacted the National Defense Education Act (NDEA) in 1958 to ensure the nation's position as a world power. This broad program of financial assistance for programs in science, mathematics, and foreign languages was designed to increase the supply of competent teachers and improve instruction, guidance, and the use of television and other media. With a curricular emphasis placed on potentially high achievers, programs encouraged elementary and secondary schools to track capable students into advanced placement and honors classes. Nearly thirty years later, financial assistance through the previously discussed Education for Economic Security Act of 1984 and Education and Training for American Competitiveness Act of 1988 addressed similar areas of the curriculum to strengthen the nation's economy relative to other countries.

Diverse programs to support military academies, finance education for children in federally impacted school systems, fund exchanges of people and ideas, and strengthen math and science curricula relate largely to the nation's defense and international relations.

Improving Nutrition and Health

Federal programs for school lunch and breakfast respond to concerns with children's nutrition; they also relieve oversupplies of farm produce. The 1935 Agricultural Adjustment Act made commodities available for school lunches, and the National School Lunch

Act of 1946 provided funds for adequate food and facilities to enable schools to operate nonprofit lunch programs. Federal support of food services expanded with the School Milk Program Act of 1954 and the 1966 Child Nutrition Act, which began breakfast programs for children of low-income families.

Education's role in raising health standards stimulated such federal actions as the National Cancer Institute Act of 1937 and the Health Professions Educational Assistance Act of 1963. The fight against drug abuse brought grants for disseminating information, developing community education programs, and training teachers under the Alcohol and Drug Abuse Education Act of 1970. Two years later, the Drug Abuse Office and Treatment Act established a special action office for abuse prevention to coordinate planning and policy, created a National Advisory Council for Drug Abuse Prevention, and provided community assistance grants to support mental health centers for treating and rehabilitating drug abusers. The 1986 Drug-Free Schools and Communities Act authorized funding for drug abuse education and prevention in coordination with community efforts.

The 1970 Environmental Education Act responded to concerns for health and the environment, providing funds for teacher training, community education programs, and dissemination of information about ecology. The 1980 Asbestos School Hazard Protection and Control Act mandated school inspections and made loans available for removal and replacement of hazardous asbestos materials. The wide range of legislative actions that finance school lunches, drug abuse prevention, and asbestos removal promotes the national interest in nutrition and health.

Expanding Educational Opportunities

The federal interest in assuring educational opportunities can be traced to the 1780s, when land grants enabled schools to form in territories. This interest continued to develop as legislation created the Freedman's Bureau to advance educational opportunities for African-Americans following the Civil War, and as the GI Bill gave World War II veterans higher educational opportunities. It was during the 1960s and 1970s that the federal interest in expanding particular groups' social and economic positions yielded large increases in financial assistance. Programs today help ensure educational opportunities for Native Americans, the educationally deprived, children with handicapping conditions, and students whose native language is not English.

Native American Education.   Treaty provisions during the 1800s obligated the federal government to educate Native American children. The government initially supported church-related mission schools, using treaty provisions and the commerce clause of the Constitution to override concerns with its entanglement with church affairs (Ryan, 1982, p. 423). By the turn of the century, financial support for sectarian schools ended, and the Bureau of Indian Affairs (BIA) assumed responsibility for administering boarding schools in remote areas and day schools in population centers. Public school districts whose boundaries overlap reservations serve the majority of Indian students today.

Federal programs to help finance Indian education in public schools began in 1934 with enactment of the Johnson-O'Malley (JOM) Act. The Indian Education Act of 1972 expanded the federal role in addressing "special educational or culturally related academic needs of Indian students, including remedial instruction, counseling, and activities to encourage regular school attendance." This act also provided funds for special programs and projects to improve educational opportunities, focusing on research, demonstration projects, and educational service projects that could develop appropriate bilingual and curriculum materials. Public school districts also benefit from impact aid payments based upon the number of Native American children enrolled; however, funds are not designated for programs targeted to these students.

Desires to limit government authority over Native Americans during the 1970s encouraged the formation of tribally controlled schools and community colleges. The 1975 Indian Self-Determination and Education Assistance Act, Title XI of the 1978 Education Amendments, and the 1978 Tribally Controlled Community College Assistance Act called for participation of Native Americans in developing and governing educational programs. These institutions receive operating funds through the Bureau of Indian Affairs of the Department of the Interior.

In FY 1988, the federal budget included $189.4 million for support of schools through the BIA, $20.4 million in JOM assistance, and $30.9 million for Indian Education programs through the Department of Education (National Center for Education Statistics, 1988, p. 299).

Educationally Deprived Students.   The 1954 *Brown* v. *Board of Education* decision set the stage for subsequent legislation to equalize educational opportunities. Programs to compensate educational deprivation regardless of students' race evolved from the interest in ending school segregation.

The Civil Rights Act of 1964, passed as part of President Johnson's War on Poverty, instituted the policy of withholding federal funds to encourage school districts to comply with federal law. Title VI prohibited discrimination based on race, religion, or national origin in "programs and activities" receiving federal financial assistance. Title VII prohibited employment-related discrimination based on these same characteristics as well as gender. Later enactment of Title IX of the Education Amendments of 1972 prohibited discrimination on the basis of gender in educational programs receiving federal funds. The Office of Civil Rights (OCR) within the Department of Education investigates and resolves reported denials of civil rights. This strategy of influencing change through such adverse consequences as legal actions and withholding transfer payments is said to hold a "stick" of enforcement over local officials. It differs from financial incentives, often referred to as "carrots," offered by categorical aid programs. The directives, or "strings," attached to these grants redirect state and local behavior toward national goals.

In 1964 Congress created the Office of Economic Opportunity and financed a number of programs, including the Job Corps to provide vocational training, Volunteers in Service to America (VISTA), Head Start, Follow Through, and Upward Bound. One year later, the Elementary and Secondary Education Act (ESEA) enlarged the federal role in the education of disadvantaged children. Title I of ESEA targeted funds to schools serving concentrations of children from low-income families, but its remedial reading and mathematics programs served pupils who scored poorly on standardized tests regardless of their family income. The Education Amendments of 1974 revised the formula to determine poverty status by including family characteristics in addition to annually adjusted income levels. The 1978 amendments targeted additional resources to districts with higher than average proportions of poor children and established a comprehensive basic skills program for reading, writing, and mathematics.

Chapter 1 of the 1981 Education Consolidation and Improvement Act (ECIA) modified Title I. Parent advisory councils were no longer required, but schools would need to assure that educational programs were designed "in consultation with parents and teachers of children being served." Services for eligible non-public school children could no longer be delivered within private schools according to the Supreme Court's holding in *Aguilar* v. *Felton* (1985). The 1988 School Improvement Act required state and local officials to assess and report the progress made by pupils served and to devise improvement plans for schools that show no gain over time. Chapter 1 is the largest program of federal financial assistance that influences children's education, providing over $4.5 billion in 1989. Table 10.3, Federal Program 3, details its intent and restrictions as a categorical aid program for disadvantaged students.

Passing the original ESEA Title I legislation required a number of compromises (Benson, 1978, pp. 379–382), and controversy continues. Nearly all school systems and many private schools receive funds, and the allocation formula directs more aid to higher-spending states. Under the assumption that poverty is a valid indicator of educational need

---

TABLE 10.3. Federal Program 3: Education Consolidation and Improvement Act, Chapter 1

Intent:	To provide supplementary educational services, particularly basic skills development in reading and mathematics, for children (1) who are educationally deprived and are enrolled in schools with concentrations of low-income families, (2) who reside in institutions for neglected and delinquent children, and (3) whose parents are migrant workers.
Enacted:	Originally enacted as Title I of the Elementary and Secondary Education Act (ESEA) of 1965; revised as Chapter 1 of the Education Consolidation and Improvement Act (ECIA) of 1981.
Appropriation:	$4,570,246,000 in FY 1989, including $3.85 billion in basic grants, $271.7 million for migrant programs, $148.2 for handicapped children, and $31.6 million for neglected and delinquent children.
Distribution:	Funds flow through State Education Agencies (SEA) to school districts with approved project applications. The amount received depends upon the number of children, including those aged 5 to 17 in institutions for neglected or delinquent children and those from low-income families, and statewide average expenditures per pupil.
Restrictions:	Chapter 1 aid is categorical in that it is targeted to schools having the highest concentrations of low-income children; all schools may benefit if the concentration is uniformly high throughout a district. Only educationally deprived children in these eligible schools receive services. ECIA eased this restriction to permit an entire school to benefit from materials, equipment, facilities, and personnel if 75% of its students are from low-income families. Chapter 1 projects are designed in consultation with parents and teachers of children served, including those in private schools. However, teachers cannot be employed by, and services cannot be delivered within, private schools. Comparability of services requires districts to use state and local funds to provide programs that are at least comparable to those provided to non–Chapter 1 students. Thus, Chapter 1 funds supplement, rather than supplant, local school programs. Maintenance of effort requires state and local agencies to continue levels of funding for eligible schools at a level of at least 90% of prior expenditures.

(*Source:* 20 USC 3801; 34 CFR 200; Final Education Department budget for fiscal 1990. [1989, December 6], *Education Week,* p. 20.)

when targeting funds to schools with the highest concentrations of low-income children, two students with the same educational needs who attend different schools receive different treatment (Jones, 1985, p. 219).

Title I program effects are scrutinized and debated more than other federal categorical aid programs because of the amount of funds appropriated. A number of studies, particularly longitudinal analyses conducted in the late 1970s after a decade of program experience, reports success in raising cognitive levels of disadvantaged children (e.g., National Assessment of Educational Progress, 1981; Stickney & Plunkett, 1983; Stonehill & Anderson, 1982). However, it is argued that effects are modest, are not sustained over time, and may be due as much to changes in schooling over the past several decades as to the programs themselves (Kaestle & Smith, 1982; Mullin & Summers, 1983). Several factors may inhibit this strategy's potential: (1) Regular staffs are relieved from the responsibility of ensuring success of lower-scoring students since Title I specialists bear this burden; (2) the school experience is fragmented for Title I students, who may learn basic skills from different texts taught in different styles in their regular and remedial classes; and (3) Title I classes are independent from core programs of schools. Organizational and political variables may also affect program successes. After 10 years of implementation, Wayson (1975) observed that local and state officials had never accepted its major priorities, programs were often installed with little regard for teachers and principals whose support was essential, and processes for securing resources often alienated school personnel.

School districts' progress toward desegregation was slow during the 1960s and 1970s, despite consistent rulings of federal courts to end de jure segregation resulting from prior state and local policies in southern as well as northern states. Congress passed the 1972 Emergency School Assistance Act (ESAA) to reward school systems that had already desegregated and to encourage others to desegregate voluntarily. However, limited funds permitted few projects, and restrictions constrained districts' policy options. Funding for ESAA ended in 1981 when it was absorbed within the block grant approach. Reducing "minority group isolation" was the stated purpose of the 1984 Education for Economic Security Act's assistance for magnet schools that offer special curricula to attract students of different races. Support of the magnet school concept also promotes the federal government's interest in expanding family or individual choice in education.

Financial assistance has expanded educational opportunities for disadvantaged students in colleges and universities. Scholarship assistance for low-income students increased in 1965 with passage of the Higher Education Act. Title IV of the act authorized the Basic (BEOG) and Supplemental Educational Opportunity Grant (SEOG) programs and established the Student Loan Marketing Association. Further modification of this act in 1968 authorized law school programs for disadvantaged students and expanded their clinical experiences in the legal profession. The Middle Income Students Act of 1978 extended the BEOG program to middle-income families and enabled independent students to receive financial aid regardless of their parents' incomes.

Education of Handicapped Children.   The education of children with handicapping conditions became a federal priority during the 1960s and 1970s. There were a few earlier programs, including the Education of Mentally Retarded Children Act of 1958, that provided funds for training teachers of handicapped children.

Financial aid for educational programs began in 1965 with benefits granted by Title

VI of ESEA and creation of Gallaudet College by the National Technical Institute for the Deaf Act. This federally funded residential institution, renamed Gallaudet University in 1986, operates model elementary and secondary schools for deaf students. The 1968 Handicapped Children's Early Education Assistance Act authorized preschool programs, and the Education of the Handicapped Act of 1970 created a Bureau of Education for the Handicapped. Section 504 of the Vocational Rehabilitation Act of 1973 prohibited discrimination against physically, mentally, or emotionally handicapped persons in schools and other federally assisted programs.

The national commitment to develop programs for handicapped children expanded with enactment of the 1975 Education for All Handicapped Children Act, often referred to as P.L. 94-142. States and school districts receive financial assistance to diagnose children's needs and to provide free, appropriate education in the least restrictive environment. Its reauthorization in 1986 provided funds for demonstration projects for severely disabled, research and technology, early childhood education, and early intervention services for handicapped children from birth to age two. Education of children with handicapping conditions is one of the largest federal programs, providing nearly $2 billion in 1989; Table 10.4, Federal Program 4, presents this legislation in greater detail.

Despite its success in expanding educational opportunities, P.L. 94-142 raises a number of concerns. The original funding goal, which would have financed 40 percent of program costs, has not been attained. The burden for meeting expanding service costs has been upon state and local money, and it is argued that funds may be diverted from meeting educational needs of nonhandicapped children. The level of program control exercised

TABLE 10.4. Federal Program 4: Education of Handicapped Children

Intent:	To ensure that all handicapped children have available a free, appropriate public education, which includes special education and related services to meet their unique needs. Federal funds supplement those of states and localities to pay the costs of this education, including testing, guidance, and other special and support services.
Enacted:	Enacted as the Education of All Handicapped Children Act (P.L. 94–142) in 1975.
Appropriation:	$1,961,288,000 in FY 1989, including $1.475 billion for general programs, $247 million for preschool programs, $70 million for infants and families, and $67 million in special funds for personnel development.
Distribution:	State Education agencies (SEAs) submit an annual program plan on behalf of school districts. Grants equal the number of handicapped children aged 3 to 21 who receive special education and related services multiplied by a given percentage of the national average per pupil expenditure for elementary/secondary schools. SEAs may retain 25% of funds for administrative expenses including financial and program audits; they allocate 75% to districts as flat grants.
Restrictions:	States have the choice of accepting these categorical funds. Each eligible child has an individual education plan (IEP) that identifies present levels of educational performance, annual goals and short-term instructional objectives, special education and related services, the extent of participation in regular educational programs (mainstreaming), and evaluation procedures to determine progress toward goals. State and local public agencies are responsible for ensuring that IEPs are prepared for private school children who receive special services from public agencies.

(*Source:* 20 USC 1401; 34 CFR 300; Final Education Department budget for fiscal 1990. [1989, December 6], *Education Week*, p. 20.)

with regard to the education of handicapped children may be eased in the future, just as deregulation affected other categorical aid programs during the 1980s.

Bilingual Education. Students whose native languages differ from English received attention in 1968 with passage of the Bilingual Education Act (Title VII of ESEA amendments). Following the *Lau* v. *Nichols* (414 U.S. 563, 1974) decision, in which the Supreme Court ruled that the denial of a "meaningful education" for non-English-speaking children violated Title VI of the Civil Rights Act, the Educational Opportunities Act of 1974 ordered districts to take appropriate steps to overcome language barriers. Funds increased, and by 1989 allocations for bilingual education amounted to over $110 million. Table 10.5, Federal Program 5, describes federal assistance for bilingual education.

Bilingual education, like other federal programs to equalize educational opportunities, has been controversial. Of primary concern is the length of time, if any, that students should receive instruction in their native language while they learn English. Some specialists advocate teaching English as a second language, with students learning basic skills in their native languages until English is mastered. Others argue for rapid transition to English and enrollment in regular classes, and a third group advocates an English-only approach, with no native language instruction in public schools.

Programs to assist immigrants and refugees also help students with limited English-language facility. The 1962 Migration and Refugee Assistance Act and the 1975 Indochina Migration and Refugee Assistance Act authorize loans and grants for education and vocational training.

TABLE 10.5. Federal Program 5: Bilingual Education

Intent:	To provide special instructional programs for students with limited English-speaking ability to ease the transition from learning in their native language to classes conducted in English.
Enacted:	Title VII of the 1968 amendments to the Elementary Secondary Education Act; Bilingual Education Act of 1974.
Appropriation:	$181,586,000 in FY 1989 for bilingual, immigrant, and refugee education, including $110.8 million for basic grants, $10.8 million in support services, $30.4 million in training grants, and $29.6 million for education of immigrants.
Distribution:	Funds are allocated on a discretionary rather than formula basis; districts apply directly to the Department of Education. There is a desire to distribute assistance equitably, and consideration is given to such criteria as the distribution of children of limited English-speaking ability, the relative needs of persons in different areas of the state, and the relative abilities of local education agencies within the state to provide services.
Restrictions:	A program of bilingual education is defined as instruction in English to the extent necessary to allow a child to progress effectively through the school system and in the native language of the child. Bilingual instruction is to be offered in all subjects in elementary schools, with full participation of limited-English-speaking students in regular classes in such subjects as art, music, and physical education.
	Programs are to be developed in consultation with parents of children with limited English-speaking ability; teachers; and where applicable, secondary school students.

(*Source:* 20 USC 880b; 34 CFR 500; Final Education Department budget for fiscal 1990. [1989, December 6], *Education Week,* p. 20.)

These categorical aid programs and civil rights mandates expand educational opportunities for diverse groups of students. In addition, improving access to education and training strengthens the economy and national defense. Indeed, important goals of the 1984 Perkins Vocational Education Act were to eliminate sex stereotyping in occupations and to expand educational opportunities for persons who are handicapped, disadvantaged, single parents, or incarcerated.

Strengthening School Programs and Improving Facilities

Many of the previously described federal programs specify target groups of students to be served. Other federal aid assists elementary, secondary, and higher education by constructing facilities or helping personnel strengthen the quality of offerings. In 1930 Congress spent $47 million to build schools, and in 1963 the Higher Education Facilities Act enabled public and private colleges and technical institutes to construct and rehabilitate classrooms, libraries, and laboratories. The Disaster Relief Act of 1965 gave financial assistance to school districts "to help meet emergency costs resulting from a national disaster."

The 1965 Higher Education Act made grants available to strengthen programs in developing institutions, financed community education and continuing education programs, and established the Teacher Corps and fellowships for teacher preparation. In that same year, the National Foundation on the Arts and Humanities Act provided grants and loans for training and research in the creative and performing arts and humanities. The 1967 Education Professions Development Act was designed to improve the quality of teaching and to relieve the shortage of adequately prepared educators.

Financial assistance for facilities and programs have encouraged schools to develop new resources and make use of technologies in instruction. Titles II and IV of ESEA helped schools improve library resources and instructional materials and initiate innovative programs. Title V funds strengthened the capacity of SEAs to provide leadership in developing curriculum, assessing educational progress, and initiating more equitable school finance structures. Desires to use the nation's educational resources effectively led to creation of the National Commission on Libraries and Information Assistance in 1970. Schools broadened their use of television and other media under the 1962 Communications Act, the 1967 Public Broadcasting Act, and the 1976 Educational Broadcasting Facilities and Telecommunications Demonstration Act. These funds assisted the construction of educational television facilities and encouraged research, demonstration, and training in broadcasting and telecommunications.

The "new federalism" of the 1980s emphasized local determination of the best use of federal funds for school improvement activities. The Education Consolidation and Improvement Act (ECIA) adopted a block grant approach to consolidate 42 categorical aid programs (National Center for Education Statistics, 1988, p. 295). Programs selected to be combined in Chapter 2 had similar developmental purposes. They strengthened the overall quality of state and local practices or stimulated activities in areas of specific national concern such as consumer education, career education, or the education of gifted and talented students (McLaughlin, 1982, pp. 564–565). The goal of ECIA was to continue federal assistance for special programs while minimizing the federal presence, reducing federal paperwork requirements, and eliminating prescriptive regulation and oversight.

Local educational agencies were to be given more discretion to spend funds where they judged improvements were most needed.

The block grant approach was described in Chapter 8 as being less prescriptive in program purposes or populations to be served than are categorical aid strategies. Chapter 2 block grants are available through states to public and non-public schools for activities related to basic skills development, school improvement and support services, and special purposes. The intents of adopting this strategy were to shift responsibilities for grant administration to states and to decentralize authority to involve local personnel: "the responsibility for the design and implementation of programs assisted under the chapter shall be mainly that of local educational agencies, school superintendents and principals, and classroom teachers and supporting personnel, because they have the most direct contact with students and are most directly responsible to parents." Chapter 3 of ECIA restricted federal and state agencies' oversight of Chapter 1 and 2 programs. Like Chapter 1 programs for disadvantaged students, Chapter 2 benefits non-public school pupils. Table 10.6, Federal Program 6, presents the intent and nature of Chapter 2 block grants.

Several additional federal programs enacted in the 1980s stimulated improvements in state and local education. The 1983 Challenge Grant Amendments Act provided matching funds to eligible institutions as incentives to seek alternative sources of funding. Legislation in 1984 created the National Talented Teachers' Fellowship Program, a Federal Merit Scholarship Program, and a Leadership in Educational Administration Program. Creation of the Fund for the Improvement and Reform of Schools and Teaching (1988) authorized grants to state and local agencies and consortia of schools with higher educational institutions. Aims of these programs included helping educationally disadvantaged

---

TABLE 10.6. Federal Program 6: Education Consolidation and Improvement Act, Chapter 2

Intent:	To combine 42 prior categorical aid programs into a single block grant, giving local school districts discretion to develop programs related to three broad goals: basic skills development, educational improvement and support services, and special projects.
Enacted:	Chapter 2 of the Education Consolidation and Improvement Act (ECIA) of 1981.
Appropriation:	$492,740,000 in FY 1989, including $463 million in block grants to states.
Distribution:	State Education Agencies (SEAs) receive grants based on pupil populations, including the number of non-public school students. SEAs distribute no less than 80% of funds to school districts by formulas that consider enrollments and such "high-cost" factors as the number of children in low-income families, economically depressed urban and rural areas, and sparsely populated areas. SEA may retain 20% for administrative costs.
Restrictions:	SEA has basic responsibility for the administration of funds and programs including financial audits; however, state agencies are not to influence districts' decisions about fund use within the three goals listed. State advisory committees assist in developing distribution formulas and processes for implementing and evaluating program success.
	School systems must involve parents and teachers in public and non-public schools in determining program priorities. Children enrolled in private schools receive "secular, neutral and nonideological services, materials and equipment" under the control and supervision of public school districts.

(*Source:* 20 USC 3811; 34 CFR 298; Final Education Department budget for fiscal 1990. [1989, December 6], *Education Week*, p. 20.)

and at-risk children meet higher standards, strengthening school leadership and teaching, encouraging school systems to reallocate resources to refocus their priorities, and providing entry-year assistance to new teachers and administrators.

The federal government has assumed an active role in strengthening programs and facilities through the diverse funding strategies described within this and previous themes. Similarly, the interest in school improvement justifies sponsorship of research and development activities.

Advancing Research and Development

The federal government serves an important role in coordinating and financing educational research and development. The goal is to further our understanding of such educational issues as teaching and learning, school organization and leadership, effective means of reaching objectives, equity in finance and programs, and uses of technologies. Federal agencies did not become involved in educational research until the 1950s, however, and federal funds for these activities are minimal in comparison with such other federal research efforts as those related to defense.

Initial creation of the U.S. Department of Education in 1867 restricted its mission to collecting and diffusing statistics that "show the condition and progress of education." One year later it was redesignated as the Office of Education within the Department of the Interior, where it maintained a low profile until 1953, when the Office of Education became a division of the Department of Health, Education and Welfare.

The Cooperative Research Act of 1954 authorized partnerships among universities and state educational agencies for educational research but provided little funding. The federal interest in educational research and development, particularly related to science and math curricula, increased with NDEA and creation of the National Science Foundation. This interest expanded in 1965 under ESEA Title IV, which authorized the Office of Education to sponsor regional laboratories, university-based research and development centers, the Educational Resources and Information Clearinghouse (ERIC), and graduate training programs for educational research (Timpane, 1982, p. 542). Individual programs supported applied research and demonstration in vocational education, special education, bilingual education, and library services during the 1960s and 1970s. There were also attempts to carry out field experiments, including the planned-variation evaluation designs for Head Start and Follow Through programs, the Experimental Schools program, performance contracting to involve private agencies in instruction, and voucher plans to encourage choice among schools.

The federal role in educational research advanced with the creation of the National Institute of Education (NIE) in 1972 to house federal research activities in an independent agency and the National Center for Education Statistics (NCES) in 1974 to coordinate the collection and dissemination of educational information. The Department of Education, created in 1979 to consolidate educational programs from several departments and agencies, brought greater visibility to the federal role in public education. The Office of Educational Research and Improvement (OERI) within the Department replaced NIE to coordinate and encourage educational research and development.

These six themes capture the primary thrusts of federal involvement in public education. Levels of funds expended for individual programs indicate relative priorities within the federal role.

TRENDS IN FEDERAL FINANCIAL ASSISTANCE

The budget of the U.S. government exceeded $1 trillion for the first time in FY 1987. Of the $1.056 trillion spent in 1988, $43.3 billion (about 4 percent) financed education and related programs, including $11.1 billion for higher education and $18.6 billion for elementary and secondary education.

The federal share of elementary and secondary school funds is much less than that of either state or local governments. The general trend for federal involvement, presented graphically in Chapter 3 (see Figure 3.1), was one of growth until the early 1980s. The federal share increased from under 1 percent in the 1930s to about 3 percent in 1950; at that time the federal government's involvement included support for school lunches, vocational education, Native American education, and impacted school systems. By 1970 the federal contribution had grown to 8.0 percent of total funds for schools, with support for a wider range of programs. The maximum proportion aided by federal funds, 9.8 percent of the total spent on education, occurred in 1980. By 1987 the federal share had declined to 6.2 percent of the total as state and local revenue increased proportionally.

This level of support represents the average percentage of total costs assumed by federal aid across the country. In actuality, the federal government's share varies among states and school districts. In 1988, a total of 6 states received over 10 percent of their revenue from this source, including a high of 15.7 percent in Mississippi. Federal revenue accounted for under 5 percent in 16 states, including a low of 3.0 percent in Wyoming (U.S. Department of Commerce, 1989, p. 140).

Priorities are evident in trends for allocations. The six largest federally funded elementary and secondary programs are ranked by 1988 outlays in Table 10.7. School lunch and milk programs account for a substantial amount of federal aid to schools. This support rose from $306 million to nearly $5 billion between 1960 and 1988. Funds for this program were eclipsed in 1970 and 1985 by financial assistance for the rapidly growing

TABLE 10.7. Federal Outlays for Selected Elementary/Secondary Education Programs, Fiscal Years 1960–1988 (in millions)

	1960	1970	1980	1985	1988*
School lunch and milk	$306	$676	$4,064	$4,135	$4,937
Grants for disadvantaged	47†	1,742‡	3,205§	4,207§	3,841§
Education of handicapped	72	48	822	1,018	1,801
Vocational education	33	181	861	658	979
Impact aid	258	656	690	647	756
Bilingual education	—	6	170	158	163

*Estimated.

†Includes various programs designed to serve educationally deprived/economic opportunity in existence prior to ESEA.

‡Includes various programs designed to serve educationally deprived/economic opportunity in addition to the Elementary and Secondary Education Act (ESEA), Title I.

§ESEA, Title I, or Education Consolidation and Improvement Act (ECIA), Chapter 1.

(*Source:* National Center for Education Statistics. [1980]. *Digest of Education Statistics, 1980,* Tables 160, 163, pp. 184, 191. Washington, DC: U.S. Department of Education; National Center for Education Statistics. [1988]. *Digest of Education Statistics, 1988,* Table 257, p. 299. Washington, DC: Department of Education.)

interest in economically and educationally disadvantaged students. Enactment of ESEA increased this aid from $47 million in 1960 to a peak level of $4.2 billion in 1985. Assistance for the education of children with handicapping conditions ($72 million) was larger than that for disadvantaged pupils in 1960. Funding declined to $48 million in 1970 but grew rapidly following enactment of P.L. 94-142 in 1975, reaching $1.8 billion in 1988.

Sponsorship of vocational education has been an important federal activity since the early 1900s. Support of secondary vocational programs grew from $33 million in 1960 to $979 million in 1988. Payments to federally impacted school districts, growing more slowly than the other programs, increased from $258 million to $756 million in this time frame. There was no support for bilingual education in 1960. This program grew rapidly in the 1970s, from $6 million in 1970 to a peak of $170 million in 1981. These funds had diminished to $163 million by 1988.

There has been a decline in federal funding, not only relative to the levels of state and local contributions, but also in adjusted dollars during the 1980s. The FY 1988 appropriation for education, when adjusted for inflation, was $2.6 billion below the cost of providing the same level of services in FY 1980 (National Education Association, 1989, p. 1). The total appropriation included funding for several programs, such as the Drug Free Schools and Communities Act and the Education for Economic Security Act, that did not exist in 1980; thus, many continuing programs experienced large declines. For example, the National Education Association reported that Chapter 1 served 5.7 million children in 1986, about 40 percent of those eligible. In comparison, Title I had served 7 million, around 65 percent of eligible students, in 1980. By 1989, federal appropriations for programs to educate children with handicapping conditions covered approximately 7 percent of the excess costs of serving these students; this funding had fallen from the 12 percent of necessary excess costs paid between 1975 and 1980. Since 1980, Chapter 2 block grants lost, in real dollars, more than $900 million compared with its antecedent programs (p. 2–3).

These declines in federal support are due in part to a deliberate policy of emphasizing state responsibility for education. They also reflect the government's desire to reduce the national deficit by making overall spending more equal to revenue.

CHANGING VIEWS OF FEDERALISM AND SCHOOL FINANCE POLICY

Different beliefs about an appropriate role of federal intervention in influencing state and local policy shape the nature of grants. General aid does not designate specific purposes, categorical aid restricts funds for particular purposes, and block grants give discretion within broad goals.

The 1929 National Advisory Committee on Education called for general aid to replace special aid programs. Proposals advanced during the Depression would have provided general aid on an equalizing basis to ensure a minimal level of education in the poorest states (Mort & Ruesser, 1941). Despite arguments that the quality of educational offerings in these states justified intervention and that a broader tax structure would reduce the large range in states' abilities to fund schools, matching grant policies continued for vocational education. Fears about expanded federal control kept the federal role at a minimal level and ensured that states would have discretion to determine the best use of federal aid.

Conditions following World War II urged greater federal intervention to strengthen economic productivity and national defense. Advocates of increased federal assistance for schools in the 1950s urged general aid, but Congress expressed its preference to support specific educational programs by enacting NDEA in 1958 and ESEA in 1965. Allocating these categorical grants without requiring state matching funds reflected a view of federalism that divides powers and duties of the federal government from those of state and local levels. Nevertheless, there has not been a strict separation, and the mixing of resources and responsibilities form a "chaotic marble cake" of American government (Grodzins, 1963, p. 4). During the decade of the 1960s, federal assistance changed from one of helping state and local governments accomplish their objectives with only perfunctory general federal review to one of using state agencies as an administrative convenience under some explicit controls for accomplishing specified federal objectives (Kirst, 1972, p. 61).

Categorical grants are targeted to particular purposes, services, or students. Entitlement programs base allocations on the number of pupils who qualify under a given program's parameters, whereas other categorical funds are distributed on a competitive basis. Guidelines shape proposals to address specified purposes, and accompanying regulations restrict recipients from using funds to benefit other purposes and from supplanting state and local money. Program evaluations and audits monitor fund use and the accomplishment of objectives; these activities increase the amount of the grants that are used for intended purposes (Barro, 1978).

However, categorical grants are not always spent in accordance with federal goals. Grants-in-aid enable the government to carry out its responsibilities "through, and in conjunction with, nonfederal institutions and individuals" (Moser, 1980). Grants create opportunities for federal–state bargaining (Ingram, 1977) in which some federal objectives may be lost because priorities of state and local agencies may differ from those of the federal government. Unless states agree with federal goals, it is difficult for the federal government to induce states to change substantive policy. Grants are administered in a variety of ways by the 50 states; differing political cultures result in programs that represent a mixture of federal priorities and frequently conflicting state priorities (Kirst, 1972; Moore et al., 1983).

Attempts to monitor fund use through regulations and reporting requirements are administratively expensive and pedagogically undesirable (Chubb, 1985, p. 294). Costs of oversight structures of entitlement and matching categorical aid programs may exceed the benefits of regulation in terms of improving program effectiveness. For example, regulations may specify that aid allocated for qualifying pupils is to supplement state and local revenue, but it is difficult to determine what would have been spent on specific services in the absence of federal aid or whether federal grants were allocated only to serve categorical purposes. Matching grants, such as those used to finance vocational education, stimulate state and local funds for designated categorical purposes. The federal government provides a proportion of state–local expenditures, thus reducing the relative cost of services. Because state and local officials give evidence of having spent their own funds for stated purposes, there may be less "leakage" of federal grant funds to directions for which they were not intended than under direct grant programs (Levin, 1982, pp. 448–453).

In the "new federalism" of the 1980s and early 1990s, federal leadership, rather than control, influences state and local priorities to meet national interests. Under this view of federalism, financial aid builds the capacity of states and localities to make education more productive. This role recognizes that "education is a federal *concern,* but a local, state, and institutional *responsibility*" (Bell, 1982, p. 378). The role of the federal government, under this view, is to give leadership, advocacy, and constructive criticism of education. Rather than directing activities, the role is one of stimulating debate, increasing awareness and concern about the status of public and private schooling, calling attention to weaknesses, and recognizing excellence. Strategies used to persuade state and local governments to address national concerns include blue-ribbon national commissions, conferences of education and business leaders, dissemination of research findings, and media campaigns.

The block grant strategy was adopted to return responsibility to states and localities. It encourages the development of diverse programs within broader goals than did the narrower federal dictates of prior categorical grants. Streamlined application and monitoring processes minimize the burden of federal and state regulatory mechanisms. However, to the degree that federal and state goals diverge, block grants may not promote federal educational goals and may function more like general aid (Vogel, 1982).

Distributive shifts occurred when funds from antecedent programs were reallocated under the Chapter 2 formula, which considered numbers of pupils rather than educational needs. Poor states, urban areas, and those with high concentrations of minority students experienced the most severe losses (Verstegen, 1985). Reductions occurring in the nation's largest cities were due also to the "erosion of political and financial support for some of the antecedent programs" (Jung & Stonehill, 1985) that began prior to Chapter 2. The consequence of both of these policy changes was to limit the concept of targeting, particularly altering the federal role in reaching equity goals. This early research on Chapter 2 did not, however, examine long-term effects, improvements in education, or state and local administrative support structures (Knapp & Cooperstein, 1986).

Deficit reduction also contributed to a diminished federal presence in the 1980s. The 1985 Balanced Budget and Emergency Deficit Control Act, commonly referred as the Gramm-Rudman-Hollings legislation after its sponsors, established declining maximum levels of annual deficits through 1991. Automatic reductions occur when deficit projections exceed these target amounts, and the process of sequestration cancels new budget authority. For example, the failure of Congress and the executive Office of Management and Budget to agree on spending reductions in FY 1990 would have resulted in a total reduction of $14.7 billion, of which $1 billion would have come from Department of Education programs. These cuts were eased by a reconciliation bill that ultimately reduced overall federal spending by only $4.6 billion (Miller, 1989, p. 19). Educational spending declined 1.4 percent for all programs except those (including impact aid and bilingual education) that had already been reduced by a percentage greater than this sequester level. Even with this reduction, educational assistance increased $1.4 billion over the prior year.

Like the redistributive effects when Chapter 2 consolidated prior categorical aids, impacts of reduced spending were anticipated to be greatest for states and localities with concentrations of disadvantaged students because they are the largest special population that depends on federal funds. However, actual effects of reductions are difficult to predict, given uncertain responses of state and local agencies that could serve proportionally fewer students or provide fewer services to similar numbers of students. Reductions could also be offset through greater efficiency in service delivery or by shifting program costs to nonfederal resources (Evans, 1986, p. 327).

The federal government's role in education changed between 1960 and 1990. In contrast to Jennings (1985) and Doyle and Hartle (1985), who observed the federal presence in the mid-1980s to be very similar to that of the 1970s, Clark and Astuto (1986) claimed that there had been "significant and enduring" changes. This era altered both the substantive context of policy preferences at federal, state, and local levels and the procedural issues that deal with the role of government levels in policy development and administration. The new federalism brought decentralization rather than intervention, disestablishment with changes in the scope and status of the Department of Education, deemphasis on education as a priority in the federal agenda, diminution in the federal budget for education, and deregulation. The federal role became "a visible presence without operational responsibilities that offers advice, counsel, support, encouragement, and exhortation to those who have operational responsibility" (Clark & Astuto, 1986, p. 12). There was a desire for the federal government once again to help state and local governments achieve their objectives.

This role is not anticipated to return to one of regulation and intervention in the 1990s. There continues to be widespread public support of the policy issues raised during the 1980s, and responsibilities of state agencies and executive offices have grown to the point that they would be reluctant to return control to the federal government. The proportion of federal financial assistance should stabilize at the 1990 level of about 6 percent of total revenue of elementary and secondary schools; this share is not likely to grow under current views of federalism. However, the influence of federal leadership will continue to be felt within states and school systems because of the importance of the national interest in education.

SUMMARY

Intergovernmental transfers of funds are important strategies of state and federal governments. The general welfare clause and judicial interpretations of the Fourteenth Amendment's equal protection and due process clauses enable the federal government to assume a role in establishing educational priorities. Federal involvement grew in importance in school finance after the Depression of the 1930s and intensified between 1960 and 1980, giving districts the means to broaden educational offerings. Six themes derived from the history of federal education legislation capture the rationale for intervention and financial assistance: strengthening national productivity, improving defense and international relations, improving nutrition and health, expanding educational opportunities, strengthening school programs and improving facilities, and advancing research and development.

The preference for categorical funding of particular programs was clearly established in 1958 with enactment of NDEA. It was not until Congress passed ESEA in 1965, however, that the level of federal aid for educational programs was of sufficient scale to affect school offerings significantly. This and other categorical aid programs influenced school priorities and created a new local-state-federal partnership. Federal funds peaked as a proportion of total revenue for schools in 1980–1981, when nearly 10 percent of all funds came from national resources and centralized policy development and regulations restricted state and local discretion. The response in the 1980s brought reduced federal involvement, deregulation, and decentralization. A block grant strategy consolidated many former categorical aid programs, and the proportion of funds derived from the federal level declined. Even though this new federalism and deficit reduction diminished federal financial assistance, the federal government's presence continues to influence state and local policies and programs.

The federated governance structure for education in the United States places control primarily at state and local levels. It is only when national interests and prevailing views of federalism favor intervention that the federal government exercises a strong role in public education. Maintaining a proper balance among governance levels is a continuing dilemma of intergovernmental transfers: To what degree should state and federal governments intervene to shape school policies and practices without jeopardizing the benefits of local control?

Part III presents state and federal leadership and fiscal programs that supplement those available at the local level. Part IV gives attention to decisions being made about the use of these resources.

ACTIVITIES

1. Debate the advantages and disadvantages of modifying the federal role in financing education with regard to
   a. increasing the proportion of revenue derived from national sources to relieve local and state tax bases,
   b. redistributing current appropriations to equalize state and local fiscal capacities, or
   c. permitting schools or states to exercise total control over the use of aid.
2. In what ways should federal finance policy be influenced by research on the impacts of categorical or block grant aid programs in terms of such criteria as changes in educational achievement, educational opportunities, and economic productivity?
3. Investigate thoroughly the rationale given for passing one federal aid program, its eventual provisions, and compliance with accompanying regulations. Locate hearings in the *Congressional Record,* the original statute in the *United States Code,* and implementing regulations in the *Code of Federal Regulations.* Interview a state or school system program coordinator to discuss experiences with compliance. What modifications in policy do you recommend?
4. Which of the general themes identified in this chapter should provide the primary rationale for federal leadership and fiscal policy in education during this decade? Which view of federalism should guide the nature of grants and implementing regulations to influence the degree to which this theme becomes important to state policymakers and school district personnel?

REFERENCES

Aguilar v. *Felton*. (1985). 473 U.S. 402.

Barro, S. M. (1978). Federal education goals and policy instruments: An assessment of the "strings" attached to categorical grants in education. In P. M. Timpane (Ed.), *The federal interest in financing schooling*. Cambridge, MA: Ballinger.

Bell, T. (1982, November). The federal role in education. *Harvard Educational Review, 52*, 375–380.

Benson, C. (1978). *The economics of public education* (3rd ed.). Dallas: Houghton Mifflin.

Brown v. *Board of Education*, 347 U.S. 483, 1954.

Chubb, J. E. (1985, Summer). Excessive regulation: The case of federal aid to education. *Political Science Quarterly, 100*, 287–311.

Clark, D. L., & Astuto, T. (1986, October). The significance and permanence of changes in federal education policy. *Educational Researcher, 15*, 4–13.

Doyle, D. P., & Hartle, T. W. (1985). Ideology, pragmatic politics and the education budget. In J. C. Weicher (Ed.), *Maintaining the safety net: Income redistribution programs in the Reagan administration* (pp. 119–153). Washington, DC: American Enterprise Institute for Public Policy Research.

Elazar, D. J. (1972). *American federalism: A view from the states* (2nd ed.). New York: Crowell.

Evans, A. M. (1986, Winter). Gramm-Rudman-Hollings and Department of Education programs. *Journal of Education Finance, 11*, 315–330.

Final Education Department budget for fiscal 1990. (1989, December 6). *Education Week*.

Goss v. *Lopez*. (1975). 419 U.S. 565.

Grodzins, M. (1963). Centralization and decentralization in the American federal system. In R. A. Goldwin, (Ed.), *A nation of states: Essays on the American federal system* (pp. 1–23). Chicago: Rand McNally.

Grubb, W. N., & Lazerson, M. (1974, March). Vocational education in American schooling: Historical perspectives. *Inequality in Education, 17*, 5–18.

Ingram, H. (1977, Fall). Policy implementation through bargaining: The case of federal grants-in-aid. *Public Policy, 25*, 499–526.

Jennings, J. (1985, April). Will Carl Perkins' legacy survive Ronald Reagan's policies? *Phi Delta Kappan, 66*, 565–567.

Jones, T. H. (1985). *Introduction to school finance: Technique and social policy*. New York: Macmillan.

Jung, R. K., & Stonehill, R. M. (1985, Winter). Big districts and the block grant: A cross-time assessment of the fiscal impacts. *Journal of Education Finance, 10*, 308–326.

Kaestle, C. F., & Smith, M. S. (1982, November). The federal role in elementary and secondary education, 1940–1980. *Harvard Educational Review, 52*, 384–408.

Kirst, M. W. (1972). Federal aid to education: Who governs? In J. S. Berke & M. W. Kirst (Eds.), *Federal aid to education: Who benefits? Who governs?* (pp. 61–76). Lexington, MA: Lexington Books.

Knapp, M. S., & Cooperstein, R. A. (1986, Summer). Early research on the federal education block grant: Themes and unanswered questions. *Educational Evaluation and Policy Analysis, 8*, 121–137.

Levin, H. M. (1982, November). Federal grants and educational equity. *Harvard Educational Review, 52,* 444–459.

McLaughlin, M. W. (1982, November). States and the new federalism. *Harvard Educational Review, 52,* 564–583.

Magers, D. A. (1977, Summer). Two tests of equity under impact aid Public Law 81-874. *Journal of Education Finance, 3,* 124–128.

Miller, J. A. (1989, November 29). Congress wraps up work on 1990 education budget. *Education Week.*

Milstein, M. M. (1976). *Impact and response: Federal aid and state education agencies.* New York: Teachers College Press.

Moore, M. K., Goertz, M. E., Hartle, T. W., Winslow, H. R., David, J. L., Sjogren, J., Turnbull, B. J., Coley, R. J., & Holland, R. P. (1983). *The interaction of federal and related state education programs: Summary report of a congressionally mandated study.* Princeton, NJ: Educational Testing Service.

Mort, P. R., & Reusser, W. C. (1941). *Public school finance: Its background, structure, and operation.* New York: McGraw-Hill.

Moser, F. C. (1980, November/December). The changing responsibilities and tactics of the federal government. *Public Administration Review, 40,* 541–552.

Mullin, S. P., & Summers, A. A. (1983, January). Is more better? The effectiveness of spending on compensatory education. *Phi Delta Kappan, 64,* 339–347.

National Assessment of Educational Progress. (1981). *Has Title I improved education for disadvantaged students? Evidence from three national assessments of reading* (ERIC ED 201 995). Denver, CO: Education Commission of the States.

National Center for Education Statistics. (1980). *Digest of Education Statistics, 1980.* Washington, DC: U.S. Department of Education.

National Center for Education Statistics. (1988). *Digest of Education Statistics, 1988.* Washington, DC: U.S. Department of Education.

National Education Association. (1989). *Federal education funding: Present realities & future needs.* Washington, DC: Author.

Ryan, F. A. (1982). The federal role in American Indian education. *Harvard Educational Review, 52,* 423–430.

Stickney, B. D., & Plunkett, V. (1983). Closing the gap: A historical perspective on the effectiveness of compensatory education. *Phi Delta Kappan, 65,* 287–290.

Stonehill, R. M., & Anderson, J. I. (1982). *An evaluation of ESEA Title I—Program operation and educational effects: A report to Congress.* Washington, DC: U.S. Department of Education.

Timpane, M. P. (1982, November). Federal progress in educational research. *Harvard Educational Review, 52,* 540–548.

U.S. Department of Commerce, Bureau of the Census. (1989). *Statistical abstract of the United States, 1989* (109th ed.). Washington, DC: U.S. Government Printing Office.

Verstegen, D. A. (1985, Spring). Redistributing federal aid to education: Chapter 2 of the Education Consolidation and Improvement Act of 1981. *Journal of Education Finance, 10,* 517–523.

Vogel, M. E. (1982). Education grant consolidation: Its potential fiscal and distributive effects. *Harvard Educational Review, 52,* 169–188.

Wayson, W. (1975, November). ESEA: Decennial views of the revolution. Part II. The negative side. *Phi Delta Kappan, 57,* 151–156.

PART IV

Improving School Finance Structures and Use of Resources

CHAPTER 11

Judicial Reviews
of School Finance Policy
under Constitutional Provisions
for Equality and Efficiency

In earlier parts of this text, we presented the nature of school finance policy-making, governance structures, and sources of revenue currently made available to schools. This section evaluates school finance policies and uses of resources in relation to the values presented in Chapter 2 and Figure 2.1: equality, fraternity, liberty, efficiency, and economic growth.

Goals of equality and efficiency are considered in this chapter as they have been weighed in judicial decisions. We examine the role courts play in assessing states' finance plans in relation to constitutional guarantees of equal protection and provisions that require uniform, thorough, and efficient educational systems. Chapter 12 continues the discussion of equality (and through equality, fraternity) from the perspectives of policy analysts. Chapter 13 focuses on educational finance policies designed to further goals of efficiency and economic growth. Opportunities for improving schools' efficiency in terms of resource use are explored more fully within Chapters 14 and 15, which address the mix of labor and technologies in education and strategies for strengthening the quality of both.

Finance policy also strives to satisfy the desire of maximizing liberty as a value. Chapter 16 examines aspects of liberty as they relate to school-based decision making (provider sovereignty), and Chapter 17 examines aspects related to family choice of schools (consumer or client sovereignty). Taken together, consumer and provider sovereignty produce marketlike conditions which, many believe, engender incentives that encourage greater efficiency (and effectiveness) in educational systems.

We begin this part with a discussion of judicial reviews of school finance structures. The judicial branch of government is the primary formal mechanism established by society for arbitrating differences which arise among its members. Since 1968, federal and state courts have heard challenges of school finance systems in a majority of states. Plaintiffs typically argue that state aid formulas fail to allocate funds in a manner that enables property-poor districts to deliver similar educational opportunities to those available in wealthier school systems. States defend finance policies that permit disparities in spending as serving the legitimate goal of promoting local control of education. In the resolution of this conflict, courts determine whether constitutional provisions disallow expenditure variations and define standards of equity and adequacy against which school finance policy should be judged.

In this chapter, we contrast the nature of judicial decision making of courts with the policy-making role of legislatures. Standards employed by the courts are then examined in relation to specific challenges to finance systems. We conclude this presentation of the judicial role with a discussion of implications for school finance policy.

THE NATURE OF JUDICIAL REVIEWS AND LEGISLATIVE RESPONSES

Judicial and legislative branches of government perform different functions in the formation of school finance policy. State and federal aid programs presented in earlier chapters illustrate the products of legislative processes. The judiciary may be asked to test whether these fiscal policies satisfy societal expectations as expressed in federal and state constitutions. This external review by the courts provides a check on legislative actions, and judicial reviews often stimulate legislatures to alter school finance policy. The courts do not, however, initiate the subjects of judicial review; they react to conflicts and problems posed by members of society.

The concept of equality of educational opportunity is one policy dilemma that continues to elicit conflicts with courts and legislatures. Federal courts have made this issue a national concern through numerous decisions originating in the Supreme Court's pronouncement in *Brown* v. *Board of Education* (1954): "Such an opportunity, where the state has undertaken to provide it, is a right which must be made available to all on equal terms." Congress responded in the mid-1960s with such legislation as Title VI of the Civil Rights Act to ease inequities in children's educational opportunities.

State policy changes in school finance structures to address inequities did not immediately follow these federal interventions. Early advocates of reform included the Lawyers' Committee for Civil Rights under Law, the National Urban Coalition, and other groups who were "outside of the normal state and local policy process and, as such, were a challenge to traditional education policy makers" (Ward, 1990, p. 235). The National Education Finance Project (NEFP) demonstrated empirically that differences in school districts' abilities to fund school programs created substantial inequities in educational opportunities. This federally sponsored project advanced model finance plans, including several presented in Chapter 8, to redistribute state revenue and equalize districts' property wealth.

Despite these varied pressures to reform finance policy to improve poor and minority students' educational opportunities, state legislatures were slow to respond. The nature of state legislative processes, characterized by "give-and-take, negotiation, and compromise" (Fuhrman, 1978, p. 160), inhibited voluntary reform of states' finance structures. Even when state legislatures responded to pressure brought by impending and actual court reviews, the equality thrust raised at the national level and within the courts deferred to consensus-building processes which shape the actual content of reform measures adopted.

Unlike judicial decision making, which is based on constitutional principles, policy development in legislatures is influenced by their representative nature, the distributive nature of school finance issues, and the ongoing nature of the decision-making process (Brown & Elmore, 1982). First, as representatives of school districts to be affected by proposed school finance reforms, legislators are often more concerned with protecting their school systems' interests than with equalizing spending for all children's education. Second, the distributive nature of finance policy requires that at least a majority of school districts benefit from reforms. Equity goals are often sacrificed in the bargaining and compromise essential in finding solutions that are premised on which districts gain and which ones lose. Finally, the resolution of school finance issues is not isolated from other concerns placed before legislators. Lining up votes on a finance proposal depends upon positions taken by legislators on prior and subsequent policy issues, rather than solely upon merits of equalizing educational opportunities.

The finance plan that results from negotiations to reach consensus may or may not reflect the equity concerns of the courts or the original proponents of reform: "The closer one gets to the process of reform in specific states, the more elusive equity seems and the more complex are the values and objectives operating on reform proposals" (Brown & Elmore, 1982, p. 113).

Unlike this legislative process that gives attention to school districts' interests and to consensus building, challenges to states' school finance policies heard in the courts are more likely to consider inequities in the treatment of pupils. For example, decisions subsequent to *Brown* determined that absolute equality of resources denies all children, particularly those who have handicapping conditions (*Mills* v. *Board of Education*, 1972) or who are English-language deficient (*Lau* v. *Nichols*, 1974), equality of educational opportunity. These decisions present the principle of equity as a broader concept than that of equality and imply that children have the right of access to instructional programs appropriate to their individual learning potentials. Equalizing educational opportunities does not necessarily mean equal dollars per pupil nor equal dollars per program; equity, in these contexts, requires additional funds for programs that serve legitimate educational needs. Many challenges to school finance systems explore the concept of equality as it relates to disparities in wealth among school districts and the impact of those disparities on districts' ability to finance educational programs.

JUDICIAL REVIEWS OF SCHOOL FINANCE STRUCTURES

The law of equity permits individuals or groups to seek judicial redress when it is believed that principles of fairness are not served by governmental policies and actions. Plaintiffs in school finance suits contend that variations in spending created by finance structures violate federal or state constitutional provisions.

Standards for Reviews

Judicial reviews of school finance challenges rely upon standards created within equal protection clauses of federal and state constitutions and within state education articles. These statements convey society's expectations for legislative policy development.

Under equal protection guarantees, people in similar situations must be treated the same. In other words, differential treatment will be upheld only if classifications created by the law are not arbitrary or irrational. When it is alleged that varying treatment of children or taxpayers is contrary to equal protection guarantees, a three-tiered test determines the reasonableness of the classification: strict scrutiny, sliding scale, and rational basis (Underwood, 1989, pp. 415–416).

If a state uses a "suspect classification" (e.g., race or national origin) to differentiate people for treatment or if a fundamental right (e.g., voting privileges) is involved, courts employ a strict level of review to determine violations of equal protection. To be upheld under the "strict scrutiny" test, the classification must be necessary to further a compelling state objective, and the state must show that there are not less intrusive methods to achieve that goal. Some courts have interpreted education to be a fundamental right and the heavy reliance on property taxation to create a suspect classification based on wealth. In this instance, students' educational opportunities may rely too heavily on the wealth of local school districts, rather than depending for primary or complete support on the wealth of the state as a whole. Sparkman (1983) notes that no state finance plan has withstood a legal challenge when courts have applied this strict scrutiny standard.

Judicial review is characterized by restraint when neither a suspect classification nor a fundamental right is involved. The less stringent "rational basis" test asks whether the classification is related to a legitimate state objective; if so, it is upheld. Many courts reason that finance structures, even when permitting program or fiscal disparities among districts, are constitutional if they are reasonably related to states' interests in promoting and preserving local control of education. Underwood and Verstegen (1990) observe that it is also possible for a court to find a finance system to be unconstitutional under this test if it determines that resulting disparities do not further a legitimate state interest: "a court could just as easily see the purpose of the funding formula to be the equitable provision of education to all children of the state, in which case disparities in funding would not be rationally related to this purpose" (p. 188).

Finally, a mid-level scrutiny requires that classifications be substantially related to an important state interest. This test has been used in cases where courts are reluctant to declare a particular class (e.g., based on gender) suspect, yet want to afford some protection (Underwood, 1989). For example, the U.S. Supreme Court employed this test in its ruling that Texas could not deny free public education to the children of illegal aliens (*Plyler* v. *Doe*, 1982). Under this test, a court recognizing a wealth-based classification within the equal protection clause may still uphold the plan if it serves an important state objective.

In addition to challenges based on equal protection clauses are judicial reviews of school finance policy that focus on education clauses within state constitutions. These articles require state legislatures to establish and maintain public education for school-age children and specify that the provision of education be "uniform," "adequate," "thorough," and/or "efficient." Individuals and groups challenging the legality of states' finance plans that permit revenue or expenditure disparities contend that these educational articles require access to equal, efficient, and adequate educational opportunities. In response, states argue that education articles require only the provision of a minimum or basic educational program and that these mandates are satisfied even though finance or program disparities are permitted. In these challenges of education articles, courts may be more concerned with the adequacy of resources, programs, and services to attain desired results than they are with fiscal equity (Sparkman, 1983, p. 99).

McCarthy (1981) contrasts equity with adequacy. Where equity connotes fair and unbiased treatment, including unequal treatment for individuals who are not similarly situated, adequacy "connotes the state of being sufficient for a particular purpose" (p. 316). Determinations of adequacy rest upon standards of sufficiency and may be quite unrelated to the standard of equity. For example, schools within a state may provide equitable educational opportunities for students but they may fall short of a standard of adequacy. Conversely, resources for educational programs may be declared to be adequate in all schools but there may be large disparities among districts.

Judicial reviews of school finance plans illustrate that courts differ in their interpretation of equity and adequacy standards as they test whether finance statutes violate equal protection clauses and state constitutional provisions for public education.

Conflicting Interpretations of Standards

Table 11.1 lists states in which challenges to school finance systems have been heard in federal and state courts between 1968 and 1989. Judicial reviews upheld state support mechanisms in 19 states and declared finance systems to be unconstitutional in 12 states, 3 of which (Texas, Montana, and Washington) had successfully defended their finance statutes in earlier challenges and 1 (Wisconsin) that subsequently satisfied court review. Nearly all reviews were heard in state courts, and their decisions differ in the way judges interpret similar constitutional provisions.

Two early reviews by federal district courts found the Illinois (*McInnis* v. *Shapiro*, 1968) and Virginia (*Burruss* v. *Wilkerson*, 1969) school finance systems to be constitutional. The courts deferred to state legislatures as the appropriate forum for policy development. For example, the *Burruss* court discussed the importance of equalizing educational opportunities but stated its limitations: "the courts have neither the knowledge, nor the means, nor the power to tailor the public moneys to fit the varying needs of these students throughout the state. We can only see to it that the outlays on one group are not invidiously greater or less than that of another" (at 574). Alexander (1982, p. 201) noted that these cases failed because the courts lacked standards against which to assess disparities in educational opportunities resulting from variations in property wealth. He attributed the absence of "discoverable and manageable standards" (*McInnis* at 335) to a lack of definitiveness in the measurement of fiscal capacity and to an inability to determine the educational standards needed to compensate disadvantaged children. Although these early cases were not successful for the plaintiffs, their arguments urged a concept of equity under which state funds would erase fiscal disparities among school districts and correct variations in educational needs.

In 1971, courts in California and Minnesota examined their states' school finance systems. The California Supreme Court applied a narrower and more measurable standard (i.e., the equality of dollar inputs) than the educational needs standard employed in the earlier *McInnis* and *Burruss* challenges. Whereas a standard of equality measured by the needs of pupils conveys the attributes of a full-blown concept of equity (Alexander, 1982, p. 202), it is complex constitutionally. The emphasis in *Serrano* v. *Priest* (1971) was

TABLE 11.1. Reviews of School Finance Systems by Federal and State Courts

Year	Finance Systems Upheld		Finance Systems Invalidated	
	Federal Review	State Review	Federal Review	State Review
1968	Illinois			
1969	Virginia			
1971			Minnesota	California
1973	Texas	Arizona		New Jersey
		Michigan		
1974		Montana		
		Washington		
1975		Idaho		
1976		Oregon		Wisconsin
1977				Connecticut
1978				Washington
1979		Ohio		West Virginia
		Pennsylvania		
1980				Wyoming
1981		Georgia		
1982		Colorado		
		New York		
1983		Maryland		Arkansas
1987	Louisiana	Oklahoma		
1988		South Carolina		
1989		Wisconsin		Montana
				Texas
				Kentucky

more simply discrimination on the basis of wealth and permitted a successful challenge to the equal protection clause of the Fourteenth Amendment. The court was asked to examine inequities in expenditures that result from differing property wealth and tax burdens among school systems. Declaring that education was a fundamental right and that school district wealth created a suspect classification, the court placed the burden on the state to demonstrate a compelling reason for maintaining such inequities. Because the state failed this "strict scrutiny" test, its finance plan was declared unconstitutional.

The court adopted the standard of fiscal neutrality as it was defined by Coons, Clune, and Sugarman (1970): "The quality of public education may not be a function of wealth other than the wealth of the state as a whole" (p. 2). Following several judicial rejections of revised finance statutes, a state appellate court in 1986 declared that the state legislature had sufficiently met this standard through good faith efforts (*Serrano* v. *Priest*, 1986). Even though the maximum disparity in spending among districts exceeded the original target of $100 per pupil, the court was satisfied by a somewhat larger range (adjusted for inflation) within which spending fell for nearly all (93%) of the state's pupils. Disparities in per pupil expenditures were declared to be "insignificant and justified by legitimate state interests" (at 616). Ward (1990) observed that fiscal neutrality had been achieved "largely because of a major event outside of the education policy-making arena, namely Proposition

13, which did change some institutional factors and created equality of spending in a way that the system itself could not" (p. 244).

Using the rationale developed in *Serrano*, federal district courts held education to be a fundamental right and found the Minnesota and Texas finance plans to violate the equal protection clause of the Fourteenth Amendment. Denying a motion to dismiss the Minnesota case, the court deferred to the state legislature to develop a satisfactory finance system (*VanDusartz* v. *Hatfield*, 1971). The district court decision in the Texas case is the only school finance dispute to be reviewed by the U.S. Supreme Court. In its 5–4 reversal of the lower court, the Court interpreted students' interests in education differently from that reached in *Serrano*.

Despite the admission that public education is "perhaps the most important function of state and local governments," the Court determined that education was not a fundamental right guaranteed by the U.S. Constitution (*San Antonio Independent School District* v. *Rodriguez*, 1973). There was no explicit or implicit right to education under the Constitution, and its importance as a state and local government service did not elevate it to the level of other fundamental interests protected at the federal level. The state's finance system enabled children to obtain at least a minimal education, and there was no absolute denial of this opportunity. In the words of the Court, ". . . no charge fairly could be made that the system fails to provide each child with an opportunity to acquire the basic skills necessary for the enjoyment of the right of speech and of full participation in the political process" (at 36–37).

Furthermore, the Texas school finance formula did not interfere with the rights of a suspect class because plaintiffs could not demonstrate that poor people clustered in districts having low property values. Without a fundamental right to an education or a finding that the finance system operated to the disadvantage of a suspect class, the Court needed only to apply the less stringent rational basis test. The Court concluded that there was a rational relationship between the funding plan and the state's interest in preserving local control over schools.

One consequence of the U.S. Supreme Court's holding in *Rodriguez* was to shift attention of the finance reform movement from federal to state courts. In the next 16 years, state courts in 10 states, including Texas, invalidated finance plans as not meeting state constitutional standards. State courts in 15 other states upheld finance structures as furthering legitimate state objectives despite resulting expenditure disparities. The only challenge in federal courts following the *San Antonio* decision was in Louisiana, where in 1987 the finance system was upheld.

Decisions Upholding Plaintiffs' Claims

In addition to California, state courts in New Jersey, Wisconsin, Connecticut, Washington, West Virginia, Wyoming, Arkansas, Montana, Kentucky, and most recently, Texas have invalidated their states' finance plans. Many of the courts adopted the *Serrano* rationale, holding finance statutes that permitted large resource or spending disparities to deny equal protection under state constitutions. For example, the Supreme Court of Connecticut held that "the right to education is so basic and fundamental that any infringement of that right must be strictly scrutinized" (*Horton* v. *Meskill*, 1977, at 373). The finance plan was declared unconstitutional because it did not correct for large disparities in communities' abilities to finance education. The court discussed the relationship between resource availability and educational programs and concluded that disparities in expenditures were closely related with disparities in educational opportunities.

The Wyoming Supreme Court also determined wealth to constitute a suspect class and education to be a fundamental right in striking down the state's finance plan (*Washakie County School District No. 1* v. *Herschler*, 1980). In a somewhat different analysis, the Arkansas Supreme Court applied the less stringent rational basis test and, unlike all other state courts that employed this test to uphold finance systems because of the goal of preserving local control, invalidated the finance statute (*Dupree* v. *Alma School District No. 30*, 1983). The court found that the finance system served no legitimate state interest. Stating that only wealthy districts benefit from local control over finance decisions, the court gave the goal of equalizing educational opportunities greater weight in its analysis.

Like *Serrano*, these rulings were based on resource inequities rather than the adequacy of available funds to meet pupils' needs. This broader standard was addressed in the New Jersey decision rendered one month after *Rodriguez*. The plaintiffs in *Robinson* v. *Cahill* (1973) expanded the wealth disparities argument presented in *Serrano*, urging the court to examine the finance plan in relation to the constitutional requirement that the state ensure a "thorough and efficient" educational system. The New Jersey Supreme Court declared that this standard included "that educational opportunity which is needed in the contemporary setting to equip a child for his role as a citizen and as a competitor in the labor market" (at 295).

The court's finding of unconstitutionality, resting on concepts of equity and adequacy, ushered in a lengthy period of legislative actions and judicial reviews. McCarthy (1981) notes that subsequent litigation increasingly focused on ensuring adequacy in educational opportunities rather than on resource inequities. In 1976 the New Jersey court enjoined the State Department of Education from allocating aid to school districts, effectively closing schools until the legislature responded by adopting a state income tax to provide the essential funds for implementing a new finance plan. In a later review of progress, the New Jersey Superior Court, Appellate Division, reviewed the plaintiff's claim that inequalities in educational resources available to children had "steadily widened" because of unequal distributions of property wealth among school districts and because of the "proclivity of the equalization formula . . . to perpetuate inequalities" (*Abbott* v. *Burke*, 1984, at 1284). This court reversed the lower court's dismissal of a challenge to the finance act, and a 1988 ruling by an administrative law judge once again held the finance system to be unconstitutional.

Two challenges in the state of Washington also reflect the shift in courts' reviews from an equity to an adequacy standard. The Washington Supreme Court's initial review (*Northshore School District* v. *Kinnear*, 1974) determined that disparities in expenditures reflecting district wealth did not violate equal protection guarantees and that children were not denied access to minimum educational opportunities. The court reached a different conclusion several years later when it examined the state's constitutional mandate: "It is the paramount duty of the state to make ample provision for the education of all children residing in its borders" (*Seattle School District No. 1 of King County* v. *State of Washington*, 1978, at 84). LaMorte (1989) comments that the court treated the definition of an "acceptable basic education" as a prerequisite to other educational reforms. A finding that the equity standard is satisfied would depend upon a prior finding that the finance plan meets the standard of adequacy.

When legislatures enact finance plans to meet equity goals, resulting redistributions of property tax revenue may in turn be challenged. In Montana, a newly enacted equalization plan was tested because it called for wealthy districts to remit property tax proceeds in excess of the foundation funding level to the state (*Woodahl* v. *Straub*, 1974). The state Supreme Court upheld this recapture feature, rejecting claims that the state-imposed tax discriminated against taxpayers in counties that paid more than was required to support their local schools. The court reasoned that the general property tax constituted "a rational method of providing for basic public education required by the Constitution" (at 777). The Wisconsin Supreme Court reached the opposite conclusion in invalidating a similar recapture provision, holding the redistribution of property tax revenue to violate the constitutional mandate for uniform taxation (*Buse* v. *Smith*, 1976). Recent reviews of these two states' finance plans also differed in interpretations of state constitutions. The Montana Supreme Court found its finance plan to be unconstitutional (*Helena Elementary School District No. 1* v. *Montana*, 1989), whereas the Wisconsin Supreme Court upheld the finance structure (*Kukor* v. *Grover*, 1989).

Two recent decisions in favor of plaintiffs expanded greatly the role of the courts and the standards to be applied in resolving school finance challenges. State courts in West Virginia and Kentucky expressed the willingness of the judiciary to influence educational structures and policies more proactively.

The West Virginia Supreme Court of Appeals declared that the requirement of a "thorough and efficient system of free schools" made education a fundamental right (*Pauley* v. *Kelly*, 1979). Rather than declare the finance plan to be unconstitutional, however, it directed the lower court to determine whether there was a compelling state interest to justify any discriminatory classification created by the finance plan. More significantly, the Supreme Court of Appeals desired an assessment of whether the failure of the school system to meet "high quality" educational standards resulted from "inefficiency and failure to follow existing school statutes" or an inadequacy of the existing system (at 878).

The trial court examined existing levels of resources available to districts in relation to standards for facilities, curriculum, personnel, and materials and equipment. In 1982, the court found all county school systems, including those with the greatest wealth, to be deficient and invalidated both the educational system and financing mechanisms as not meeting the thorough and efficient standard. The court ordered the development of a master plan for the "constitutional composition, operation and financing" of the state's educational system. The Supreme Court of Appeals subsequently reaffirmed the State Board of Education's "duty to ensure delivery and maintenance of a thorough and efficient" educational system as embodied in the committee's "Master Plan for Public Education" (*Pauley* v. *Bailey*, 1984). Camp and Thompson (1988) noted that the judiciary had assumed a new role in delineating for the state characteristics of a quality education: "Though the court was not trying to usurp the power of the legislature, it needed standards to evaluate the system" (p. 237).

In a similar ruling (*Rose* v. *Council for Better Education*, 1989), the Kentucky Supreme Court declared its state's entire system of precollegiate education unconstitutional in 1989 (Walker, 1989, p. 1). The district court had previously issued a narrower decision, holding only that the formula violated the efficiency clause of the education article. The Kentucky Supreme Court ultimately ordered the legislature to "re-create and re-establish" the entire system of public education:

> This decision applies to all the statutes creating, implementing and financing the *system* and to all regulations, etc. pertaining thereto. This decision covers the creation of local school districts, school boards and the Kentucky Department of Education to the Minimum Foundation Program and Power Equalization Program. It covers school construction and maintenance, teacher certification—the whole gamut of the common school system in Kentucky. (cited by Walker, 1989, p. 14)

The court deferred to the General Assembly to devise a plan to provide adequate funding but specified clearly that any plan relying on real and personal property taxation would have to assess all property at 100 percent of market value and would necessitate uniform tax rates throughout the state.

In 1989, the Texas Supreme Court agreed unanimously that the finance system violated the state constitution's mandate that there be "support and maintenance of an efficient system of public free schools" to foster a general diffusion of knowledge (*Edgewood Independent School District* v. *Kirby,* 1989). In defining the term "efficient," the court rejected such terms as "economical" and "inexpensive": " 'Efficient' conveys the meaning of effective or productive . . . results with little waste. . ." (at 395). The extreme range in abilities of districts (from $20,000 to $14 million in property valuation per pupil) enabled the wealthiest districts to exert far less effort. Because state allocations did not sufficiently equalize spending and resulting educational opportunities, the Texas Supreme Court concluded that the finance plan did not meet the constitutional mandate: "The present system . . . provides not for a diffusion that is general, but for one that is limited and unbalanced. The resultant inequalities are thus directly contrary to the constitutional vision of efficiency" (at 396).

The court called for a "direct and close correlation" between districts' tax efforts and their educational resources. An efficient system does not preclude the ability of communities to exercise local control over the education of their children: "It requires only that the funds available for education be distributed equitably and evenly" (at 398). The court noted the "implicit link" between goals of equality and efficiency. An efficient system recognizes the value of local control in decisions about the amount of spending and equalizes districts' abilities to finance desired educational programs.

In contrast to these judicial reviews are rulings in which states have successfully defended challenges to finance structures.

Decisions Upholding States' Finance Systems

In two decisions referred to previously, federal courts upheld school support mechanisms in Illinois and Virginia. Subsequent to the U.S. Supreme Court's decision in *San Antonio Independent School District* v. *Rodriguez* (1973) that school finance is a matter for resolution within states, there have been state court validations of finance plans in Arizona, Michigan, Montana, Washington, Idaho, Oregon, Ohio, Pennsylvania, Georgia, Colorado, New York, Maryland, Oklahoma, South Carolina and Wisconsin. A federal Circuit Court of Appeals upheld the Louisiana finance system in 1987.

With the exception of Arizona, decisions testing finance plans against equal protection clauses declared that education was not a fundamental interest. The appropriate level of scrutiny was the less stringent rational basis test, under which states successfully demonstrate a nexus between the finance plan and such goals as promoting local control over educational decisions. Even though the Arizona Supreme Court declared that children are guaranteed a basic right to education under the state constitution, it determined that the educational finance system need be "only rational, reasonable, and neither discriminatory nor capricious" (*Shofstall* v. *Hollins*, 1973, at 592). More typical of these decisions was the Oregon Supreme Court's determination that the state finance plan enabled all districts to finance adequately at least a minimal level of education while also permitting local districts to exercise control over decisions about spending for programs beyond the level guaranteed by the state (*Olsen* v. *Oregon*, 1976).

For similar reasons, the Colorado Supreme Court reversed a state district court ruling that had found the state's finance system to violate both federal and state constitutions. The lower court noted in 1979 that educational needs varied among school districts because of "geographical, ecological, social, and economic factors" but that neither the legislature nor the Department of Education had taken steps to formulate a plan to satisfy the constitution's "thorough and uniform" mandate. In overturning this decision, the Colorado Supreme Court ruled that the state constitution did not establish education as a fundamental right, nor did it require the General Assembly to develop a centralized school finance system that would restrict schools to equal expenditures per pupil (*Lujan* v. *Colorado State Board of Education*, 1982). The court upheld the state's argument that the reliance on property taxation was rationally related to its objective of fostering local control over schools: "Taxation of local property has not only been the primary means of funding local education, but also of insuring that the local citizenry direct the business of providing public education in their school district" (at 1021).

State courts in New York and Maryland rejected plaintiffs' desires to broaden the concept of equity to include conditions of urban districts. Twenty-seven poor school districts in New York initially called into question disparities in spending related to variations in property wealth. These plaintiffs were joined by New York State's four largest cities, who challenged the distribution of state aid on two additional grounds. First, the large cities argued that the state plan relied on an "arbitrary and inadequate" measure of local capacity. They claimed that urban districts were actually poorest among the state's districts in school finance resources because of the general poverty of their residents, which required a higher level of municipal as well as educational services. But the aid formulas treated them as if they were wealthy, causing them to receive less state aid than they felt was justified. Second, the big cities claimed that the aid formula "arbitrarily and inequitably grants less and inadequate aid per pupil" in urban districts having the highest concentrations of pupils requiring compensatory schooling services (*Levittown Union Free School District* v. *Nyquist*, 1978, at 611).

Goertz (1981) described the urban interveners' complaints as a failure of the state to recognize four overburdening conditions—municipal overburden, educational overburden, cost differentials, and absenteeism overburden. Cities face higher costs of educating disproportionate numbers of low-achieving, language-deficient, and other high-cost students; greater demands for municipal services; and higher prices for purchasing goods and services. Nevertheless, state aid formulas often overstate cities' wealth and understate their educational needs, school tax effort, and higher costs.

The lower court employed the previously discussed "sliding scale analysis" to find that the finance plan violated federal and state equal protection clauses. This mid-level scrutiny required the court to determine whether the statutory classification satisfied a substantial (rather than a compelling) state interest. The state failed its burden of showing such an interest to be served by the state aid formula. The court also concluded that the method of financing schools did not satisfy the state constitutional requirement for the legislature to "provide for the maintenance and support of a system of free common schools."

The highest state court in New York, the Court of Appeals, reversed this decision (*Levittown Union Free School District* v. *Nyquist*, 1982). The court determined that the finance system did not offend equal protection clauses or the state constitution's education provision. Accepting the rational basis test as the appropriate level of review, the court held that the "preservation and promotion of local control of education" was a legitimate state interest to which the finance system was reasonably related. Disparities in spending and educational opportunities did not violate the education article because there was no reference to any requirement that the education provided in districts "be equal or substantially equivalent." Finally, the court determined that "municipal dollars flow into cities' treasuries from sources other than simply real property taxes—sources similarly not available to non-municipal school districts" (at 649). Despite the various dimensions of overburden of large urban areas relative to other districts, the court reasoned that these alternative revenue sources countered the argument that the aid distribution plan denied equal protection. Similar justification was given to uphold the Maryland finance plan (*Hornbeck* v. *Somerset County Board of Education*, 1983).

Judicial reviews in the late 1980s once again examined finance plans under the equal protection clause of the Fourteenth Amendment. The Oklahoma Supreme Court invalidated the complaint of a nonprofit corporation whose members included the boards of education of 38 school districts. The court denied their challenge of the finance system on both federal and state constitutional grounds, declaring that education was not a fundamental right and that "equal educational opportunity in the sense of equal expenditures per pupil" was not guaranteed by the state constitution (*Fair School Finance Council of Oklahoma* v. *State*, 1987, at 1136). Because children received a basic adequate education, they were not denied equal protection even though there were disparities in spending among districts. This court's reasoning mirrored the U.S. Supreme Court's arguments in the *Rodriguez* decision.

Relying on a similar rationale, the Fifth Circuit Court of Appeals upheld Louisiana's school finance plan. Two school districts brought suit under the federal statute (42 U.S.C. Section 1983) which protects individuals from state denial of federal constitutional rights and under the Fourteenth Amendment's equal protection clause. Once again reinforcing the view that school finance is a state issue, the court applied the rational basis test and upheld the constitutionality of the state plan as being rationally related to the goals of "providing each child in each school district with certain basic educational necessities and of encouraging local governments to provide additional educational support on a local level, to the extent that they choose to and are financially able to do so" (*School Board of the Parish of Livingston* v. *Louisiana State Board of Elementary and Secondary Education*, 1987, at 572). Most recently, the South Carolina Supreme Court employed the rational basis test to uphold the state's finance system under the Fourteenth Amendment (*Richland County* v. *Campbell*, 1988).

These decisions illustrate judicial tolerance for spending disparities, permitting states to defend finance structures that promote local control of educational decisions.

IMPLICATIONS FOR SCHOOL FINANCE

Differing interpretations of constitutional provisions evidenced in these judicial reviews of states' school finance systems suggest a number of policy implications.

1. Whereas courts may provide the stimulus for reform, policy development is a legislative prerogative.

The judiciary performs an important function as a check on legislative actions, testing whether finance structures satisfy constitutional provisions and stimulating policy change. Lehne (1978) describes the courts' role in advancing finance reform issues as an "agenda-setting" rather than a "decision-making" function. The courts specify which issues will be considered rather than act as institutions that develop concrete policies. The courts motivate change whether states are under direct orders to reform unconstitutional finance systems, have cases in process, or are threatened by the possibility of judicial reviews (Fuhrman, 1978, p. 162).

Courts are reluctant to overstep their role to assume that of policymaker. The U.S. Supreme Court, for example, despite its conclusion in *Rodriguez* that the Texas finance system satisfied legal tests, commented that improvements and "solutions must come from the lawmakers and from the democratic pressures of those who elect them." The courts recognized the complexity of problems in financing a statewide school system and that "there will be more than one constitutionally permissible method of solving them." The Idaho Supreme Court, in its decision upholding the state finance system, also refrained from entering the legislative domain whereby the court "would convene as a 'super-legislature,' legislating in a turbulent field of social, economic and political policy" (*Thompson* v. *Engelking*, 1975, at 640). Many state courts validated finance policies when states demonstrated convincingly that objectives served fell within the prerogative of lawmakers, despite resulting expenditure variations. In these states, advocates of reform must work within legislative processes, rather than rely upon the judiciary, to further goals of equity and adequacy.

Even in states in which finance plans are declared invalid under constitutional mandates, courts typically reserve the formation of remedies to legislatures. However, moving the reform agenda from the courts to the legislative arena permits individual legislators representing special interests of school districts to shape finance policies. When principled decision making yields to political interests, the goal of equalizing wealth and educational opportunities may be sacrificed. Brown and Elmore (1982) observe that fiscal limitations and social realities may result in school finance systems that are more "rational" by some standard but not necessarily more "equitable" by the criteria of reformers and courts.

Demonstrating successfully to a court that disparities in funds, facilities, and faculties because of wealth variations among school systems inhibit students' access to similar educational opportunities may be only the first step in the reform of school finance policy.

Conflicting interpretations of similar constitutional provisions illustrate that there is not a clear role for the courts in school finance reform. Sparkman (1990) concludes,

> There is a profound sense that something is at work in the courts' deliberations that is not reported in the decisions. It is clear that the courts frequently struggle with the various issues and often express concern about the disparities, but they continue to defer to the legislature with the anticipation that the political process might rectify the problems. What seems to be missing in the decisions is a discussion of the basic sense of fairness. (p. 216)

This conjecture suggests that principled decision making by the courts may be as uncertain as the politicized decision making within legislatures.

2. Standards of equity, adequacy, and efficiency continue to evolve, both to judge policy and to guide finance policy development.

Constitutions provide broad statements concerning the protection of individual rights and the maintenance of public school systems. In the absence of firm criteria for judicial reviews and legislative action, many approaches to financing schools are possible. Early decisions evidenced a lack of an equity standard to relate disparities in wealth or pupils' needs to constitutional provisions. The standard of fiscal neutrality was clearly advanced by the *Serrano* court, but policymakers were assigned the task of defining the structure and parameters for making educational finance a function of state wealth. The court's concern was equity in resource inputs; 15 years later, during which several judicial reviews of policy changes took place, the court's standard was satisfied.

Such vague standards as "uniform," "adequate," "thorough" and "efficient" in education articles similarly frustrate courts and legislatures. A number of state courts followed *Robinson*'s lead, placing as great an emphasis on adequacy of school resources and programs as they placed on fiscal neutrality. Once again, policymakers were given the task of determining what level of funding and distribution plan would satisfy such standards as "adequate" or "thorough and efficient." Where the earlier *McInnis* and *Burruss* plaintiffs were unable to protect children's educational needs under the U.S. Constitution, the *Robinson* court accepted the argument that education must be adequate to meet the state constitution's mandate.

Many courts recognize that an equitable distribution of resources alone does not improve educational programs and services. Equity is a necessary, but not a sufficient, condition for attaining equal educational opportunities. Recent decisions suggest a trend toward a larger judicial role in defining standards, not only for judicial decision making, but also for policy formulation. These holdings also evidence the courts' interest in judging whether states' entire educational systems, not just aid distributions, satisfy constitutional expectations.

3. Fiscal neutrality is not incompatible with the goal of preserving and promoting the local choice of spending levels or total tax effort.

The value of maintaining local control over school finance decisions is addressed in many federal and state court decisions. The school finance reform movement, in encouraging states to adopt finance plans that stress the goal of equity over that of preserving local control, erased many of the benefits of school district autonomy. Ward (1990) states, "Rather than increasing democratic participation in public decision making, the net effect of the school finance reform cases was increased centralization and bureaucratic decision making" (p. 246). Local voters had less discretion and school programs became more standardized. The response to this movement in the 1980s was to return control of educational decisions to school districts and schools within them.

Courts adopting the standard of fiscal neutrality have proclaimed that the quality of a child's education may not be a function of wealth other than that of the entire state. Variations in tax effort and spending levels are tolerated under this standard if the result is that districts choosing to exert the same effort have the same levels of resources available. Reformers have advanced, and states have adopted forms of, model formulas that blend the goal of fiscal neutrality with that of preserving local control (see various forms of tax base equalization presented in Chapter 8). For example, rich and poor districts desiring the same expenditure per pupil would tax local property at the same rate, and the state would provide unequal amounts of aid to raise these districts to that desired spending level. Expenditures vary among districts, but the finance system is fiscally neutral because local wealth is equalized by the state. Disparities are a function only of local decisions about educational programs. The Texas Supreme Court holding in *Edgewood* concluded that the goals of equity and efficiency are both satisfied when local control is encouraged within such an equalized finance plan.

4. In the absence of legislative action to promote equity, adequacy, and efficiency, courts may assume a more activist role.

When the New Jersey legislature failed to agree on a funding plan to satisfy standards, the state Supreme Court declared that no public funds could be spent for schools until the issue was resolved (*Robinson* v. *Cahill*, 1976). Lehne (1978) discussed this decision in relation to the growing activism of the judiciary: "The expansion of government in society and the progressive logic of constitutional positions once taken may have propelled courts beyond the point where they can retreat from a dynamic role in policy debates" (p. 5). He continues,

> While judicial decisions have traditionally been negative statements proscribing specified actions, in recent decades, courts more frequently demand positive actions from government to achieve specified goals. The judiciary is now more likely to require the executive, the legislature, and the public to deal with an issue but also to leave them an uncertain latitude to determine exactly how to deal with it. (p. 16)

Perhaps because of the vagueness of constitutional calls for equal treatment and language within education articles, or because of legislative resistance to change and processes of negotiations and compromise which frustrate reformers' desires to reduce inequities, courts have assumed strong roles in recent decisions. The West Virginia and Kentucky rulings indicate the courts' willingness to effect change in educational governance structures and programs in addition to finance plans. Persons desiring reforms in the future may turn more eagerly than ever to the courts, hoping to influence the shape of reform through judicial reviews rather than through lawmakers' votes.

SUMMARY

Courts have played important roles in defining standards and stimulating change in school finance policy. Interpretations of constitutional provisions that guarantee equal treatment and define legislative responsibilities for education establish standards for later policy development. Developments at the national level that focused attention on equal educational opportunity led to reviews of states' school finance systems. Denied reviews under the U.S. Constitution, reformers turned to state courts.

The choice of the appropriate level of judicial scrutiny for reviewing challenges of finance plans under equal protection clauses results in differing state court interpretations of similar societal standards. A strict scrutiny analysis, which is premised on findings that public education is a fundamental right or that disparities are a consequence of a suspect wealth-based classification, places a very difficult burden on states to justify spending variations among school districts. States have been more successful in satisfying the less stringent rational basis test, showing disparities under finance systems to be related to the legitimate objective of maintaining local control.

Court reviews that use these tests to assess whether finance systems meet equal protection provisions of federal and state constitutions focus on a narrow equity standard. Other decisions rest on educational provisions of state constitutions and broaden the concepts of equity and adequacy as they require states to satisfy standards of uniformity, thoroughness, and efficiency. Several recent judicial reviews of state policies exhibit the expanding roles of courts in defining standards and declaring entire educational systems to be unconstitutional.

Judicial reviews represent one way for determining whether finance policies are satisfying goals of equality and efficiency. The next chapter continues to focus on the value of equality (and through equality, fraternity), but from the perspectives of policy analysts.

ACTIVITIES

1. Read and contrast several of the court decisions cited in this chapter.
2. Contrast legislative and judicial roles in the development of educational policy in your state. Investigate conditions that were or may be related to an actual or threatened challenge to the finance structure. What legislative enactments, if any, have responded to judicial pressure?
3. Debate the appropriateness of elevating school finance policy issues to a strict level of scrutiny to determine violations of the equal protection clause.

4. Speculate about the role of the judiciary in educational policy development in the coming decade, given the Kentucky Supreme Court's finding that the entire system of public education is unconstitutional.

REFERENCES

Abbott v. *Burke*, 477 A. 2d 1278 (1984); 495 A. 2d 376 (1985).

Alexander, K. (1982). Concepts of equity. In W. W. McMahon & T. G. Geske (Eds.), *Financing education: Overcoming inefficiency and inequity* (pp. 193–214). Urbana: University of Illinois Press.

Brown, L. L., Ginsburg, A. L., Killalea, J. N., Rosthal, R. A., & Tron, E. O. (1978, Fall). School finance reform in the seventies: Achievements and failures. *Journal of Education Finance, 4,* 195–212.

Brown, P. R., & Elmore, R. F. (1982). Analyzing the impact of school finance reform. In N. H. Cambron-McCabe & A. Odden (Eds.), *The changing politics of school finance* (pp. 107–138). Cambridge, MA: Ballinger.

Brown v. *Board of Education*, 347 U.S. 483 (1954).

Burruss v. *Wilkerson*, 310 F. Supp. 572 (1969); Affirmed, 397 U.S. 44 (1970).

Buse v. *Smith*, 247 N.W. 2d 141 (1976).

Camp, W. E., & Thompson, D. C. (1988, Fall). School finance litigation: Legal issues and politics of reform. *Journal of Education Finance, 14,* 221–238.

Coons, J. E., Clune, W. H., & Sugarman, S. D. (1970). *Private wealth and public education.* Cambridge, MA: Harvard University Press (Belknap Press).

Cubberley, E. P. (1906). *School funds and their apportionment.* New York: Teachers College, Columbia University.

Dupree v. *Alma School District No. 30*, 651 S.W. 2d 90 (1983).

Edgewood Independent School District v. *Kirby*, 777 S.W. 391 (1989).

Fair School Finance Council of Oklahoma, Inc. v. *State*, 746 P. 2d 1135 (1987).

Fuhrman, S. (1978, Fall). The politics and process of school finance reform. *Journal of Education Finance, 4,* 158–178.

Goertz, M. (1981). School finance reform and the cities. In K. F. Jordan & N. H. Cambron-McCabe (Eds.), *Perspectives in state school support programs* (pp. 113-142). Cambridge, MA: Ballinger.

Guthrie, J. W. (1980). United States school finance policy 1955–1980. In J. W. Guthrie (Ed.), *School finance policies and practices, The 1980s: A decade of conflict* (pp. 3–46). Cambridge, MA: Ballinger.

Helena Elementary School District No. 1 v. *Montana*, 769 P. 2d 684 (1989).

Hornbeck v. *Somerset County Board of Education*, 458 A. 2d 758 (1983).

Horton v. *Meskill*, 376 A. 2d 359 (1977).

Kukor v. *Grover*, 436 N.W. 2d 568 (1989).

LaMorte, M. W. (1989, Spring). Courts continue to address the wealth disparity issue. *Educational Evaluation and Policy Analysis, 11,* 3–15.

Lau v. *Nichols*, 414 U.S. 563 (1974).

Lehne, R. (1978). *The quest for justice: The politics of school finance reform.* White Plains, NY: Longman.

Levittown Union Free School District v. *Nyquist*, 408 N.Y.S. 2d 606 (1978); Affirmed, 443 N.Y.S. 2d 843 (1981); Reversed, 453 N.Y.S. 2d 643 (1982); Cert. denied, 459 U.S. 1139 (1983).

Lujan v. *Colorado State Board of Education*, 649 P. 2d 1005 (1982).

McCarthy, M. M. (1981). Adequacy in educational programs: A legal perspective. In K. F. Jordan & N. H. Cambron-McCabe (Eds.), *Perspectives in state school support programs* (pp. 315–351). Cambridge, MA: Ballinger.

McInnis v. *Shapiro*, 293 F. Supp. 327 (1968); Affirmed, *McInnis* v. *Ogilvie*, 394 U.S. 322 (1969).

Mills v. *Board of Education of the District of Columbia*, 348 F. Supp. 866 (1972).

Northshore School District No. 417 v. *Kinnear*, 530 P. 2d 178 (1974).

Olsen v. *Oregon*, 554 P. 2d 139 (1976).

Pauley v. *Kelly*, 255 S.E. 2d 859 (1979); *Pauley* v. *Bailey*, 324 S.E. 2d 128 (1984).

Plyler v. *Doe*, 457 U.S. 202 (1982).

Richland County v. *Campbell*, 364 S.E. 2d 470 (1988).

Robinson v. *Cahill*, 303 A. 2d 273 (1973); 355 A. 2d 129 (1976).

Rose v. *Council for Better Education*, 790 S.W.2d 186, 1989.

San Antonio Independent School District v. *Rodriguez*, 411 U.S. 1 (1973).

School Board of the Parish of Livingston v. *Louisiana State Board of Elementary and Secondary Education*, 830 F. 2d 563 (1987).

Seattle School District No. 1 of King County v. *State of Washington*, 585 P. 2d 71 (1978).

Serrano v. *Priest*, 487 P. 2d 1241 (1971); 557 P. 2d 929 (1976); 226 Cal. Rptr. 584 (1986).

Shofstall v. *Hollins*, 515 P. 2d 590 (1973).

Sjogren, J. (1981). Municipal overburden and state aid for education. In K. F. Jordan & N. H. Cambron-McCabe (Eds.), *Perspectives in state school support programs* (pp. 87–111). Cambridge, MA: Ballinger.

Sparkman, W. E. (1983). School finance litigation in the 1980s. In S. B. Thomas, N. H. Cambron-McCabe, & M. M. McCarthy (Eds.), *Educators and the law: Current trends and issues* (pp. 96–108). Elmont, NY: Institute for School Law and Finance.

Sparkman, W. E. (1990). School finance challenges in state courts. In J. K. Underwood & D. A. Verstegen (Eds.), *The impacts of litigation and legislation on public school finance: Adequacy, equity, and excellence* (pp. 193–224). New York: Harper & Row.

Thompson v. *Engelking*, 537 P. 2d 635 (1975).

Underwood, J. K. (1989, Winter). Changing equal protection analyses in finance equity litigation. *Journal of Education Finance, 14*, 413–425.

Underwood, J. K. & Verstegen, D. A. (1990). School finance challenges in federal courts: Changing equal protection analyses. In J. K. Underwood & D. A. Verstegen (Eds.), *The impacts of litigation and legislation on public school finance: Adequacy, equity, and excellence* (pp. 177–191). New York: Harper & Row.

VanDusartz v. *Hatfield*, 334 F. Supp. 870 (1971).

Walker, R. (1989, June 14). Entire Kentucky school system is ruled invalid: Court tells Assembly to create it anew. *Education Week, 8*, 1, 14.

Ward, J. G. (1990). Implementation and monitoring of judicial mandates: An interpretive analysis. In J. K. Underwood & D. A. Verstegen (Eds.), *The impacts of litigation and legislation on public school finance: Adequacy, equity, and excellence* (pp. 225–248). New York: Harper & Row.

Washakie County School District No. 1 v. *Herschler*, 606 P. 2d 310 (1980); Cert. denied, 449 U.S. 824 (1980).

Woodahl v. *Straub*, 520 P. 2d 776 (1974).

CHAPTER 12

Equality and Fraternity

Courts are the formal mechanisms created by society for evaluating social policy within parameters established by constitutional and statutory authority. The previous chapter examined the assessments made by courts of school finance policy in the United States, where equity and fraternity are primary, but not exclusive, concerns. In this chapter, we view equity (and through equity, fraternity) from the perspectives of policymakers and policy analysts who are not constrained by the same parameters and procedures as those in judicial reviews.

Equality and fraternity, along with liberty, are described in Chapter 2 as "ethical" values which influence decisions about school finance. Equality was defined as the state, ideal, or quality of being equal, as in enjoying equal social, political, and economic rights. The operational definition of equality within the sociopolitical context also includes factors of condition, placing emphasis on the *appropriateness* of treatment. As such, "equality" has taken on the broader connotations of "equity," defined in Morris (1969) as "the state, ideal, or quality of being just, impartial and fair" (p. 443). In this chapter, the term "equity" is used instead of "equality" as more accurately reflecting modern usage in reference to public policy.

Fraternity was defined as a common bond, producing a sense of unity, community, and nationhood. Public policies which further the realization of equity also frequently advance the realization of fraternity. For example, policies of school desegregation were implemented to make the educational opportunities of minority children equivalent to those of majority children (e.g., separate is inherently unequal). Policies of desegregation could have been advanced just as well to further realization of the concept of fraternity in that a desegregated school provides a common experience for all children, uniting them at a tender age—an argument used by Horace Mann in the nineteenth century while lobbying for the "common" school.

Fraternity and equity also interrelate with liberty in a similar fashion. Achieving equity and building a sense of fraternity or community require constraints on the behaviors of individuals; thus, both restrict liberty. During the latter half of the twentieth century, equity considerations have dominated fraternal ones in public policy debates even though many of the policies implemented have promoted both objectives. Following the flow of the discourse, policy analysts have designed their analyses around equity constructs. Few, if any, analyses have been built around the concept of fraternity. The discussion in this chapter will thus focus on equity, although the reader should keep in mind that much which has been said about equity pertains to fraternity as well. We describe a number of measures of equity that policy analysts employ to evaluate school finance policies, and we review the outcomes of several analyses intended to inform policymakers.

Alexander (1982) has written one of the most comprehensive discussions of the concepts of equity as they relate to the provision of educational services. Figure 12.1 represents his reconciliation of philosophical equity, legal equity, and the practice of school finance. The figure shows an equity hierarchy ranging from the lowest philosophical level of commutative equity through equal distribution and restitution to positivism. School finance practices are associated with each philosophical level. A position toward the left of the figure is more in keeping with conservative political and economic philosophies, whereas a position toward the right is more in keeping with liberal views.

Commutative equity entitles a person to something on the basis of property rights alone

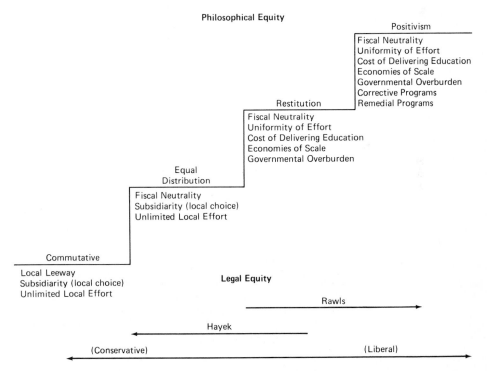

Figure 12.1. Alexander's Equity Hierarchy. (*Source:* K. Alexander. [1982]. "Concepts of Equity." In W. W. McMahon and T. G. Geske [Eds.], *Financing Education: Overcoming Inefficiency and Inequity* [pp. 193–214]. Urbana: University of Illinois Press. p. 211. Reprinted by permission.)

and leaves the distribution produced by the marketplace unaltered. Such a philosophy would not support any public intervention in school finance. Given that some intervention is inevitable, however, subscribers to commutative equity would endorse the greatest possible local discretion in using local tax bases—which moves us toward distributive equity.

Distributive equity is concerned with correcting inequitable conditions created by the design of government. This has direct relevance to school finance since a primary source of inequity, variation in school district tax bases, lies in the school district structure, a creation of state government. Holders of this position would endorse the concept of fiscal neutrality, power equalization formulas, and no restraints on local effort.

Restitution endorses the correction of inequitable conditions arising out of social and economic circumstances as well as those created through government action. Restitution focuses on weaknesses of the system only and not on the personal educational needs of children. In addition to fiscal neutrality, persons accepting this view would endorse public policies of uniform tax effort and adjustments for regional cost variations, economies of scale, and municipal overburden. Full state funding would be an acceptable means of financing public schools.

Positivism introduces the concept of the educational needs of children. Holders of this position justify intervention designed to assist the least advantaged. It demands that unique and high-cost corrective, remedial, and compensatory programs be fully financed. Alexander (1982) identified several features which would need to be included in an ideal model of education finance in order to satisfy this highest philosophical level of equity: adequate financing of basic educational programs, complete fiscal equalization of each district's tax-paying ability, uniform tax effort, and supplemental standards for corrective and remedial educational programs.

DIMENSIONS OF EQUITY

In analyzing the impact of a policy on equity concerns, an analyst must be fully aware of the level of equity the policy is intended to address. In addition, regardless of the level addressed, the methodology employed should consider the horizontal and vertical dimensions of equity. These concepts were introduced in Chapter 4 in the context of taxation policy. Horizontal equity refers to the equal treatment of equals—the traditional meaning of "equality." Vertical equity recognizes that equal treatment is not always fair and just for persons (or school districts) experiencing abnormal conditions such as poverty and physical, psychological, and mental handicaps (or high costs of living, dispersed populations, and municipal overburden). Thus vertical equity refers to the appropriate unequal treatment of unequals. Some analysts add a third dimension, equal opportunity, defined in the negative as no differences in treatment according to characteristics (such as race or national origin) that are considered illegitimate (Berne & Stiefel, 1984, p. 17). Other analysts treat equal opportunity as a condition of horizontal equity, the position taken in this text.

Virtually all studies of school finance equity deal only with the horizontal dimension (including equal opportunity). The lack of agreement on "appropriate" treatment for abnormal populations makes the analysis of vertical equity very difficult, if not impossible; nevertheless, recognition of the concept is very important in designing school finance policy.

The most comprehensive treatment of equity in school finance has been made by Berne and Stiefel (1984). They organize their analysis around four questions:

1. What is the makeup of the groups for which school finance systems should be equitable?
2. What services, resources, or, more generally, objects should be distributed fairly among members of the groups?
3. What principles should be used to determine whether a particular distribution is equitable?
4. What quantitative measures should be used to assess the degree of equity? (p. 7)

In reference to the first question, two groups have been the focus of studies of school finance equity, schoolchildren and taxpayers. Alternative concepts involved in the analysis of equity for children as identified by Berne and Stiefel (1984) are shown in Figure 12.2.

The objects to be distributed equitably among schoolchildren are divided into inputs, outputs, and outcomes. Inputs are the resources used in the schooling process. They may be measured in dollars or actual amounts of physical resource employed. Dollar inputs are the most commonly used, and they may be analyzed as revenues and/or expenditures. Revenues may be subdivided according to source; expenditures may be subdivided according to purpose (e.g., operating expenditure or instructional expenditure). Some categories of revenues and expenditures are of greater interest than others from a policy perspective, and the selection needs to be made with care. Berne and Stiefel also recommend the use of price-adjusted dollars to correct for regional variations which exist within many states and among states.

Inputs may also be measured by the actual amount of physical resources available such as pupil–adult ratios, average class size, characteristics of teachers, and number of library books. The advantage of using measures of actual resources is that the measurements are not affected by regional price variations or inflation over time. On the other hand, the major disadvantage is that there is no satisfactory way of aggregating quantities of different resources.

Outputs and outcomes relate to goals and objectives of schooling. Outputs represent the immediate products of the schools, often measured in terms of pupil achievement and behavioral changes. Outcomes include such long-range effects of schooling as lifetime earnings and quality of life.

The list of possible objects of analysis is almost infinite and there is no general agreement on what inputs, outputs, and outcomes should be equitably distributed. Objects selected for analysis need to be closely related to the stated or implied purposes of the policy being analyzed.

Figure 12.2 conceptualizes school finance equity in terms of objects of concern and the principles of horizontal and vertical equity and equal opportunity; it also lists various statistics policy analysts use to assess the degree to which distributions of inputs satisfy equity principles. Those most commonly used are described in the next section.

A portrayal of concepts related to taxpayer equity would look similar to Figure 12.2 except for objects of analysis. In evaluating taxpayer equity, the primary interests are tax rates and revenue generated.

Alternative for Each Component

Component of
Equity Concept

Who?
The Group
Children

What?   *Inputs*   *Outputs*   *Outcomes*
The Object   Dollars   Student Achievement   Earning Potential
              Price-adjusted   Behavioral Output Measures   Income
              Dollars   Satisfaction
              Physical
              Resources

How?   *Horizontal Equity*   *Vertical Equity*   *Equal Opportunity*
The   Equal Treatment   Unequal Treatment of Unequals   No Discrimination on the Basis
Principle   of Equals   More of the Object to the Needier   of Property Wealth in School
              Minimize Spread   District or Other Categories
              in Distribution   Minimize Undesirable Systematic
                                                                         Relationships

How much?   *Univariate Dispersion*   *Relationship*
The   Range   Simple Correlation
Summary   Restricted Range   Simple Slope
Statistic   Federal Range Ratio   Quadratic Slope
              Relative Mean Deviation   Cubic Slope
              The McLoone Index   Simple Elasticity
              Variance   Quadratic Elasticity
              Coefficient of Variation   Cubic Elasticity
              Standard Deviation of Logarithm   Constant Elasticity
              Gini Coefficient   Adjusted Relationship Measure from Simple Regression
              Atkinson's Index   Adjusted Relationship Measure from Quadratic Regression
              Theil's Measure   Adjusted Relationship Measure from Cubic Regression
                                                   Implicit Weight
                                                   Averaged Implicit Weight

Figure 12.2. Berne and Stiefel's Alternative Concepts of School Finance Equity for Children. (*Source:* R. Berne and L. Stiefel. [1984]. *The Measurement of Equity in School Finance: Conceptual, Methodological, and Empirical Dimensions.* Baltimore, MD: The Johns Hopkins University Press, p. 9. Reprinted by permission.)

MEASURING EQUITY

Two categories of statistics used for assessing equity are discussed in this section. The most commonly used measures of dispersion of a single object include range, coefficient of variation, McLoone index, and Gini coefficient. Measures of relationships among two or more objects include correlation coefficient, slope, and regression coefficient.[1]

---

[1]Technical definitions are not provided in this text for standard statistics, that is, mean, standard deviation, correlation coefficient, and regression coefficient. Readers desiring such technical information are referred to a basic statistics textbook.

To illustrate the concepts behind each statistic, Table 12.1 presents a set of values for 20 hypothetical school districts representing two hypothetical states. The districts are arranged in ascending order according to the object of interest, in this case, expenditure per pupil. Each district has 100 pupils and each state has 2,000 pupils. The mean and median expenditure per pupil for both states is $3,450 and the range is the same, $2,500 to $4,400; distributions within that range vary considerably, however. Data are also presented for property values per pupil and percentage of minority students.

Dispersion of a Single Object

Range.   The spread between the highest and lowest expenditure districts in both states is $1,900 (see Table 12.1). On the surface, this would suggest comparable equity; but on closer examination, one can see that the distribution of expenditures among districts is quite different because of differing property values and tax rates. Districts in State A are evenly distributed across the range, whereas districts in State B cluster more closely around the median ($3,450).

One way of eliminating the distortion of outlying cases is to use a restricted range— say between the 10th and 90th percentiles. The restricted range for State A is $1,500 (from $2,700 in District 3 to $4,200 in District 18). The smaller restricted range for State B ($700) reflects the greater equity we observed by inspection.

The restricted range provides a simple, easily understood way of comparing equity in two or more states at a given time; but because of the historic effects of inflation, restricted range does not provide accurate comparisons over time. To illustrate, if five-year comparisons are to be made and costs double every five years, districts would have to double their expenditures to provide the same level of services. This would increase the range for both states to $3,800, and the restricted range for State A would increase to $3,000 and for State B to $1,400. Both sets of statistics suggest that equity has suffered in both states, especially within State A, in spite of the fact that the actual distribution of services has not changed.

To correct for the effects of inflation, the federal range ratio was developed. It divides the restricted range for the middle 90 percent of students (eliminating from consideration the top and bottom 5 percent) by the value of the object (in the case of our illustration, expenditure per pupil) for the pupil at the fifth percentile. Since both of our states have 2,000 students, we remove from consideration 100 students at the top and bottom of the expenditure range in each state, that is, Districts 1 and 20. For State A, the restricted range becomes $1,700; when this is divided by the expenditure for the student at the fifth percentile, $2,600, the federal range ratio is 0.65. For State B, the federal range ratio is 0.26, calculated as ($3,850 − $3,050)/$3,050. The smaller the ratio, the greater the equity. Perfect equity (all districts with the same expenditure) results in a federal range ratio of zero. When the impact of inflation is equal for all districts, the ratio remains unchanged even though the values of the objects of analysis increase over time.

Coefficient of Variation.   Although it is easy to compute and to understand, the range statistic is determined by only two cases in a distribution. A statistic like the standard deviation, which encompasses all cases, is preferable. The standard deviation measures the extent of dispersion of the cases in a distribution about its mean. In a normal distribution, one-third of the cases fall between the mean and 1 standard deviation above the

TABLE 12.1. Equity-related Data for Two Hypothetical States, Each with 20 Districts and 2,000 Students

District Number	Pupils		Percentile	State A			State B		
	Number	Accumulative Number		Expenditure per Pupil	Full Property Value per Pupil	Percentage Minority	Expenditure per Pupil	Full Property Value per Pupil	Percentage Minority
1	100	100	5	$2,500	$ 50,000	10	$2,500	$ 45,000	41
2	100	200	10	2,600	45,000	48	3,050	60,000	64
3	100	300	15	2,700	60,000	1	3,100	55,000	29
4	100	400	20	2,800	62,000	50	3,150	70,000	50
5	100	500	25	2,900	55,000	11	3,200	62,000	19
6	100	600	30	3,000	70,000	1	3,250	85,000	20
7	100	700	35	3,100	75,000	20	3,300	80,000	48
8	100	800	40	3,200	68,000	11	3,350	100,000	1
9	100	900	45	3,300	80,000	16	3,400	90,000	10
10	100	1,000	50	3,400	90,000	17	3,450	105,000	20
11	100	1,100	55	3,500	85,000	41	3,450	120,000	11
12	100	1,200	60	3,600	100,000	64	3,500	110,000	22
13	100	1,300	65	3,700	95,000	3	3,550	130,000	11
14	100	1,400	70	3,800	110,000	7	3,600	115,000	7
15	100	1,500	75	3,900	120,000	20	3,650	150,000	16
16	100	1,600	80	4,000	115,000	29	3,700	130,000	17
17	100	1,700	85	4,100	130,000	19	3,750	140,000	7
18	100	1,800	90	4,200	140,000	7	3,800	180,000	0
19	100	1,900	95	4,300	135,000	0	3,850	175,000	1
20	100	2,000	100	4,400	150,000	22	4,400	200,000	3

mean. Another one-third fall between the mean and 1 standard deviation below the mean. Ninety-five percent of the cases fall within 2 standard deviations above and below the mean. The standard deviations of the expenditure per pupil measure for states A and B are $592 and $391, respectively. The smaller statistic for State B indicates greater equity.

The standard deviation suffers from the same problem as the range in that it is sensitive to changes in scale. The solution is similar to that used in correcting the range to get the federal range ratio; the standard deviation is divided by the mean of the distribution, producing the coefficient of variation. The coefficients of variation for states A and B are 0.17 and 0.11, respectively. The smaller statistic for State B indicates greater equity. If all districts in a state spent exactly the same, the coefficient of variation would be zero.

The Gini Coefficient. Economists use the *Lorenz curve* to illustrate inequalities in income; it is equally useful in illustrating inequities related to educational resources. The Lorenz curves for states A and B are shown in Figure 12.3. The horizontal axis represents the percentage of pupils and the vertical axis represents the percentage of total expenditure. Perfect equity is represented by the diagonal that bisects the quadrant; 25 percent of the pupils would have access to 25 percent of the total expenditures, 50 percent of the pupils would have access to 50 percent of the total expenditures, and so on. In reality, for State A, the first 25 percent of the pupils have access to only 19.6 percent of the total expenditures; thus, the Lorenz curve, representing the actual distribution, sags below the diagonal. The greater the area between the ideal (diagonal line which represents perfect equity) and the actual distribution (Lorenz curve), the greater the inequity.

The extent of inequity is measured quantitatively by dividing the area between the Lorenz curve and the diagonal by the area of the triangle formed by the diagonal, the *x*-axis and the right side of the graph. The resulting ratio is known as the Gini coefficient (Berne & Stiefel, 1984, pp. 66–68).

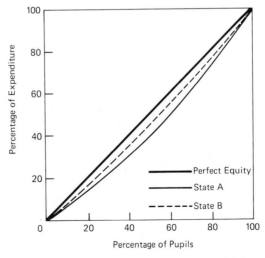

Figure 12.3. Lorenz Curve for Expenditures and Pupils for States A and B

In the case of perfect equity, the actual distribution line would be superimposed on the diagonal. The area between the two lines would be zero, as would the Gini coefficient. If total expenditures were available to students in only one district, the case of greatest inequity, the line of actual distribution would follow the x-axis to the right side of the graph and upward to the (100 percent, 100 percent) coordinate; the Gini coefficient would be 1.0. In our example, the Gini coefficients for states A and B are .10 and .05, respectively. The smaller coefficient for State B represents greater equity.

The McLoone Index.   The statistics discussed to this point measure attributes of the total distribution. Such statistics are appropriate in evaluating policies in which the intent is to treat all individuals in the group alike. But few state finance plans are intended to accomplish this goal. More typically, for example, foundation and flat grant plans, states attempt to ensure a basic level of support above which districts are free to spend to the extent local resources permit. The McLoone index is designed to assess equity under these latter assumptions (Harrison & McLoone, 1960).

The McLoone index is the ratio of (1) the sum of the actual expenditures of all districts at or below the median expenditure for the state to (2) what expenditures would be if all such districts actually spent at the median level. Unlike previous statistics, perfect equity is represented by 1.00 and the greatest amount of inequity is represented by zero. For states A and B, the McLoone indices are 0.855 and 0.992, respectively. The *higher* index for State B represents *greater* equity.

Relationship

All of the statistics in the previous section address equity in terms of a single object. There are instances, however, when we are interested in relationships, or the lack thereof, between two or more objects (variables). Berne and Stiefel's equal opportunity dimension represents such a class. Here we are interested in the relationship between an object of distribution, such as expenditure per pupil, and a characteristic of children, such as race or family income.

To measure the impact of percentage equalizing and guaranteed tax base programs, it is also necessary to resort to relationship analyses. These finance programs are not intended to eliminate differences in expenditures among pupils but rather to uncouple the linkage between expenditures and the wealth of districts and/or tax rates.

Correlation Coefficient.   The strength of the relationship between two variables is commonly described by the Pearson product moment correlation coefficient. The coefficient ranges in size from -1.00 to $+1.00$. A zero coefficient indicates no relationship between the two variables—the desired state in analyses of equal opportunity. A coefficient of 1.00 (either positive or negative) indicates a perfect correspondence between the two variables; there is no unexplained variation. A positive coefficient indicates that the two variables increase in size together; a negative coefficient indicates that as one variable increases in size, the other variable decreases.

Figure 12.4 shows the scattergrams and regression lines of expenditures against the percentage of minorities for states A and B. For State A, the plots are widely scattered, suggesting no relationship between the two variables. This is confirmed by a low correlation coefficient (-0.12) and nearly horizontal regression line. There is a very definite pattern

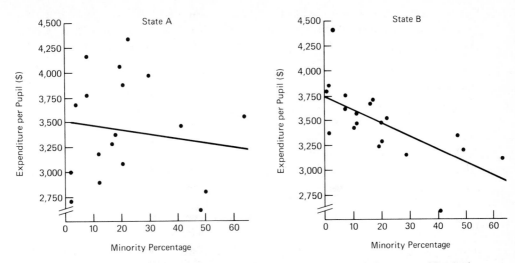

Figure 12.4. Scattergram and Regression Line of Expenditure per Pupil with Percentage Minority for States A and B

for State B, however. As the percentage of minorities increases, the expenditure per pupil decreases. This is reflected in a high and negative correlation coefficient of −0.68 and a downward-sloping regression line. In terms of equal opportunity, State A is more equitable than State B.

Slope.   Figure 12.5 shows the scattergrams of expenditure per pupil against property value per pupil for states A and B and their respective regression lines. The correlation in both states is high and positive, 0.98 and 0.93, respectively. But, from an equity perspective, the situation is more serious in State A than in State B because an increase in property value per pupil is associated with a much larger increase in expenditure per pupil in State A. In other words, the slope of the regression line for State A is steeper than for State B. The slope of a distribution measures the increase in the dependent variable (*y*-axis), on

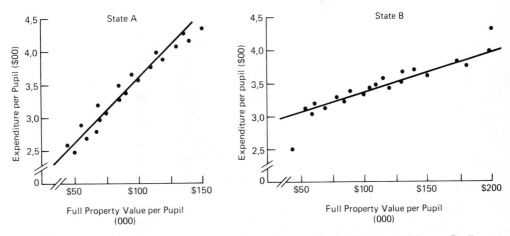

Figure 12.5. Scattergram and Regression Line of Expenditure per Pupil with Property Value per Pupil for States A and B

average, associated with one unit increase of the independent variable (*x*-axis). The slope is measured by the regression coefficient, and the larger the slope, the greater the inequity. The regression coefficients for states A and B are .02 and .01, respectively.

Multivariate Methods.   Despite a variety of conflicting equity goals, virtually all analyses of school finance equity have used univariate or bivariate methods as described in previous sections. A primary exception is a study by Garms (1979) which pioneered the use of multivariate techniques to permit the comparison of states or one state with itself over time. Garms points out that "any attempt to separately analyze the effects of multiple goals must have a way of separating the allocations for those goals" (p. 416). Since this is impossible in an accounting sense (a single allocation may be directed toward several ends), Garms employs multivariate statistics which enable "the separation of provisions for differences in district wealth from differences in tax rate, and both of these from differences in provision for needs and costs" (p. 435). Although acknowledging some problems that may limit its applicability, Garms promotes the method as providing a more comprehensive view of school finance systems than any previously proposed.

Equity Measures for the States

Moving from the hypothetical to the actual, Table 12.2 shows selected equity measures of per pupil operating expenditures and rankings by states for 1984–1985 as reported by Schwartz and Moskowitz (1988). The ranking among states corresponds quite closely for the federal range ratio (FRR), the coefficient of variation (CV), and the McLoone index (MI). Each of these is unidimensional, that is, involving only one variable, expenditure per pupil. On these measures, Iowa, Nevada, and West Virginia are among the most equitable states, and Alaska, Montana, and Vermont are among the least equitable.

There is generally a substantial discrepancy, however, between a state's ranking on the first three measures and the correlation coefficient (CC), which is bivariate, measuring the strength of the relationship between expenditure per pupil and property valuation per pupil. Expenditures in New Hampshire, for example, are shown to be quite inequitable by the first three measures, but the state's school expenditures are among the most equitable on the correlation coefficient measure. Apparently there is considerable variation among districts in New Hampshire in expenditure per pupil, but state policy has succeeded in decoupling this variation from variation in property values.

New York is shown to have an inequitable variation among districts in expenditure per pupil by the FRR and the CV, and the CC indicates that this variation is directly related to variation in property valuation. On the other hand, New York is among the most equitable of states on the MI, indicating that low-spending districts cluster close to the expenditure for the median child in the state. The inequity shown by other measures indicates that some districts spend well above the median, whereas the high equity rating of the MI shows that few districts spend far below the median.

In using these measures of equity, it is important to recognize that each examines a somewhat different aspect of the concept. The measure selected for evaluating the effectiveness of a particular policy should correspond closely to the intended effect of that policy.

TABLE 12.2. Measures of Equity for the States, 1984–1985

State	Federal Range Ratio		Coefficient of Variation		McLoone Index		Correlation Coefficient*	
	Ratio	Rank	Coefficient	Rank	Index	Rank	Coefficient	Rank
Alabama	.40	9	.11	7	.95	7	.21	6
Alaska	1.57	49	.52	48	.85	45	.39	15
Arizona	.58	22	.17	26	.91	28	.31	13
Arkansas	.48	14	.13	13	.92	18	−.07	2
California	.43	13	.13	12	.92	20	NA	NA
Colorado	.34	6	.12	9	.88	41	.63	36
Connecticut	.74	32	.21	36	.91	31	.31	13
Delaware	.41	11	.13	11	.84	48	.56	29
Florida	.37	7	.09	4	.91	12	.55	27
Georgia	.80	36	.18	31	.90	34	.31	13
Idaho	.56	21	.17	25	.91	22	.56	29
Illinois	1.21	46	.25	44	.85	46	.63	36
Indiana	.53	20	.15	16	.90	33	.16	3
Iowa	.25	3	.07	2	.96	3	.40	17
Kansas	.59	25	.16	21	.93	13	.70	41
Kentucky	.63	28	.17	24	.94	10	.75	43
Louisiana	.41	12	.13	10	.93	11	.52	26
Maine	.59	26	.18	30	.90	32	NA	NA
Maryland	.60	27	.15	17	.94	9	.80	45
Massachusetts	.91	43	.24	42	.90	35	.56	29
Michigan	.75	33	.20	35	.86	44	.39	15
Minnesota	.58	23	.16	20	.92	17	.58	34
Mississippi	.52	19	.17	23	.91	27	.44	20
Missouri	.96	44	.22	37	.90	38	.65	38
Montana	1.44	47	.74	49	.84	47	NA	NA
Nebraska	.90	41	.23	40	.86	43	.69	40
Nevada	.19	1	.10	6	1.00	1	.57	32
New Hampshire	.97	45	.27	45	.91	25	.21	6
New Jersey	.76	34	.18	29	.87	42	.30	11
New Mexico	.48	15	.16	18	.91	26	.17	4
New York	.89	39	.22	38	.96	2	.48	25
North Carolina	.33	5	.09	3	.94	8	.42	19
North Dakota	.80	35	.28	46	.91	29	.20	5
Ohio	.90	40	.24	41	.90	36	.47	23
Oklahoma	.59	24	.19	33	.92	21	.28	9
Oregon	.50	17	.13	14	.92	14	.26	8
Pennsylvania	.89	38	.19	34	.89	40	.45	21
Rhode Island	.32	4	.11	8	.91	24	.41	18
South Carolina	.40	8	.10	5	.96	5	−.09	1
South Dakota	.66	30	.18	32	.90	37	.47	23
Tennessee	.70	31	.18	27	.89	39	.71	42
Texas	.64	29	.18	28	.91	23	.60	35
Utah	.40	10	.16	22	.92	15	.57	32

(Continued)

TABLE 12.2. *(Continued)*

State	Federal Range Ratio		Coefficient of Variation		McLoone Index		Correlation Coefficient*	
	Ratio	Rank	Coefficient	Rank	Index	Rank	Coefficient	Rank
Vermont	.47	48	.31	47	.82	49	NA	NA
Virginia	.90	42	.22	39	.91	30	.56	29
Washington	.51	18	.16	19	.95	6	.47	23
West Virginia	.22	2	.07	1	.96	4	.65	38
Wisconsin	.50	16	.14	15	.92	16	.29	10
Wyoming	.88	37	.24	43	.92	19	.75	43
Mean	.65	—	.19	—	.91	—	.45	—

*District per pupil property valuation and district operating expenditures. (*Source:* Compiled from various tables reported in M. Schwartz and J. Moskowitz. [1988]. *Fiscal Equity in the United States, 1984–85.* Washington, DC: Decision Resources Corporation. Reprinted by permission.)

FINDINGS FROM STUDIES OF SCHOOL FINANCE EQUITY

Interest in school finance equity peaked during the decade of the 1970s and has waned since then. Beginning in the 1960s with the civil rights movement and the related compensatory educational programs of President Johnson's Great Society, concerns over the equality of educational opportunities dominated the educational agenda. In the 1970s, attention focused on the equity of state school finance systems as litigation was brought in over half the states challenging their constitutionality (as discussed in Chapter 11). The 1970s were dubbed the decade of school finance reform as state after state restructured their finance systems to improve their equity—under court order and at their own initiative. Researchers from several disciplines joined with jurists, policymakers, interest groups, task forces, and national foundations during this decade to sharpen the understanding of equity problems and to evaluate the effectiveness of attempted remedies.

In the 1980s, national attention shifted to excellence and efficiency; interest in equity declined but did not disappear completely. In reviewing approximately 140 pieces of equity research since 1980, Barro (1987) referred to them as a "holding operation" (p. 3). He found no newly developed concepts or methods of analysis. The decline in research on school finance equity parallels a decline in the demand and funding for such studies over that which was available in the prior decade.

One might suspect—or at least hope—that, with all the attention given to it during the 1970s, there would have been substantial gains in school finance equity, but this does not seem to be the case. Berne and Stiefel (1983) reviewed equity studies using data going back to 1940. They found that, prior to the school finance reform movement, from 1940 to 1960, horizontal equity improved in an overwhelming number of states. School district consolidation and increased state aid contributed indirectly to this goal. During the 1960s and 1970s, when concern over equity was an explicit issue, the trend was toward a worsening of equity.

Brown, Ginsburg, Killalea, Rosthal, and Tron (1978) also found that disparities in per pupil expenditures among districts in most states actually increased or remained constant between 1970 and 1975. The pattern was somewhat different among the 19 states that reformed their finance structures during that period. Ten of the 19 had reduced interdistrict disparities, although 4 remained among the 10 states with the greatest expenditure disparities. In 1970, reform states as a group had larger wealth-related disparities than nonreform states; by 1975, the situation was reversed.

Brown and co-workers (1978) take the most optimistic interpretation of their rather disappointing findings by pointing out that the reform states were "swimming against a tide of increasing disparity" (p. 212) and that inequities might have been even worse without reform. The lack of greater progress toward expenditure equity was attributed by them, in part, to the desire to provide property tax relief. Considerable relief was provided and did lead to lower correlations between wealth-related measures and expenditures in reform states. It is also of interest that the six states with the least expenditure disparity operate relatively few school systems of comparatively large size.

A study by Carroll (1979) also provided little cause for optimism. He analyzed the impact of school finance reform in five states, California, Florida, Kansas, Michigan, and New Mexico, and concluded that the results were mixed: "Reform has brought about some advances; but judged in relation to the major goals that the proponents of reform have championed, the scattered victories of reform appear somewhat hollow" (p. v). Reform reduced the linkage between district wealth and expenditure per pupil and it increased statewide spending for education. Reform did not, however, change the distributions of revenues and instructional expenditures. In other words, taxpayer equity appears to have increased, but child equity did not.

Carroll (1979) offered two probable explanations for the ineffectiveness of the reforms in equalizing spending outcomes and opportunities. The first was that states simultaneously pursued diverse and conflicting objectives such as equalizing revenues, preserving some local control over spending, trying to avoid the political hazards of cutting back high-spending districts, providing tax relief, and avoiding excessive growth in state spending for schools. Carroll's second explanation is that each state made add-ons and adjustments to the basic plan; these policy changes had disequalizing effects. Kansas, for example, introduced income tax rebates and Florida introduced a cost-of-living adjustment. Both procedures provided more state aid to wealthy districts than to poor ones.

Of the states studied by Carroll, only New Mexico showed substantial equity among districts on both revenues and expenditures. New Mexico has assumed virtually full responsibility for school finance, while retaining the district as the operating unit (see Table 8.7, School Finance Plan 6). No local discretion is allowed to school districts in setting tax rates or determining revenues. In a subsequent study, King (1983) attributed New Mexico's wealth neutrality to property tax limitations, uniform tax rates, and a steady increase in state financial support. Commenting on King's conclusions, Hickrod and Goertz (1983) speculate that "midwestern and northern state legislators will find these restrictions on local control too high a price to pay for greater education finance equity" (p. 3).

In a similar vein, Lake (1983), in a study of the public school systems in the four provinces of Atlantic Canada, found the greatest equity in New Brunswick, where schools are fully funded by the province.

> If one focuses on Nova Scotia and New Brunswick, a policy implication of some importance arises. New Brunswick, the full provincial assumption case, made more progress toward equity than did Nova Scotia, the combined provincial/local funding case. However, in terms of sufficiency, Nova Scotia made more progress than did New Brunswick. This suggests, though it certainly does not rigorously prove, that the act of full provincial (state) assumption may help the educational community accomplish the equity goal at the expense of the sufficiency goal. (p. 460)

Using the federal range ratio and coefficient of variation for all states except Montana, Berne (1988) analyzed changes in horizontal equity for the periods 1970–1977 and 1977–1985. For the first period, Berne found that horizontal equity improved by more than 5 percent on both measures in 6 states and worsened in 18 states. For the 1977–1985 period, equity improved by more than 5 percent in 14 states and became worse in 16 states. For the two periods combined, 1970–1985, 11 states improved and 18 became worse. He concluded that, even though it is a very crude indicator, there is some evidence that equity fared somewhat better during the more recent period. "During the first period, the general trend was towards worsening equity, while during the second period equity ups and downs were more nearly equal" (p. 177).

Heinold (1983) studied the impact of federal aid on horizontal equity of revenues among states between 1960 and 1981. The coefficient of variation and the McLoone index showed movement toward greater equity among the states during the decade of the 1960s and movement away from equity during the 1970s. Federal aid enhanced equity for all years, but especially during the period from 1965 through 1976.

In discussing the policy implications of his research, Heinold (1983) contrasts the situation in the United States to that in Canada.

> During the period of years analyzed, the federal government portion of the funding of elementary and secondary public education ranged from three to nine per cent of the total revenues. In contrast, the level of funding by the federal government of Canada was 19 per cent of the total revenues in 1978, representing an effort greater than twice that of the United States government. This increased effort on the part of Canada has been rewarded by reductions in disparities among provinces to levels below the levels of disparities among states in the United States. While progress has been made in movement toward equity among the provinces in Canada, a reverse trend in the United States has been identified by this study. (p. 473)

Bezeau (1985) used public school systems of the United States and Canada to test relationships between equity and centralization of governance. Unlike Lake (1983), Bezeau found that centralization had no effect on the magnitude of expenditures per pupil; but it did appear to be associated with greater equity, although the relationship was small.

The lack of progress in bringing about greater equity in expenditures per pupil has also been confirmed, with a few exceptions, by numerous single-state studies. Hickrod, Chaudhari, and Hubbard (1983) report on a longitudinal study of the reform adopted by the state of Illinois in 1973. They found that the state had made progress toward established equity goals of less expenditure disparity and greater wealth neutrality for a period of three years; then a reversal began to set in. They attribute the reversal primarily to "smaller and smaller amounts of new state funds that were available after the middle of the 1970s" (p. 34).

Berne and Stiefel (1984) analyzed data for the state of Michigan for the years 1970 through 1978. They found that criteria of horizontal equity started and ended at about the same point but worsened during the middle of the period. With respect to equal opportunity, they found that children in wealthier districts enjoyed better educational provision. They also found inequities by region of the state and with respect to race.

Kearney and Chen (1989) continued the study of Michigan where Berne and Stiefel left off—extending the analysis to 1985. Although 1984 and 1985 had brought about some improvements in most criteria of horizontal equity, they concluded that the goal was much further from attainment in 1985 than it had been in 1979. Equal opportunity continued to worsen over the period of the analysis.

Berne and Stiefel (1984) also conducted a study of equity in New York for a 14-year period beginning in 1965 and ending in 1978. On most criteria of horizontal equity, they found improvements to about 1969; conditions then worsened for five years and remained level or improved slightly during the remainder of the period. As a result, there was greater inequity in educational opportunities in the latter part of the 1970s than in the 1960s. There were consistently positive correlations between indicators of levels of educational services and equalized property wealth per pupil in all of the 14 years the study covered.

Goertz (1983) found that in spite of a doubling in state aid in New Jersey, disparities in per pupil expenditures had not narrowed significantly. She concluded,

> New Jersey has created a "zero-sum" game in its state aid program. State policy makers must examine the alternatives carefully: increase state support of education, redistribute funds within the state pot, or accept the movement away from greater equity in the system. (p. 489)

Minnesota reformed its school finance structure in 1971, one of the first states to do so. Krupey and Hopeman (1983) studied the impact on equity using data for 1972–1973, 1978–1979, and 1981–1982. They found that during the first seven years of reform, the state had made progress toward reducing revenue and tax rate disparities and in making the system more fiscally neutral. As a result of subsequent legislation and increased use of referendum levies, however, revenue disparities increased and the system became less fiscally neutral.

Three states that seem to have bucked the general trend toward greater inequity are New Mexico (King, 1983), Texas (Verstegen, 1987), and South Carolina (Cohn & Smith, 1989). The success of the New Mexico reforms in terms of equity has already been discussed.

Verstegen (1987) analyzed data from the Texas school finance system for 1976 through 1986 to determine if legislative action had improved financial equity in the wake of the Supreme Court decision in 1973 (*San Antonio Independent School District* v. *Rodriguez*, 1973). She found that all measures studied (coefficient of variation, federal range ratio, restricted range, McLoone index, simple correlation, and elasticity) showed improvement, indicating greater equity over time. The improvement was even greater when the upper 5 percent of students ranked by revenue per pupil were excluded from the analysis.

The South Carolina study examined the impact of the state's Educational Finance Act of 1977 on wealth neutrality only. Cohn and Smith (1989) concluded that the act had had a marked impact on wealth neutrality and that unlike many other states, it appears that the positive impact has sustained itself at least through 1985. They suggest that the success may be attributed to the nature of the aid formula itself and to increased state resources that have been made available to school districts.

DISCUSSION AND CONCLUSIONS

On the whole, the evidence leaves little room for optimism about substantial improvements in school finance equity. Ironically, the greatest improvements in equity were made when equity was not an explicit issue. Jones (1985) points to the necessity of considering allocation and distribution patterns across time, covering periods of policy reform and periods of stability, to monitor the sustained effects of efforts to change public policy.

The most likely explanation of the lack of predictability of policy initiatives on equity appears to be that equity is only one of many policy objectives of school finance reform. Equity collides with the goals of improving adequacy and efficiency, meeting educational needs, maintaining local control, providing property tax relief, and increasing public choice (Brown & Elmore, 1982). Hickrod and Goertz (1983) observe,

> A legislative body is the appropriate forum to try to strike a balance between conflicting values such as equity and local control. It may have to be aided and abetted from time to time by the judicial branch, but it is the right place to make the decision. A compromise will be struck for these conflicting values for a given point in time with certain knowledge that that compromise is never final. The voice of the people speaks through a majority which is forever shifting through time. Each successive legislative body will change the balance point between egalitarian goals and libertarian goals and they will continue to do that so long as the democratic process is allowed to freely operate. (p. 418)

The 1980s saw a shift in favor of libertarian goals. Efficiency and standards moved to center stage; "school finance reform" became "school reform," and there was little recognition that the two might in some way be connected. Existing fiscal and educational inequities among school districts may be exacerbated by allocations of state funds for educational reform which are not equalized for wealth variation among districts. Without equalized funds, wealthy, high-spending districts will be able to initiate program reforms in ways and in magnitudes that are denied to poor, low-spending districts.

> There is little recognition in the "education reform" literature that school districts differ in their abilities and need for additional funding, to implement these reforms. These reports, for example, leave the impression that all districts are equally affected by the economic disincentives for persons to enter and stay in the teaching profession. They ignore that low salaries and poor working conditions for teachers tend to be greater problems for poor school districts than for those endowed with large tax bases and that these factors may produce teaching staffs of unequal quality. . . . Some children may actually be harmed by these reforms if equity issues are ignored. Higher educational standards, without more [resources], are likely to result in more educational failures,

more retentions in grade, and more drop-outs. And the children most affected are minority and poor. (Long, 1986, pp. 341–342)

With constrained resources, equity objectives can be realized only through the reallocation of resources. This is a very unpopular strategy—and politically dangerous. "Leveling up" poor districts, on the other hand, is very expensive and may be possible only with higher or new taxes—also unpopular and politically dangerous.

SUMMARY

In this chapter, we have discussed the philosophical levels of equity and their horizontal and vertical dimensions. The more common criteria used by policy analysts in measuring equity were described. Studies monitoring the progress, or the lack of such, toward school finance equity goals since World War II were reviewed. In the remaining chapters of this section, we shift our attention to other objects of social policy such as liberty, efficiency, and economic growth, which compete for the attention of policymakers.

ACTIVITIES

1. Using data from a state or region, calculate several of the equity measures described in this chapter. Which are the most relevant measures for evaluating school finance policy in that state or region? What are the implications for policy initiatives?
2. Selecting the equity measure which most closely reflects the policy objectives of the state studied in Activity 1, calculate the measure for each year over a period of a decade or more. Examine the trends in relation to changes in state policy. Have the policies been effective? What changes, if any, would you propose in state policy to improve school finance equity?

REFERENCES

Alexander, K. (1982). Concepts of equity. In W. W. McMahon & T. G. Geske (Eds.), *Financing education: Overcoming inefficiency and inequity* (pp. 193–214). Urbana: University of Illinois Press.

Barro, S. M. (1987). *School finance equity: Research in the 1980s and the current state of the art.* Washington, DC: Decision Resources Corporation.

Berne, R. (1988). Equity issues in school finance. *Journal of Education Finance, 14,* 159–180.

Berne, R., & Stiefel, L. (1983). Changes in school finance equity: A national perspective. *Journal of Education Finance, 8,* 419–435.

Berne, R., & Stiefel, L. (1984). *The measurement of equity in school finance: Conceptual, methodological, and empirical dimensions.* Baltimore: Johns Hopkins University Press.

Bezeau, L. M. (1985). Level and inequality of per pupil expenditure as a function of finance centralization. Paper presented at the Annual Meeting of the Canadian Society for the Study of Education, Montreal, Quebec, Canada.

Brown, L. L., Ginsburg, A. L., Killalea, J. N., Rosthal, R. A., & Tron, E. O. (1978). School finance reform in the seventies: Achievements and failures. *Journal of Education Finance*, *4*, 195–212.

Brown, P. R., & Elmore, R. F. (1982). Analyzing the impact of school finance reform. In N. H. Cambron-McCabe & A. Odden (Eds.), *The changing politics of school finance* (pp. 107–138). Cambridge, MA: Ballinger.

Carroll, S. J. (1979). *The search for equity in school finance: Summary and conclusions*. Santa Monica, CA: Rand Corporation.

Cohn, E., & Smith, M. S. (1989). A decade of improvement in wealth neutrality: A study of school finance equity in South Carolina, 1977–1986. *Journal of Education Finance*, *14*, 380–389.

Garms, W. I. (1979). Measuring the equity of school finance systems. *Journal of Education Finance*, *4*, 415–435.

Goertz, M. E. (1983). School finance in New Jersey: A decade after *Robinson v. Cahill. Journal of Education Finance*, *8*, 475–489.

Goertz, M. E. & Hickrod, G. A. (1983). Evaluating the school finance reforms of the 1970s and 1980s: Part 2. *Journal of Education Finance*, *9*, 1–4.

Harrison, F. W., & McLoone, E. P. (1960) *Profiles in school support 1959–60* (Misc. 32). Washington, DC: U.S. Department of Health, Education, and Welfare.

Heinold, D. (1983). Impact of federal monies on equity among states in K–12 public school finance. *Journal of Education Finance. 8*, 461–474.

Hickrod, G. A., Chaudhari, R. B., & Hubbard, B. C. (1983). The decline and fall of school finance reform in Illinois. *Journal of Education Finance, 8*, 17–38.

Hickrod, G. A., & Goertz, M. E. (1983). Introduction: Evaluating the school finance reforms of the 1970s and early 1980s. *Journal of Education Finance*, *8*, 415–418.

Jones, T. (1985). *State fiscal behavior: A study of resource allocation and distribution*. Paper presented at the Annual Meeting of the American Educational Research Association, Chicago.

Kearney, C. P., & Chen, L. (1989). Measuring equity in Michigan school finance: A further look. *Journal of Education Finance*, *14*, 319–367.

King, R. A. (1983). Equalization in New Mexico school finance. *Journal of Education Finance*, *9*, 63–78.

Krupey, J. E., & Hopeman, A. (1983). Minnesota school finance equity, 1973–1982. *Journal of Education Finance*, *8*, 490–501.

Lake, P. (1983). Expenditure equity in the public schools of Atlantic Canada. *Journal of Education Finance*, *8*, 449–460.

Long, D. C. (1986). An equity perspective on educational reform. In V. D. Mueller & M. P. McKeown (Eds.), *The fiscal, legal, and political aspects of state reform of elementary and secondary education* (pp. 325–344). Cambridge, MA: Ballinger.

Morris, W. (Ed.). (1969). *The American heritage dictionary of the English language*. Boston: Houghton Mifflin.

San Antonio Independent School District v. *Rodriguez*, 411 U.S. 1 (1973).

Schwartz, M., & Moskowitz, J. (1988). *Fiscal equity in the United States, 1984–85*. Washington, DC: Decision Resources Corporation.

Verstegen, D. A. (1987). Equity in state education finance: A response to *Rodriguez. Journal of Education Finance, 12*, 315–330.

CHAPTER 13

Efficiency, Adequacy, and Economic Growth

Equity is an important consideration in developing public policy; but concerns over equity must be balanced against other objects of public policy. Policy analysts have developed modestly sophisticated measures for evaluating the success of public school finance policy in meeting numerous societal objectives. In this chapter, we examine existing systems of education within the context of efficiency, adequacy, and economic growth. More specifically, we look at the role played by educational institutions in incorporating technological advances into the economy and the implications for economic growth. We also look at the efficiency of the operation of schools and the economies and diseconomies of scale experienced by them.

A primary stimulus of the school reform movement launched in the 1980s was concern over the ability of the United States to compete in international markets. Fears stemming from economic competition replaced the threat of military conflict as a fundamental stimulant of social action. The technological revolution, which had been gaining momentum since World War II, emerged into a new social and economic order which substantially upgraded educational requirements for those who were to participate fully in it. Coupled with the demographics of fewer entrants into the labor market and longer working careers, business and industrial leaders recognized how critical it is for workers to have the basic mathematical and language skills needed to provide a foundation for learning other skills (McDonnell & Fuhrman, 1986). As a result, improving the efficiency of the educational system was seen as critical to any strategy for strengthening the nation's economic condition.

Chapter 2 refers to efficiency and economic growth as "derived values" that enhance the realization of the ethical values of liberty, equality, and fraternity. Efficiency and economic growth became primary objectives of public policy only during the twentieth century. Efficiency is improved by increasing desired outputs produced from available resources or by maintaining a given level of output while using fewer resource inputs. Improving efficiency also improves productivity, a similar concept.

Hanushek (1986, p. 1166) defines economic efficiency as "the correct share of input mix given the prices of inputs and the production function." Production function is defined as the causal relationship between inputs and outcomes. He cautions against confusing economic efficiency and technical efficiency. The latter considers only the process of combining inputs to produce outcomes and does not take into account the prices of inputs. Both concepts are important considerations in designing educational systems, but the primary focus in this chapter is on economic efficiency.

There are two aspects of economic efficiency, external and internal. External efficiency considers contributions to national economic growth made by the scarce resources allocated by society to various sectors of production. With respect to education, we are interested in the returns on investments in education relative to the returns from other investment opportunities. Internal efficiency relates to the allocation of resources *within* educational enterprises in order to maximize output (e.g., achievement, skill development, and behavioral and attitudinal changes among students) from the resources committed.

The decision matrix of Chapter 2 poses a series of questions to be resolved by policymakers. Analyses of external efficiency assist in making decisions about the amount of resources to be committed to and among educational services and in determining the level of societal investment in population quality in order to promote economic growth. In other words, studying external efficiencies addresses the issues of how much to spend for educational services and of which kinds of services to provide in order to create the greatest amount of economic benefit. Internal efficiency relates to the means by which educational services are produced. Studying internal efficiency is directed toward gaining the maximum benefit from the resources committed to an institution. Whereas internal efficiency is studied through educational production functions and cost-benefit and cost-effectiveness analysis, external efficiency is studied through rate of return analysis.

We begin this chapter by looking at external efficiencies. The theory of human capital is described, and studies estimating the contribution of investments in education to national economic growth are reviewed. The discussion of external efficiency ends with an assessment of the adequacy of expenditures for education in the United States. The second section of this chapter focuses on internal efficiency. In reviewing evidence from studies of both the technical and economic efficiency of schools, it is concluded that there are significant opportunities for redirecting resources already committed to education in such ways that the outcomes of schools would be substantially improved.

EXTERNAL EFFICIENCY

In Parts II and III of this book, we discussed the processes by which public revenues are raised for the support of educational services and how they are distributed to school districts. The discussion assumed that we know how much we want to spend on education. As developed in Part I, deciding how much to spend for educational services is largely a political process and the decisions made may not be efficient from an economic—or technical—perspective. Economic analysis can estimate the efficiency by which we are using scarce resources for educational services; but economic efficiency is only one of many often-conflicting objectives of social policy—although an important one. Other social concerns must be balanced against the concern for improving economic efficiency.

The rate of return on investments in education has been studied at two levels: the individual and society. The human capital approach assumes that schooling endows an individual with knowledge and skills which enable him or her to be more productive and thereby receive higher earnings. This result is, of course, beneficial to the individual. The accumulation of benefits derived by all individuals is beneficial to society as a whole through greater total production, higher tax yields, and possible spillover benefits which may contribute to a generally improved quality of life for all.

The concept of human capital has been recognized as an essential force for economic progress since the beginning of economics as a discipline. In his *Wealth of Nations*, first published in 1776, Adam Smith (1976) included this concept in his definition of fixed capital. He referred to

> . . . the acquired and useful abilities of all the inhabitants or members of the society. The acquisition of such talents, by the maintenance of the acquirer during his education, study, or apprenticeship, always costs a real expense, which is capital fixed and realized, as it were, in his person. Those talents, as they make a part of his fortune, so do they likewise of that of the society to which he belongs. The improved dexterity of a workman may be considered in the same light as a machine or instrument of trade which facilitates and abridges labour, and which, though it costs a certain expense, repays that expense with a profit. (p. 298)

Despite the early recognition of the concept of human capital, and of education as a formal means for developing it, the investment aspects of education were almost completely neglected by economists through the nineteenth and the first half of the twentieth centuries (Blaug, 1970).

Causes of Economic Growth

In analyzing causes of economic growth, economists have traditionally considered only increases in the quantity of labor and physical capital and have largely ignored improvements in their quality. Schultz (1981, p. 11) condemns this assumption that capital is qualitatively homogeneous. Claiming that each form of capital has specific properties, he introduces the concept of variation in the quality of both physical and human capital.

Schultz, who received the Nobel Prize in economics in 1979 for his work with developing countries, is generally credited with sparking a renewed interest in human capital theory. He turned attention to the economics of education, observing that the concepts commonly used to "measure capital and labor were close to being empty in explaining the increases in production that occur over time" (Schultz, 1963, p. viii). Schultz was referring to the fact that quantitative increases in labor and physical capital accounted for less than one-third of the rate of economic growth in the United States between 1929 and 1957 (Blaug, 1970).

In attempting to explain the cause of the remaining two-thirds of growth, called "the residual," Schultz (1963) drew an analogy between additions of stock to physical capital and increases to the amount of education available in the population at large. Schultz's thesis was that traditional measures of labor and capital understated the true investment.

By adding together income forgone by students in pursuing an education (opportunity costs) and the resources used in providing it, he estimated total annual investment in education during the period 1900 to 1956. Although the value of physical capital, that is, nonhuman wealth, was still over twice as much as that of human capital stock in 1956, the value of human capital had grown 849 percent over the period whereas nonhuman wealth had grown only 450 percent. Schultz concluded that the unexplained economic growth

> . . . originates out of forms of capital that have not been measured and consists mainly of human capital. . . . The economic capabilities of man are predominantly a produced means of production and . . . most of the differences in earnings are a consequence of differences in the amounts that have been invested in people. (pp. 64–65)

Extending Schultz's analysis, Benson (1978, p. 72) estimated that the net "investment" through education accounted for approximately 21 percent of the growth in real national income of the United States between 1929 and 1957—or nearly half of the residual.

Denison (1962) took a different approach to measuring the contribution of education to economic growth. He examined earning differentials attributable to education as a measure of its economic value rather than the costs of input factors, as did Schultz. Denison estimated an aggregate statistical model of the American economy and then attempted to resolve the unexplained residual of economic growth. A more recent analysis indicated that real national income grew at an average annual rate of 3.85 percent between 1948 and 1969 (Denison, 1974). Of that amount, Denison attributed 0.41 percent to the higher level of education of the work force and 1.19 percent to advances in knowledge and technology. This latter factor is closely related to the mission of educational institutions—especially higher education—since advances in technology and growth in knowledge are among the products of colleges and universities, although not in their domain exclusively.

Rate of Return Approach

The Schultz and Denison studies showed that education contributed significantly to economic growth. Those studies did not address the adequacy of investment in education, however. With respect to education, rate of return analysis is intended to inform policymakers about how much to spend on different kinds of programs (Benson, 1978, p. 91). Rate of return analysis compares the profit (increased earnings) to the expense of acquiring knowledge and skills including earnings forgone (opportunity costs) in the process.

When supply and demand for persons possessing a particular set of knowledge and skills are in equilibrium, the rate of return approximates that which is generally expected from other types of investments. If the rate is much higher, there is an apparent shortage of persons with these skills, permitting them to command higher wages. This encourages more people to acquire similar training and enter the work force until wages and the rate of return drop to the expected level. If, on the other hand, the rate of return is much lower than that which can be obtained from other investments, there is a surplus of persons with similar skills—more than the market can absorb. Competition for employment drives wages down, discouraging people from acquiring such skills until supply again equals demand and the rate of return from earnings over expenditures equals the expected level. (See the discussion of the interaction between supply and demand in Chapter 1, pp. 5–9, and in Murphy & Welch, 1989.)

Table 13.1 reports the private and social rates of return calculated by McMahon and Wagner (1982) for three levels of postsecondary education in five types of institutions in the United States. The estimates are based on a sample of 2,765 white, male students surveyed in 1976. Private returns are calculated by comparing net cost to students attending each type of institution with expected earnings of students graduating from each type of institution. Net costs include fees, books and supplies, and income forgone minus part-time earnings, grants, scholarships, and tuition wavers. With 10 percent serving as a benchmark of expected return from investments generally (i.e., in stocks, bonds, real estate, etc.), securing a bachelor's degree from public and private research universities and comprehensive four-year colleges appears to provide an exceptional return for the individual. Large returns are also derived from earning master's degrees from private research universities and doctoral or professional degrees from public research universities.

Private rates of return are good guides for individual behavior, but social policy must consider total cost. The price of an education in both public and private institutions is subsidized by public funds and/or private endowments. To calculate the social rate of return, the amount of subsidization to individuals (e.g., the difference between tuition charged to the student and actual cost, scholarships, and fellowships) is also included. Doing so reduces the rates of return, as shown in Table 13.1. As a general rule, social

TABLE 13.1. Percentage of Private and Social Rates of Return to Educational Investment of White Males by Degree Level and Type of Institution Attended

Degree	Research University		Comprehensive Four-Year College		Liberal Arts College
	Public	Private	Public	Private	Private
	Mean Private Rate of Return				
Bachelor's	19.0	26.0	21.0	18.5	8.7
Master's	9.6	17.3	6.2	−0.7	7.7
Doctor's/ Professional	19.3	11.6	9.0	−1.8	10.3
	Mean Social Rate of Return				
Bachelor's	15.5	18.01	17.7	15.9	7.1
Master's	8.0	15.0	4.8	−1.4	6.9
Doctor's/ Professional	17.9	10.5	9.3	−5.0	10.1

(*Source:* From W. W. McMahon and A. P. Wagner. [1982]. "The Monetary Returns to Education as Partial Social Efficiency Criteria." In W. W. McMahon and T. G. Geske [Eds.], *Financing Education: Overcoming Inefficiency and Inequity.* Urbana: University of Illinois Press, p. 167.)

rates of return to education are lower than private rates of return—an argument for having the cost of higher education paid in part by students' tuition and not totally subsidized by government.

Evaluating social policy by computing internal rates of return for investments in education was the focus of the pioneering work by Becker (1960, 1964). He estimated the social rate of return for white, male college graduates to be between 10 percent and 13 percent. Assuming that rates for college dropouts and nonwhites would be lower, he estimated the rate for all college entrants to be between 8 percent and 11 percent. Becker (1964, p. 121) concludes, "The rates on business capital and college education seem, therefore, to fall within the same range." Rates of return for high school students were higher, and they were highest for elementary students. Becker cautions, however, that adjustments for differential ability would probably reduce or eliminate the differences in rates among levels of schooling. Estimates of rates of return from expenditures for secondary and higher education between 1939 and 1976 showed that the returns were falling, although not by a large amount (Woodhall, 1987). This trend appears to have reversed itself dramatically during the 1980s (Murphy & Welch, 1989) because of increasing demand for highly trained workers and correspondingly higher wages relative to workers with less training.

Others have also discovered a lower rate of return for higher levels of education. Hanoch (1971, p. 205) found a rate of return in excess of 100 percent for Caucasians completing elementary school. The rate of return for a high school graduate fell to 16 percent, and for a college graduate holding a baccalaureate degree to 12 percent. All are respectably above the 10 percent benchmark. In another study, Davis and Morrall (1974) estimated rates of return ranging from 5 percent to 11 percent for graduate education. They concluded, "The implications for policy makers are that relatively more funds should be devoted to the lower levels of schooling than are now being allocated" (p. 51).

Psacharopoulos (1973, 1981, 1985) surveyed rate of return studies across nations. Findings from his 1985 study for 61 countries are summarized in Table 13.2. This table shows the average private and social rates of return for primary, secondary, and higher education for countries grouped according to stage of development and region. All results, except for the social rate of return for higher education for advanced and intermediate countries, are at or above the 10 percent benchmark commonly expected from capital investment. Returns of 8 percent and 9 percent for higher education may indicate that

TABLE 13.2. International Comparison of Social and Private Rates of Return by Education Level, Stage of Development, and Region

Region/ Country Type	Rate of Return (in percent)					
	Social			Private		
	Primary	Secondary	Higher	Primary	Secondary	Higher
Africa	26	17	13	45	26	32
Asia	27	15	13	31	15	18
Latin America	26	18	16	32	23	23
Intermediate	13	10	8	17	13	13
Advanced	NA	11	9	NA	12	12

Note: NA = not available because of lack of a control group of illiterates. (Source: G. Psacharopoulos. [1985]. "Returns to Education: A Further International Update and Implications." Journal of Human Resources, 20, 586.)

advanced countries and intermediate are spending at or slightly above the optimum for those levels, given the current organization of education.

The highest returns at all levels of development are for primary education. This is a function of the interaction between the low cost of primary education relative to other levels and the substantial productivity differential between primary school graduates and those who are illiterate. Rates of return at all levels of education tend to decline with development. This is explained by the relative scarcity of human-to-physical capital within each group of countries. In all countries, private returns exceed social returns because education is publicly subsidized. Not shown in Table 13.2, Psacharopoulos (1985) found that expenditures on education of women were at least as profitable as were those for men and that expenditures on the general curriculum produced higher yields than did those for vocational education. The optimal investment strategy for countries appears to vary according to level of economic development and other demographic characteristics.

Spending Levels for Education

When 10 economically advanced countries are compared in educational expenditures as a percentage of gross national product (GNP), the United States stands about in the middle, consuming 6.8%. Educational spending consumes more of the GNP in Sweden (9.1%), Canada (7.1%), the Soviet Union (7.4%), and the Netherlands (6.9%). Countries that devote proportionally less include Australia (6.8%), France (5.8%), Japan (5.6%), the United Kingdom (5.2%), and West Germany (4.6%) (U. S. Department of Commerce, 1983, 1988).

Investment in education in the United States for the period 1959 through 1986 is reported in Table 13.3 along with the percentage of the total population enrolled in precollegiate and higher education. The percentage of GNP spent for all educational institutions rose steadily from 4.8 percent in 1959 to 7.5 percent in 1970. It then declined to 6.7 percent in 1980 and 1985, rising to 6.9 percent in 1988. The peak allocation of

TABLE 13.3. Percentage of Gross National Product (GNP) Spent on Education and Percentage of Total Population Enrolled in Educational Institutions, 1959–1986

Year	Elementary and Secondary Schools		Higher Education		Total	
	Percentage of GNP	Percentage Enrollment of Population	Percentage of GNP	Percentage Enrollment of Population	Percentage of GNP	Percentage Enrollment of Population
1959	3.4	23.0	1.4	2.0	4.8	25.0
1965	4.0	24.9	2.2	3.0	6.2	28.0
1970	4.7	25.0	2.7	4.2	7.5	29.2
1975	4.7	23.1	2.7	5.2	7.4	28.2
1980	4.1	20.3	2.6	5.3	6.7	25.6
1985	4.0	18.8	2.7	5.1	6.7	24.0
1986	4.1	18.8	2.7	5.2	6.8	24.0
1988	NA	18.7	NA	5.1	6.9	23.8

(*Sources:* U.S. Department of Education, Office of Educational Research and Improvement. [1988]. *Digest of Education Statistics, 1988,* Tables 3 and 23. Washington, DC: U.S. Government Printing Office; U.S. Department of Commerce, Bureau of the Census. [1988]. *Statistical Abstract of the United States, 1988,* p. 7. Washington, DC: U.S. Government Printing Office.)

GNP to education (1970) corresponds to the peak in the percentage of the population enrolled in educational institutions.

For elementary and secondary school expenditures, the percentage of GNP rose from 3.4% in 1959 to 4.7% in 1970 and 1975. Although expenditure per pupil continued to increase in constant dollars (see Figure 3.2), the percentage of GNP declined to 4.0% in 1985. In 1986, the figure stood at 4.1%. The decline in the percentage of GNP spent for education can be attributed at least in part to the smaller proportion of the total population attending elementary and secondary schools. Enrollment peaked in 1970 at 25.0%, subsequently declining to 18.7% in 1988.

The percentage of GNP spent on colleges and universities rose from 1.4% in 1959 to 2.7% in 1970. Since 1970 the statistic has ranged between 2.6% and 2.7%. Actual enrollments in postsecondary education rose from 3,640,000 in 1959 to 8,581,000 in 1970 and have continued to increase to over 12 million. The percentage of the population enrolled in higher education in 1959 was 2.0%. It rose to 5.3% in 1980 and has remained relatively stable between 5.1% and 5.2% since then, parallelling the leveled percentage of GNP devoted to those institutions.

As already noted, rate of return studies suggest that advanced countries, including the United States, are probably spending at or near the optimal rate for educational services, given the existing state of educational technology. If the rate of investment in education were increased, it can probably be best justified at the elementary level. The percentage of GNP allocated to education may continue to fluctuate along with the proportion of the population engaged in schooling.

INTERNAL EFFICIENCY

We now turn to consideration of the efficiency with which resources allocated to schools are used in the education of children. The ability of such resources to improve individual and societal welfare will be enhanced or diminished according to the efficiency with which they are used. If the tentative policy conclusion of the previous section is correct that the United States (along with other advanced nations) is spending about the optimal amount on education, given the technology currently in use, then improvements in the educational performance of American students will depend more on improving the internal efficiency of schools and school systems than on the addition of more resources.

Studies of the efficiency of schooling which relate outcomes to inputs are generally traced to the report by James Coleman (1966), *Equality of Educational Opportunity* (EEO). This line of study has been classified under the economic terms "educational production functions" and "input-output analysis," even though the studies are not the exclusive domain of economists. Such research has been pursued in an effort to improve educational productivity.

A production function may be conceptualized as a set of relations among possible inputs and a corresponding set of outputs for a firm or industry—in this case, schools and education (Burkhead, 1967, p. 18). According to Hanushek (1987), "A firm's production possibilities are assumed to be governed by certain technical relationships, and the production function describes the maximum feasible output that can be obtained from a set of inputs" (p. 33).

A production function may be expressed simply as output (O) being a function of inputs (I):

$$O = f(I)$$

With respect to schooling, outputs include behavioral and attitudinal changes in pupils induced through school activities. Inputs studied have ranged from student background (e.g., socioeconomic status of family, student IQ, and previous achievement) to material provision (e.g., expenditures, teacher characteristics, and characteristics of buildings) to process (e.g., time on task, teaching methods, and student–teacher interactions).

The existence of such relationships assumes that there is a common underlying technology in education, an assumption that may come as a surprise to many educators because production technologies in education are inexact. Nevertheless, the sameness of American schools (and schools around the world, for that matter) lend credibility to an assumption of an implicit technology. School buildings are typically arranged with classrooms and certain ancillary spaces such as libraries, auditoriums, and gymnasiums. Each classroom is usually presided over by one teacher only, and there is a large degree of similarity in the ways teachers organize and manage classrooms.

The assumption of a common technology was tested by Klitgaard and Hall (1975). They examined the distributions of residual student achievement once the effects of socioeconomic status had been controlled statistically. They hypothesized that if there were schools functioning under different pedagogical assumptions, the distribution of residuals would be multimodal. Although their findings were not definitive, they concluded that it is reasonable to assume that all schools, including highly effective ones, function under the same pedagogical technology.

Monk (1989) identified two traditions with respect to the study of the production of educational services. The first attempts to estimate the parameters of the educational production function. The second is less developed but uses "the production function as a gateway to broader economic theories and reasoning that can be used to guide inquiry" (p. 31). After discussing studies that illustrate the first tradition, we want to address educational production in the light of several related topics: effective schools research, psychological studies, comparisons with private schools, and economies and diseconomies of scale.

Estimating Educational Production Functions

The EEO study (Coleman, 1966) was one of the first and remains one of the largest production function studies ever attempted. It involved over one-half million students in 4,000 schools and thousands of teachers. It is perhaps the best-known and most controversial of all the input-output studies. The controversy extends not only to its conclusions, that schooling has little potential for closing the achievement gap between white and minority students, but also to the methodology used. Among the critics are Bowles and Levin (1968), Cain and Watts (1970), and Mostellar and Moynihan (1972). The shortcomings of the early studies have been summarized by Benson (1988):

> They used achievement scores at one point in time. The unit of analysis was the school, or even the school district, and the consequent averaging of results weakened the power

of the findings. Each variable on the right-hand side of the regression (independent and control variables) was treated as wholly independent of the other variables. In considering the effects of teacher characteristics on achievement, no account was taken of the fact that the child's progress in school is not determined by his or her current teacher alone but is the result of the cumulative actions of all the teachers in the child's school career. (p. 365)

Criticisms of the EEO led to more sophisticated studies and conceptualizations of the problem (Bridge, Judd, & Moock, 1979; Dreeben & Thomas, 1980; Madaus, Airasian, & Kellaghan, 1980; Murnane, 1975; Rutter, Maughan, Mortimore, & Ouston, 1979; and Summers & Wolfe, 1975). Murnane (1983) discusses the methodological learnings gained from more than fifteen years of controversy. These include the importance of using the individual child as the unit of observation rather than the school or school district. In estimating educational effectiveness, a child's progress as measured by growth in achievement over a period of time should be used instead of the student's achievement level at one point in time. School resources should be measured according to what is available to a specific child and not according to average resources in the school or school district. Murnane also points out that the types of resources examined have broadened and have become more sophisticated. Early studies focused on factors that were easy to quantify such as school size, the number of books in the library, and student–teacher ratios. More recent studies have focused on the quality and intensity of student–teacher interaction, student time on task, and characteristics of teachers and classmates.

A most significant finding of studies of school effectiveness, beginning with the EEO study, is the very strong relationship between family background and pupil achievement. The relationship is so strong that findings of these studies have frequently been misinterpreted to mean that schools have relatively little impact on pupil achievement. It is well documented that schools have not been very effective in closing achievement gaps among racial and ethnic groups and among socioeconomic classes; nevertheless, schools do have enormous impacts on the development of all children.

Even the most gifted of children learn—or at least develop—their basic academic skills in schools. Children come into schools as nonreaders and leave with varying levels of literacy skills. Similar statements could be made about mathematics, writing, and other academic skills, as well as about knowledge and attitudinal development. Mayeski and co-workers (1972) stated it very well in a reanalysis of the EEO data: "Schools are indeed important. It is equally clear, however, that their influence is bound up with that of the student's background" (p. ix). Very little of the influence of schools can be separated from the social backgrounds of their students, and very little of the influence of social background on learning can be separated from the influence of the schools. According to Mayeski, schools, as presently constituted, produce the greatest amount of learning and foster the greatest amount of motivation among students from higher socioeconomic strata and white and oriental-American backgrounds; the effect of schools on achievement and attitudes grows for all groups with the length of time a student spends in school.

Hanushek (1987) has identified in the literature some 144 separate studies of production relationships in education completed since the EEO study in 1966. Two recent reviews of such studies have been made by Hanushek (1986) and MacPhail-Wilcox and King (1986). Per pupil expenditures generally correlate positively with student achievement and socioeconomic status. But these two reviews agree that when appropriate statistical control is made for socioeconomic status, relationships for all students between per pupil expenditure levels and achievement are weak or nonexistent. Teachers' verbal ability appears to provide the strongest relationship between any school characteristic and student achievement. Schools with higher-achieving students, when socioeconomic factors are taken into account, quite consistently pay their teachers more than lower-achieving schools. The evidence is mixed, however, concerning any relationships between teachers' experience and advanced degrees and pupil achievement. This lack of relationship is particularly important given that the structure of most salary schedules is based on longevity in teaching and degrees and/or graduate credits earned (see Chapter 14).

Hanushek (1986) and MacPhail-Wilcox and King (1986) differ sharply in their interpretations of findings with respect to relationships between class size and achievement. Hanushek unequivocally states that there is no consistent evidence of a relationship. According to Hanushek, of 112 studies investigating teacher–student ratios, only 9 found positive statistically significant relationships with achievement. Fourteen found significant negative relationships; in the remaining 89 studies, there were no significant relationships.

MacPhail-Wilcox and King (1986), on the other hand, found "overwhelmingly" significant relationships between small classes and higher achievement. They observe that relationships are stronger, however, where opportunities for direct student–teacher instructional interaction are measured more precisely, that is, the size of the specific class, specific staff-to-pupil ratios versus average class size, and overall pupil–teacher ratios. They also note that the presence of paraprofessionals appears to enhance opportunities for pupil–adult interactions and improved achievement.

A meta-analysis of class size research by Glass and Smith (1979) may provide an explanation for the conflicting conclusions of Hanushek and MacPhail-Wilcox and King. Glass and Smith found little relationship between class size and achievement over the normal range of classes. In smaller classes *where instruction was individualized*, better achievement was found. Unless the mode of teaching in small classes is individualized, however, the potential of the small class is not realized.

Benefits of small classes and individualized instruction seem to be more critical to the good performance of at-risk children than for other children (MacPhail-Wilcox & King, 1986). The negative effect of ability grouping is also greatest for at-risk children. Ability grouping is associated with lower performance among low socioeconomic and minority students, whereas heterogeneous grouping is associated with higher achievement among such students and does not harm the achievement of high socioeconomic and majority students (Summers & Wolfe, 1975).

In light of their analysis of findings from production function studies, MacPhail-Wilcox and King (1986) are concerned that a primary focus of recent educational reform efforts is on improving the credentials of teachers and standardizing teacher approaches to the instruction of all students.

> Focused largely on teacher quality, these educational reforms overlook the obviously important role which students play in learning. They fail to acknowledge that teacher effects vary by the type of student, instructional context, and organizational characteristics. Despite more than fifteen years of research confirming these propositions, current reforms proceed on unwarranted assumptions that uniform teacher qualities, standard

pedagogical practices, and existing organizational arrangements will eradicate the purported ills of public education. (p. 191)

Effective Schools Research

Effective schools research is a variation of the production function approach. Education production functions research takes a normative approach in studying school efficiency. Effective schools research focuses on exceptions and usually ignores cost considerations; thus, its findings relate more to technical efficiency than to economic efficiency. It consists largely of case studies of schools and classrooms which have unusually positive effects on pupil achievement in order to identify practices which might cause or contribute to that effectiveness (Brookover & Lezotte, 1979; Edmonds, 1979; Jackson, Logsdon, & Taylor, 1983; Reed, 1985; Venezsky & Winfield, 1980; Weber, 1971).

Effective schools are characterized by effective classroom teaching practices, which include high teacher expectations, good classroom management techniques, and greater time on task than one would find in most schools. These schools are also characterized by strong leadership, usually in the person of the principal, which provides for the coordination of the instructional program at the building level in a manner which is tightly coupled but not bureaucratic. The principal appears to be a key factor in establishing a common school culture and sense of community consisting of "shared goals; high expectations for student performance; mechanisms to sustain motivation and commitment; collegiality among teachers, students, and the principal; and a school-wide focus on continuous improvement" (Odden & Webb, 1983, p. xiv). Given current assumptions about schooling, effective schools research is identifying some ways for schools to make more efficient use of the resources they already have.

Psychological Studies

Psychological studies of schooling also have important implications for the technical efficiency of schools. For the most part, like effective schools research, psychological studies do not take into account the price of inputs. Psychological studies have produced results which provide grounds for greater optimism about the impact of schools on pupil achievement than those conducted by economists and sociologists.

Walberg (1984) analyzed nearly 3,000 investigations of the productive factors in learning conducted during the 1970s. Table 13.4 summarizes his synthesis of the effects of various approaches to improve teaching and learning. Relationships between achievement and socioeconomic status (.25) and peer groups (.24) are relatively small when compared with many of the instructional interventions reported in Table 13.4.

Reinforcement (1.17) and instructional cues and feedback (.97), both of which are psychological components of mastery learning, rank first and fourth in effect. Acceleration programs (1.00), which provide advanced activities to high-achieving students, ranked second. Ranking third was reading training (.97), which involves skimming, comprehension, finding answers to questions, and adjusting reading speeds. Other highly effective techniques include cooperative learning (.76), graded homework (.79), and various approaches to individualized instruction. High teacher expectations (.28) have a moderate impact, as do time on task, advanced organizing techniques, morale or climate of the

TABLE 13.4. Walberg's Syntheses of Effects on Learning

Method	Effect	Size
Reinforcement	1.17	xxxxxxxxxxx
Acceleration	1.00	xxxxxxxxxx
Reading Training	.97	xxxxxxxxxx
Cues and Feedback	.97	xxxxxxxxxx
Science Mastery Learning	.81	xxxxxxxx
Graded Homework	.79	xxxxxxxx
Cooperative Learning	.76	xxxxxxxx
Class Morale	.60	xxxxxx
Reading Experiments	.60	xxxxxx
Personalized Instruction	.57	xxxxxx
Home Interventions	.50	xxxxx
Adaptive Instruction	.45	xxxxx
Tutoring	.40	xxxx
Instructional Time	.38	xxxx
Individualized Science	.35	xxxx
Higher-Order Questions	.34	xxx
Diagnostic Prescriptive Methods	.33	xxx
Individualized Instruction	.32	xxx
Individualized Mathematics	.32	xxx
New Science Curricula	.31	xxx
Teacher Expectations	.28	xxx
Computer Assisted Instruction	.24	xx
Sequenced Lessons	.24	xx
Advance Organizers	.23	xx
New Mathematics Curricula	.18	xx
Inquiry Biology	.16	xx
Homogeneous Groups	.10	x
Class Size	.09	x
Programmed Instruction	−.03	−.
Mainstreaming	−.12	−x.

Note: The x symbols represent the sizes of effects in tenths of standard deviations. (*Source:* H. J. Walberg. [1984]. "Improving the Productivity of America's Schools." *Educational Leadership, 41* [8], Figures 3–4, p. 24. © 1984 by ASCD.)

classroom, and home interventions. Reduced class size has little impact at all. Walberg (1984) concludes,

Synthesis of educational and psychological research in ordinary schools shows that improving the amount and quality of instruction can result in vastly more effective and efficient academic learning. Educators can do even more by also enlisting families as partners and engaging them directly and indirectly in their efforts. (p. 26)

Comparisons with Private Schools

Coleman returned to the center stage of school policy controversy with his comparison of public and private high schools (Coleman, Hoffer, & Kilgore, 1981). His methodology involved multiple regression similar to his EEO study and other production function studies. Data for this study came from High School and Beyond, an ongoing national study of achievement and other high school outcomes sponsored by the National Center for Education Statistics and carried out by the National Opinion Research Center. More than 50,000 students in over 1,000 schools participated in the initial data collection in 1980. The schools included approximately 80 Catholic and 25 other private high schools. Because of the small number of "other" private high schools, few conclusions were drawn concerning them. Longitudinal data became available in 1984.

The researchers found greater achievement growth in verbal skills and in mathematics between the sophomore and senior years among students in Catholic high schools than in public high schools when statistical controls were made for differences in student background characteristics (Coleman & Hoffer, 1987). The magnitude of the difference was equivalent to one grade on average, and it was greater for minority, low socioeconomic status, and other at-risk students than for other students. No differences were found in science knowledge and civics. Coleman's conclusions have been challenged but not refuted by others (Alexander, 1987; Alexander & Pallas, 1987; Willms, 1987). The challenges reinforce our understanding of the subjectivity of even quantitative research. In reviewing Coleman's work and the challenges to it, Haertel (1987) concludes,

> Given our present state of knowledge, all of the authors' different choices are defensible. They are dictated by different *conceptions* of school policy, of the sources of individual differences in learning, of what is taught during the last two years of high school, and of appropriate public policy. (p. 16, emphasis added)

Haertel also points out that none of the analysts found public school achievement to be superior to that in Catholic schools; the argument was over the size of the Catholic school advantage and whether or not it was significant from a policy perspective. Noting this, Hoffer, Greeley, and Coleman (1987) discuss the policy implications of even no difference in achievement between the two sectors:

> It has often been assumed by American educators and educational researchers that Catholic schools were academically inferior—class room size was larger, teacher training was less professional, resources more limited, per-pupil cost far smaller, religious narrowness perhaps more restrictive to thought and imagination. It might have been an undisturbing finding that, for all their apparent weakness, Catholic schools were not worse than public schools. To suggest that in terms of academic outcomes that they might be somewhat better is such a reversal of the conventional received truth, that one might well have expected intense debate. (p. 86)

Hoffer, Greeley, and Coleman (1987) attribute the greater success of the Catholic schools to their higher demands on students. These schools place larger proportions of their students in the academic track including many who would be relegated to general or vocational tracks in public high schools. Catholic high schools also demand more course work, more advanced course work, and better discipline. The researchers found that at-risk pupils did especially well in Catholic schools and that the productive characteristics of this school climate could be successfully replicated in public schools.

> Catholic schools are especially beneficial to the least advantaged students: minorities, poor, and those whose initial achievement is low. For these students, the lack of structure, demands, and expectations found in many public schools is especially harmful. *Our*

analyses show that those public schools which make the same demands as found in the average Catholic school produce comparable achievement. (p. 87, emphasis added)

The description of the average Catholic high school culture sounds very much like that characterized by "effective" public schools.

Coleman and Hoffer (1987) attribute the ability of Catholic high schools to make greater demands on their students to their greater "social capital." Social capital, discussed in Chapter 7 in the context of partnerships and volunteerism, consists of the relationships between people. Social capital provides norms and sanctions, which in turn "depend both on social relations and the closure of networks created by these relations" (p. 222). The religious communities surrounding Catholic schools provide the social capital which is not found in most public and independent schools today.

In a simpler time, public schools were part of a functioning community; this is still the case in many rural areas, where achievement tends to be unexpectedly high given the relatively low average socioeconomic status of rural communities. But functional communities in metropolitan areas, where most Americans live, are no longer based on residence, as are public school attendance boundaries; functional communities have been replaced by value communities. Residential proximity is no longer the source of dense interaction and thus is incapable of providing public schools organized around residential proximity with norms, sanctions, and networks in support of the schools' educational missions. To bring significant amounts of social capital to public schools, Coleman and Hoffer (1987) urge choices among schools built around value communities: "Policies which would bring about expansion of choice should contain provisions that encourage the growth of social structures that can provide the social capital important to a school" (p. 243).

Chubb and Moe (1985) expanded the data base used by Coleman, Hoffer, and Kilgore to include organizational and environmental information. Their findings are discussed at length in Chapter 16 in reference to school-based management.

Economies and Diseconomies of Scale

If one assumes a universal educational production function, economies of scale are realized when average production costs decline as more units are produced or serviced. Conversely, there are diseconomies of scale when average production costs increase as more units are produced or serviced. These are important concepts in the efficient organization of educational enterprises.

School district consolidation is directed toward realizing economies of scale, whereas decentralization of large city school districts is directed toward avoiding diseconomies of scale. Likewise, during periods of declining enrollments, closing underutilized buildings is a strategy for minimizing operating costs. Reorganizing very large schools into "houses" or "schools within schools" is a strategy for realizing the benefits of both large and small units while minimizing their disadvantages. Interest in scale economies derive from concern over economic efficiency.

Policy implications drawn from studies on relationships between school and district size and pupil achievement and cost have taken a dramatic turn in recent years. From the beginning of this century through the 1960s, the overwhelming evidence seemed to support large schools and school districts in terms of economies and the higher number, diversity, and caliber of professional and administrative personnel which they could attract. These early studies were concerned primarily with inputs (costs) and gave little, if any, attention to outputs and ratios of outputs to inputs. As researchers began to take into account total cost and socioeconomic status of pupils, and to include measures of output such as achievement, pupil self-image, and success in college, economies of scale evaporated at relatively low numbers of pupils. The disadvantages of large size became readily apparent.

The new emphases in research on the relationships between size and quality of schooling may have been a byproduct of the disenchantment with large city schools in recent years. City educational systems had served through the 1950s as the standard for measuring the quality of educational opportunities. But in the 1960s and to the present, evidence of low cognitive pupil achievement, low attendance rates, and high dropout rates has surfaced in urban school systems. This finding, coupled with their inability to use substantial federal and state funds to raise significantly the achievement levels of most disadvantaged children, severely marred the image of urban schools. It now appears that, given present assumptions about how schools (and school districts) should organize, the relationships between size and quality of schooling are curvilinear. The benefits brought by larger enrollments increase to an optimal point and then decline following an inverted U-shaped curve (Fox, 1981; Riew, 1981, 1986).

Scale research has two foci: the district and the school. For very small districts, these are the same thing. Large districts have choices, however, as they may operate schools over a wide range of sizes. Thus, a large district may operate small schools as a matter of district policy, though most do not. Large schools also have the option of organizing "schools within schools" to secure the advantages inherent in both large and small schools.

What size should a school be? Barker and Gump (1964) were not specific, but they provided a useful guide as they concluded their classical work:

> The data of this research and our own educational values tell us that a school should be sufficiently small that all of its students are needed for its enterprises. A school should be small enough that students are not redundant. (p. 202)

Barker and Gump (1964) concluded that large school size has an undesirable influence on the development of certain personal attributes of students. Specifically, they found that in most large schools, leadership is dominated by just a few students, whereas in small schools proportionally more students take an active part. The actual proportion of students who participated in extracurricular activities and the satisfaction of students with their schooling clearly supported small, local schools over large, centralized ones.

Although more varieties of subjects are available to students in large schools, Barker and Gump (1964) observed that a given pupil participates in proportionally fewer of these electives than do students in small schools. They concluded, "If versatility of experience is preferred over opportunity for specialization, a smaller school is better than a larger one; if specialization is sought, the larger school is the better" (p. 201).

A 1986 study by the U.S. Department of Education updates the Barker and Gump findings. This study reports that participation rates in extracurricular activities were consistently greater for small high schools (200 or fewer seniors) than for large ones. Small schools also compared favorably with large schools with respect to course credits taken by students, hours of homework, test scores and grade average, and involvement in extracurricular activities (Sweet, 1986). Lindsay (1982), in another replication of Barker and Gump, using a representative national sample of 328 elementary schools, found higher participation in extracurricular activities, student satisfaction, and attendance in small schools (fewer than 100 in each grade level).

Newman (1981) reports the optimum size of secondary schools to fall in the range of 500 to 1,200 pupils. Student participation in school activities and general interaction are greatest, and vandalism and delinquency are lowest, in that range.

> The opportunity that small schools provide for sustained contact among all members is a significant safeguard against alienation. The larger the school, the more difficult it is to achieve clear, consensual goals, to promote student participation in school management, and to create positive personal relations among students and staff. (p. 552)

Goodlad (1984), in his comprehensive national study of *A Place Called School*, observes,

> Most of the schools clustering in the top group of our sample on major characteristics were small, compared with the schools clustering near the bottom. It is not impossible to have a good large school; it is simply more difficult. What are the defensible reasons for operating an elementary school of more than a dozen teachers and 300 boys and girls? I can think of none. (p. 309)

With respect to secondary school size, Goodlad writes,

> Clearly we need sustained, creative efforts designed to show the curricular deficits incurred in very small high schools, the curricular possibilities of larger schools, and the point where increased size suggests no curricular gain. . . . The burden of proof, it appears to me, is on large size. Indeed, I would not want to face the challenge of justifying a senior, let alone a junior, high of more than 500 to 600 students (unless I were willing to place arguments for a strong football team ahead of arguments for a good school, which I am not). (p. 310)

Current research clearly suggests that small schools have the edge over large schools. Berlin and Cienkus (1989), after co-editing an issue of *Education and Urban Society* devoted to the subject of the size of school districts, schools, and classrooms, concluded that "smaller seems to be better."

> Why does smaller seem to work better? . . . The literature on educational change repeats the answer. That is, people seem to learn, to change, and to grow in situations in which they feel that they have some control, some personal influence, some efficacy. Those situations in which parents, teachers and students are bonded together in pursuit of learning are likely to be the most productive. Small size by itself can only aid the complex process. (p. 231)

In Boyer's (1983) report of the Carnegie Foundation's study, *High School*, it is noted that research over the past several decades suggests that small schools provide greater opportunity for student participation and greater emotional support than large ones. Acknowledging the difficulty of knowing the exact point at which a high school becomes too large, Boyer proposes that schools enrolling 1,500 to 2,000 students are good candidates for reorganization into smaller units (using a school within a school concept). Turning to the issue of the small high school, Boyer raises this question:

> Can a small school provide the education opportunities to match the social and emotional advantages that may accompany smallness? We believe the preferred arrangement is to have bigness *and* smallness—a broad education program with supportive social arrangements. (p. 235)

Optimum school and district size is a function of desired standards, available technology, and governing structures. The criteria defining these have changed over time. In the past, providing diversity in the curriculum and support services at an affordable cost were the primary justifications for large, urban schools and rural school consolidation. Now the disadvantages of bigness and the virtues of smallness have been well documented. Additionally, technological advances characteristic of the "information age" have made it possible for any individual in almost any place to find curricular diversity easily. These developments combine to impel a reassessment of the large school policies of central cities and state school consolidation policies for rural areas. Fowler (1989) concludes,

> It is apparent that public school size and district size both influence schooling outcomes, and although other evidence of this relationship has accumulated, policy makers seem to ignore the finding and its significance. Much litigation has been undertaken to equalize expenditures per pupil, or to assure equivalent staff characteristics in an effort to increase learning; however, it appears that keeping schools relatively small might be more efficacious. (p. 21)

Schools of any size, but especially small schools, require support services which they cannot provide themselves in a cost-effective manner. In rural areas, such services are increasingly being provided through intermediate districts and other cooperative arrangements. This trend needs to be greatly accelerated if rural schools are to keep up with modern demands, but outright consolidation is no longer necessary.

Creation of regional service units greatly lowers the minimum functional size of schools and school districts by making it possible for a number of small schools and districts to provide jointly selected services none could provide alone. Occupational education and education of the severely handicapped are examples which involve relatively small proportions of enrollments. Regional centers also provide certain technological services with respect to educational television, interactive video, and computer-assisted instruction.

In enlarging the domain of decision making at the building level, and in reducing the domain of decision making at the district level, central city districts may begin to take on the characteristics of intermediate districts. In this respect, it is interesting to note that Illinois has radically changed the governance of education in Chicago (Hess, 1990). The new arrangement does away with the former Board of Education and places control of schools in the hands of school councils consisting of parents, other local residents, and teachers. Day-to-day authority resides in the hands of principals—who are selected by the councils. The councils also have authority to set the budget and to dismiss incompetent teachers. We see this as a precursor of things to come.

In summary, relationships between size and effectiveness and economy appear to be curvilinear. Although there are disadvantages in being very small, there are also disadvantages in being very large. There is little agreement on an optimal size, which appears to be a function of circumstances. The challenge before us is to provide stimulating learning environments with broad educational programs characteristic of large schools along with the supportive social structure characteristic of small schools.

Policy Implications for Improving Internal Efficiency

Studies relating to the efficiency of public schools indicate with great consistency that schools are not using the resources entrusted to them to full advantage. Given current organization and practice, the problem is not so much the lack of resources but rather the nature of available resources and the way in which they are being used.

Hanushek (1986, p. 1167) draws one simple policy conclusion from the production function studies: "increased expenditures, by themselves, offer no overall promise for improving education." He proposes that we stop requiring and paying for things that do not matter. Noting that about 70 percent of school costs are for professional services and that these are strongly tied to class size and teacher training and experience, Hanushek points out,

> There is little apparent merit for schools to pursue their ubiquitous quest for lower class sizes. Nor should teachers be required, as they are in many states, to pursue graduate courses merely to meet tenure requirements or to get an additional salary increment. More teacher experience by itself does not seem to have much value. (p. 1167)

The psychological and scale studies, effective schools research, and comparisons with private schools, in general, support the conclusions drawn by Hanushek. More important, they have identified instructional and organizational interventions which do affect achievement: structure, discipline, high demands, high expectations, and a supportive community. Most, if not all, of these interventions require no new resources but rather a redirection of existing resources.

The effective schools research, scale studies, and the Coleman works point to the importance of the social climate of schools. Coleman finds that building supportive climates is facilitated when schools are organized around value communities to which the families of children subscribe rather than around residential areas. This suggests that the prevailing neighborhood school policy be replaced with a policy of schools of choice and that district governance yield to greater involvement of parents and teachers in policymaking and the operation of schools.

Monk (1989) criticizes the direction that school effectiveness research has taken. According to Monk, the estimation approach to education production functions is, with a few exceptions, void of economic content because analysts have been forced to make so many simplifying assumptions. He finds the same fault with effective schools research and refers to it as "backwards-looking." Monk calls effective schools "sites of excellence

. . . making exemplary use of traditional, labor intensive instructional technologies" (p. 38). Effective schools accept all the parameters of the present system, and the methodology condemns them only to refine the current system's very labor-intensive and expensive organization and practice rather than to permit them to discover and use new technologies.

Instead of becoming further involved in increasingly sophisticated applications of econometrics which hold very limited value for educational policymakers, Monk (1989) encourages the application of economic reasoning to educational problems. "The goal . . . is instead to apply economic reasoning to the manifold instances of resource allocation that have bearing on educational activities" (p. 38). Using the production function as analogy, we could say that Chapters 14 through 17 analyze the financial implications of proposals for the fundamental restructuring of the organization and delivery of educational services. We examine personnel remuneration policies in relation to teacher supply and demand as well as teacher motivation and quality in Chapter 14. We then turn our attention in Chapter 15 to the potential of educational technology in terms of relative prices, substitution effects, and tradeoffs. The next two chapters examine the financial implications of policies directed toward enhancing educational choice and the social objective of liberty. Chapter 16 focuses on the implications for school finance policy in enhancing the sovereignty of education providers, and Chapter 17 addresses the implications of enhancing consumer sovereignty.

SUMMARY

In this chapter, we have looked at evidence concerning the economic efficiency of elementary and secondary schools. We concluded that in terms of external efficiency, the United States, along with most other advanced nations, devotes about the optimal proportion of its resources (GNP) to education, given the current state of educational technology. If there are to be improvements in educational outcomes, they will result primarily from improvements in internal efficiency—not from the application of additional resources. A review of educational production function studies, effective schools research, psychological studies, and comparisons with private schools showed that we already possess the knowledge of policies and practices which could enhance the internal efficiency of schools. In the chapters which follow, we will pursue in greater detail the potential of proposed structural reforms of education for improving the economic efficiency of schooling.

ACTIVITIES

1. Has the investment in your own education "paid off"? Estimate in current dollars the cost of your education beyond high school, including the income forgone. Find the present value of your investments by compounding annually each cost from the time it was incurred at a 10 percent rate of interest. Now estimate the earning differentials in current dollar values between the positions you have held and the positions you would probably have held if you had terminated your education at high school graduation. Estimate the present value by compounding the differentials from the times they were incurred at a 10 percent rate of interest. Is the present value of the sum of the

earnings differentials as large as or larger than the present value of the sum of the costs? If so, you have at least broken even; if not, from an economic standpoint, it would have made more sense to have entered the work force directly after high school or to have pursued another career.

2. List and discuss arguments for and against using the educational production function as a paradigm for analyzing resource allocations within public schools.

3. Chapter 13 concludes that the United States is already devoting an adequate proportion of its resources to formal education and that any improvements in education will have to come from using those resources more wisely (more efficiently). Do you agree with this position? List and discuss arguments supporting it and those which do not.

4. Using the information provided in the Internal Efficiency section of Chapter 13, devise one or more configurations for using public school resources which are likely to be more efficient than configurations typically employed at the present time.

5. Visit a large school and a small school serving the same grade levels and look for answers to the questions which follow. Alternatively, form a study group made up of persons with experience in different sizes of schools and compare experiences as you discuss these questions:

   a. Do you find any differences between schools which can be attributed to their differences in size?

   b. What are the advantages and disadvantages of being large? Of being small?

   c. What strategies might best neutralize the negative effects of school size?

REFERENCES

Alexander, K. L. (1987). Cross-sectional comparisons of public and private school effectiveness: A review of the evidence and issues. In E. H. Haertel, T. James, & H. M. Levin (Eds.), *Comparing public and private schools: Vol. 2, School achievement* (pp. 33–66). New York: Falmer Press.

Alexander, K. L., & Pallas, A. M. (1987). School sector and cognitive performance: When is a little a little? In E. H. Haertel, T. James, & H. M. Levin (Eds.), *Comparing public and private schools: Vol. 2, School achievement* (pp. 89–112). New York: Falmer Press.

Barker, R. G., & Gump, P. V. (1964). *Big school, small school.* Palo Alto, CA: Stanford University Press.

Becker, G. S. (1960). Underinvestment in college education? *American Economic Review* (Papers and proceedings), *50*, 345–354.

Becker, G. S. (1964). *Human capital: A theoretical and empirical analysis, with special reference to education.* New York: National Bureau of Economic Research.

Benson, C. S. (1978). *The economics of public education* (3rd ed.). Boston: Houghton Mifflin.

Benson, C. S. (1988). Economics of education: The U.S. experience. In N. J. Boyan (Ed.), *Handbook of research on educational administration* (pp. 355–372). White Plains, NY: Longman.

Berlin, B., & Cienkus, R. (1989). Size: The ultimate educational issue? *Education and Urban Society, 21*, 228–231.

Blaug, M. (1970). *An introduction to the economics of education.* Harmondsworth, England: Penguin Books.

Bowles, S. S., & Levin, H. M. (1968). The determinants of scholastic achievement: An appraisal of recent findings. *Journal of Human Resources*, *3*, 3–24.

Boyer, E. L. (1983). *High school: A report on secondary education in America*. New York: Harper & Row.

Bridge, R. G., Judd, C. M., & Moock, P. R. (1979). *The determinants of educational outcomes: The impact of families, peers, teachers and schools*. Cambridge, MA: Ballinger.

Brookover, W., & Lezotte, L. (1979). *Changes in school characteristics coincident with changes in student achievement*. East Lansing, MI: State University, College of Urban Development.

Burkhead, J. (1967). *Input and output in large-city high schools*. Syracuse, NY: Syracuse University Press.

Cain, G. G., & Watts, H. W. (1970). Problems in making policy inferences from the Coleman report. *American Sociological Review*, *35*, 228–252.

Chubb, J. E., & Moe, T. M. (1985). *Politics, markets, and the organization of schools*. Stanford, CA: Institute for Research on Educational Finance and Governance, School of Education, Stanford University.

Coleman, J. S. (1966). *Equality of educational opportunity*. Washington, DC: U.S. Government Printing Office.

Coleman, J. S., & Hoffer, T. (1987). *Public and private high schools: The impact of communities*. New York: Basic Books.

Coleman, J. S., Hoffer, T., & Kilgore, S. (1981). *Public and private high schools*. Washington, DC: National Center for Education Statistics.

Davis, J. R., & Morrall, J. F., III. (1974). *Evaluating educational investment*. Lexington, MA: Lexington Books.

Denison, E. F. (1962). *The sources of economic growth in the United States*. New York: Committee for Economic Development.

Denison, E. F. (1974). *Accounting for United States economic growth, 1929–1969*. Washington, DC: The Brookings Institution.

Dreeben, R., & Thomas, J. A. (1980). *The analysis of educational productivity, Vol. I: Issues in microanalysis*. Cambridge, MA: Ballinger.

Edmonds, R. (1979). Effective schools for the urban poor. *Educational Leadership*, *37*: 15–24.

Fowler, W. J., Jr. (1989). *School size, school characteristics, and school outcomes*. Paper presented at the Annual Meeting of the American Educational Research Association, San Francisco.

Fox, W. F. (1981). Reviewing economies of size in education. *Journal of Education Finance*, *6*, 273–296.

Glass, G. V., & Smith, M. L. (1979). Meta-analysis of research on the relationship of class-size and achievement. *Educational Evaluation and Policy Analysis*, *1*, 2–16.

Goodlad, J. I. (1984). *A place called school: Prospects for the future*. New York: McGraw-Hill.

Haertel, E. H. (1987). Comparing public and private schools using longitudinal data from the HSB study. In E. H. Haertel, T. James, & H. M. Levin (Eds.), *Comparing public and private schools: Vol. 2, School achievement* (pp. 9–32). New York: Falmer Press.

Hanoch, G. (1971). An economic analysis of earnings and schooling. In B. F. Kiker (Ed.), *Investment in human capital*. Columbia: University of South Carolina Press.

Hanushek, E. A. (1986). The economics of schooling: Production and efficiency in public schools. *Journal of Economic Literature*, *24*, 1141–1177.

Hanushek, E. A. (1987). Education production functions. In G. Psacharopoulos (Ed.), *Economics of education: Research and studies* (pp. 33–42). Oxford: Pergamon Press.

Hess, G. A., Jr. (1990). *Chicago school reform: What it is and how it came to be*. Chicago: Chicago Panel on Public School Policy and Finance.

Hoffer, T., Greeley, A. M., & Coleman, J. S. (1987). Catholic high school effects on achievement growth. In E. H. Haertel, T. James, & H. M. Levin (Eds.), *Comparing public and private schools: Vol. 2, School achievement* (pp. 67–88). New York: Falmer Press.

Jackson, S., Logsdon, D., & Taylor, N. (1983). Instructional leadership behaviors: Differentiating effective from ineffective low-income urban schools. *Urban Education, 18*, 59–70.

Klitgaard, R. E., & Hall, G. R. (1975). Are there unusually effective schools? *Journal of Human Resources, 10*, 90–106.

Lindsay, P. (1982). The effect of high school size on student participation, satisfaction, and attendance. *Educational Evaluation and Policy Analysis, 4*, 57–65.

McDonnell, L. M., & Fuhrman, S. (1986). The political context of school reform. In V. D. Mueller & M. P. McKeown (Eds.), *The fiscal, legal, and political aspects of state reform of elementary and secondary education* (pp. 43–64). Cambridge, MA: Ballinger.

McMahon, W. W., & Wagner, A. P. (1982). The monetary returns to education as partial social efficiency criteria. In W. W. McMahon & T. Geske (Eds.), *Financing education: Overcoming inefficiency and inequity*. Urbana: University of Illinois Press.

MacPhail-Wilcox, B., & King, R. A. (1986). Production functions revisited in the context of educational reform. *Journal of Education Finance, 12*, 191–223.

Madaus, G. F., Airasian, P. W., & Kellaghan, T. (1980). *School effectiveness: A reassessment of the evidence*. New York: McGraw-Hill.

Mayeski, G. W., Wisler, C. E., Beaton, A. E., Jr., Weinfeld, F. D., Cohen, W. M., Okada, T., Proshele, I. M., & Tabler, K. A. (1972). *A study of our nation's schools*. Washington, DC: U.S. Government Printing Office.

Monk, D. H. (1989). The education production function: Its evolving role in policy analysis. *Educational Evaluation and Policy Analysis, 11*, 31–45.

Mostellar, F., & Moynihan, D. P. (1972). *On equality of educational opportunity*. New York: Vintage Press.

Murnane, R. J. (1975). *The impact of school resources on the learning of inner city children*. Cambridge, MA: Ballinger.

Murnane, R. J. (1980). *Interpreting the evidence on school effectiveness* (Working Paper No. 830). New Haven, CT: Yale University, Institution for Social and Policy Studies.

Murnane, R. J. (1983). Quantitative studies of effective schools: What have we learned? In A. Odden & L. D. Webb (Eds.), *School finance and school improvement: Linkages for the 1980s* (pp. 193–209). Cambridge, MA: Ballinger.

Murphy, K., & Welch, F. (1989). Wage premiums for college graduates: Recent growth and possible explanations. *Educational Researcher, 18* (4), 17–26.

Newman, F. M. (1981). Reducing student alienation in high schools: Implications of theory. *Harvard Education Review, 51*, 546–564.

Odden, A., & Webb, L. D. (1983). Introduction: The linkages between school finance and school improvement. In A. Odden & L. D. Webb (Eds.), *School finance and school improvement: Linkages for the 1980s* (pp. xiii–xxi). Cambridge, MA: Ballinger.

Psacharopoulos, G. (1973). *Returns to education: An international comparison*. Amsterdam: Elsevier.

Psacharopoulos, G. (1981). Returns to education: An updated international comparison. *Comparative Education, 17*, 321–341.

Psacharopoulos, G. (1985). Returns to education: A further international update and implications. *The Journal of Human Resources, 20,* 583–604.

Reed, L. (1985). *An inquiry into the specific school-based practices involving principals that distinguish unusually effective elementary schools from effective elementary schools.* Unpublished doctoral dissertation, State University of New York at Buffalo.

Riew, J. (1981). Enrollment decline and school reorganization: A cost efficiency analysis. *Economics of Education Review, 1,* 53–73.

Riew, J. (1986). Scale economies, capacity utilization, and school costs: A comparative analysis of secondary and elementary schools. *Journal of Education Finance, 11,* 433–446.

Rutter, M., Maughan, B., Mortimore, P., & Ouston, J. (1979). *Fifteen thousand hours: Secondary schools and their effects on children.* London: Open Books.

Schultz, T. W. (1963). *The economic value of education.* New York: Columbia University Press.

Schultz, T. W. (1981). *Investing in people: The economics of population quality.* Berkeley: University of California Press.

Smith, A. (1976). *An inquiry into the nature and cause of the wealth of nations.* Chicago: University of Chicago Press.

Summers, A. A., & Wolfe, B. L. (1975). *Equality of educational opportunity quantified: A production function approach.* Philadelphia: Federal Reserve Bank of Philadelphia, Department of Research.

Sweet, D. A. (1986, September). Extracurricular activity participants outperform other students. *Office of Educational Research and Improvement Bulletin* (CS 85-2136).

U.S. Department of Commerce, Bureau of the Census. (1983). *Statistical abstract of the United States, 1983.* Washington, DC: U.S. Government Printing Office.

U.S. Department of Commerce, Bureau of the Census. (1988). *Statistical abstract of the United States, 1988.* Washington, DC: U.S. Government Printing Office.

Venezsky, R., & Winfield, L. (1980). *Schools that exceed beyond expectations in the teaching of reading: Studies on education* (technical report 1). Newark: University of Delaware.

Walberg, H. J. (1984, May). Improving the productivity of America's schools. *Educational Leadership, 41,* 19–27.

Weber, G. (1971). *Inner city children can be taught to read: Four successful schools.* Washington, DC: Council for Basic Education.

Willms, J. D. (1987). Patterns of academic achievement in public and private schools: Implications for public policy and future research. In E. H. Haertel, T. James, & H. M. Levin (Eds.), *Comparing public and private schools: Volume 2, School achievement* (pp. 113–134). New York: Falmer Press.

Woodhall, M. (1987). Human capital concepts. In G. Psacharopoulos (Ed.), *Economics of education: Research and studies* (pp. 21–24). Oxford: Pergamon Press.

CHAPTER 14

Personnel Quality and Remuneration

Labor is the most critical, and the most costly, resource for education. It is an important factor in the educational production function introduced in Chapter 13. The desire to improve the internal efficiency of schools must inevitably consider the capabilities of teachers and instructional support personnel. For these reasons, strategies to improve personnel quality and remuneration have received much attention in the recent educational reform movement.

In this chapter, we examine the teacher labor market in relation to economic and social considerations. Trends in the demand for teachers' services and policy options for increasing supplies of highly capable teachers are presented. We also discuss traditional remuneration of teachers through the single salary schedule, strategies for strengthening the relationship between compensation and performance, and the involvement of teachers in collective bargaining and decision-making processes.

THE LABOR MARKET FOR TEACHERS' SERVICES

In Chapter 1 we introduced the concepts of supply and demand in the context of the flow of resources between households and producers in a market-oriented society. Households purchase products and offer labor, and businesses hire workers for production processes, creating supply and demand sides of product and labor markets. In this section, we differentiate the teacher labor market from the operation of the larger economy and discuss conditions of supply and demand that affect educators.

Differing Labor Markets

Conditions of supply and demand in a free-market economy influence the level at which equilibrium is reached for prices of goods and services (see Figure 1.2). The prevailing wage for labor is the amount of money necessary to ensure that there are qualified applicants (supply) for available jobs (demand). Wage differentials attract workers to occupations in which the demand for labor is the greatest and away from those in which the demand is the least (Butler, 1963). Differentials exist between job assignments within a given business, among different business firms within a given industry, and among the many industries employing people with the same occupation.

Setting wages in the private sector assumes that consumers exercise free choice among available products and that employers exercise choice among similarly skilled laborers. Workers are also assumed to be free and willing to move among jobs and geographic locations in response to conditions of labor surplus and shortages. In reality, such a "perfect" free-market economy does not exist. Workers are not uniform in motivation, attitudes, ability, and mobility, nor do they have information about all the alternatives in their labor market choices (Kreps, Somers, & Perlman, 1974). In our mixed economy, the government intervenes in the marketplace by setting minimum wages and specifying such benefits as Social Security and unemployment insurance. The public sector also influences wages in the private sector by its ability to attract labor into public employment, and vice versa.

The supply of labor that households are willing to provide private and public sectors is influenced by personal and economic considerations. The desire for income is balanced with individual and family decisions about alternative uses of their talents, including working within the household itself, obtaining additional education, and volunteering time and effort in any number of pursuits. Employers control the amount of compensation offered and the nature of working conditions, using them to entice people to enter the work force and to prepare for particular occupations. Not all individuals who are willing and capable of performing a given job, however, find satisfactory employment. Supplies of willing workers do not dictate demands of employers for their services; the latter depends on the public's consumption of goods and services and on opportunities to alter the mix of labor and capital required in production processes. The goal of maximizing profits encourages private sector businesses to increase workers' productivity and to substitute capital for labor in production processes.

Teachers and other certified personnel constitute a labor market that operates somewhat differently, but not independently, from the larger economy. Public schools produce a service that is not marketed at a price to their clients, and it is difficult to determine how much an individual teacher contributes to this "product." Compensation and working conditions are determined by legislatures and school boards through processes of political compromise; in most states teachers' unions affect salary determination through collective bargaining.

The supply of potential employees is restricted by states' licensing requirements that define the minimum qualifications to enter the profession, although exceptions are readily granted. Tenure statutes and state retirement systems, as well as personal and family preferences, restrict teachers' mobility to respond to changes in labor markets. Broader changes in social behavior, such as the exodus of women and minorities from teaching to other professions during the 1980s, further influence supply conditions. The number of teachers seeking employment varies greatly among subjects and geographic areas.

The demand for teachers also differs from free-market assumptions. There is not necessarily a large number of buyers (school systems) demanding teachers' services. Because there is less competition among public and private schools, or between schools and other sectors of society, than in other labor markets, teachers' salaries are less responsive to market conditions. The teacher labor market approaches a "monopsony," a market in which there is effectively one demander of labor (Fleisher & Kniesner, 1980). In such restricted markets, wages tend to be lower than they might be in competitive marketplaces.

The public sector labor market does not operate in isolation, however, and school systems experience similar forces of supply and demand as they compete with private sector employers in the broader labor market. The supply curve in Figure 1.2 suggests that more individuals will prepare for careers in teaching and more people in the reserve pool of certified teachers will reenter the profession as salaries increase. Once this larger supply meets the demand, salaries will stabilize at a new equilibrium level. The demand curve suggests that as society requires additional teachers to serve more children, reduce class size, or provide diverse services, the equilibrium price rises (assuming that supply remains the same).

When the supply of teachers differs from demand, instabilities in the marketplace result in shortages and surpluses. The labor market is slow to respond to these changes because of the lengthy period between realizations of demand for teachers, encouragement for individuals to select different college majors, and graduation of new entrants to the profession. Periods of high teacher demand, such as that in the 1950s and 1960s, result in aggressive recruitment and relatively higher salaries. There is eventual oversupply, as occurred in the 1970s at the time of rapidly declining enrollments, and salaries stabilize or decrease in terms of purchasing power. The quality of teacher candidates may be related to conditions of supply and demand, assuming that higher-ability teachers are more responsive to changes in wages paid among various employment opportunities (Thangaraj, 1985).

Predicting supply and demand in the teacher labor market is complex. Some reports predicted shortages for the 1990s (e.g., Carnegie Forum, 1986), whereas others projected sufficient numbers of teachers to meet the demand (e.g., Feistritzer, 1986; Hecker, 1986). Fox (1988) discusses three problems in making accurate projections. First, demand depends on assumptions made about pupils to be served and on policy decisions regarding class size and the number of supplementary teachers needed. For example, growth in birthrates, particularly in low-income households, and the expansion of public school offerings for preschool children stimulate the demand for teachers. This demand is expected to peak in 1991 (Hecker, 1986), but if new programs are financed to serve the educational needs of children in poverty, the demand for early childhood educators is likely to grow beyond this time frame (Anthony, 1988).

Second, it is more difficult to determine the supply of educators than it is for that of other professions. College graduates do not necessarily begin teaching careers immediately upon completion of preparation programs, nor do they remain in classrooms until retirement. The number of teacher candidates depends on the number of college students who prepare to teach and the number in the reserve pool of people who are qualified to teach but do not actively seek a teaching position. The number enrolled in college programs fell steadily between the early 1970s and the mid-1980s, along with the demand for teachers. As teacher demand increases in the 1990s, improving financial incentives and working conditions have positively influenced teacher supply.

Third, definitions of teacher quality influence projections. It is desirable to attract and retain a teaching force of sufficient quantity and quality, but defining "sufficient" is an issue about which there is little agreement. However, there is evidence of continuing supplies of poor-quality teachers: (1) A large number of teachers are assigned to teach classes outside their subject certification; (2) prospective teachers score lower on tests of academic ability than do individuals preparing for other professions (Fox, 1984; Sykes, 1983); and (3) those who are attracted to and retained in teaching are the least academically able, and those who abandon the profession are often the most academically able (Vance & Schlechty, 1982, p. 24).

Trends in Teacher Demand

The demand for teachers is conditioned largely on the number of children enrolled. However, policy decisions in recent years that expanded the ranks of instructional support personnel better to serve particular student populations (e.g., special education and disadvantaged) and that reduced class size have altered demand conditions.

The growing demand for educators doubled the number of full-time equivalent (FTE) teachers and support personnel from 2 million in 1960 to over 4 million in 1987. The growth was greatest during the 1960s, when student enrollments increased and educational services expanded. However, the share of this growth represented by the number of FTE classroom teachers—a 66 percent growth rate, from 1.35 million to 2.24 million—was overshadowed by the larger increase in the number of noninstructional personnel employed in schools and central offices—a 170 percent increase, from 0.74 million in 1960 to 2.00 million in 1987 (Stern, 1988, p. 98).

Table 14.1 examines more closely the relative growth in numbers of teachers and

TABLE 14.1. Full-Time Equivalent Personnel Employed in Public Schools

Type of Personnel	1983	1984	1985	1986	1987
Number (in thousands)					
Classroom teachers	2,121	2,126	2,168	2,207	2,243
Instructional support*	396	387	399	421	449
Administrators and administrative support[†]	511	512	511	516	540
Other support[‡]	899	883	984	1,016	1,015
Total	3,927	3,908	4,063	4,161	4,247
Percentage Distribution					
Classroom teachers	54.0	54.4	53.4	53.0	52.8
Instructional support*	10.1	9.9	9.8	10.1	10.6
Administrators and administrative support[†]	13.0	13.1	12.6	12.4	12.7
Other support[‡]	22.9	22.6	24.2	24.4	23.9
Total	100.0	100.0	100.0	100.0	100.0

*Includes instructional aides, guidance counselors, and librarians.
[†]Includes school and district administrators and the associated clerical staff.
[‡]Includes employees not listed above, such as media personnel, bus drivers, security officers, cafeteria workers, and so on. Totals are rounded. (*Source:* J. D. Stern. [1988]. *The Condition of Education: Elementary and Secondary Education, 1988.* Vol. 1, p. 99. Washington, DC: National Center for Education Statistics.)

support personnel during the middle 1980s. The total number of FTE personnel employed in schools grew from 3.9 million in 1983 to 4.2 million in 1987. During this period of relative stability in student enrollment, classroom teachers declined as a percentage of total employment (from 54.0% to 52.8%). The growth in personnel was accounted for by instructional support staff, including classroom aides, guidance counselors, and librarians (from 10.1% in 1983 to 10.6% in 1987), and such other support staff as media personnel, bus drivers, security officers, and cafeteria workers (from 22.9% to 23.9%). There was a slight decline in the percentage employed in building and central office administrative capacities (from 13.0% to 12.7%) during these years.

The introduction of computers, television, and other capital equipment that has the potential of enabling teachers to work with large groups has not reduced demand. Class size itself is smaller today than in the past. Declining enrollments, the growth of special education, and a pervasive belief among educators and laypersons alike that teachers can work more effectively with small groups of children encourage smaller classes. In Chapter 3 we discussed trends in pupil–teacher ratios (PTR) in public elementary and secondary schools; Table 3.9 indicated a steady decline, from 26 to 17 pupils per teacher, between 1961 and 1988. Large variations in class sizes among states illustrate differing beliefs about the internal efficiencies of schools. Pupil–teacher ratios ranged in 1986–1987 from 14 in Connecticut and Wyoming to over 23 in California and Utah (see Table 3.11).

The decline in class size in the United States is similar to that in other industrialized nations. Table 14.2 presents an international comparison of staffing practices in public and private schools. Average class sizes were smaller than in the United States in 6 of the 12 countries providing recent data, and each nation reduced class size between 1960 and 1984. Class sizes diminished over time in each nation's elementary schools, but secondary

TABLE 14.2. Pupils per Teacher in Public and Private Schools in Selected Countries, 1960 to 1984

Country	Elementary			Secondary			All Schools		
	1960	1970	1984	1960	1970	1984	1960	1970	1984
Australia	33	28	15	18	21	12	27	25	14
Canada	26	23	16*	24	17	18*	26	21	17*
France	34	26	21†	26	16	16†	31	20	18†
Italy	22	22	15†	12	12	10†	17	16	12†
Japan	35	26	24	25	18	18	30	22	21
Mexico	44	46	36*	13	15	18*	36	35	28*
Netherlands	34	30	20*	21	15	15*	29	23	18*
Sweden	NA	20	16†	NA	10	12†	NA	16	14†
United Kingdom	24	23	18†	18	16	15†	21	20	17†
United States	29	25	20	21	20	16	26	22	18
USSR	16	11	10	16	NA	NA	16	NA	NA
West Germany	30	26	17*	23	12	14*	27	19	14*
Yugoslavia	33	27	23	13	22	18	28	24	20

NA = Not available.

*Data from 1983.

†Data from 1982. (*Source:* National Center for Education Statistics. [1988]. *Digest of Education Statistics, 1988,* Table 285, p. 339. Washington, DC: U.S. Department of Education.)

school classes grew slightly between 1970 and 1984 in Canada, Sweden, and West Germany.

In addition to smaller class size, increasing enrollments and teacher retirements will continue to raise the demand for teachers during the 1990s. Darling-Hammond and Berry (1988) anticipate that the supply of graduating teacher candidates would satisfy only 60 percent of this demand.

Reforms to Alter Teacher Supply

Many social and economic conditions affect the supply of teachers. Fluctuating birthrates bring cycles of growth and decline, creating demand for teachers at one grade level while other grade levels have short-term surpluses. Population shifts from cities to suburbs and from northern to southern and western states have produced oversupplies in some districts and shortages in others. Racial conflicts and drugs, lack of parental involvement, reduction of public tax support for schools, level of teachers' salaries relative to those of other occupations, and teachers' work conditions affect the relative attractiveness of careers in education. Minorities and women have more diverse career opportunities than in the past, and college graduates in selected fields like mathematics and computer science find readily available employment alternatives (Darling-Hammond, 1984). Educational reforms of the 1980s addressed many of these root causes of declining supplies of high-quality teachers (MacPhail-Wilcox & King, 1988). This section addresses several policy options that promise to strengthen the quality of initial and experienced teachers.

Nearly all reform reports of the 1980s advocated changes to elevate teaching from its status as a "semi-profession." Sykes (1987) observes that a profession develops and enforces standards of good practice in exchange for autonomy and the right to practice free of bureaucratic supervision and external regulation. Professionals are presumed to employ specialized knowledge and skills in a competent manner and stay abreast of developments in their field of knowledge. They desire to attract new entrants who are capable of acquiring and applying expert knowledge, and then they provide a lengthy period of training for the acquisition of skills and socialization to the norms of the profession.

The ascension of teaching to professional status, like that of other occupations throughout history, is questioned for advantages sought primarily for members themselves (Metzger, 1987). Professionalism may not be socially desirable if it means that the emphasis on a technical knowledge base erodes concerns for caring and compassion in public schools, that the greater social distance created between professionals and clients works to the detriment of democratic ideals of schooling, or that setting standards in the name of professionalism works against equity goals by shrinking the pool of minorities attracted to teaching (Sykes, 1987). On the other hand, Darling-Hammond (1984) claims that the bureaucratic orientation of public schools negatively affects the retention of teachers: "Lack of input into professional decisionmaking, overly restrictive bureaucratic controls, and inadequate administrative supports for teaching contribute to teacher dissatisfaction and attrition, particularly among the most highly qualified members of the teaching force" (p. v.). It is believed that changes in entry standards and working conditions will result in a more professional atmosphere and ultimately in a higher quality teaching force.

The demonstration of specialized subject knowledge is one prerequisite to entry into a profession. Georgia and Mississippi in 1975 were the first to require written competency tests for licensure, and by 1987 a total of 43 states (U.S. Department of Education, 1988, p. 123) conditioned initial licensure on passing exams on generic knowledge or specific subject matter. Concerns are raised about the content validity and predictive validity of competency tests for initial licensure, as well as about the role of these tests in defining the professional knowledge base (Darling-Hammond, 1986; Madaus & Pullin, 1987). To address these limitations, Shulman (1987) urged simulations, assessment center exercises, and closely supervised field experiences to enrich the measures of knowledge and skills of potential teachers. By 1988, 25 states had initiated beginning teacher programs; 18 of these states required new entrants to pass a formal performance assessment before qualifying for permanent certification (Darling-Hammond & Berry, 1988).

Initial licensing of teacher candidates to enforce minimal standards would differ from professional certification under recommendations of the Carnegie Forum (1986). This report advocated the creation of a teacher-controlled National Board for Professional Teaching Standards to develop high standards for professional competence and to certify teachers meeting those standards. Jordan (1988) notes that not all teachers would volunteer to be considered for this certification, but all teachers in a given state would be subject to licensing requirements.

Alternative routes to licensure attract people who have not completed formal teacher education prior to employment. For example, the New Jersey lateral entry program attracts applicants who hold a bachelor's degree and 30 credit hours or equivalent work experience in the subject field they intend to teach (Cooperman & Klagholz, 1985). School systems assign these new teachers to a team (consisting of an administrator, peer teacher, college faculty member, and curricular specialist) that oversees their development and evaluates their performance. This strategy holds promise for increasing the supply of applicants with greater depth of preparation and/or practical experience in particular subjects. However, it is not clear if district-administered approaches to licensure lower entry standards to the disadvantage of pupils or to teaching as a profession.

Reform reports that advocate changes in teacher preparation also address concerns with subject matter expertise. The National Commission on Excellence in Education (1983), which included elementary, secondary, and university personnel as well as public officials; the Carnegie Forum (1986), which was broadly representative of public, business, and educational leaders; and the Holmes Group (1986), which was made up of deans of selected colleges of education, recommended a fifth-year of professional education beyond a four-year liberal arts degree. A lengthened preparation program would increase graduates' mastery of a broad liberal education, the subject matter of their teaching fields, the literature of professional education, and reflective practice. However, there were concerns that the additional investment in preparation without the promise of commensurate future compensation would make the profession less attractive. The more recent reports of the Consortium for Excellence in Teacher Education (Travers & Sacks, 1987) and the Association of American Colleges (1989) contend that four-year undergraduate programs can successfully integrate the liberal arts with professional studies.

Financial aid programs and forgiven loans provide incentives for less financially able students, who are in many cases minorities, to prepare for teaching careers. For example, statewide initiatives such as Massachusetts's payment of college expenses in exchange for future teaching within the state, New Jersey's Minority Teacher Program, and North

Carolina's teaching fellows program, were designed to attract capable candidates to teaching careers.

Examining the likelihood of alternative strategies to affect the supply of teachers, Hawley (1986) concluded that tests and other screening devices to control entry would not attract better-qualified people because of the failure to alter rewards. On the other hand, Manski (1985) speculated that raising salaries without increasing entrance standards would yield a substantial growth in the size of the pool of teachers but minimal improvement in its quality. In contrast, policies that restructure the workplace by giving greater responsibility, fostering collegiality, and maximizing the time teachers teach are low-cost reforms that have positive effects on recruitment and improve teacher effectiveness. Darling-Hammond and Berry (1988) observed that the emphasis of reform proposals shifted in 1986 toward decentralizing decision making and professionalizing teaching. Rigorous preparation, licensing, and selection processes to ensure teaching competence would be acceptable tradeoffs for fewer rules prescribing what would be taught, when, and how. They stated, "The test of the experiment in professionalization is whether other conditions of teaching work will prove sufficiently attractive to sustain an adequate supply of individuals able and willing to meet these requirements" (p. 37).

It appears that a three-pronged strategy is necessary to increase both the supply and quality of teachers: Raise entrance standards, improve working conditions, and improve wages relative to other professions.

STRATEGIES FOR REMUNERATION

Among the most important aspects of personnel policies are the nature of compensation packages offered to employees and the relationship that responsibilities and job performance have with remuneration. The presumption that these factors affect the internal efficiencies of schools and future supplies of capable teachers made them the subject of recent educational reforms.

The National Commission on Excellence (1983) stated that maintaining current levels of salaries would not be sufficient to attract and retain high-quality teachers: "Salaries for the teaching profession should be increased and should be professionally competitive, market-sensitive, and performance-based" (p. 30). Because salaries are indicators of the economic health of the profession and of teachers' status in the community (Salmon, 1988), they influence people's career choices.

In this section, we discuss teachers' salaries in relation to the cost of living and to wages paid other workers. We explore structures of salary schedules, particularly their presumed relations between teachers' experience and training and outcomes of schooling, and we examine merit pay and career ladders as strategies to relate compensation with performance and responsibilities.

Salaries and Fringe Benefits

In Chapter 3, we presented trends in teachers' salaries. Teachers lost purchasing power in the 1970s, but by 1988 they had recouped their position relative to the cost of living. Table 3.10 indicated that the value of the average salary earned in 1981 had declined to

$23,595, a loss of $3,937 in purchasing power from that earned in 1973. Teachers' salaries in 1988 ($28,044) represented an increase of $4,449 in constant dollars over the 1981 level. By 1988–1989 the average salary earned by teachers was $29,567 (National Education Association, 1989, p. 18).

Teachers in the United States have generally greater purchasing power than their foreign counterparts (Lawton, 1988). Table 14.3 compares 1985 salaries in U.S. dollars for primary teachers in 22 countries. Teachers in Switzerland, Canada, Luxembourg, and Australia earned higher salaries than primary teachers in selected U.S. cities. Although teachers earn as much as 34 percent more in Switzerland, 17 other countries paid average salaries between 29 percent and 93 percent of the level earned in the United States.

Comparisons of teachers' compensation with that of other occupations give an indication of relative economic status. One recent ranking placed teachers last among professions

TABLE 14.3. Teachers' Salaries in Selected Countries, 1985

Country*	Salary in U.S. Dollars	Ratio to U.S. Salary	Ratio of Maximum to Minimum Salary		Years to Maximum
			Elementary	Secondary	
Switzerland	$33,070	1.34	NA	NA	NA
Canada	30,294	1.23	1:2.1	1:1.8	13
Luxembourg	29,359	1.19	1:2.0	1:1.8	24
Australia	24,809	1.01	NA	NA	NA
United States	24,600	1.00	1:2.0	1:2.0	15
Japan	22,876	.93	1:3.3	1:3.1	39
West Germany	20,944	.85	1:1.8	1:1.8	30
Ireland	20,143	.82	1:1.6	1:1.6	14
Denmark	20,034	.81	1:1.3	1:1.5	18
Spain	19,781	.80	1:1.4	1:1.4	42
Sweden	18,753	.76	1:1.4	1:1.4	16
Norway	18,251	.74	1:1.3	1:1.5	24
United Kingdom[†]	18,220	.74	1:2.3	1:2.3	13
Scotland	NA	NA	1:1.5	1:1.6	12
Netherlands	18,171	.74	1:2.0	1:2.6	22
Belgium	17,991	.73	NA	NA	NA
Italy	16,126	.66	1:1.4	1:1.5	40
Finland	14,530	.59	1:1.6	1:1.6	20
Greece	14,510	.59	NA	NA	NA
France	13,764	.56	1:1.5	1:2.2	30
Austria	13,656	.56	1:2.2	1:2.5	38
Portugal	12,052	.49	NA	NA	NA
Turkey	7,176	.29	NA	NA	NA
Gilbraltar	NA	NA	1:2.3	1:2.3	13
Malta	NA	NA	1:1.8	1:1.9	11
Average	19,505	.78	1:1.8	1:1.9	23

NA = Not available.
*For many of the countries, salaries are determined from one or several major cities.
[†]Includes data of United Kingdom for salaries and data of England and Wales for ratios of maximum to minimum salaries. (*Source:* S. B. Lawton. [1987]. "Teachers' Salaries: An International Perspective," pp. 73, 77. In K. Alexander and D. H. Monk (Eds.). *Attracting and Compensating America's Teachers* [pp. 69–89]. Copyright © 1988 by American Education Finance Association. Used by permission of Harper Business, a division of HarperCollins Publishers.)

in both 1979–1980 and 1985–1986 (Salmon, 1988, pp. 255–256). Salaries paid teachers were more comparable to technical occupations than to professions. However, during these six years, teachers had moved from midpoint among technical occupations to the top of this group. Feistritzer (1986) found teachers to be 26th of 35 occupations; of the 10 ranked below teachers, only 2 (social worker and priest) demanded a college degree. When the Carnegie Forum (1986) compared salaries of 12 selected occupations, only plumbers, airline ticket agents, and secretaries earned less than teachers.

Salaries may affect teacher retention. The majority (53 percent) of teachers surveyed by Feistritzer (1986) reported that they would leave teaching for a position paying at least $5,000 more. A large number of teachers moonlight in evening, weekend, and summer jobs to supplement salaries. Wisniewski and Kleine (1984) contend that "teaching will remain at best a semiprofession as long as so many of its members are taking nonprofessional work for nonprofessional wages and benefits" (p. 555).

The amount of salaries, the most visible reward for work, overshadows the diversity of fringe benefits offered and the proportion of their cost paid by school districts. The labor intensity of schooling is apparent in the large percentage of budgets, generally between 85 percent and 90 percent, devoted to personnel costs including fringe benefits. The total compensation package may affect school districts' competitiveness in the marketplace for certified personnel and for classified secretarial and custodial staff.

Rebore (1987) defines a fringe benefit as "a service made available to employees as a direct result of a fiscal expenditure by the school district" (p. 298). Individual employees and school districts contribute to the cost of federally sponsored Social Security and workmen's compensation plans (see Chapter 5). Most also share the expense of statewide teachers' retirement programs and group health, dental, disability, and life insurance plans. School boards bear the cost of liability insurance to protect themselves and their employees from negligence suits.

Several other benefits are available to certified personnel. Favorable income tax policies enable teachers to invest funds for retirement in annuities that shelter tax obligations until they can take advantage of lower tax brackets. School districts bear the cost of substitute teachers when health, personal, and extended sabbatical leaves are granted. In some districts, a "sick leave incentive cash payment plan" (Candoli, Hack, Ray, & Stollar, 1984, p. 367) accumulates unused leave to a maximum number of days over a career, giving teachers large payments upon retirement or leaving the profession. Other districts enable employees to choose from a number of benefits in a "cafeteria" approach in order to make compensation more attractive to employees who do not require standard, family-oriented benefit packages.

The desire to improve internal efficiencies through compensation must involve more than the amount of salary and extent of fringe benefits. There is concern that the predominant structure of salary schedules does not encourage or reward specific aspects of teaching that are related to instructional quality.

The Single-Salary Schedule

A uniform salary schedule for all teachers in a school district emerged early in the twentieth century in response to inequities based on elementary and secondary grade levels, subjects taught, gender, number of dependents, political affiliations, and bargaining between individual teachers and school boards. The principle of equal pay for equal qualifications called for the same salary for teachers of equal training and experience.

Table 14.3 illustrates that not all countries disregard grade-level differences in determining salaries. For example, the maximum paid to an elementary teacher in France is 1.5 times the minimum paid; the ratio of 2.2 indicates a larger range in remuneration for secondary teachers. Elementary teachers have a higher range in possible earnings than secondary teachers in Canada, Luxembourg, and Japan. In the remaining countries, salaries for elementary and secondary teachers have similar ranges. Although Table 3.10 indicates that salaries of elementary teachers are lower than those of secondary teachers in the United States, this difference is due to lower levels of experience and professional training of elementary teachers rather than to a deliberate differentiation by grade levels.

The salary structure in place in nearly all U.S. school systems differentiates teachers' pay in accordance with experience and advanced preparation, with additional pay only for such extra services as coaching teams and overseeing extracurricular activities. The experience dimension of the typical schedule brings salary increases to a stated maximum after a given number of years. Teachers receive from 10 to 20 annual "step" increases for longevity; Table 14.3 shows the average for selected school systems to be 15 years. Schedules in other countries range from 11 to 40 years to achieve the maximum salary. Lawton (1988, p. 78) comments that pay scales with 15 steps or fewer are limited to countries with British connections; other countries prefer to have scales with 20 or more steps.

The second dimension included in salary schedules rewards and encourages continued preparation in professional education and subjects taught. Four to six training categories typically range from having no degree to earning a doctoral degree. In some cases, teachers advance along this continuum upon completion of specified numbers of graduate hours. The effect of experience and training dimensions is generally to double salaries from the initial cell of the matrix (e.g., first-year teacher with a bachelor's degree) to the last cell (e.g., teacher with 12 years of experience and a doctoral degree). In addition to these increments, actual annual increases in salaries, including those of experienced teachers who are "frozen" on the top step, depend upon legislative or school board actions. All cells of the matrix are changed, reflecting increases in the cost of living and the results of negotiations with teacher unions and associations among other factors.

Table 14.4 indicates trends in experience and preparation of teachers between 1961 and 1986. The median number of years in teaching declined from 11 to 8 in the 1960s, but increased thereafter to 15 years in 1986. The declining percentage of first-year teachers, from 9.1 percent in 1971 to 2.4 percent in 1981, reflects the declining enrollments and fiscal conditions of the 1970s that served to discourage new hiring and turnover among veteran teachers. At the same time, the length of academic preparation increased. The percentages of teachers without a bachelor's degree declined from 15 percent in 1961 to less than 1 percent in 1986, and with only a bachelor's degree from 70 percent in 1971 to 48 percent in 1986. The proportion of teachers with advanced preparation grew substantially, from under a quarter in 1961 to over one-half of all teachers holding a graduate degree in 1986.

Advances in these mean experience and training levels translate into substantial increases in average salaries because schedules depend on these two dimensions. A more experienced teaching force today than a decade ago appears to be paid higher average

TABLE 14.4. Teachers' Experience and Training, 1961–1986

	1961	1971	1981	1986
Median years of experience	11.0	8.0	12.0	15.0
Percentage teaching for first year	8.0	9.1	2.4	3.1
Highest degree held (percent)				
Less than bachelor's	14.6	2.9	0.4	0.3
Bachelor's	61.9	69.6	50.1	48.3
Master's or specialist	23.1	27.1	49.3	50.7
Doctor's	0.4	0.4	0.3	0.7

(*Source:* U.S. Department of Education. [1988]. *Digest of Education Statistics, 1988*, p. 70. Washington, DC: Department of Education; National Education Association. [1987]. *Status of the American Public School Teacher, 1985–86*. Washington, DC: National Education Association.)

salaries, but the average teacher is only marginally better off in terms of purchasing power (see Table 3.10). Larger salaries reflect movements on salary schedules and general salary increases provided by state legislatures and school boards.

In response to calls for changing compensation systems, advocates of maintaining a single salary schedule argue that it

> promotes positive working relationships among teachers and between teachers and administrators,
> is a relatively inexpensive and unburdened system for allocating pay when compared with other systems,
> has minimal impacts on productive school processes, such as teachers' intrinsic motivations to perform and principals' decisions for effectively using skills of teachers, and
> avoids racial, ethnic and gender discrimination among teachers (National Education Association, 1985, p. 19).

On the other hand, the single-salary schedule is flat, with no opportunity for teachers to be given recognition of their performance. Rather than raises that depend upon individual productivity, teachers' pay is subject to collective decisions made by groups external to school districts, such as statewide salary schedules or bargaining processes between teachers' associations and boards of education in states that permit or mandate bargaining. The structure of the schedule itself rewards only the number of graduate courses completed, rather than their usefulness or relevance to subjects taught, and the number of years teachers have taught, rather than their performance. These dimensions permit little or no recognition of teachers' initiative, enthusiasm, efficiency, innovation, cooperation, ability, or improvements in performance. These factors may affect teachers' decisions to leave the profession voluntarily or school boards' decisions to dismiss teachers for poor classroom teaching, but they are not determinants of annual salaries.

An important goal of processes that reward and compensate individuals is to improve teacher quality (Castetter, 1986, p. 427; Rebore, 1987, p. 238). Rewarding training and experience is most defensible if they are related to instructional quality or pupil performance. These assumed relationships were challenged in Chapter 13. Policymakers have considered alternative compensation plans that relate remuneration with measures of performance or redefined job responsibilities.

Merit Pay and Career Ladders

Rewarding meritorious work performance and differentiating responsibilities of teachers are the most visible strategies advanced for improving teachers' compensation and productivity. The National Commission on Excellence (1983) urged performance-based salaries and the development of career ladders that "distinguish among the beginning instructor, the experienced teacher, and the master teacher" (pp. 30–31). Rather than two-dimensional salary schedules, the argument is made that school boards should adopt compensation strategies that relate salary with performance, as measured by gains in pupil achievement or by supervisors' or peers' evaluations of teaching abilities, or with clearly differentiated roles.

Merit pay is premised on Vroom's expectancy theory, which suggests that harder work is forthcoming when valued rewards are anticipated. People shape their behavior to increase the likelihood of achieving rewards they believe are attainable (Johnson, 1986). Merit pay is also based on equity theory, which proposes that dissatisfaction results when individuals perceive that they are unjustly compensated in relation to others (Frohreich, 1988). Career ladders and other differentiated staffing patterns rest upon job enrichment theory, which states that productivity is improved when job responsibilities are varied and challenging. These varied incentives presume that teachers can be motivated by financial rewards and that opportunities for extra compensation can effectively motivate teachers' behavior throughout their careers.

Merit pay assumes that extrinsic, or external and material, rewards including salary increases, travel funds for professional meetings, and nonmonetary benefits such as relief from assigned duties motivate teachers to be more productive. Some salary incentive plans grant a one-time pay bonus based on superior performance and others advance teachers on the salary matrix, thus raising their salaries into the future. Herzberg's two-factor theory suggests that extrinsic rewards, including monetary incentives, play an important role in teacher retention, but compensation strategies must be more attentive to intrinsic rewards if they are to improve performance (Jacobson, 1988, p. 163). Career ladders expand considerably the range of motivators to include intrinsic, or internal and intangible, rewards such as recognition, responsibility, and a sense of achievement. Lawler (1981) contends that career ladders offer stronger potential for changing behaviors and for retaining capable teachers because they provide both intrinsic and extrinsic rewards.

The push for merit recognition is cyclical. It became popular in the early 1960s after Sputnik raised concern about schools' productivity, and it reappeared in the more recent context of educational reform. Murnane and Cohen (1986, p. 2) observe that "while interest in paying teachers according to merit endures, attempts to use merit pay do not." Astuto (1985) found very few school districts (4 percent) to have any form of pay for performance. More districts that had tried merit pay had dropped their plans than had retained this approach to compensation. Districts with plans invested very little money in merit awards, in many cases less than the cost of a single teacher's salary. The majority of approaches to determine merit assessed input data (e.g., subject knowledge and evidence of preparation) to evaluate teachers, and fewer than 20 percent of the plans linked merit pay to student achievement or other output data.

There are many advantages and disadvantages of merit pay for teachers (Frohreich, 1988; National Education Association, 1984). On the one hand, supporters argue that

performance-based pay provides a competitive environment with higher pay for superior performance;

more public support flows to schools when teachers are paid in accordance with their performance;

evaluation processes improve and more individuals become involved in the apppraisal and improvement of instruction;

intrinsic recognition of the value of outstanding teaching motivates as much as do monetary rewards; and

merit compensation helps attract and retain effective teachers while discouraging ineffective ones from continuing in the profession.

On the other hand, merit pay's detractors contend that

there is no clear agreement on what constitutes effective teaching or on which teacher qualities influence pupil achievement;

competition among teachers lowers morale and decreases cooperation among colleagues;

most evaluation systems do not provide valid or comprehensive indicators of teaching abilities; and

the cost and time necessary to develop and implement an effective plan detract from more critical responsibilities.

The National Education Association's (1984) definition of merit pay reflects these limitations: "any plan to increase salary compensation of individual teachers that is based upon politics, favoritism, or the subjective evaluation of teachers by administrators or others" (p. 4).

The failure of merit plans to motivate teachers has been due largely to the difficulty of developing defensible and objective criteria to measure performance. Merit pay, in the absence of differential work assignments, also poses a logistical problem in justifying the assignment of some pupils to teachers of recognized merit and other pupils to teachers of lesser quality. Murnane and Cohen (1986) concluded that successful merit plans supplemented already high salaries and good working conditions and compensated teachers for extra responsibilities outside classrooms, rather than determining relative abilities of teachers within classrooms.

Career ladders and other differentiated staffing approaches restructure salary schedules with more formal status and pay differentiation among teachers than in the case of merit pay. The Holmes Group (1986) called for three levels within a "staged career that would make and reward formal distinction about responsibilities and degrees of autonomy." The first-level "instructor" would teach for several years under the supervision of experienced teachers. The majority of autonomous classroom teachers would hold the title of "professional teacher." The highest level, the "career professional," would include teachers who are capable of using their pedagogical expertise to improve other teachers' work. Similarly, the Carnegie Forum (1986) report called for more responsibilities to be given to board-certified teachers who would serve in the role of "lead teacher."

Early career ladders advanced teachers in accordance with years of experience, advanced preparation, and evaluations of teaching abilities. For example, Tennessee's Comprehensive Education Reform Act of 1984 included a five-step career ladder, and North Carolina piloted a three-step career ladder in 16 districts. Each of these states' plans called for a standardized appraisal system to assess performance in the classroom. Nevertheless, without a reasonable and valid way to distinguish good from excellent teachers (Cornett, 1985), more teachers than anticipated qualified for advancement. Because career ladders require funds for development, implementation, and evaluation in addition to salary supplements and fringe benefits paid to teachers, these plans require a long-term commitment to increase the funds as more teachers advance in the profession. Career ladders were found in many districts to breed suspicion, aggressive and circumventing behavior, and poor morale among teachers (MacPhail-Wilcox & King, 1988, p. 111). Because of these limitations, some states placed a cap on participation or withdrew funding entirely.

More effective career ladders differentiate responsibilities and salaries through the expansion or redesign of teaching roles. Although promotion to one of the designated levels may depend upon performance, differentiated pay reflects additional responsibilities rather than performance. For example, school boards, administrators, teachers, and parents were given latitude in Utah to develop programs cooperatively to include one of four incentives: performance bonuses, supplemental pay for expanded job responsibilities or special projects, job redesign, or extended contracts to reward teachers for curriculum development or other duties during additional work days. Career ladders that included job expansion or redesign were superior to those based on merit pay (Malen, Murphy, & Hart, 1988). Similarly, Astuto (1985) concluded that career ladders are more effective than traditional merit pay and encouraged states to support local districts' experiments with diverse approaches.

Another strategy, a career development plan, enables continuous professional growth for teachers without status differentiation. Unlike merit pay and career ladders, career development recognizes that teachers have different skills and abilities depending on their stage of growth as professionals. Increases in salary follow a uniform salary schedule with experience and advanced preparation dimensions. In a similar approach, the Collegial Research Consortium offered a "career lattice" (Pipho, 1988) of roles, including mentor, peer coach, and knowledge producer, from which teachers design individual professional development plans appropriate to their stages in the career cycle. Unlike merit pay plans that emphasize extrinsic rewards, a career lattice stresses intrinsic rewards in giving greater job satisfaction, varied responsibilities, and a voice in decision making without differentiating pay.

Table 14.5 indicates the status of states' incentive programs, including reforms in individual teachers' compensation and rewards for improved school performance. Cornett (1990) reports local initiatives ongoing in 15 states, state-financed or state-assisted pilot projects continuing to be supported in 11 states, incentives being fully implemented in 15 states, and incentive programs being developed in 9 states. Teacher incentives, including various plans to tie compensation with performance measures, are called for in 17 states, with local efforts present in 10 states and full implementation in 5 states. Career ladders

TABLE 14.5. Status of Teacher and School Incentive Programs, 1989

State	Local Initiative	State-Funded/ Assisted Pilots	Full Implementation of State Program	State Program Under Development	Type of Program
Alaska	x				Teacher incentive
Arizona		x			Career ladder
Arkansas		x*			Career development
California			x		Mentor teacher
Colorado		x			Teacher incentive
				x*	Teacher/school incentive
Connecticut				x	Teacher incentive/ mentor teacher
Florida			x		School incentive
Georgia				x†	Career ladder
Hawaii				x	Mentor teacher
Idaho				x	Career compensation/ mentor teacher
Illinois	x				Teacher incentive
Indiana		x			Career ladder
			x		Mentor teacher
			x		School incentive
Iowa			x		Teacher incentive
Kansas	x				Teacher incentive
Kentucky		x†			Career ladder
Louisiana		x			Career options
				x	School incentive
Maine			x		Tiered certification
Maryland	x				Career development
Massachusetts			x		Teacher incentive
				x	Mentor teacher
Michigan	x				Teacher incentive
		x			
Minnesota	x				Teacher incentive
		x			Mentor teacher
Missouri			x		Career ladder
Montana	x				Teacher incentive
New Hampshire	x				Teacher incentive
New Jersey			x		Teacher incentive
New York			x		Teacher incentive
		x			Mentor teacher
	x				Distr/school incentive
North Carolina			x		Career ladder
				x	Differentiated pay
North Dakota	x				Career development
Ohio		x		x	Career ladder
Oklahoma	x				Teacher incentive
Oregon		x			Career development/ mentor teacher

(Continued)

298

TABLE 14.5. *(Continued)*

State	Local Initiative	State-Funded/ Assisted Pilots	Full Implementation of State Program	State Program Under Development	Type of Program
Pennsylvania		x			Career development
			x		Mentor teacher
			x		School incentive
South Carolina				x	Teacher incentive
			x		Principal/school incentive
South Dakota	x				Mentor teacher
Tennessee			x		Career ladder
Texas			x		Career ladder
				x	School incentive
Utah			x		Career ladder
Vermont				x	Mentor teacher
Virginia	x	x[†]			Career ladder/ teacher incentive
Washington		x			School incentive
			x		Mentor teacher
Wisconsin	x				Mentor teacher
Wyoming	x				Career ladder/ teacher incentive

*Reform called for but not funded.
[†]Funding for pilot terminated. (*Source:* L. M. Cornett. [1990]. "Paying for Performance: Important Questions and Answers." *Career Ladder Clearinghouse.* Atlanta: Southern Regional Education Board. Reprinted by permission.)

result from local initiative, or are piloted or fully implemented statewide, in 10 states. Several other states provide differentiated pay or tiered certification to recognize career progression. Six states are reported to encourage professional growth without status differentiation through local- or state-financed career development programs. Mentor teacher programs are implemented or being developed in 13 states to reward or provide released time for exemplary teachers who assist new and other experienced teachers. Teachers benefit indirectly in nine states from school and district incentives that tie additional resources to measures of productivity, including student achievement.

In some cases, reforms in compensation plans that alter the nature of teachers' responsibilities involve them in school- and district-level decisions that affect work conditions. The discussion shifts to these situations in the next section.

COLLECTIVE BARGAINING AND SHARED DECISION MAKING

The involvement of teachers in decision-making processes may influence the internal efficiency of schools. Recent reform reports have urged school systems to give teachers a larger role in building-level decisions that directly influence working conditions. This thrust differs from the adversarial posture taken when teachers' unions and management define work conditions through collective bargaining.

In the 1960s and 1970s, professional associations gained a voice in district-level determinations of salaries and working conditions in most states. With a unionized teaching force came a bifurcated profession. Labor and management resolved disputes about personnel policies through collective bargaining. Along with the improvement of many aspects of teachers' work conditions came changes in personnel relations. A once-complacent teaching force whose needs were defined by school boards and administrators became actively involved in political action at local, state, and federal levels. Their numbers and political power forced policymakers to grant teachers a larger voice in decisions. At the same time, state policymakers, school boards, and administrators resisted demands and narrowed the scope of collective bargaining. Carefully defined management prerogatives restricted the extent of shared decision-making power.

The confrontational model has yielded slowly to shared and more collegial decision-making processes. In response to the 1960s drive to centralize small school districts, the concepts of school site management and budgeting emerged during the 1970s to give principals and their advisory councils a larger role in determining priorities for resources. The Carnegie Forum (1986) recommended decentralized authority to lodge greater control over educational decisions with principals and their leadership teams. Teachers would be "empowered to make principled judgments and decisions on their students' behalf" and lead teachers would be in a position to affect school operations more broadly:

> This means the ability to make—or at least to strongly influence—decisions concerning such things as the materials and instructional methods to be used, the staffing structure to be employed, the organization of the school day, the assignment of students, the consultants to be used, and the allocation of resources available to the schools. (p. 58)

Lead teachers would coordinate the work of the school's instructional staff, and they would be held accountable for the performance of the entire school (Tucker & Mandel, 1986, p. 25). In Chapter 16, we discuss more fully the involvement of teachers and communities in building-level governance and decision making.

Views of work change as teachers become involved in decision making and as principals increase their instructional leadership responsibilities (Cornett, 1987; Far West Laboratory, 1987). There is a more collegial environment as management processes are reformed. Rather than reporting policy directions defined externally and dictating procedures for internal operations, the principal shares information with and guides school-based teams toward consensus. Once the team identifies goals for a given program direction, the principal provides leadership in finding and coordinating resources to achieve those goals.

The roles of district offices and teachers' associations also change in a model that emphasizes building-level governance. Central offices provide leadership and technical assistance as their personnel assist school-based teams. Bargaining at the district level (or perhaps at the regional level in the future) resolves salary issues, but a number of items formerly placed on the bargaining table are reserved for building-level negotiations. More important, changes in the role of the professional teacher promise to strengthen schools and attract more highly qualified teaching candidates.

SUMMARY

The teacher labor market differs from that of the private sector in several important ways. Traditional economic assumptions about supply and demand do not adequately describe the setting of wages in the public sector. The availability of teachers (supply), requirements of school systems for teachers (demand), and teachers' salaries are influenced by a host of social and political considerations.

Improving the efficiency of schools depends in large part on refinements in personnel policies. Demand for teachers grew with expanding programs and services; the number of personnel who support instruction has grown more rapidly during the past decade than has the number of teachers required.

The desire for increasing the supply of qualified candidates leads to reforms to improve the cognitive abilities of individuals preparing for teaching roles. Policies that address several areas will contribute to efforts to attract and retain highly capable teachers: raising initial qualifications, expanding professional growth opportunities, increasing the level of compensation relative to other professions, relating compensation to individual performance and responsibilities, and improving conditions of the workplace.

There is agreement that compensation plans influence teachers' motivation and performance. Unlike the single-salary schedule that rewards limited but easily measured characteristics of teachers, merit pay and career development plans strive to relate remuneration with actual teaching performance and responsibilities. However, these performance-based plans may interfere with cooperative working relationships among teachers. Support is building to grant teachers greater autonomy and more opportunities for exercising professional judgment. Experiments with school governing councils will determine whether an even larger role in guiding school operations is warranted.

Policy changes that affect the number and qualifications of personnel directly influence school finance policy because of the high cost of labor relative to total school budgets. Effective merit pay and career ladder plans are costly strategies. However, improved working conditions and personnel quality promise to enhance the internal efficiencies of schools. Chapter 15 continues this discussion of educational production by examining the potential of increased use of information technologies as teachers' responsibilities change in the future.

ACTIVITIES

1. Examine teacher supply and demand conditions in a given state, region, or school district. Construct a chart or spreadsheet that compares the number of applicants for teaching positions with the number of personnel hired for different grade levels and subjects, over a 10-year period. Interview state and local officials about the trends evidenced and steps that had been or might be taken to stimulate supply, particularly in high-demand subjects.

2. Research and debate the advantages of merit pay plans that condition additional compensation on teachers' performance versus career ladder programs that differentiate salaries in accordance with redefined responsibilities.

3. Develop a career ladder remuneration plan that includes three to five progressions for

professional advancement as teachers grow in their capabilities and assume varied responsibilities. Include a second dimension for years of experience or for another indicator of continued professional growth at each of the three to five progressions. How does this plan differ in its rewards and motivations from traditional salary schedules?

4. Investigate the potential impact of shared decision making through governing councils that include teachers and parents at the school-building level upon collective negotiations between school boards and teachers' associations at the district level. In what ways are the scope of bargaining issues and the roles of various actors in these processes altered as decision making is decentralized?

REFERENCES

Anthony, P. (1988). Teachers in the economic system. In K. Alexander & D. H. Monk (Eds.), *Attracting and compensating America's teachers* (pp. 1-20). Cambridge, MA: Ballinger.

Association of American Colleges. (1989). *Those who can: Undergraduate programs to prepare arts and sciences majors for teaching*. Washington, DC: Author.

Astuto, T. A. (1985). *Merit pay for teachers: An analysis of state policy options*. Educational Policy Studies Series. Bloomington: Indiana University.

Butler, A. D. (1963). *Labor economics and institutions*. New York: Macmillan.

Candoli, I. C., Hack, W. G., Ray, J. R., & Stollar, D. H. (1984). *School business administration: A planning approach* (3rd ed.). Boston: Allyn & Bacon.

Carnegie Forum. (1986). *A nation prepared: Teachers for the 21st century*. New York: Carnegie Forum on Education and the Economy.

Castetter, W. B. (1986). *The personnel function in educational administration* (4th ed.). New York: Macmillan.

Cooperman, S., & Klagholz, L. (1985). New Jersey's alternate route to certification. *Phi Delta Kappan, 66*, 691–695.

Cornett, L. M. (1985). Trends and emerging issues in career ladder plans. *Educational Leadership, 43*, 6-10.

Cornett, L. M. (1987). More pay for teachers and administrators who do more: Incentive pay programs, 1987. *Career ladder clearinghouse*. Atlanta: Southern Regional Education Board.

Cornett, L. M. (1990). Paying for performance: Important questions and answers. *Career ladder clearinghouse*. Atlanta: Southern Regional Education Board.

Darling-Hammond, L. (1984). *Beyond the commission reports: The coming crisis in teaching* (R-3177-RC). Santa Monica, CA: Rand Corporation.

Darling-Hammond, L. (1986). Teaching knowledge: How do we test it? *American Educator, 10*, 18–21, 46–47.

Darling-Hammond, L., & Berry, B. (1988). *The evolution of teacher policy* (JRE-01). Santa Monica, CA: Rand Corporation, Center for Policy Research in Education.

Far West Laboratory. (1987). *Evaluation of Utah's career ladder system, Interim report*. San Francisco: Author.

Feistritzer, C. E. (1986). *Profile of teachers in the U.S.* Washington, DC: National Center for Education Information.

Fleisher, B. M., & Kniesner, T. J. (1980). *Labor economics: Theory, evidence, and policy.* Englewood Cliffs, NJ: Prentice-Hall.

Fox, J. M. (1984). Restructuring the teacher work force to attract the best and the brightest. *Journal of Education Finance, 10,* 214–237.

Fox, J. M. (1988). The supply of U.S. teachers: Quality for the twenty-first century. In K. Alexander & D. H. Monk (Eds.), *Attracting and compensating America's teachers* (pp. 49–68). Cambridge, MA: Ballinger.

Frohreich, L. E. (1988). Merit pay: Issues and solutions. In K. Alexander, & D. H. Monk, (Eds.), *Attracting and compensating America's teachers* (pp. 143–160). Cambridge, MA: Ballinger.

Hawley, W. D. (1986). Toward a comprehensive strategy for addressing the teacher shortage. *Phi Delta Kappan, 67,* 712–718.

Hecker, D. (1986). Teachers' job outlook: Is Chicken Little wrong again? *Occupational Outlook Quarterly, 30,* 13–17.

Holmes Group. (1986). *Tomorrow's teachers: A report of the Holmes Group.* East Lansing, MI: Author.

Jacobson, S. L. (1988). Merit pay and teaching as a career. In K. Alexander & D. H. Monk (Eds.), *Attracting and compensating America's teachers* (pp. 161–177). Cambridge, MA: Ballinger.

Johnson, S. M. (1986). Incentives for teachers: What motivates, what matters? *Educational Administration Quarterly, 22,* 54–79.

Jordan, K. F. (1988). Teacher education recommendations in the school reform reports. In K. Alexander & D. H. Monk (Eds.), *Attracting and compensating America's teachers* (pp. 21–47). Cambridge, MA: Ballinger.

Kreps, J. M., Somers, G. G., & Perlman, R. (1974). *Contemporary labor economics: Issues, analysis, and policies.* Belmont, CA: Wadsworth.

Lawler, E. E. (1981). *Pay and organization development.* Reading, MA: Addison-Wesley.

Lawton, S. B. (1988). Teachers' salaries: An international perspective. In K. Alexander & D. H. Monk (Eds.), *Attracting and compensating America's teachers* (pp. 69–89). Cambridge, MA: Ballinger.

McDonnell, L. M., & Pascal, A. (1988). *Teacher unions and educational reform.* Santa Monica, CA: Rand Corporation.

MacPhail-Wilcox, B., & King, R. A. (1988). Personnel reforms in education: Intents, consequences, and fiscal implications. *Journal of Education Finance, 14,* 100–134.

Madaus, G. F., & Pullin, D. (1987). Teacher certification tests: Do they really measure what we need to know? *Phi Delta Kappan, 69,* 31–38.

Malen, B., Murphy, M. J., & Hart, A. W. (1988). Restructuring teacher compensation systems: An analysis of three incentive strategies. In K. Alexander & D. H. Monk (Eds.), *Attracting and compensating America's teachers* (pp. 91–142). Cambridge, MA: Ballinger.

Manski, C. F. (1985). *Academic ability, earnings, and the decision to become a teacher: Evidence from the national longitudinal study of the high school class of 1972* (Working Paper No. 1539). Cambridge, MA: National Bureau of Economic Research.

Metzger, W. P. (1987). The spectre of "professionism." *Educational Researcher, 16,* 10–18.

Murnane, R. J., & Cohen, D. K. (1986). Merit pay and the evaluation problem: Why most merit pay plans fail and a few survive. *Harvard Educational Review, 56,* 1–17.

National Center for Education Statistics. (1988). *Digest of Education Statistics, 1988.* Washington, DC: U.S. Department of Education.

National Commission on Excellence in Education. (1983). *A nation at risk: The imperative for educational reform*. Washington, DC: U.S. Department of Education.

National Education Association. (1984). *Merit pay: Promises and facts*. Washington, DC: Author.

National Education Association. (1985). *The single salary schedule*. Washington, DC: Author.

National Education Association. (1987). *Status of the American public school teacher, 1985–86*. Washington, DC: Author.

National Education Association. (1989). *Estimates of school statistics, 1988–89*. Washington, DC: Author.

Pipho, C. (1988). Career ladders are changing. *Phi Delta Kappan*, *69*, 550–551.

Rebore, R. W. (1987). *Personnel administration in education: A management approach* (2nd ed.). Englewood Cliffs, NJ: Prentice Hall.

Salmon, R. G. (1988). Teacher salaries: Progress over the decade. In K. Alexander & D. H. Monk (Eds.), *Attracting and compensating America's teachers* (pp. 249–261). Cambridge, MA: Ballinger.

Shulman, L. S. (1987). Assessment for teaching: An initiative for the profession. *Phi Delta Kappan*, *69*, 38–44.

Stern, J. D. (1988). *The condition of education: Elementary and secondary education, 1988* (Vol. 1). Washington, DC: National Center for Education Statistics.

Sykes, G. (1983). Public policy and the problem of teacher quality: The need for screens and magnets. In L. S. Shulman & G. Sykes (Eds.), *Handbook of teaching and policy* (pp. 97–125). White Plains, NY: Longman.

Sykes, G. (1987). Reckoning with the spectre. *Educational Researcher*, *16*, 19–21.

Thangaraj, E. P. (1985). *The impact of teacher labor market forces on characteristics of the teacher aspirant pool*. Unpublished doctoral dissertation, State University of New York at Buffalo.

Travers, E. F., & Sacks, S. R. (1987). *Teacher education and the liberal arts: The position of the Consortium for Excellence in Teacher Education*. Swathmore, PA: Swathmore College.

Tucker, M., & Mandel, D. (1986). The Carnegie report—A call for redesigning the schools. *Phi Delta Kappan*, *68*, 25–27.

U.S. Department of Education. (1988). *Digest of education statistics, 1988*. Washington, DC: Author.

Vance, V. S., & Schlechty, P. C. (1982). The distribution of academic ability in the teaching force: Policy implications. *Phi Delta Kappan*, *64*, 22–27.

Wisniewski, R., & Kleine, P. (1984). Teacher moonlighting: An unstudied phenomenon. *Phi Delta Kappan*, *65*, 553–555.

CHAPTER 15

Educational Technology and Staffing Decisions

We introduced the concepts of educational production functions and input-output analysis in Chapter 13 in reference to the internal efficiency of educational enterprises. In Chapter 14, we examined efficiency aspects of the input of labor; in this chapter, we continue our analysis of efficiency but focus on the mix of inputs—specifically, labor and capital. While productivity can be enhanced by higher outputs, it can also be improved through lower costs. Any rearrangement of inputs which lowers total cost without changing the quality of education delivered is an increase in productivity. Resulting decreases in total cost represent decreases in the amount of real resources (human and nonhuman) which society must commit to current educational processes, freeing those resources to satisfy other human aspirations or permitting investment in new educational pursuits.

The chapter begins with a general discussion of education and technology. It then presents one vision of the integration of state-of-the-art information and communication technologies into elementary and secondary schooling. The chapter concludes with a discussion of the politics of technological change in education and the implications for school administration and finance.

TECHNOLOGICAL CHANGE AND EDUCATION

Technology is the application of science to control the material environment for human benefit through the use of tools and intellect. When used prudently, technologies allow society to produce more and better goods and services from a fixed amount of resources. Advances in technology have permitted humankind to live longer and more comfortably; but they have also led to undesirable results including environmental exploitation, unemployment, and the capacity for total human annihilation.

Educational technology is the application of scientific knowledge, including learning theory, to the solution of problems in education. Education and technology are at the same time cause and effect to one another. Technological developments place continuing pressure on educators to keep curriculum and instructional methods up to date. At the same time, educational institutions are essential to the generation and assimilation of new technology.

Although society in general has tended toward enhanced technological sophistication and increased capital intensity, the educational sector has retained a traditional, labor-intensive, craft-oriented technology. Vaizey, Norris, and Sheehan (1972, p. 228) refer to education as "the part of the economy where time has stood still." This "standing still" creates both sociological and economic problems. From an economic standpoint, labor-intensive education is unnecessarily expensive and, in general, does not produce a work force with the prerequisite attitudes and skills needed for the workplace. From a sociological standpoint, technologically unsophisticated schools are losing their credibility and thereby their effectiveness with pupils because they are no longer congruent with the larger society.

Continuing reference has been made in this book to the growing labor intensity of education. Figure 3.2 shows the dramatic increases since 1950 in expenditures per pupil in constant dollar purchasing power. The fourfold increase, from $960 to $3,752, was sufficient to allow for significant program expansion in terms of smaller classes; more specialists; more electives; and new programs for gifted, handicapped, and learning-disabled children. The growing labor intensiveness of education is further developed in Chapter 14. For the American economy as a whole, approximately 66 percent of total product cost is for labor; for education, the range is between 85 percent and 90 percent. There is strong evidence that during the 1970s and 1980s, higher expenditures and program enhancements were not accompanied by improved academic achievement, a primary, although not an exclusive, outcome of schooling (Astin, Green, & Korn, 1987).

In nonservice industries, for example, manufacturing, it is generally understood that "technological structure" is not inalterably fixed, especially under market conditions of competition. Instead, there is an ongoing search for alternative, more efficient methods of producing a desired product; each alternative production possibility is judged by its potential cost and effectiveness versus the potential cost and effectiveness of every other alternative. Education, however, as a state monopoly and in the absence of market incentives for efficiency, appears to be locked into one mode of production. Even when parents enter the educational marketplace, they exercise choice among public and private schools that differ in size and philosophies but are remarkably similar in basic technologies.

Baumol (1967, p. 415) argued that "inherent in the technological structure" of such service industries as education "are forces working almost unavoidably for progressive and cumulative increases in the real costs incurred in supplying them." If productivity is to be enhanced in education, there must be a willingness to develop alternative means of providing educational services including modifications in the technological structures of schooling.

There is a tendency among educators to think of educational technology as being very expensive. But this is not necessarily the case. Even allowing for substantial increases in teacher salaries, Willett (1973) estimated the cost per pupil of an instructional system optimally integrating human and machine capabilities to be well below that of the existing system because:

there would be fewer teachers, but with higher qualifications;

technology would largely take over the information transfer function;

extensive use would be made of relatively low-cost paraprofessionals under the supervision of teachers; and

there would be extensive use of community resources.

Because the cost of instructional technology is even lower today relative to other costs and the sophistication of the technology is much greater than when Willett made his analysis, it is likely that cost comparisons would be even more favorable.

The National Governors' Association (1986) report on education noted,

> despite extensive purchase and high expectations, most American schools have not become significantly more cost-effective or more efficient because of technology. The structure of most schools has not changed significantly because technology is available. (p. 123)

A 1987 report by the National School Boards Association (Perelman, 1987) criticized the school reform movement because it failed to address the issue of increasing efficiency in education. This report anticipates an inevitable technological transformation of teaching and learning in the United States and elsewhere in the world.

Levin and Meister (1985) comment that educational technologies have been characterized by promise rather than realization of that promise. During this century, the educational potential of new inventions such as radio, motion pictures, television, videocassettes, compact disks, and computers has been touted, only to be followed by disappointment as the invention remains ancillary to traditional instructional procedures. These authors diagnosed the generic failure of educational technologies as being due largely "to a misplaced obsession with the hardware and neglect of software, other resources, and instructional setting that are necessary to successful implementation" (p. 9). They point out that equipment purchase represents only about 10 percent of the total costs of an innovation.

To improve the situation, Levin and Meister (1985, p. 38) propose three initiatives: (1) more coordinated market information, (2) improved decision mechanisms in schools, and (3) large-scale institutional approaches to software development and funding. The decision mechanism they propose provides for district-wide coordination of the purchase and installation of technology, integration of software in relation to district curricular objectives and materials, and training of professional and support staff in the use of hardware and software (p. 43).

In a similar vein, a 1982 report by the Office of Technology Assessment of the U.S. Congress pointed to the desirability of integrating technology into the instructional system. After presenting a series of case studies of the use of information technology in education, the report concluded that "information technologies can be most effectively applied to tasks when they are well integrated in their institutional environments" (p. 9).

This is not the way technology has been used in schools, however. The purpose of technology is to make labor go further by replacing it, to the extent possible, with mechanical devices and more efficient organization in order to produce a better product or service and/or to reduce the costs of production (Benson, 1961). Yet labor-intensive strategies, such as those discussed in Chapter 14, are the most common reforms suggested to improve public education.

It isn't that schools have totally neglected new technologies; the concern expressed is over the way in which schools have chosen to accommodate them. Technological devices have been used as "add-ons" to assist or supplement teachers rather than as integral parts of new instructional systems which combine the capabilities of people and machines to achieve results that people cannot achieve alone. When technology is used as an add-on or as enrichment, rather than reducing costs and increasing efficiency, costs are increased and efficiency is decreased unless there is evidence of greatly improved outcomes.

This is not a recent phenomenon. In a 1972 study, Vaizey, Norris, and Sheehan noted that teacher costs account for at least half of all school costs and that unless increases in pupil–teacher ratios took place as a result of new technologies, the new technologies must necessarily add to total costs. The authors accurately predicted that increases in pupil–teacher ratios would not happen:

> it seems unlikely that any teacher substitution will occur—certainly none has yet taken place. Thus for new methods to be used on a wider scale, the decision will have to be taken that the educational benefits are worth the resulting increases in costs. (p. 234)

Becker (1982), in assessing the educational potential of the microcomputer, concluded that "disappointment and poorly utilized resources" will result without forethought about the integration of technology with traditional classroom instruction. He sees as the biggest problem overcoming the contrast between the computer's profitable interaction with a single student and the group-based organizational structure of schools.

We now turn our attention to some of the design and implementation issues which will arise *if* schools took full advantage of the instructional potential of information and communication technologies. In the next section we describe one possible approach to redesigning schools in a fashion which integrates instructional technology and human resources. The resulting design redefines the roles of teachers and students and increases the use of paraprofessionals and community volunteers.

AN APPROACH TO INTEGRATING EDUCATIONAL TECHNOLOGY INTO THE PROCESS OF INSTRUCTION

In an increasingly literate and sophisticated society, ways need to be found to meet the unique needs of individual students. At the same time, there needs to be improved effectiveness of schools in meeting these needs at current, or perhaps reduced, levels of resources. No longer are these two goals mutually exclusive. They are obtainable if educators (1) restructure the ratio of human and capital inputs in the schooling process and (2) take advantage of existing information and communication technologies.

The move from the nineteenth century American Common School to "mass education" in the twentieth century appears to have been at least partly dictated by new least-cost combinations of inputs which made larger schools economically viable. Likewise, present technological changes in information processing, transmission, and retrieval are making necessary a reexamination of the relative prices of educational inputs and a reconsideration of the scale of educational production functions. A number of production possibilities exist in any educational situation. It would be rare to have some improvement in resource allocation without having a resulting positive effect on both unit cost and productivity.

Since early in this century, industrial concepts of standardization and economies of scale have dominated thinking about the organization and administration of schools (Callahan, 1962). Increasingly larger schools have enabled a greater variety of course offerings and specialists. But this same trend has made the system so rigid that it cannot adequately respond to individual differences of students or changing conditions in the environment. This point was developed more fully in the discussion of economies of scale in Chapter 13.

In our current school organization, too little recognition is given to the fact that learning is primarily a function of the interest, motivation, and hard work of the student. We frequently assume that learning takes place best in the physical presence of a teacher to guide and supervise learning activities from moment to moment. The practical effect of this assumption has been to claim that for a child to learn, a course has to be established. More critically, that course requires a certified teacher, and cost considerations require approximately 20 or more pupils per class. Under these assumptions, "individualization" requires many courses, many teachers, and many students.

Contemporary schooling has become "rigidified" and "standardized" in ways that actually thwart learning and fail to educate young people for productive lives in a society now facing accelerating change and diversity. Rather than create self-directed learners who can function independently and interpret change, the school has continued to create teacher-dependent role players. Instead, school regimens and instructional methods need to be more flexible to provide students with programs and content which are individualized according to learning abilities and personal interests. School curricula need to be interrelated across subject boundaries in order to permit the integration of ideas and to emphasize the interrelatedness of problems.

New Roles for Teachers

In an information-rich society, the teacher as a primary source of information is rapidly becoming obsolete. Libraries, textbooks, television, videodisks and cassettes, audiotapes, CD-rom data bases, computer software, and information systems provide the means whereby any student, knowing how to read and to use these resources, can obtain most information needed in a manner of presentation which is at least as effective as today's typical teaching. This portends new roles for educational professionals. They will need to become experts in managing information resources and in designing learning experiences for individual students relevant to their needs, growth, and development; they need not, for the most part, be purveyors of information. Teachers—if we continue to call them that—will need to be involved primarily in the diagnosis of learning needs, prescription of learning experiences (i.e., curriculum design), motivation of students, and evaluation of the results (Nelson, 1978). In carrying out these functions, the primary interaction with students will be, of necessity, on a one-to-one basis, in essence eliminating the classroom as we know it.

The new focus of schools needs to be on learning rather than on teaching. With the nearly unlimited accounting capabilities of mainframe and minicomputers, emphasis can be placed on *continuous* rather than discontinuous learning which is *individualized* to capitalize on student strengths and to remedy student weaknesses as these are diagnosed. For nearly two decades, it has been the law of the land that children with learning disabilities and other handicapping conditions receive individual diagnoses and education prescriptions; all children should be so treated in the future.

A multimedia approach to learning does not eliminate traditional teaching; but traditional teaching becomes only *one* of many methods. Other media include books, drill, computer-assisted instruction (CAI), videodisk enhanced by computer, audiotape and audiodisk, lecture (large group), discussion (small group), drama, chorus, band, athletic teams, tutors (teacher, aide, volunteer, or other student), laboratory, and field experiences. The learning experience can be a function of all life experiences, not just those in a school. Student–teacher ratios are relevant only when particular group sizes can be shown to contribute to greater efficiency in the *learning* process.

Combining teacher assessments of individual student needs with a multimedia approach to instruction makes possible the development of an individualized educational plan for each student. But, simultaneously, the individualization of instruction increases the problems of scheduling and custodial functions of schools in society. Means need to be devised to build into instructional management software a capability for handling far greater complexities of scheduling resulting from the use of a variety of resources on an individual basis.

The difficulty of the task is not to be understated. It is of such magnitude that general systems and material need to be developed at the state and national levels with adaptations made at the district and school levels. Although some good software packages do exist, they need to be adapted and others need to be developed. Each media package needs extensive review, and objectives obtainable with each package need to be listed and cross-referenced in schools' information systems. The curriculum development effort required is substantial; but the existence of complex, computerized military defense systems; inventory and financial control systems in business; and on-line reservation systems for airlines, hotels, and entertainment events suggests that the problem is not insurmountable. Such systems are beyond the capacities of schools and most school districts to design, however.

To take full advantage of available technology, planned reliance needs to be placed on the machine for its complete range of capabilities, but subject to human direction, planning, and control. Teachers are still absolutely essential, but their role is changed from one of director, leader, and final authority to one of diagnostician, prescriber, motivator, facilitator, and evaluator. Teachers, students, and aides are seen as multidimensional human resources leading to specialization and division of labor, breaking the self-contained classroom mold of today's schools. Tasks requiring professional judgment are separated from those which are routine. High-cost, professionally trained persons are assigned to the former and lower-cost paraprofessionals are assigned to the latter. The pupil–teacher ratio is likely to increase, but the pupil–adult ratio is likely to remain the same or even decline from current levels. Teachers would be perceived as managers— managers of instruction—supervising students and paraprofessionals with the aid of contemporary technological inventions.

Economic Costs

In using existing technology to enhance the educational productivity and effectiveness of teachers, paraprofessionals, and students, and in dividing control tasks into those which require professional training and those which do not, an overall design is permitted which, using the most conservative estimates, is no more expensive than today's labor-intensive school. Willett, Swanson, and Nelson (1979) argue that the cost would be much less. Based on studies by McCusker-Sorensen (1966), they determined that schools can be operated with an adult–pupil ratio of only 30 per 1,000. This compares to a nationally prevailing professional–pupil ratio of over 60 per 1,000. They estimated the cost of an integrated human-machine schooling system to be less than 60 percent of its contemporary counterpart.

Levin, Glass, and Meister (1984) made cost-effective analyses of four commonly proposed reform interventions: reducing class size, lengthening the school day, CAI, and cross-age tutoring. The interventions were treated as modifications of current practice and not as complete redesigns of the instructional system. They found the interventions of CAI and cross-age tutoring to be cost effective in reading instruction. As an add-on, CAI was not cost effective in improving achievement in mathematics, although cross-age tutoring was. Reducing class size and extending the school day are not relevant concepts to the design of schools as previously set forth. But CAI and cross-age tutoring are, and they could prove to be even more cost effective as part of a total redesign package which reduces reliance on expensive labor.

Staffing

Intelligent direction for schools of the future depends upon the professional educators associated with them, and school-based decision making is likely to be the norm (see Chapter 16). Teachers need to be experts in learning theory, curriculum design, motivational techniques, and developmental procedures. They need highly specialized skills in diagnosing the strengths and weaknesses of individual students with various intellectual skills and backgrounds and in prescribing the best combinations of available learning resources.

Student assistants (Johnson & Johnson, 1987; Lippitt, 1975) and paraprofessional adults can become valuable staff members in schools. The roles of both can be arranged to complement and supplement the role of the highly trained professionals who have the prime responsibility for guiding student instruction. The use of these two ancillary groups results in distinct advantages to the professional personnel: Each professional can specialize in the areas of expertise to which that individual is best suited by personality and training; and the required "omniscience in the classroom," assumed under the present system as necessary for the professional, will be relaxed.

Until recently, teacher salaries have been so low and teacher supply so abundant that little attention has been given to maximizing the time available for making decisions which require professional discretion. As a result, teachers have been expected to assume assignments, such as collecting lunch money; typing worksheets; and monitoring cafeterias, lavatories, and hallways, which could be accomplished as well—and, in some cases, better—by persons without professional teacher training. With a growing shortage of teachers and salaries which are beginning to reach professional levels in some districts, it becomes imperative that teachers' time be concentrated on tasks requiring professional discretion. Less expensive persons can be employed to carry out clerical and routine tasks.

Graduate study at the doctoral level could easily be justified for teachers functioning in the preceding mode; teachers need to be truly "reflective practitioners" (Schon, 1983). Differentiated staffing and multimedia instructional delivery systems can release sufficient resources to enable salaries, especially those of teachers with a master teacher classification, to be raised to a level competitive with other professions.

THE POLITICS OF IMPLEMENTATION

Redesigning educational systems to make optimal use of technology holds the potential for contributing to the solution of a number of current policy problems including upgrading teaching roles to professional levels, paying teachers professionally competitive salaries, and making the system more effective and more efficient. Other distinct advantages can accrue: (1) The savings in per pupil per year expenditures over present costs can literally "buy us into" a new system; (2) the steady increase in the cost in education can be slowed in absolute dollars and in further increases as a percentage of GNP; and (3) the professionalization of educators can continue, rather than be aborted for the lack of money.

When changes in productivity are positive, unit costs fall; when changes in productivity are negative, unit costs rise. In the case of public education, the benefits derived from declining unit costs may be shared by the public in the form of declining or stabilized tax rates and by the employees of the system, teachers and support personnel, in the form of higher wages. Although in the short run the reduction in unit costs is made possible by a reduction in the numbers of professionally trained persons employed, in the long run positive changes in productivity generally result in employment of more people.

The arguments which have been presented in support of redesigning elementary and secondary schooling through the use of available technology are derived from economic and pedagogical considerations. However, the decision to modernize or not to modernize is political in that 90 percent of elementary and secondary schooling is provided through the public sector. Because of the highly decentralized structure for policy-making in education and because of the incremental nature of democratic policy development, modernization is likely to come about as a series of decisions over an extended period of time made in a variety of legislative forums.

Any strategy for change will have to take into account two factors which tend to perpetuate the status quo. The first is the strong, articulate constituency of professional and auxiliary employees of public schools who have a vested interest in maintaining current arrangements. The second is that even with their recognized shortcomings, elementary and secondary schools as presently constituted are familiar; the proposed is unknown. A new system could be better, but, then, it could be worse. Under such circumstances, the prudent person is likely to opt for the known until there is convincing evidence of the merits of the proposed.

Reforms will be accomplished most quickly if they can be done in collaboration with professional organizations. To obtain collaboration will require a recognition on the part of state and local officials that proposed innovations pose threats to the psychological and economic security of employees and their associations. An incremental strategy of implementation allows time for building a base of experience and alleviating fear derived from its lack (Lindblom, 1968).

The costs and benefits for the present members of the teaching profession are mixed. For teachers of the future, the benefits should far exceed the costs. But for those currently teaching, significant changes in their professional duties would be required as the role of teacher is redefined, and some might face the possibility of losing their positions. Both possibilities can cause an inordinate amount of trauma. Movements of labor are essential if society is to improve its productivity through technological change, but it does not follow that it needs to be a financial burden to those directly concerned. There will be start-up costs to be borne by the public to offset economic losses to individuals because of early retirement or to cover costs of retraining and relocating younger educational personnel. Providing fair guarantees of economic security to present teachers represents a major challenge to teacher organizations, local school leadership, and the state and federal governments.

On the positive side, reorganizing schools along the lines suggested would facilitate realization of proposed reforms in personnel policies as discussed in Chapter 14. There would be substantially higher salaries for those remaining in teaching. The possibility of more interesting job definitions which are wholly professional in nature and the possibility of career advancement without leaving the field of teaching would assist efforts to recruit and retain capable teachers.

The implications for administrators at both the district and school levels are significant. Change requires professional leadership; at the initial stages this is most likely to come from professionally alert principals and central office administrators. At the central office level, a strategic plan needs to be developed and implemented for moving from the status quo to desired future states. The board of education, the professional staff, and the community need to be convinced of the merits of the plan and its strategy. Tough negotiations can be expected with unions representing teachers and other personnel, especially if there are to be cutbacks in personnel and redefinitions of duties. Extensive staff development programs have to be initiated. Political action and strategic planning at state and federal levels are necessary to secure essential technological infrastructures, human support systems, and start-up financing.

The most dramatic change in roles is likely to be at the school level. High-caliber and highly trained teachers are needed to be responsible for curricular and instructional decisions made at the school. Principals and lead teachers need to stimulate and coordinate the redesign process and establish and maintain wholesome school environments; they also need to provide properly functioning support systems. School leaders of the future, first and foremost, must be visionaries. They also need to be politically astute, diplomats, planners, negotiators, and trainers.

SUMMARY

There is a recursive relationship between education and technological innovation. Technological innovations place social and economic pressures on educational institutions to change; and educational institutions are the means by which scientists, engineers, planners, and designers are given their underlying knowledge base from which they create new technological innovations.

The world is currently going through a basic shift in its technoeconomic paradigm, from manufacturing to information processing, which is affecting the very structure and conditions of production and distribution for almost all sectors of the economy. This paradigm shift is manifesting itself in educational institutions in what has been called the "educational reform movement." An educational system designed for an industrial age is slowly adapting to the requirements of an information society. Instead of making better use of traditional labor-intensive technologies, as Monk (1989) states has been the predominant mode of educational reform, schools of the future must employ very different strategies in their uses of labor *and* capital.

This chapter has described one vision of the probable impact of technological changes on schools. Schools are seen as needing to integrate efficiently information and communication technologies into their instructional systems, making schooling compatible with a technologically sophisticated world. Such integration transforms the role of elementary and secondary teachers from purveyors of information to managers of instruction. The role of student is changed from passive to active participant. Increasing numbers of paraprofessionals are used in the instructional process. To implement such changes, school leaders need to be visionaries, planners, coordinators and negotiators as they provide liaison with the community and other levels of government.

ACTIVITIES

1. Describe an educational system which maximizes the utilization of human and machine capabilities as is suggested in the following statement:

   > In order to take full advantage of available technology, planned reliance needs to be placed on the machine for its complete range of capabilities, but subject to human direction, planning, and control.

2. Table 3.9 reports national statistics on the continuing decline in pupil–teacher ratios and average class size.
   a. Under what circumstances would this represent a decline in the efficiency of public schools, an increase in the quality of educational services, or some combination of these?
   b. What is the rationale for your response?

3. Technologically sophisticated schools may have important implications for other reform proposals such as the raising of academic expectations and standards, the professionalization of teaching, school site management, and family choice of schooling. Describe the potential interrelationships and indicate whether technology is likely to facilitate or inhibit each of the reforms.

REFERENCES

Astin, A. W., Green, K. C., & Korn, W. S. (1987). *The American freshman: Twenty year trends*. Los Angeles: University of California, Graduate School of Education, Cooperative Institutional Research Program.

Baumol, W. J. (1967). Macroeconomics of unbalanced growth: The anatomy of urban crisis. *American Economic Review*, *57* (3), 415–426.

Becker, H. (1982). *Microcomputers in the classroom: Dreams and realities* (Report No. 319). Baltimore, MD: Johns Hopkins University, Center for the Social Organization of Schools.

Benson, C. (1961). *The economics of public education*. Boston: Houghton Mifflin.

Callahan, R. (1962). *Education and the cult of efficiency: A study of the social forces that have shaped the administration of the public schools*. Chicago: University of Chicago Press.

Johnson, D. W., & Johnson, R. (1987). *Learning together and alone: Cooperative, competitive, and individualistic learning* (2nd ed.). Englewood Cliffs, NJ: Prentice Hall.

Levin, H., Glass, G., & Meister, G. (1984). *Cost-effectiveness of four educational interventions* (Project Report No. 84–A11). Stanford, CA: Stanford University, Stanford Education Policy Institute.

Levin, H., & Meister, G. (1985). *Educational technology and computers: Promises, promises, always promises* (Project Report No. 85–A13). Stanford, CA: Stanford University, Stanford Education Policy Institute.

Lindblom, C. S. (1968). *The public policy-making process*. Englewood Cliffs, NJ: Prentice Hall.

Lippitt, P. (1975). *Students teach students*. Bloomington, IN: The Phi Delta Kappa Educational Foundation.

McCusker, H., & Sorensen, P. (1966). The economics of education. In P. H. Rossi, & B. J. Biddle (Eds.), *The new media and education: Their impact on society*. Chicago: Aldine.

Monk, D. H. (1989). The education production function: Its evolving role in policy analysis. *Educational Evaluation and Policy Analysis*, *11*, 31–45.

National Center for Education Statistics. (1988). *The condition of education: Elementary and secondary education*. Washington, DC: U.S. Department of Education.

National Governors' Association. (1986). *Time for results: The governors' 1991 report on education*. Washington, DC: Center for Policy Research and Analysis.

Nelson, E. (1978). Occupational education in New York State: The transition from vocational to career education (Occasional Paper No. 28). Albany: Unpublished monograph, New York State Education Department, School Finance Law Study Project.

Office of Technology Assessment, Congress of the United States. (1982). *Informational technology and its impact on American education*. Washington, DC: U.S. Government Printing Office.

Perelman, L. (1987). *Technology and the transformation of schools*. Alexandria, VA: National School Boards Association.

Schon, D. A. (1983). *The reflective practitioner: How professionals think in action*. New York: Basic Books.

Vaizey, J., Norris, K., & Sheehan, J. (1972). *The political economy of education*. New York: Wiley.

Willett, E. J. (1973). *Designs for structuring capital-intensive (rather than labor-intensive) education production functions for the promotion of individualized learning below college level*. Unpublished doctoral dissertation, State University of New York at Buffalo.

Willett, E., Swanson, A., & Nelson, E. (1979). *Modernizing the little red schoolhouse: The economics of improved schooling*. Englewood Cliffs, NJ: Educational Technology Publications.

CHAPTER 16

School-based Decision Making: Provider Sovereignty

Several proposals for restructuring educational systems attempt to generate marketlike incentives to improve their efficiency. These proposals bring with them the added benefit of simultaneously enhancing the societal objective of liberty by permitting more choice among consumers and providers alike. Elmore (1988) has identified two fundamental questions associated with choice. The first is whether or not parents and students should be empowered to choose among schools or among programs within schools. He calls this the "demand side" question. "It poses the question of whether the consumers of education should be given the central role in deciding what kind of education is appropriate for them" (p. 79). Chapter 17 focuses on this issue through the lens of market concepts, acknowledging the fact that there is no universal agreement on the desired outcomes of schooling.

Elmore's second question is whether or not educators should be empowered to organize and manage schools, to design educational programs, and to receive public funds for providing education to students. He refers to this as the "supply side" question. "It poses the issue of whether the providers of education should be given the autonomy and flexibility to respond to differences in judgments of consumers about appropriate education" (p. 79). The supply side issue is addressed in this chapter by considering proposals for school-based management as a strategy for stimulating alternative means of combining schooling inputs to obtain desired outputs. Combining the concepts of family choice (the focus of the next chapter) with genuine schooling options made possible through school-based decision making (the focus of this chapter) holds the potential for generating marketlike forces in education which encourage efficiency and accountability.

School-based management (SBM) is known by many names including self-managing schools; school site management; school site decision making; shared governance; decentralized management; and, the more narrowly focused term, school-based budgeting. This strategy is founded on the premise that the school is the fundamental decision-making unit within the educational system and that its administrators, teachers, and other professional staff constitute a natural management team. Each school is considered a relatively autonomous unit, with the principal in the role of chief executive officer.

Under SBM, school personnel may develop the budget, select staff, and refine the school's curriculum to meet the specific needs of its pupils within legal constraints set by the school district or higher levels of government (Cawelti, 1989). Such decisions may be made by the principal alone or the responsibility may be shared with teachers, parents, and upper-grade students (Lindelow, 1981). The school district continues to set general priorities within which all schools must function; develop overarching educational objectives and the curriculum to meet those objectives; allocate lump sums of money to schools based on student needs; negotiate labor contracts; and provide facilities and other support services such as transportation, payroll, and accounting.

Cuban (1988) would classify SBM, along with most of the other reforms considered in Part IV of this book, as second-order changes, "which involve visions of what ought to be that are different from those imbedded in the existing organization. Putting those visions into practice alters fundamental roles, routines, and relationships within an organization" (p. 229). First-order changes assume that existing organizational goals and structures are adequate and only minor adjustments in current policies and practices are needed to correct their deficiencies. First-order changes are matters of quality control, whereas second-order changes involve system redesign. The latter is far more difficult to bring about.

In this chapter, we examine the rationale for SBM as expressed by its leading advocates. Since SBM is intended to simulate in public schools many of the perceived organizational advantages of private schools, a study which contrasts public and private school organizations and environments is reviewed. Actual experiences of districts experimenting with SBM are reported. The chapter closes with a description of a model for implementing SBM at the school level.

REFORMERS' ARGUMENTS FOR SCHOOL-BASED MANAGEMENT

One of the first proposals for SBM was made by New York State's *Fleischmann Report* (1973) in conjunction with a proposal for full state funding. Referring to studies by the Committee for Economic Development (1970) and the Urban Institute (1972), the commission concluded that

> centralization and decentralization are not inconsistent concepts and that it is quite possible to have financing at one level and policy-making and other kinds of control at another, with the implication that state financing is not inconsistent with decentralized operating units.
>
> The Commission strongly urges greater powers of decision-making in the *local school*. . . . The effective point for expression of citizen and parent-citizen interest in education is the school, not the school district, for the school is the basic operating unit and cost center in the provision of educational services. (pp. 86–87)

To facilitate citizen involvement in the educational process, the commission called for a Parent Advisory Council (PAC) for every public school in the state. The PACs would participate in the selection of principals and would provide criteria for the employment of teaching staff; however, the final selection of staff would be the principal's responsibility (*Fleischmann Report*, 1972). These commission recommendations were never implemented.

Well before the advent of "effective schools" research, the commission saw the principal as having the greatest potential for improving the quality of education. According to the commission, the principal should be the major voice in setting the educational tone of the school. But principals were to work closely with local citizens, parents, faculty, and students, subject to strengthened measures of accountability and constraints imposed by higher levels of the educational hierarchy.

A decade later, the National Governors' Association (1986) renewed the call of the *Fleischmann Report* for SBM. Their Task Force on Leadership and Management recommended that states provide districts with incentives and technical assistance to promote school site management and improvement. They proposed the identification and removal of legal and organizational barriers and the encouragement of local experimentation in school-based budgeting, school-based hiring of teachers, and provision of discretionary resources at the school level. Lamar Alexander, governor of Tennessee and chair of the association at the time the report was issued, commented that *if* schools and school districts were held accountable for results, "Then, we're ready to give up a lot of state regulatory control" (p. 4).

Sizer (1985) claims that hierarchical bureaucracy is paralyzing American education: "The structure is getting in the way of children's learning" (p. 206). Sizer's first imperative for better schools is to give room to teachers and students to work and learn in their own, appropriate ways. He sees decentralized authority as allowing teachers and principals to adapt their schools to the needs, learning styles, and learning rates of students individually. Although not denying the need to upgrade the overall quality of the educating profession, Sizer believes that, if empowered, there are enough fine teachers and administrators to lead a renaissance of American schools.

Goodlad (1984) identifies the school as *the* unit for improvement. The approach to educational reform which Goodlad believes most promising is the one "that will seek to cultivate the capacity of schools to deal with their own problems, to become largely self-renewing" (p. 31). He does not see the schools as being "cut loose," but rather as being linked to the hub (district office) and to one another in a network. State officials should be responsible for developing "a common framework for schools within which there is room for some differences in interpretation at the district level and for some variations in schools resulting from differences in size, location, and perspective" (p. 275). According to Goodlad, the district should concern itself with the balance in curricula presented, the processes employed in planning, and the equitable distribution of funds. "What I am proposing is genuine decentralization of authority and responsibility to the local school within a framework designed to assure school-to-school equity and a measure of accountability" (p. 275).

Boyer (1983) also sees heavy doses of bureaucracy "stifling creativity in too many schools, and preventing principals and their staffs from exercising their best professional judgement on decisions that properly should be made at the local level" (p. 227). For

Boyer, "Rebuilding excellence in education means reaffirming the importance of the local school and freeing leadership to lead" (p. 316). Among his recommendations for accomplishing this are the following:

> Principals and staff at the local school should have more control over their own budgets, operating within the guidelines set by the district office. Further, every principal should have a School Improvement Fund, discretionary money to provide time and materials for program development and for special seminars and staff retreats. Principals should also have more control over the selection and rewarding of teachers. Acting in consultation with their staffs, they should be given responsibility for the final choice of teachers for their schools. (p. 316)

Cuban (1988) argues that the bureaucratic organization of schooling is responsible for the lack of professional leadership.

> Autonomy is the necessary condition for leadership to arise. Without choice, there is no autonomy. Without autonomy, there is no leadership. . . . Schools as they are presently organized press teachers, principals, and superintendents toward managing rather than leading, toward maintaining what is rather than moving to what can be. The structures of schooling and the incentives buried within them produce a managerial imperative. (pp. xx–xxi)

Cuban also recognized the need for federal, state, and district regulations and their accompanying forms of accountability. He called for balanced procedures which permit sufficient discretion to those delivering a service while allowing prudent monitoring by higher levels of authority. Such procedures would focus "less on control through regulation and more on vesting individual schools and educators with the independence to alter basic organizational arrangements (if necessary) to reach explicit goals and standards" (p. 248).

SCHOOL-BASED MANAGEMENT AND PRIVATIZATION

It has been argued that SBM can introduce into public schools some of the incentives for productivity and client satisfaction which are believed to be more prevalent in private schools while still protecting the public interest through limited regulation and control. The debate over the relative merits of public and private schools stimulated by the Coleman, Hoffer, and Kilgore (1981) study was introduced in Chapter 13. Chubb and Moe (1985, 1989) supplemented the high school and beyond (HSB) data base used by Coleman and his colleagues with a new survey aimed at organizational and environmental factors. The survey was administered to the principal and 30 teachers, among others, in nearly 500 of the HSB schools including most of the more than 100 private schools. The findings are instructive concerning the mechanisms by which SBM may permit the more effective use of human and physical resources in the educating process.

Chubb and Moe (1985) note the very different environments in which public and private schools exist. The former is characterized by politics, hierarchy, and authority, and the latter by markets, competition, and volunteerism. The researchers hypothesize, however, that the differences these environments make for school organization may not be due entirely, or even primarily, to qualities that are inherently public or private. Rather, they suggest that organizational differences may derive from environmental characteristics, such as control, constraint, and complexity, that differentiate school environments regardless of sector. Thus, through organizational redesign, the strengths characteristic of schools in one sector may be incorporated into schools in the other.

As expected, Chubb and Moe (1985) found outside authority exerting a much stronger influence on public schools than on private schools. Because of strong external influences, public schools have less freedom in choosing how to respond to the more difficult environments since they are more constrained by formal rules and regulations and informal norms. Unexpectedly, however, the external influence on Catholic schools was even less than that experienced by other private schools even though, unlike other private schools, Catholic schools are part of a rather substantial hierarchy. This last finding supported the conclusion that bureaucracy need not necessarily be the stultifying force it often becomes.

Among the other findings, teachers in private schools rated their principals as better all-around leaders than did teachers in public schools. Private school principals were also rated by their teachers as being more helpful than were their counterparts in the public sector. Further, private school teachers indicated that the goals of their schools were clearer and more clearly communicated by the principal than did public school teachers. Teachers in private schools were also more likely to rate their principals as encouraging, supportive, and reinforcing. The findings by Chubb and Moe (1985) that public school principals are likely to take on the roles of manager and representative are consistent with those of Cuban (1988). According to Chubb and Moe, private school principals have greater freedom to pursue the role of leader and to direct their schools according to their best professional judgments.

Chubb and Moe (1985) found that private schools delegate significantly more discretion to their teachers and are more likely to involve them in school-level policy decisions than are public schools. Private schools also seem to do a better job of relieving teachers of routine and paperwork. There is a higher level of collegiality among private school staff; teachers are more likely to know what their colleagues are teaching and to coordinate the content of their courses. Private school teachers spend more time meeting to discuss curriculum and students and observing one another's classes. Private school teachers feel that they have more influence over school policies governing student behavior, pupil assignment to classes, curriculum, and in-service programs. Within their classrooms, private school teachers feel that they have more control than do public school teachers over text selection, course content, teaching techniques, and student discipline. Private school teachers even feel that they have more influence over hiring and firing practices than do public school teachers.

Of all the potential barriers to hiring excellent teachers, not one was rated higher by private school principals than by their public school counterparts. Public school principals regard "central office control" and "excessive transfers from other schools" as particularly onerous. They also face substantially greater obstacles in dismissing teachers for poor performance than do private school principals. The complexity of formal dismissal procedures was the highest barrier to firing cited by public school principals. For private school principals, it was "a personal reluctance to fire."

Public school pupils were less likely to know what comprises school policy than were students in private schools. Public school students also regarded their school policies as less fair and effective.

Parents are much more involved and cooperative in private schools. In public schools, parents are more likely to be required to communicate with school officials through formal channels and school officials have less flexibility in addressing reasonable grievances.

Chubb and Moe (1985) concluded that the external environment places complex and conflicting expectations on public school principals:

> Public schools relative to private, live in environments that are complex, demanding, powerful, constraining, and uncooperative. As a result, their policies, procedures, and personnel are more likely to be imposed from the outside. Public principals make the best of this environment by blending two roles, the middle manager and the politician. Like the middle manager, he consolidates whatever power is given him and guards the school's few prerogatives against the influence of a staff over which he has inadequate control. In the same role he emphasizes efficient administration as a safe way to please the administrative hierarchy of which he is a part. But the principal must also deal with a more complex and less friendly environment than the private principal—an environment that is politicized by school boards, state politicians, superintendents, local communities, and last but not least, parents. To do so, he plays the role of a politician, campaigning for the support of his school from a host of sometime hostile constituencies. (p. 41)

Is it possible that SBM in public schools can relieve the pressures of external authorities, permitting public schools to take on some of the desirable characteristics of private schools? Or might SBM create even greater conflict among principals, teachers, and community representatives—conflicts that they could ignore or push off to the school district for resolution under current arrangements? In the next section we look for clues to the answers to these questions by reviewing the results of some SBM experiences.

EXPERIENCES WITH SCHOOL-BASED MANAGEMENT

Edmonton

Edmonton, located in Alberta, Canada, has been functioning under a SBM configuration for more than 10 years. Decisions related to the allocation of resources have been decentralized to schools for teaching and nonteaching staff, maintenance, utilities, equipment, and supplies. Schools contract for consultant services as needed from district providers or outside vendors. The district also operates a professional development program that derives its funds by charging school-based budgets.

A survey of Edmonton principals and teachers (Brown, 1990) reveals that principals see flexibility, efficiency, and staff involvement in decision making as strongly positive attributes of SBM. Resource allocation is a problem for some, but time demands and stress accompanying decentralization are viewed as its major disadvantages. Teacher involvement appears to be primarily consultative rather than advisory. Seventy-nine percent of the principals would recommend that other districts consider SBM.

Teachers in Edmonton identify flexibility and staff involvement in decision making as being the major advantages of SBM. As with the principals, teachers see the primary weakness of SBM as the time demand. This was followed by problems with the allocation of resources, heightened stress, and the increased authority of the principal.

The Edmonton school district has instituted formal procedures for monitoring SBM. In addition to standardized tests administered on a regular basis, parents, students, and staff are surveyed to measure their level of satisfaction with matters affecting them. Results are compiled by school, with district averages indicated. Satisfaction among the three groups has steadily improved under SBM; the growth in satisfaction has been particularly strong among parents and students at the secondary level (Brown, 1990).

The Edmonton program was implemented gradually. The pilot project lasted four years and involved seven volunteer schools which represented the variety in the district. Community support for the concept grew, and eventually the Board of Education voted to implement the idea district-wide (Brown, 1990).

Dade County

Dade County, Florida, which includes the City of Miami, began implementing its school governance experiment, School-Based Management/Shared Decision Making (SBM/SDM) during the 1987–1988 school year. Dade County is the fourth-largest school district in the United States, with over a quarter of a million students.

SBM/SDM is a four-year pilot program designed to give teachers and administrators the opportunity to voice and implement their ideas on how students should be taught. Thirty-three schools participated the first year; additional schools were added in subsequent years. To participate in the program, a school or group of schools must submit a proposal to the district office. The proposal must carry the approval of the principal, union steward, and two-thirds of the faculty. Technical assistance in developing proposals is available from the district office. Proposal assessment criteria include educational impact/accountability, collegial process, shared decision-making model, targeted changes, feasibility for implementation, rationale, community involvement, school climate, and replication.

Schools selected for participation have significantly increased flexibility in both budgeting and staffing. The decisions on how to allocate funds, as well as how to organize instructional plans, are left to SBM/SDM schools. Parents and other community representatives may participate in the school's decision-making process as advisors and as supportive and helpful partners. These schools report directly to the central office, bypassing mid-level management. School board rules, teacher contract provisions, and State Department of Education regulations may be waived. The school board has suspended requirements regarding maximum class size, length of school day, number of minutes per subject, and distribution of report cards. The union has allowed teachers to give up planning periods, work longer hours for no additional pay, and engage in peer evaluation programs (Mojkowski & Fleming, 1988).

Under district guidelines, the participating schools receive the same level of funds as non-SBM/SDM schools. The budgets for SBM/SDM schools are based on a lump-sum allocation. Average district salaries plus fringe benefits are used for the purchase of additional units of staff or the return of the dollar equivalent of staff relinquished for reallocation to other purposes. Equivalent dollars for the special services that once were provided at the area or district level are distributed to participating schools. Such funds may be used to purchase services from the district or private vendors as determined by the school.

Alternative arrangements proposed by schools vary considerably. Some schools have opened on Saturdays; others have added programs before and after school. Several are modifying staffing patterns by hiring aides in place of assistant principals, employing teachers by the hour, and creating new positions (Mojkowski & Fleming, 1988).

Initial evaluations have been generally positive. Teachers indicate some increase in involvement in decision-making activities usually considered management's prerogative. Teachers also indicate a shift in their attitudes in favor of a collegial approach to school operation. Principals feel that SBM/SDM has had a favorable impact on the school environment. It is seen as facilitating the generation of instructional ideas, design of specific interventions, and provision for feedback. Principals acknowledge that SBM/SDM is more time-consuming than previously employed management methods and that it makes their jobs more complex (Collins, 1988).

Timar (1989) links the Dade County experience with state actions dating back to 1971, when Governor Ruben Askew appointed the Citizens' Committee on Education. Among other things, the committee recommended that decision making be placed at the level of instruction. Enabling legislation was subsequently adopted. Within the district, the school board, administration, and teachers' union have cooperated fully in the development and implementation of SBM/SDM. According to Timar, "Restructuring was not something that one side wanted and the other resisted; hence it could not be held hostage and used as a bargaining chip" (p. 272). Timar sees cause for optimism in the Dade County experience that genuine restructuring is possible.

Of the situations studied by Timar (1989), only Dade County has state, district, and union authorities working in concert. In contrast to Dade County, he studied schools in suburban Seattle, Washington, and Jefferson County, Kentucky, where SBM had not been so successful. For successful implementation, Timar underscores the importance of a policy climate which fosters an integrated and organizationally coherent response to restructuring—one which redefines the roles and responsibilities of just about every party connected with schools: teachers, administrators, professional organizations, policymakers, parents, students, and colleges and universities. He concludes that an integrated response to restructuring at the school level is not likely to occur in politically balkanized and programmatically fragmented districts and states.

Chicago

Although it is too early to evaluate its effectiveness, one of the most ambitious attempts at school-based management is in Chicago. The plan was adopted by the Illinois legislature in December 1988 in a desperate attempt to reform a school system that was alleged to contain the worst schools in the country by realigning its incentives and power structure (Hess, 1990). The plan is being phased in over a five-year period. Ten goals of the reform are identified in the act, but the primary goals are to raise student achievement, attendance rates, and graduation rates to national norms for *all* schools.

The key for achieving the goals of the act are Local School Councils (LSCs) made up of six parents, two community representatives, two teachers, and the principal. For high schools, they also include one nonvoting student. Except for teacher representatives and the principal, employees of the system may not serve as members of LSCs. District employees are also barred from voting in elections of parent and community representatives. This configuration was designed to give parents a major voice in the educational decisions affecting their children and to avoid the problems encountered in New York City, where employees have been able to dominate elections to the 32 community Boards of Education that govern elementary schools in the city (Hess, 1990).

The councils have the responsibility for adopting a school improvement plan, developing a budget to implement that plan based upon a lump-sum allocation, and selecting a new principal or retaining the incumbent. The amount of discretionary funds available to each school annually should average about $450,000 in five years.

Although never stated explicitly, the Chicago School Reform Act is built upon the assumption that the principal is the chief instructional leader in each school (Hess, 1990). Principals are given the right to select teachers, aides, counselors, clerks, hall guards, and any other instructional program staff for vacant or newly created positions. Principals are responsible for initiating a needs assessment and a school improvement plan in consultation with the LSC and the Professional Personnel Advisory Committee (PPAC). They are also responsible for drafting a budget for amendment and/or adoption by the LSC. Principals hold no tenure rights in the position other than those they hold as teachers.

Unlike most other school-based management plans, the Chicago plan places greater responsibility with parents and community representatives than with teachers. The importance of participatory decision making was recognized, however, in relationships mandated between the LSCs and the professional staff. A PPAC is to be created in each school to advise the principal and the LSC on the educational program. The PPAC is made up of teachers and other professional personnel in the school.

Subdistrict councils were established for each administrative division in the city. They are made up of one parent or community representative from each school. The subdistrict councils serve in a coordinating capacity for schools within the division. They also have the power to retain, terminate, or select a subdistrict superintendent. Each subdistrict council elects one representative to a system-wide Board Nominating Commission. The commission is charged with providing the mayor with a slate of three persons for each vacancy on the city's Board of Education. The mayor must appoint from among the slate or reject the entire slate and ask for another.

The subdistrict superintendent (DS) was changed from a line officer with authority over principals and school employees into a staff officer who monitors and facilitates school improvement (Hess, 1990). The DS is charged with providing training to the LSCs, to mediate disputes at local schools, and to monitor the development and implementation of a school improvement plan at each school.

The city Board of Education consists of 15 members serving four-year staggered terms. The new board was given most of the powers of the previous board, with the exception of powers granted to the LSCs. To recognize the existence of these new semiautonomous LSCs, the powers of the board were redefined from "management of" to "jurisdiction over" the public education and the public school system of the city (Hess, 1990). Among other responsibilities, the board is charged with establishing "system-wide curriculum objectives and standards which reflect the multicultural diversity of the city."

A Multidistrict Analysis of SBM

Brown (1990) analyzed the implementation of SBM in five districts including Edmonton and Cleveland. The other districts were Langley (a suburb of Vancouver) and two rural districts in British Columbia. He interviewed district personnel in SBM districts and five selected centralized districts and examined district documents.

Brown (1990) identified two main processes as part of the structure of SBM: the mechanism by which resources are allocated to schools and the budgeting process within the school. Schools receive the bulk of their allocations by multiplying their enrollments by a district-established amount such that "the money follows the child." Adjustments are made for special programs and for school attributes. Districts provide schools with system-wide goals and objectives, and schools respond with their own curricular plans and budgets for implementation, which is mostly absorbed by personnel costs. Teachers are usually purchased from the district at a uniform rate, and those not located in a particular school are placed within the district pool for selection.

Brown's (1990) analysis found that the SBM school boards became more concerned with policy matters than with the administration of schools. Under SBM, the district hierarchy is sharpened, whereby each person has only one supervisor; nonline central office staff assume a strictly advisory, on-call relationship with school-level personnel. "Most importantly, authority and responsibility are largely brought together, particularly for the school principal, but also for others in the administrative structure" (p. 2).

Still, many things remain the same. Brown (1990) detected little change in the accountability model employed under SBM; ultimate authority comes from the electorate and is directed through school boards and administrators. Thus the school board is still responsible for establishing the general direction for the district through the setting of goals. The district remains the reservoir of funds, whether they come from local sources such as the property tax or from the state or federal governments. Collective bargaining remains a district prerogative, and the district continues to provide financial and other support services. The district retains responsibility for monitoring and evaluating school performance.

Under SBM, specific budgetary and personnel decisions are made at the school level, but the school board sets the general parameters by which the school's lump-sum allocation is determined. The school board must answer such questions as these: What should the size of the pupil allocation be? Should it vary according to type of program, for example, elementary, secondary, vocational? Should the allocation vary according to the characteristics of children served, for example, socioeconomic status, learning disabled, gifted, or handicapped? Should the allocation vary according to the characteristics of the school, for example, size and complexity of services offered? In many respects, decisions made by school boards under SBM are similar to those made by state governments.

By the same token, many of the decisions made at the school level under SBM are similar to those made by school boards today. School-level authority approaches that of a single-building rural district; the primary differences are that the school does not control the size of its budget (it has no authority to levy taxes or to charge tuition) and it cannot set wage scales. The role of principal takes on aspects of a superintendent of a small district (David, 1989; Jacobson, 1988). Although SBM introduces substantial procedural changes at the district level, the changes are revolutionary at the school level.

Brown (1990) found that under SBM, schools are considered to be much more able to adapt resources and procedures to student needs as perceived by school personnel. He reports that it may be a viable avenue for school improvement because of the flexibility it accords schools, but it does not appear to be a key stimulus for innovation. In the five districts, Brown observed tradeoffs between personnel and material. Examples of personnel-related decisions included more dollars for professional development, teacher choice of school, swaps of personnel, and increases in personnel allocations for specific learning tasks.

Principals strongly favor SBM in the five districts studied; they feel that it enhances their ability to be educational leaders. Teachers are less positive in their endorsement. Teachers and principals agree that the primary strength of SBM is greater flexibility at the school level, and that the greatest weakness is the additional time that it requires. Most school staff are consulted during the budgeting process, but they do not control the planning process or school decision making. Some teachers and support staff want to be involved in the process whereas others do not. Parents are only tangentially involved, if at all.

Surveys conducted by Brown (1990) indicate that SBM is not intended as a vehicle to cut costs in the districts studied. Illustrations are offered, however, to show that funds are being used more effectively under SBM than they were prior to its implementation. For example, the practice of permitting schools to accumulate surpluses is thought to lead to more efficient use of funds than spending just to meet financial deadlines. Hoarding of supplies was common under centralized management but is no longer necessary under SBM. There is also some evidence that central office staffs are slightly smaller in SBM districts. Interviewees generally believe that school staffs have gained a greater awareness of costs and have tried to reduce unnecessary ones. The allocation rule that the dollar follows the child is felt to provide a more equitable distribution of resources among children than did previous centralized procedures.

The experiences of SBM districts clearly show that SBM is no trivial change from traditional centralized decision making. It involves new relationships between the district and the school and among people within the school itself. Brown (1990) found that district interest in SBM is usually stimulated by one person. After the adoption decision, leadership from other sources becomes very important. The experience of other districts with SBM appears to be a primary consideration in making the adoption decision. Extensive preparations are required for successful implementation of SBM, including several years of pilot experiments. Despite the difficulties entailed in implementing SBM, Brown observed little tendency to recentralize once SBM was fully implemented.

The discussion of decision making in Chapter 2 indicates that the debate concerning the appropriate allocation of authority over education is not limited to the United States. Illustrations of the centralization/decentralization controversy come from England and Australia; the extensive references here to Edmonton and British Columbia districts suggest that it is a matter of interest in Canada also. Of all of the models for implementing SBM, we are most impressed with one developed in Australia. It is Caldwell and Spinks' (1988)

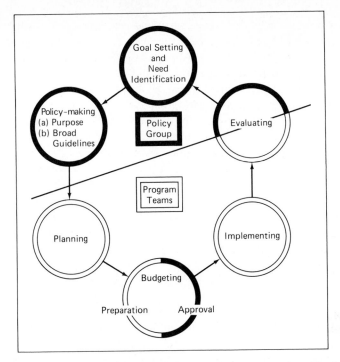

Figure 16.1. Caldwell and Spinks's Collaborative School Management Model. (*Source:* B. J. Caldwell and J. M. Spinks. [1988]. *The Self-managing School,* p. 37. Sussex, England: Falmer Press. Reprinted by permission.)

Collaborative School Management Model, which we will describe in some detail.[1] The model has been used extensively in the Australian state of Victoria (Melbourne) and it is gaining in popularity in England as state schools assume the budgetary authority granted to them by the Education Reform Act of 1988. We feel that it offers an appropriate guide also for American districts interested in SBM.

THE COLLABORATIVE SCHOOL MANAGEMENT MODEL

The Collaborative School Management Model (CSM) is illustrated in Figure 16.1. It integrates the management functions of planning, budgeting, implementing, and evaluating with the governance functions of goal setting and policy-making. CSM focuses on the central function of schools—learning and teaching—and is designed to involve administrators, teachers and other staff, students, parents, and other members of the community.

---

[1]The reader who is planning to implement a school-based management system should consult the cited source. It provides much greater detail about the system including sample goals, policies, program descriptions, evaluations, and so on. It also provides helpful suggestions for designing the system and implementing it.

The management of the school is organized around "programs" which correspond to the preferred patterns of work in the school.

The composition of the policy group varies according to the setting. In Victoria, it would be the legally established School Council. In England, it would be a school's Board of Governors. In the United States, where there are no formally established school governing boards, the nature of the policy group could be established by the state, as in the case of Chicago; by the district as in the case of Dade County; or left to the discretion of the school. The group could consist of the principal alone or be supplemented with representatives of teachers, students, parents, the community, and/or the district office. The policy group is solely responsible for goal setting, need identification, and policy-making, although it is likely to seek advice broadly in carrying out these responsibilities. It must approve program budgets prepared by program teams, ensuring that the proposals reflect established policy and are supportable by the resources allocated to the school. The policy group is responsible for summative evaluation of the programs, making judgments on the effectiveness of each program and on the effectiveness of policy supporting program efforts.

Program teams consist primarily of teachers, who are supplemented by others as appropriate. The teams prepare plans for their areas of responsibility within a framework constructed by the policy group and identify the resources needed to support those plans. The teams are responsible for the implementation of their plans as approved by the policy group. They are also responsible for formative evaluation of their respective programs and for submitting information to the policy group as required for their summative review. Although the division of responsibility is clear, some individuals are likely to serve on both the policy group and one or more program teams, thereby facilitating a high level of formal and informal communication.

On the surface, CSM resembles the largely discredited planned programming budgeting systems (PPBS) which were attempted in the United States during the 1960s and 1970s. Although they are similar in concept, they are very different in design. The creators of the CSM model learned much from the failures of PPBS and have largely succeeded in avoiding them. PPBS was very rigid, giving too much attention to the minutia of budgeting and requiring excessive paperwork.

> To these shortcomings may be added an inappropriate emphasis on the specification of performance requirements or criteria for evaluation. PPBS assumed a greater degree or capacity for rational or analytical planning than existed or was possible. In short, PPBS suffered from the "paralysis through analysis" which is to be avoided if effectiveness along the lines studied by Peters and Waterman (1982) is to be attained. (Caldwell & Spinks, 1988, p. 68)

With CSM, paperwork is deliberately kept to a minimum. Each goal is to be limited to a single sentence; policies are limited to one page, program plans and budgets to two pages, and evaluation reports to one or two pages. Criteria for evaluation are kept simple and clearly related to learning and teaching. Priorities can be reordered quickly and simply as new needs emerge. All written material is to be free of technical jargon so that it can be easily read and understood by all members of the school community.

Ideally, a school should enter the CSM cycle at the goal-setting phase and proceed counterclockwise through the remaining phases as illustrated in Figure 16.1. This is not always possible, however. In actuality, a school may enter the cycle at any phase, completing the other phases in a manner appropriate for each setting. The model provides a comprehensive portrayal of all that must eventually be accomplished.

The goals are general statements which set the direction and tone of the school. They usually are directed toward desired educational outcomes for students; but they may also relate to learning experiences for students, provision of resources, and school management.

Once the goals are in place, the policy group must determine in practical terms where the school should be in the immediate future. Then a careful assessment is made of where the school is in relation to where it should be. A "need" exists when there is a significant gap between where it is and where it wants to be. Schools typically have far more needs than their resources permit them to address, so priorities must be established concerning which are the most pressing. Caldwell and Spinks (1988) suggest that one consideration in setting priorities is the extent of identifiable harm caused by each gap or need.

Caldwell and Spinks (1988) define a policy as a statement of purpose accompanied by one or more guidelines concerning how that purpose is to be achieved. The policy provides a framework for the operation of the school or a program, and it may allow discretion in its implementation. The statement of purpose should be derived from the school's statement of philosophy or from a goal statement or statements. The guidelines should clearly state the intent of the policy and the desired pattern of action without becoming so specific as to prohibit professional judgment by those concerned with implementing the policy.

A program is defined as an area of learning and teaching, such as English, mathematics, art, and music, or a support service, such as administration, audiovisual media, and maintenance of buildings and grounds. A program team is usually made up of everyone involved in the delivery of the program service. Each team should have a designated leader, usually a person with formal authority related to the program such as a subject coordinator or head of department.

Caldwell and Spinks (1988) define planning as "determining in advance what will be done, when it will be done, how it will be done and who will do it" (p. 43). CSM recognizes three levels of planning: program, curricular, and instructional.

> Program planning is determining in general terms how a program is to be implemented, specifying such things as the manner in which students will be grouped vertically (among grade or year levels) and horizontally (within a grade or year level); the number and nature of teachers and support staff associated with the program; the supplies, equipment and services required and initiatives (additions or deletions) which are noteworthy. Curriculum planning provides a relatively detailed specification of what will be taught, how it will be taught and when it will be taught. Instructional planning is considered here to be planning undertaken by individual teachers when implementing a curriculum plan in their own classrooms. (pp. 43–44)

The budget is a financial plan which forecasts expenditures and income. It is through a budget that an organization (or program) aligns its resources with its purposes (Guthrie, Garms, & Pierce, 1988). Thus, a budget is a financial translation of an educational plan for a program or a school. In order to convert into dollars the cost of time allocations of personnel to specific tasks, an allocation for salaries must be made in program and school budgets even though the actual salaries may be paid by the district. The salary rate used is the average salary for the district (plus cost of fringe benefits) rather than the actual salaries paid to personnel assigned to a program. Caldwell and Spinks (1988) write that "the inclusion of such [salary] estimates is an acknowledgement that the major resource in a school is the staff and that the most important task in resource allocation each year is making the school timetable [i.e., the master schedule]" (pp. 46–48).

A program budget is a comprehensive plan for a program. It contains a statement of the program's purpose, a listing of broad guidelines about how the purpose is to be achieved, a plan for implementation with elements listed in order of priority, an estimate of resources required to support the plan, and a plan for evaluation. All must be reported in two pages or less.

The program budgets for all programs in the school are brought together in a single document for submission to the policy group for review, possible revision, and eventual approval. During the process of reconciliation, program expenditure requests will be adjusted, if necessary, so that combined approved expenditures will fall within the school's estimated income.

With the adoption of the program budget by the policy group, program teams are authorized to proceed with the implementation of their plans in the forthcoming year. There is no need for further reference to the policy group during the course of the year unless a program team desires to make a major change in its plan.

The final phase of the CSM cycle is evaluation, defined by Caldwell and Spinks (1988) as

the gathering of information for the purpose of making a judgment and then making that judgment. Two kinds of evaluation should occur during or following the implementation of program plans. One is evaluation of learning, where information is gathered to form judgments about the progress or achievement of students. Another is evaluation of programs, when information is gathered to form judgments about the extent to which progress toward goals has been made, needs have been satisfied and policies have been implemented. (p. 49)

The policy group holds the major responsibility for program evaluation and may call in external authorities to assist them in the process. Planning teams have a similar, but more detailed, interest and gather much of the information needed for program evaluation for their own purposes and for use by the policy group. Minor evaluations are carried out annually and their reports are limited to one page. Major evaluations are scheduled for a three- to five-year frequency, and their reports are limited to two pages. "The emphasis is on a manageable and usable approach to program evaluation, in contrast to the frequently exhausting approach to school review and evaluation which has been encountered in many schools in recent years" (Caldwell & Spinks, 1988, p. 50).

The CSM cycle is completed when judgments in program evaluation result in the setting of new goals, the identification of new needs, the formulation of new policies, or the introduction of new programs.

SUMMARY

In this chapter, we have addressed Elmore's (1988) "supply side" question; that is, should providers of education be given the autonomy and flexibility to respond to differences in the judgments of consumers about appropriate education? We looked at the implications for finance policy of decentralized decision making through various approaches to school-based management. School-based management was defined and the rationale for its adoption was reviewed through the words of some of its leading advocates. Since SBM is intended to simulate, in part, private sector conditions within the public sector, the study by Chubb and Moe (1985) of organizational and environmental attributes of public and private schools was reviewed in some detail. Several studies of the implementation of SBM were described. Finally, Caldwell and Spinks' (1988) Collaborative School Management Model was presented as a well-designed strategy for implementing SBM.

In the next chapter, we address Elmore's (1988) "demand side" question; that is, should consumers of education be given a central role in deciding what kind of education is appropriate for them? In that chapter, we examine the implications of family choice proposals for school finance policy. The combination of SBM and family choice represent the most radical form of educational decentralization short of complete privatization.

ACTIVITIES

1. Imagine a policy board for each public school made up of the principal, serving as the chief executive officer, and representatives of teachers, parents, and students.
    a. What are the advantages and disadvantages of such an arrangement?
    b. Would you add representation from any other group?
    c. Would you eliminate representation of any group?
    d. Assuming each representative has one vote, how many representatives should there be from each group?
    e. What constraints, if any, would you place on the decision-making powers of the board?
    f. Provide the rationale for each of your responses.
2. Within the context of the decision matrix presented in Figure 2.1, what educational decisions are best placed at the school level? What safeguards need to be implemented to protect societal and family interests? Give the rationales for your responses.
3. Can the public interest be protected without the bureaucratization of schools? If so, how?
4. To what extent, if any, should public control and regulation follow public finance? Give examples of alternative patterns of providing publicly financed support and the levels of control and regulation accompanying each.
5. Under a school-based budgeting scheme, what factors should be taken into account in determining the amount of a school's lump-sum distribution?
6. Review the literature on PPBS in search of the reasons for its failure to be widely implemented in public schools. Is the fate of a system like the CSM, described in this chapter, likely to be any different? Provide the rationale for your response.

REFERENCES

Boyer, E. L. (1983). *High school: A report on secondary education in America*. New York: Harper & Row.

Brown, D. J. (1990). *Decentralization and school-based management*. London: Falmer Press.

Caldwell, B. J., & Spinks, J. M. (1988). *The self-managing school*. London: Falmer Press.

Cawelti, G. (1989). Key elements of site-based management. *Educational Leadership*, *46*, 46.

Chubb, J. E., & Moe, T. M. (1985). *Politics, markets, and the organization of schools*. Stanford, CA: Institute for Research on Educational Finance and Governance, School of Education, Stanford University.

Chubb, J. E., & Moe, T. M. (1989). Effective schools and equal opportunity. In N. E. Devins (Ed.), *Public values, private schools* (pp. 161–183). London: Falmer Press.

Coleman, J. S., Hoffer, T., & Kilgore, S. (1981). *Public and private schools*. Final report to the National Center for Education Statistics (Contract No. 300-78-0208). Chicago: National Opinion Research Center.

Collins, R. A. (1988). *Interim evaluation report, School-based management/shared decision making Project, 1987–88, Project-wide findings*. Miami, FL: Dade County Public Schools, Office of Educational Accountability.

Committee for Economic Development. (1970). *Reshaping government in metropolitan areas*. New York: Author.

Cuban, L. (1988). *The managerial imperative and the practice of leadership in schools*. Albany: State University of New York Press.

David, J. L. (1989). Synthesis of research on school-based management. *Educational Leadership*, *46*, 45–53.

Elmore, R. F. (1988). Choice in public schools. In W. L. Boyd & C. T. Kerchner (Eds.), *The politics of excellence and choice in education* (pp. 79–98). New York: Falmer Press.

Fleischmann report on the quality, cost and financing of elementary and secondary education in New York State (Vol. 3). (1972). Albany: Author.

Fleischmann report on the quality, cost and financing of elementary and secondary education in New York State (Vol. I). (1973). New York: Viking Press.

Goodlad, J. I. (1984). *A place called school: Prospects for the future*. New York: McGraw-Hill.

Guthrie, J. W., Garms, W. I., & Pierce, L. C. (1988). *School finance and education policy: Enhancing educational efficiency, equality and choice*. Englewood Cliffs, NJ: Prentice Hall.

Hess, G. A., Jr. (1990). *Chicago school reform: What it is and how it came to be*. Chicago: Chicago Panel on Public School Policy & Finance.

Jacobson, S. L. (1988). The rural superintendency: Reconsidering the administrative farm system. *Research in Rural Education*, *5* (2), 37–42.

Lindelow, J. (1981). School-based management. In S. C. Smith, J. A. Mazzarella, & P. K. Piele (Eds.), *School leadership: Handbook for survival* (pp. 94–129). Eugene: Clearinghouse on Educational Management, University of Oregon.

Mojkowski, C., & Fleming, D. (1988). *School-site management: Concepts and approaches*. Andover, MA: Regional Laboratory for Educational Improvement of the Northeast and Islands.

National Governors' Association. (1986). *Time for results: The Governors' 1991 report on education*. Washington, DC: Author.

Peters, T. J., & Waterman, R. H. (1982). *In search of excellence: Lessons from America's best-run companies*. New York: Warner Books.

Sizer, T. R. (1985). *Horace's compromise: The dilemma of the American high school*. Boston: Houghton Mifflin.

Timar, T. (1989). The politics of school restructuring. *Phi Delta Kappan, 71* (4), 265–275.

Urban Institute. (1972). *Public school finance: Present disparities and fiscal alternatives, A report to the President's Commission on School Finance* (Vol. I, Chap. 5). Washington, DC: U.S. Government Printing Office.

CHAPTER 17

Family Choice of Schooling: Consumer Sovereignty

The National Governors' Association (1986) had given its endorsement to the concept of family choice of schooling in its report on education:

> We believe that we can remain dedicated to a system of public schools and still increase consumer sovereignty. . . . If we implement broader choice plans, true choice among public schools, then we unlock the values of competition in the educational marketplace. Schools that compete for students, teachers and dollars will, by virtue of their environment, make those changes that allow them to succeed. (p. 12)

Although the governors confine their support of choice to public schools, others argue that public funds should also be made available to private schools through vouchers or tax credits for parents' expenses including tuition.

Chubb and Moe (1985) aptly describe what the governors meant by "consumer sovereignty" and "the values of competition in the educational marketplace":

> Public schools have their resources allocated to them by authorities who do not directly consume their services while private schools receive their resources in a direct exchange for services rendered. The resources of public schools are therefore less closely connected to the school's performance. Effectiveness may be rewarded by the environment or it may not; the same is true of ineffectiveness. Public schools therefore operate under considerable uncertainty, never confident that their efforts will pay off. They must depend upon the beneficence of various political processes that include a host of participants other than parents, and on their own ability to bargain for funds from their local superiors. For private schools, resources are not necessarily easier to acquire. To the contrary, competition with other schools, coupled with parental demands for excellence, may make resources harder to acquire. But the resource problem is a simpler one, with a clear connection between school success in accomplishing goals and school rewards

from the environment. "Perform or perish" brings considerable certitude to the relationship between private schools and their environments. (pp. 9–10)

Family choice is proposed by theoreticians as a means of strengthening the linkages among resources allocated to schools by government, schooling outcomes, and client satisfaction. This is accomplished by placing the authority over pupil assignment with parents rather than with school boards and by allowing publicly provided resources to "follow the child." The process increases consumer sovereignty while still vesting in public bodies authority to regulate societal concerns.

In reality, however, most public school plans of choice have been initiated to facilitate school desegregation. In an alternative strategy to forced cross-district busing for controlling the racial or ethnic mix of school enrollments, some school boards designed magnet schools to *attract* children of different backgrounds who seek particular programs. Representing a compromise between consumer sovereignty and social justice, this procedure appears to have avoided creating fears on the part of parents for the safety and well-being of their children which are frequently engendered by "forced busing" plans. Thus, school choice is advocated to improve two quite different aspects of schools and school districts: their internal efficiency and the racial distribution of students.

Opponents argue that choice may lead to stratification of students according to socioeconomic characteristics and academic ability. They are concerned that inequitable distribution of resources will result and that if choice is eventually extended to private schools, the wall of separation between church and state will be bridged and the public schools will be abandoned by all but the poor. On no issue do the values of liberty and efficiency on the one hand and equality and fraternity on the other come into potentially sharper conflict than over the issue of school choice.

It is not the purpose of this chapter to weigh the merit of the arguments over school choice, but rather to look at the financial implications of various choice proposals. (For comprehensive discussions of the issues involved in school choice and the privatization of education see Boyd and Kerchner, 1988; Coons and Sugarman, 1978; Friedman, 1962, Chap. 6; Friedman and Friedman, 1980, Chap. 6; Gwartney and Wagner, 1988; James and Levin, 1988; Kearns and Doyle, 1988; Levy, 1986; Lieberman, 1989.) We begin the discussion by reviewing some of the options already available. We continue by examining the reform proposals of educational vouchers and tuition tax credits and deductions. To assess the impact of choice plans on diversity in schooling, we turn to studies of The Netherlands and Canada. We close by considering constitutional constraints.

CURRENT SCHOOLING OPTIONS

For many years, students in Vermont school districts that do not operate high schools have been able to choose among public and nonsectarian private schools at public expense. More recent policy changes permit Minnesota parents to enroll their children in virtually any public school district in the state they choose (Nathan, 1989; Pearson, 1989). Iowa and Arkansas have similar plans, and numerous other states are likely to follow suit (Snider, 1989a). For over twenty years, Massachusetts has encouraged and financed interdistrict transfer of pupils which improves racial balance in the schools involved

(Glenn, 1986). Similarly, Saint Louis City and County school districts voluntarily exchange students to improve racial balance as part of a court-ordered desegregation plan.

A number of large cities have developed open enrollment plans within their districts. For generations, New York City has operated a variety of specialty schools, including the prestigious Bronx High School of Science, which draw their students from throughout the city. The Boston Latin School dates to colonial times.

District 4 in New York City's East Harlem has received much attention in recent years for the academic success of its students and its open enrollment policies. The district serves a generally poor population, with 80 percent of its 14,000 students eligible for free or reduced lunch. Ninety-five percent of the students are from minority populations, Hispanics constituting the majority of its enrollment. The average achievement gains of its students are impressive, although district critics attribute those gains to factors other than open enrollment, such as the small size of its schools (about 300 pupils each) and favored treatment to academically stronger students (Snider, 1989b).

The Boston Public Schools have recently embraced a school choice plan as an alternative to forced busing imposed by the courts to remedy racial imbalances in the district. The plan includes decentralized decision making and school-based management. At least a dozen other large cities have used a variety of school choice plans to end racial segregation. One of the most successful has been the magnet school program in Buffalo, New York.

Parental choice of *public* schools regardless of district of residence is supported by 60 percent of the adult population according to a series of annual Gallup polls sponsored by Phi Delta Kappa (Elam & Gallup, 1989). The support given to the concept by parents with children in school is even higher: 64% of parents with children in public schools and 68% of parents with children in private schools. Support is stronger among nonwhites (67%) than among whites (59%) and among younger persons than older persons (67% of the 18–29 age group, 64% of those between 30 and 49, and 51% of those over 50). Regionally, support for choice is least in the East (53%) and strongest in the West (64%).

Traditionally, parents were able to choose between public and private schools; but even this option was seriously challenged during the 1920s. Then, in 1925, the U.S. Supreme Court in its landmark decision in *Pierce* v. *Society of Sisters* (1925) recognized the constitutionally protected right of private schools to exist as an alternative to public schools. In so doing, the Court recognized parental rights to direct the education and upbringing of one's own children, foreclosing the possibility of a public monopoly. On the other hand, *Pierce* and other decisions permit reasonable regulation of private schooling by government without requiring public subsidization of the choice of private schooling.

Without subsidization, schooling costs can become very expensive, forcing most parents out of the private school market. In the absence of public support, it is primarily religious groups that have the financial capacity and are so organized and motivated to sponsor nongovernmental schooling to the point where it becomes a feasible option for sizable numbers of families. Table 3.7 reports that nearly 11 percent of elementary and secondary pupils have chosen private school options. Table 3.8 indicates that of those enrolled in private schools, 87 percent are enrolled in religiously affiliated schools and 57 percent attend Roman Catholic schools. The percentages in private schools and in religiously affiliated schools have remained quite stable over the years, but the nature of religious affiliation is rapidly changing from being almost exclusively Catholic to a heterogeneous mixture of denominations.

Some public assistance is provided to students enrolled in private schools, which to a small degree facilitates the possibility for family choice. Many states provide public support of transportation, health services, testing and remedial services, and textbooks to children enrolled in private schools.

At the federal level, until 1965, the issue of aid to private schools—or the lack of it—often led to the defeat of aid proposals for public schools. The Elementary and Secondary Education Act (ESEA) was the first federal program which required that federally funded services be provided to private elementary and secondary school children. Compromise was reached among contending interest groups over a child-benefit approach to federal aid which focused on educationally disadvantaged children wherever they were enrolled. Services were provided to the child under public control and supervision—not to the school.

Subsequently, services purchased through federal funds were extended to private school students for vocational education, bilingual education, education of handicapped children, and instructional and library materials. It was estimated that about 25 percent of school districts in 1980 provided services to students in private schools, representing less than 4 percent of total private school enrollments (Jung, 1982). Enactment of the Education Consolidation and Improvement Act in 1981 brought substantially greater support for programs serving private school children (see Chapter 10). Recent court decisions, however, have placed severe constraints on the manner in which such services may be delivered to children attending private schools (*Aguilar* v. *Felton,* 1985; *Pulido* v. *Cavazos,* 1989); this, in turn, may affect the number being served.

Within the public sector, there is also a degree of choice. The most widespread choice is selection of courses at the high school level. Here, choice is so extensive that Powell, Farrar, and Cohen (1985) likened the high school curriculum to the availability of goods in a shopping mall. In addition, Elmore (1988) estimates that about one-third of big-city school districts offer another kind of choice in the form of magnet and/or specialty schools. Magnet schools and other configurations were discussed in the previous section.

But the most common vehicle of school choice in the public sector is through the selection of a residence. Murnane (1986) points to compelling evidence that families pay premiums for housing in school districts with reputations for good schools. Kutner, Sherman, and Williams (1986) report on a survey of a national random sample of approximately 1,200 households with school-age children. About half of the parents indicated that the public schools their children would attend influenced the choice of a place to live; 18 percent said that it was the most important factor in their choice of residence.

Tiebout (1956) presents a theory for the existence of local governments which argues that they permit people with similar tastes for public services to cluster together within jurisdictions. Variety in local government offers households arrays of public services that are significantly different in type and quality. Choice of residence becomes equivalent to consumer choice in the market; it becomes a middle ground between a free market and centralized governmental control. This appears to be what has happened with respect to educational services in metropolitan areas, where persons with high demands for educational services cluster in specific suburbs—usually affluent—and persons with low demand, or unable to afford the cost of high levels of service, cluster in central cities and other suburbs—usually blue collar.

The Balkanization of local government, and of school districts in particular, does advance to a limited extent libertarian objectives. But it also creates serious inequities and impedes the realization of fraternal objectives. This phenomenon was illustrated in Table 3.2, using data drawn from the Los Angeles metropolitan area. Balkanization works to the advantage of a rich or upper-middle-class household because such a household has sufficient resources to choose a community whose array of services includes those most desired by the household. Resources in these households are sufficient to the degree that the provision by the community of additional services to which a household is indifferent does not present an insurmountable economic barrier to its living there. This is not the case with poor households. Those with a strong desire for education might be able to afford to meet the cost of a high level of service by sacrificing in other areas such as housing and transportation. But in linking educational services with residence, this decision is not possible because high levels of educational services are usually provided in concert with high housing costs and in communities where public transportation is not readily available. This may account for the strong interest in choice plans by racial and ethnic minorities (Elam & Gallup, 1989).

In a random survey of the attitudes of Minnesota residents about educational choice, Darling-Hammond and Kirby (1988) found impressive evidence of the Tiebout effect. Households that had considered the quality of public schools in making residential location decisions had a lower propensity to express interest in private schools even with governmental subsidies. They felt that their educational needs were already well served by the public schools of the communities they had selected.

According to Kutner, Sherman, and Williams (1986), the most common reasons given by public school parents for choosing the schools they did were school assigned (28%), transportation (24%), and academic quality (17%). The most common reasons given by private school parents included academic quality (42%), religious instruction (30%), and discipline (12%). Nearly half of the children in private schools had once attended public schools, and 17% of those attending public schools had once attended private schools. Reasons given for switching from private to public schools included cost (24%), change of residence (21%), and availability of public alternatives (17%). Reasons for switching from public to private schools included academics (27%), discipline (25%), religious instruction or values orientation (25%), and quality of teachers (12%).

In the Kutner study, respondents with a child in private school tended to be better educated, earn a higher income, be Catholic, have attended private schools themselves, and live in large or medium-size cities. Parents sending their children to public schools were more likely to live in nonmetropolitan environs and to have attended only public schools themselves. The researchers conclude that for any given level of funding, "access and choice would be expanded most for low-income and minority families by increasing the proportion of tuition eligible" (p. 80).

Reports of similar findings concerning preferential differences among public and private school parents have been made by Darling-Hammond and Kirby (1988) and Erickson (1986) in surveys in Minnesota and British Columbia, respectively. Erickson also found that among parents with children in private schools, the preferential differences were much more pronounced among school types [i.e., Catholic, Calvinistic and High-Tuition] than among social class strata. The data suggest that private school types, rather than being mere vehicles of social stratification, attracted parents with different preferences, with limited regard to social class. The schools were products, as it were, of different preference structures. (pp. 95–96)

Whereas public schools are financed through taxation and are tuition free, private schools depend primarily upon tuition, donations, and volunteer or low-priced labor. In addition to the indirect services already noted, governments provide assistance to nonprofit private schools, sectarian and independent alike, through exemption from property taxation; and as an incentive to private contributors, donations to nonprofit private schools may be deducted from the contributor's taxable income.

As government agencies, public schools are subject to direct control by state governments. Their policies are also subject to limitations placed on governmental activities imposed by state and federal constitutions and courts. Private schools need not comply with constitutional requirements imposed on public schools. Private schools are subject to the same general laws that apply to any private business, however, and may be further regulated by state governments, but such regulations tend to be minimal.

EDUCATIONAL VOUCHERS

An educational voucher is an entitlement extended to an individual by a government permitting that individual to receive educational services up to the maximum amount specified. The voucher can normally be redeemed according to the preference of the holder at any institution or enterprise approved by the granting agency. According to Guthrie, Garms, and Pierce (1988),

> Regardless of operating details, voucher plans possess a common fundamental principle. Their intent is to enfranchise households as the basic decision-making unit. Vouchers do not eliminate government interest in education. Rather, voucher plans retain the prospect of government responsibility for financing and otherwise maintaining a marketplace of education providers, which would require regulation. (p. 356)

The differences between the public and private sectors in making decisions about resource allocation were described in Chapter 1. Each household can maximize its satisfaction, within the amount of purchasing power it has, in the private sector because multiple decisions are allowed. In the public sector, however, a single decision is required, which tends to reflect the opinion of the average voter, making it difficult for households deviating from the average to match their tastes with their resources.

Noting that public schooling is the worst where parents have the fewest or no options, Friedman (1962) argued that equity and fraternal ends as well as libertarian and efficiency goals would be better served through governmentally financed vouchers. Vouchers separate the current nexus among public support of education, place of residence, and the public ownership of educational enterprises. Under the Friedman scheme, parents sending their children to private schools would be paid a sum equal to the estimated cost of educating a child in a public school, providing that at least that amount was spent on education in an approved school. If the cost of the private school were greater, the parent would have to make up the difference. Such a plan, Friedman argued, would greatly expand the educational options currently available to poor families.

> One way to achieve a major improvement, to bring learning back into the classroom, especially for the currently most disadvantaged, is to give all parents greater control over their children's schooling, similar to that which those of us in the upper-income classes now have. Parents generally have both greater interest in their children's schooling and more intimate knowledge of their capacities and needs than anyone else. Social reformers, and educational reformers in particular, often self-righteously take for granted that parents, especially those who are poor and have little education themselves, have little interest in their children's education and no competence to choose for them. This is a gratuitous insult. (Friedman & Friedman, 1980, p. 150)

Critics of the Friedman plan argue that unregulated vouchers would merely enable private schools to raise their tuition, still keeping them out of the reach of low-income families. At the same time, unregulated vouchers would make private schools more accessible to higher-income families, encouraging them to abandon the public schools, which would become havens for the poor. This, they claim, would further stratify society. Some critics do see merit in the general concept of vouchers, however, and propose modifications to the original plan which they believe would overcome perceived inequities while retaining what they consider to be its more attractive features.

The Center for the Study of Public Policy (CSPP, 1970) analyzed the potential impact of seven voucher models including Friedman's unregulated market model. Its report concluded that regulations were required to ensure more equitable distribution of resources over the present system; but the regulations themselves would probably generate greater segregation in the schools by ability and/or income than currently exists. Only their regulated compensatory model, described below, was judged likely to give the poor a larger share of the nation's educational resources. In addition to lotteries and quota systems, economic incentives that encourage schools to accept disadvantaged and handicapped students would be needed to give such students a reasonable chance of getting into the schools of their choice. The fundamental political and pedagogic danger posed by most voucher plans was reported to be that at least a few publicly managed schools would become dumping grounds for the students which oversubscribed public and private schools did not want. Oversubscribed schools under an unregulated model would become sanctuaries of privilege.

Under the center's regulated compensatory model, every child would receive a voucher roughly equivalent to the cost of the public schools in the area. A supplement would be paid for children who were in some way disadvantaged because of poverty or physical, psychological, or other learning handicaps. The receiving school would not necessarily have to spend the supplement exclusively on the child for which it was given; for example, it could be used to reduce class size in general throughout a school. No school could charge tuition beyond the voucher amount awarded for a given student. Schools wishing to increase their revenue beyond the voucher amount could seek subventions from such sponsors as churches and businesses or from special purpose grants from the federal government and foundations. Income could also be increased by proportionally increasing the enrollment of disadvantaged students. Schools would have considerable latitude in developing their curricula and in setting their expenditure levels (by admitting larger numbers of students qualifying for supplements). Parents desiring high-expenditure programs would only be able to find them in schools accommodating significant numbers of disadvantaged children. Thus, the basic choice for parents under the plan would be between schools with high financial resources or with more able classmates; parents could continue to finance fully their children's education at schools not participating in the voucher plan.

Coons and Sugarman (1978) took a different approach to family choice through a plan designed to promote variety in the quality of schools rather than uniformity. Their plan has been called both family power equalizing (FPE) and the quality choice model (QCM). QCM would allow schools to charge whatever tuition they wanted within a very broad, but specified, range. Tuition would be paid partly by the parents and partly by the state. State subsidies would be based on tuition charged and family income so that poorer parents, in some meaningful sense, could afford high-priced schools as easily as the rich. The actual formula would work in a fashion similar to district power equalization, discussed in Chapter 8, with families being the focus of wealth equalization rather than school districts. Even the poorest would be required to pay something to establish a personal stake in the choice. No additional charge would be imposed on families with more than one child in school. After the first child, tuition would be fully subsidized by the state. The financial obligation of families sending their children to differently priced schools would be based on the average of tuition amounts charged. Open access to participating schools would be assured by having oversubscribed schools make selections of students on a random basis.

Coons and Sugarman (1978) acknowledge social science research which questions the relationship between cost and quality in schooling. They project that QCM "would encourage families to exercise their own judgement about the efficacy of extra school purchases compared to other goods and services" (p. 200). Enactment of this plan would constitute a marked departure from the current financing of public schools in that, for the first time in this century, tuition would be charged for such schools. (Tuition and "rate bills" were commonly charged by public schools in the nineteenth century; see Chapter 4.) This could significantly alter the educational burden between users and nonusers.

The Reagan administration unsuccessfully proposed a number of times that the more than $3 billion provided annually through Chapter 1 of the Education Consolidation and Improvement Act for supplementary educational services for educationally disadvantaged children in schools serving low-income families be distributed through "minivouchers." Under the Reagan proposal, states and local school districts would give low-income parents vouchers to spend on their children's education to enable choice among public schools within or outside their home district or at private schools.

Another proposal, by Senator Daniel Patrick Moynihan of New York, was modeled on the Pell Grants available for higher education. Families sending their children to elementary and secondary schools qualifying as nonprofit corporations under Section 501(c)(3) of the IRS code would be eligible for financial assistance. Grant allowances would be based on family financial need and the costs of private schooling. Grants would be larger for families with relatively low incomes. By permitting children of poor parents access to private and other public school options, such plans are intended to increase parent leverage on their public schools, encouraging those schools to improve services.

Matching Pupils to Schools

Family choice plans may create the problem of allocating human as well as financial resources to schools. In extensive studies of The Netherlands, James (1986) found certain policy implications for the United States, where we are concerned that privitization may lead to class segmentation in education. She concluded that the Dutch experience suggests that placing restrictions on tuition and salaries can prevent this from happening. As already noted, the CSPP (1970) report concluded that equal access to schools for disadvantaged students could not be ensured by financial incentives alone; regulations would also be required limiting application, admission, and transfer procedures.

Applications and Admissions.   Any marketlike plan for distributing educational services depends upon parents making informed choices in selecting schools for their children. Parents must be able to obtain accurate, relevant, and comprehensive information about the advantages and disadvantages of *all* available alternatives. In the absence of a public initiative, private information sources would probably develop, as has been the case with higher education, but such sources are likely to charge fees for services and would, therefore, not be readily available to the poor. Hence, providing a public information system must become a responsibility of a coordinating public agency. The CSPP (1970) proposed that such responsibilities should include

> collecting information about each school on matters of social and parental concern;
> compiling information in clear and comprehensible printed formats;
> providing counselors who can explain the printed information to those who do not understand it;
> monitoring information provided to parents, protecting them against misleading advertising claims;
> investigating claims of fraud, discrimination and deception, and taking appropriate remedial action where these claims are verified. (pp. 62–63)

The CSPP recommends a procedure whereby parents would have to appear personally at an office of the coordinating agency to fill out the necessary voucher application forms. At this time a counselor would provide information on available options and review procedures for making application. Individual schools would probably establish their own recruiting procedures.

The CSPP (1970) found the most promising device for preventing discrimination in admissions by oversubscribed schools to be some kind of lottery for at least half of their admissions. In recognition that there needs to be some correlation between the curriculum of a school and the characteristics of its students, a case was built for allowing schools some discretionary admissions as long as their criteria do not reinforce patterns of invidious discrimination.

> The idea of favoring cellists over pianists, for example, seems harmless because it does not aggravate any of the more general problems of the educational system. The idea of favoring Spanish-speaking or black applicants seems acceptable to us for the same reason. The idea of discriminating against children against whom everyone else also discriminates is less acceptable. (p. 77)

There are other reasons justifying discretionary admissions. Families with one child already in a school, for a number of very good reasons, would probably want to enroll younger brothers and sisters in the same school. To encourage new schools, which would enhance variety, parents who establish schools would need to be guaranteed a place for their children in recognition of their efforts. As long as the number of founders was limited to a reasonable number, and as long as all founders were listed when the school was incorporated, the CSPP saw no serious difficulty in this procedure.

Transfers among Schools.   Transfers are initiated by either the school or the parent. A parent may become dissatisfied with a school or find with experience that it has not lived up to expectations. In either case, parents should have the option to withdraw their children from a school at any time as long as they can continue to meet compulsory attendance laws by enrolling them in other schools. Admission counselors should be available to them.

Schools also enroll students they would rather not have. Private schools usually persuade such children to withdraw; public schools are constrained by compulsory attendance laws but deal with the situation by placing problem children in "special" schools or programs, by removing them through suspension or expulsion, or by encouraging them to "drop out." Private schools have a great deal of flexibility in eliminating misfits, but public schools must follow formal bureaucratic procedures. The CSPP (1970) could see no justification for providing publicly and privately managed schools with the same amount of money and then allowing the private schools to shirk the responsibilities that are placed on public schools. They recommend that the constraints placed on public schools in these matters be extended to private schools receiving vouchers.

Normally it should be assumed that once a child is admitted to a school and surrenders a voucher, the school is obliged to provide for the education of the child until he or she has completed the course of study or elects to transfer. If a school finds it necessary to expel a child, evidence supporting such action should be submitted to an impartial arbitrator. Both the school and the parents of the child should have access to professional consultation. Parents should also have access to the services of an educational ombudsman to ensure the protection of their rights.

TUITION TAX CREDITS AND DEDUCTIONS

Another approach to aiding persons attending private schools, rather than subsidizing the schools directly, is through tax credits and deductions. A tax credit reduces the amount of the tax (usually an income tax) owed up to a specified sum. Tuition payments (or a percentage of them, depending on how the law is written) can be subtracted from the computed tax amount owed.

Tax deductions apply to income taxes exclusively and are not as favorable for qualifying taxpayers as tax credits. Tax deductions reduce the amount of taxable income upon which the tax is computed. Thus the reduction in tax liability is only a percentage (the marginal tax rate) of tuition payments. Such deductions are allowed in Minnesota, for example. In computing their state income tax liability, the Minnesota law allows parents with children in public and private schools to deduct from their taxable income educational expenses of up to $650 per elementary school child and $1,000 per secondary school child. Expenses eligible for deduction include tuition and cost of secular textbooks, transportation, school supplies, and fees. With marginal tax rates in Minnesota ranging from 1.6 percent to 16 percent, the maximum reduction in tax liability per secondary school child ranges from nothing, for nontaxpayers, to $160. The Minnesota law has been reviewed at all levels of the court system and was upheld by the U.S. Supreme Court in 1983 (*Mueller* v. *Allen*).

Opponents of tax credits and deductions argue that the benefits flow disproportionately to high-income persons. To qualify for either a credit or a deduction, a person has to incur a tax liability and file a return. Thus, the very poorest would not benefit. Such parents could be brought into a tax credit scheme through refundability provisions; that is, the government would reimburse to the individual the amount of the credit. This would still require the filing of a tax return.

Proposals usually contain civil rights guarantees based on school eligibility requirements. Credits and deductions would be allowed only for expenditures incurred in schools which had received governmental approval.

IMPACT ON DIVERSITY

Although the intent of vouchers and tax credits is to provide parents with more educational options for their children, some evidence suggests that there is actually a narrowing in the range of choice—but more people may participate in that narrower range. Currently, with no governmental aid and with only a small percentage of the population attending private schools, there is very little governmental regulation or oversight of private schools. Adoption of increased fiscal support of private schools can come only as a result of extensive political compromises that recognize other objectives such as equality and fraternity. Greater aid and greater participation would thus, undoubtedly, be accompanied with greater governmental control and regulation. This restricts the flexibility of private schools, making them more acceptable to the "average voter" but not necessarily to their original clientele.

Policies on the support of public, private, and religious schools in Canada vary markedly from province to province, providing an excellent setting for the empirical study of the impact of alternative policies. Erickson (1986) reports on such a series of studies, beginning in 1975, which involved interviews of persons associated with Catholic school systems in Alberta, Saskatchewan, and Ontario, where Catholic schools were fully supported with public funds, and in Manitoba and British Columbia, where they were not. Evidence from the interviews convinced Erickson that the lengthy period of total support has significantly "deprivitized" Catholic schools in Alberta, Saskatchewan, and Ontario, attenuating or obliterating numerous characteristics which elsewhere distinguished Catholic schools from public schools. (pp. 99–100)

In 1978, British Columbia embarked on a new policy of partial support of private schools. Most private schools are now funded at 30 percent of the per pupil public school operating cost. Regulations which would protect the public interest have been held to a minimum to avoid homogenizing the private schools. Erickson subsequently launched a follow-up in British Columbia to his 1975 study.

In Catholic elementary schools in British Columbia, dramatic declines were detected in teacher commitment as perceived by parents and in parent commitment as perceived by teachers. The most pronounced negative consequences of increased public assistance were in the Catholic secondary schools. At this level,

> there was a notable decline in the sense among parents that their schools needed their help, in the extent to which parents viewed their schools as responsive, in teacher commitment as perceived by both parents and students, in parent commitment as perceived by teachers, in student affection toward teachers and classes, and in the perception by students that their schools, rather than being just like public schools, were doing something special. (p. 102)

Erickson (1986) concludes that the Canadian examples do not lend much credence to efforts to encourage educational diversity by extending public funds to private schools.

> In one important sense, what the British Columbia government is attempting to do is far from unusual. Faced with the evidence of what they have done to bias the marketplace, governments have often attempted to rectify the situation by returning to the citizens, for their unbiased use, some of the funds previously extracted from them through taxation. It soon turns out, unfortunately, that the money has been transformed by passing through the public pipeline. It cannot be freely used. It has become a political instrument, laden with constraints produced by the anxieties, pressures, and concerns of public officials. (p. 106)

Erickson suspects that the negative effects would not have been nearly so great if the aid had been provided directly through parents in the form of vouchers, tax credits, or tax deductions. Such strategies would encourage less centralization and loss of parental influence.

James (1986) has come to remarkably similar conclusions in a study of school finance and control in The Netherlands, where private schools have been almost wholly supported by public funds for most of this century. At the primary level, 31% of the children are enrolled in public schools, 28% in Protestant schools, 38% in Catholic schools and 3% in other schools (p. 118). At the secondary level, the corresponding percentages are: 28%, 27%, 39%, and 6%.

Families are free to choose the schools for their children to attend. Teachers are prorated to schools on the basis of school enrollments; teacher salaries in all schools are fully paid by the central government. Private schools may supplement neither the staffing levels nor teacher salaries. Buildings are provided by municipal governments for both public and private schools. A small fund for operating expenses is allocated to each school, public or private, which may be used according to its discretion for such items as maintenance, cleaning, heating, libraries, and instructional supplies. Private schools have severely limited rights to supplement the fund with student fees; public schools do not have such rights. James (1986) comments, "Both society in choosing its system, and private schools, in choosing where they fit into the system, would then face a trade-off between autonomy and more funds" (p. 122). James concludes that private schools sacrifice their individuality when they accept public support:

> Cultural heterogeneity often generates a demand for private education and for government subsidies to help cover the associated costs. The subsidies facilitate private sector growth, but they also allow government to impose regulations, particularly over inputs and other behavioral characteristics. Thus, the initial demand for differentiation, if successful, sets in motion forces which make the private sector quasi-governmental; subsidized private sectors are very much like public sectors. If we [in the United States] institute a voucher scheme or other privitization policies, we may end up with a private sector which is larger but less distinctive than the one we have now. (p. 135)

Hirschoff (1986), after a thorough review of the legal structure of schooling in the United States, finds that a significant degree of choice already exists. She cautions that the expansion of family choice bought by increased public funding of private schools has to be weighed against the increased governmental regulation that is sure to follow and the resultant loss of flexibility. She closes her analysis: "Particularly with regard to fiscal change, then, one might conclude that the present legal structure of the mixed system—with perhaps minor adjustments—maximizes parental choice more than would the major changes on which public discussion usually focuses" (p. 52).

CONSTITUTIONAL CONSTRAINTS

There appear to be no constitutional restrictions on family choice among public schools as long as the civil rights of children are not violated in the process. This is probably also true with respect to independent private schools. Direct aid to religiously affiliated private schools, however, is a different matter. Here, there is potential conflict with the First Amendment to the U.S. Constitution, which bars governmental actions "respecting the establishment of religion"; several state constitutions have even more restrictive terminology that bars any form of public assistance to religious institutions. It remains to be determined whether or not aid to parents through vouchers or tax credits which may then be used in religious or other schools is constitutional. We noted that state income tax deductions for tuition and other educational expenses for both public and private school children have been determined to be constitutional (*Mueller* v. *Allen*, 1983).

In *Lemon* v. *Kurtzman*, the Supreme Court established a three-point test to determine whether statutes violate the establishment clause: (1) The statute must have a secular legislative purpose; (2) its principal or primary effect must be one that neither advances nor hinders religion; (3) the statute must not foster an excessive government entanglement with religion. Applications of this test to various forms of governmental aid preclude direct subsidy of private schools. Thus, the constitutional amendment that protects the right of parents to select a private school for their children under the free exercise clause virtually prohibits direct aid to most private schools, which would lighten the burden of choosing a private option, under the establishment clause.

Aid to parents may be another matter, however. Anthony (1987) detects a change in position by the U.S. Supreme Court on this issue. Ten years prior to their *Mueller* decision, the Court had found deductions unconstitutional in a New York case (*Levitt* v. *Committee for Public Education and Religious Liberty*, 1973). A critical difference in the two cases, according to the Court, is that in the Minnesota statute all parents could take advantage of the deduction, whereas in the New York case only parents paying tuition to private schools could benefit.

Anthony (1987) relates the change in this and other interpretations to the shift in the composition of the Supreme Court from liberal domination to conservative domination during the Reagan administration. She sees a softening in the Court's position on parochial aid as a result, drawing on the *Mueller* decision in particular in support of her position. First, she notes the majority's unsolicited endorsement of Minnesota's efforts to defray costs for parents of parochial school children. Because of the heavy burden borne by parents in educating their children in parochial schools, the majority found "whatever unequal effect may be attributed to the statutory classification can fairly be regarded as a rough return for the benefits . . . provided to the state and all taxpayers by parents sending their children to parochial schools" (at 3070).

As a second piece of evidence of the Court's softening position, Anthony (1987) refers to the majority's opinion concerning the Founding Fathers' interpretation of the establishment clause.

> Here, again, Rehnquist [writing for the majority] suggests that the Court no longer needs to be concerned about the separation of church and state. Thus he writes, "At this point in the 20th century we are quite far removed from the dangers that prompted the Framers to include the Establishment Clause in the Bill of Rights. . . . The risk of significant religious or denominational control over our democratic processes—or even of deep political division along religious lines—is remote" (at 3069). (p. 599)

Anthony concludes that the application of the "original intent" doctrine to future parochial school aid is likely to result in decisions which hold public funding of parochial schools constitutional. "However, due to the tendency of conservative jurists to uphold precedent, one can expect a gradual chipping away at previous parochiaid decisions rather than a total renunciation of those rulings" (p. 604).

SUMMARY

One of the most controversial issues on the school reform agenda is family choice of schooling. In this chapter, we looked at implications for school finance policy of possible mechanisms for enhancing choice. Considered were educational vouchers, tax credits, and tax deductions. Mechanisms for choice within public schools were also discussed, including magnet schools and open enrollment plans. Attention was given to the probable loss of flexibility and diversity in the private school sector resulting from public regulation, which would, in all likelihood, accompany the funding of private schools. Finally, constitutional barriers to the use of tax monies in support of religiously affiliated schools were considered in light of changing legal interpretations of the issue initiated by the new conservative majority controlling the U.S. Supreme Court. Consumer sovereignty as discussed in this chapter and provider sovereignty as discussed in the previous chapter are critical elements in imbuing the public education sector with marketlike incentives for efficiency and for permitting individual liberty with respect to schooling.

This chapter concludes our evaluation of possible school finance structures and strategies for the use of resources based on criteria of equity, fraternity, liberty, efficiency, economic growth, and adequacy. In the next chapter, and final section of the book, we return to the decision model presented in Chapter 2 to consider the alternatives before us in organizing school governance and finance in the decade ahead.

ACTIVITIES

1. Within the context of the decision matrix presented in Figure 2.1, what educational decisions are best placed with parents? What safeguards need to be implemented to protect legitimate social and professional interests? Provide the rationale for your responses.

2. If parents have freedom to choose the schools their children attend, how might their interests best be represented in the design of educational programs (assuming school-based management)?

3. Do you believe that education vouchers issued directly to parents would violate the prohibitions of the First Amendment of the U.S. Constitution against the establishment of religion if some parents chose to enroll their children in religiously affiliated schools? Why?

4. Examine the provisions of your state constitution governing church-state relationships. Compare them with the provisions in the U.S. Constitution. Are your state's provisions more or less restrictive with respect to making public monies available in support of children attending religiously affiliated schools? Provide the rationale for your response.

5. Discuss the advantages and disadvantages of alternative arrangements for expanding diversity in schooling options:
   a. The current arrangement of free, publicly financed and operated schools with direct aid to private schools prohibited but allowing supporting services which benefit children attending private schools
   b. Educational vouchers, with options among public and private schools
   c. Tax deductions for tuition and other expenses incurred in public and private education
   d. Tax credits that rebate the cost of tuition up to a specified amount
   e. Direct aid to private schools, for example, as in The Netherlands
   f. Open enrollment among public schools without public aid for private schools

6. Design a voucher scheme which would enhance family choice of schools while protecting equity considerations.

REFERENCES

Aguilar v. *Felton*. 473 U.S. 402 (1985).

Anthony, P. (1987). Public monies for private schools: The Supreme Court's changing approach. *Journal of Education Finance*, *12*, 592–605.

Boyd, W. L., & Kerchner, C. T. (1988). *The politics of excellence and choice in education*. New York: Falmer Press.

Center for the Study of Public Policy (CSPP). (1970). *Education vouchers: A report on financing education by grants to parents*. Cambridge, MA: Author.

Chubb, J. E., & Moe, T. M. (1985). *Politics, markets, and the organization of schools*. Stanford, CA: Institute for Research on Educational Finance and Governance, School of Education, Stanford University.

Coons, J. E., & Sugarman, S. D. (1978). *Education by choice: The case for family control*. Berkeley: University of California Press.

Darling-Hammond, L., & Kirby, S. N. (1988). Public policy and private choice: The case of Minnesota. In T. James & H. M. Levin (Eds.), *Comparing public and private schools: Vol. 1, Institutions and organizations* (pp. 243–267). New York: Falmer Press.

Elam, S. M., & Gallup, A. M. (1989). The 21st annual Gallup poll of the public's attitudes toward the public schools. *Phi Delta Kappan*, *71* (1), 41–54.

Elmore, R. F. (1988). Choice in public education. In W. L. Boyd & C. T. Kerchner (Eds.), *The politics of excellence and choice in education* (pp. 79–98). New York: Falmer Press.

Erickson, D. A. (1986). Choice and private schools. In D. C. Levy (Ed.), *Private education: Studies in choice and public policy* (pp. 57–81). New York: Oxford University Press.

Friedman, M. (1962). *Capitalism and freedom*. Chicago: University of Chicago Press.

Friedman, M., & Friedman, R. (1980). *Free to choose: A personal statement*. New York: Avon Books.

Glenn, C. L. (1986). The Massachusetts experience with public school choice. *Time for results: The governors' 1991 report on education*. Supporting works, *Task Force on Parent Involvement and Choice*. Washington, DC: National Governors' Association.

Guthrie, J. W., Garms, W. I., & Pierce, L. C. (1988). *School finance and education policy: Expanding educational efficiency, equity and choice*. Englewood Cliffs, NJ: Prentice Hall.

Gwartney, J. D., & Wagner, R. E. (Eds.). (1988). *Public choice and constitutional economics*. Greenwich, CT: JAI Press.

Hirschoff, M. U. (1986). Public policy toward private schools: A focus on parental choice. In D. C. Levy (Ed.), *Private education: Studies in choice and public policy* (pp. 33–56). New York: Oxford University Press.

James, E. (1986). Public subsidies for private and public education: The Dutch case. In D. C. Levy (Ed.), *Private education: Studies in choice and public policy* (pp. 113–137). New York: Oxford University Press.

James, T., & Levin, H. M. (Eds.). (1988). *Comparing public and private schools: Vol. 1, Institutions and organizations*. New York: Falmer Press.

Jung, R. (1982). *Nonpublic school students in Title I ESEA programs; A question of "equal" services*. McLean, VA: Advanced Technology.

Kearns, D. T., & Doyle, D. P. (1988). *Winning the brain race: A bold new plan to make our schools competitive*. San Francisco: Institute for Contemporary Studies.

Kutner, M. A., Sherman, J. D., & Williams, M. F. (1986). Federal policies for public schools. In

D. C. Levy (Ed.), *Private education: Studies in choice and public policy* (pp. 57–81). New York: Oxford University Press.

Lemon v. *Kurtzman*, 403 U.S. 602 (1970).

Levitt v. *Committee for Public Education and Religious Liberty*, 413 U.S. 472 (1973).

Levy, D. C. (Ed.). (1986). *Private education: Studies in choice and public policy*. New York: Oxford University Press.

Lieberman, M. (1989). *Privitization and educational choice*. New York: St. Martin's Press.

Mueller v. *Allen*, 463 U.S. 388 (1983).

Murnane, R. J. (1986). Comparisons of private and public schools: The critical role of regulations. In D. C. Levy (Ed.), *Private education: Studies in choice and public policy* (pp. 138–152). New York: Oxford University Press.

Nathan, J. (1989). Helping all children, empowering all educators: Another view of school choice. *Phi Delta Kappan, 71*, 304–307.

National Governors' Association. (1986). *Time for results: The governors' 1991 report on education*. Washington, DC: Author.

Pearson, J. (1989). Myths of choice: The governor's new clothes? *Phi Delta Kappan, 70*, 821–823.

Pierce v. *Society of Sisters*, 268 U.S. 510 (1925).

Powell, A. G., Farrar, E., & Cohen, D. K. (1985). *The shopping mall high school: Winners and losers in the educational marketplace*. Boston: Houghton Mifflin.

Pulido v. *Cavazos*, 728 F. Supp. 574.

Snider, W. (1989a). Iowa, Arkansas enact "choice"; proposals gain in other states. *Education Week, 8* (25), 1, 19.

Snider, W. (1989b). Known for choice, New York's District 4 offers a complex tale for urban reformers. *Education Week, 9* (9), 1, 13.

Tiebout, C. M. (1956). A pure theory of local expenditures. *Journal of Political Economy, 64* (5), 416–424.

PART V

Synthesis

CHAPTER 18

Implications of Educational Restructuring for School Finance Policy: The Economics and Politics of School Finance

We hope that this journey through the concepts and issues that make up the field of school finance has been an enlightening one. It is our purpose in this chapter to bring together the themes of this book in an integrated discussion of the problems that must be addressed during the 1990s and to assess some of the more promising alternatives before us.

Because the provision of elementary and secondary education is made largely through the public sector, educational decisions are political and must be understood as such. But because the public sector functions within a market economy, where two-thirds of our GNP is allocated through decisions made by private choice, the implications of political decisions about financing education must be studied by using economic paradigms (see Chapter 1).

Using economic terminology, we see the lack of internal efficiency as being the paramount educational policy issue before us. All of the reform proposals of the 1980s addressed the task of making the educational system work better, so that the attitudes and achievements of children and young people might be improved. Throughout the preceding chapters we have seen the blame for failures of the system placed on teachers and administrators who are, allegedly, of low competence; poor methods of preparing teachers and administrators; lack of adequate resources; poor curriculum; outmoded instructional procedures; and a bureaucratic system that stifles initiative and change and promotes lethargy, uniformity, and impersonalization. In Part IV, proposals for correcting each of these weaknesses were considered in terms of their implications for school finance policy.

Chapters 11 and 12 show the lack of equity in distributing resources to be a major problem also. We place this problem second only because the evidence is very strong that diverting more resources to poor and at-risk children will not improve their achievements unless the instructional system itself is made more effective. The evidence is quite consistent that the persons most affected by the inefficiencies of the educational system are children at risk. A review in Chapter 13 of educational production function studies, effective schools research, psychological studies, and comparisons with private schools shows that we already possess the knowledge of policies and practices which could enhance the internal efficiency of schools. But the inertia of the system effectively blocks most attempts at reform. School finance policy in the future must be directed in a fashion to overcome this inertia and improve first, the efficiency of the system, and second, its equity.

The decision matrix presented in Figure 2.1 depicted what decisions have to be made about financing schools, who the primary decision makers are, and the value context which influences the nature of the decisions made. The process was shown to be a dynamic one, causing the nature of acceptable decisions to change along with the political-economic environment and with the priorities given to intrinsic social values. As a vehicle for synthesizing the concepts and issues discussed in this text, we now take that matrix and place it within Easton's (1965) simplified model of a political system (see Figure 1.4).

The result is Figure 18.1. The decision matrix, in its new context, is called the Political-Economic System. The intrinsic values of liberty, equality, and fraternity along with the derived values of efficiency and economic growth of Figure 2.1 are treated as "demand" inputs to the policy-making process in the new model. Other demand inputs include existing knowledge and requirements for a qualified work force. The latter requirement is, at the same time, a "support" input in that trained personnel are required to implement any policies which are made, and indeed, the qualifications of available labor will strongly influence which policy alternatives are feasible and which are not. Other supportive inputs are the economic base from which resources must be drawn to finance implementation and the behavior of citizens in general, which sustains the political-economic system through obeying laws, paying taxes, and accepting outcomes of elections. The outputs of the process are educational policies, categorized in the figure under the five types of issues which must be addressed. The policies are derived from decisions made by society, the profession, and the family.

In this chapter, we will discuss each of the five types of educational policy issues in terms of policy alternatives considered in earlier chapters and the peculiar interests of society, the teaching profession, and family clients. Where there appears to be evidence about the effectiveness of a particular alternative, this will also be reported.

SETTING GOALS AND OBJECTIVES FOR THE EDUCATIONAL ENTERPRISE

The history of public education in the United States has been a history of centralization of authority. Compulsory school attendance legislation in the nineteenth century was one of the first acts of centralization in that it removed the right of parents to decide *not* to educate their children. The establishment of the common school with the use of public funds did leave the setting of educational goals and objectives with school districts, which for the most part were very small and easily controlled by family constituents.

At the same time, parents continued the privilege of enrolling their children in private schools at *their* expense, if they so desired—an important accommodation for those whose values orientations were not satisfied by the philosophy and orientation of the public schools or who were dissatisfied with the quality of public school services. The combined

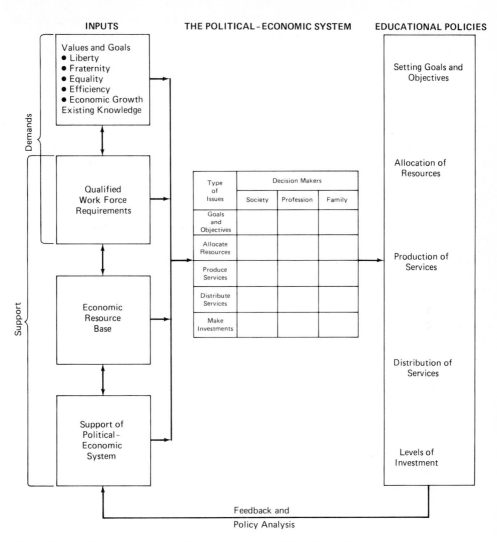

Figure 18.1. A Model of the Political-Economic System of Educational Policy Development

effect of compulsory attendance laws, publicly financed and operated schools, and privately financed private schools was to improve the societal objectives of fraternity and equality of educational opportunity within, but not among, school districts while minimizing the diminution of liberty for family clients. This political compromise balanced interests of society with those of parents.

During the first half of the twentieth century, through the natural growth of cities and the deliberate policy of consolidation of rural and suburban school districts, control over the direction of schools by family clients became more and more remote, strengthening the authority of the teaching profession over those decisions. Teachers and administrators received much better professional preparation during this period than they had previously.

Efficiency of schools was enhanced at the expense of liberty for the 90 percent of parents sending their children to public schools.

Following World War II, the state and federal governments began to play a larger role in shaping the direction of public schooling through legislation and litigation. Increasing proportions of young people found it necessary to complete secondary school in order to qualify for a satisfactory job. This increased the cost of education beyond that which most communities could support through the property tax alone and magnified the disparities among school districts in their ability to finance educational services and in the quality of services offered. States responded by gradually assuming a greater proportion of the financial support of public schools and, along with it, a greater degree of control over them. Objectives of equality and efficiency motivated the actions, again at the expense of the liberty of family clients, of local communities, and of the profession.

In the pursuit of equality and fraternity objectives, litigants successfully challenged through federal courts the practices in schools of segregation by race and gender discrimination. Court-ordered desegregation, hiring quotas, limits on the disciplinary discretion of educators, and curricular change resulted. Disparities in spending that result from state school aid formulas were also successfully challenged in several states. State and federal legislation reinforced the decisions of courts on all issues, making specific decisions universal. Little discretion was left to family clients within public schools; the discretion of independent teaching professionals was severely constrained by bureaucratic rules and regulations and compounded by collective bargaining. Objectives of fraternity and equality came into sharp conflict with efficiency and client liberty.

Centralization continued with the first wave of educational reform in the 1980s, which responded to the national concern over global economic competition. In an effort to increase student achievement (efficiency), states instituted more rigorous curricula, more stringent high school graduation requirements, statewide standardized testing, and higher certification standards for teachers and administrators. The centralization of decision making had become nearly complete.

Centralization of authority did not always produce the results desired, and by the mid-1980s, there was a realization that it might be necessary to differentiate among decisions about which were appropriate to be made by central authorities and which were not. From the mid-1960s through the early 1980s, efficiency and equity had been pursued through centralized authority. Policy implementation studies of that period showed that central governments are particularly effective in dealing with issues of equity and access, but they appear to be less effective in dealing with matters of efficiency and "production," that is, how a school is organized and operated. Learning from our experience, there is a growing movement to pursue efficiency through decentralized authority and equity through centralized authority.

School-based decision making (discussed in Chapter 16) and family choice (discussed in Chapter 17) represent important tactics in an overall strategy of decentralization. These tactics return some decision-making authority to parents and teachers in order to induce marketlike forces into the public school sector for the purpose of increasing its efficiency. In responding to the issue of who should set goals and objectives for educational enterprises, these chapters concluded that extreme centralization had sapped public schooling of much of its vitality and efficiency and had alienated a significant proportion of its family clients. Nevertheless, it was recognized that there are important societal interests that have to be protected. Societal interests become paramount where there are significant spillover of benefits and where there are redistributive considerations, as is the case of providing educational services.

There are legitimate concerns about the goals and objectives of education at all levels of the sociopolitical hierarchy; the critical issue is achieving an acceptable balance among legitimate interests. Although some decisions concerning equity and access can be made best by central authorities, teaching professionals hold the technical expertise of schooling. Parents are the guardians of interests and needs of individual children. The family holds the most intimate knowledge about, and caring concern for, the child. It is through the family that the child's voice can best be heard (see Chapter 17).

ALLOCATING RESOURCES TO AND AMONG EDUCATIONAL SERVICES

Two basic policy decisions must be made concerning the allocation of resources to education:

Should there be governmental intervention?
If there is to be governmental intervention, what should be its nature and extent?

In Chapters 1 and 2, the case for governmental involvement in the financing of education was developed. Such involvement ensures that societal interests in a literate citizenry are satisfied and promotes equality of educational opportunity within the population. The current practice of public ownership and operation of schools, however, is only one form of intervention. This leaves open for consideration as public policy alternatives aid to privately owned and operated schools and direct aid to parents in the form of educational vouchers. Nevertheless, it is our assessment that the most likely scenario for the 1990s is a continuation of the near public monopoly of the ownership and operation of elementary and secondary schools. Accommodation of efficiency and liberty concerns are more likely to be made through incremental adjustments to the current system, such as school-based decision making and open enrollment in public schools, than through more radical reforms that would privatize education.

Federal involvement in the financing of education is likely to continue near its current level until the federal deficit is brought under control and other federal social service programs are reorganized (see Chapter 10). The proportion of school costs derived from local taxation will continue to fall because of the inelasticity of the property tax base (see Chapter 6). Even though private funds will increase through partnership activities in many school systems, these funds are not likely to make a difference in poor or rural districts. The slack in financial support of elementary and secondary schools will be picked up by the broader and more elastic tax bases of state governments (see Chapter 5). This growing state involvement in school finance makes the structuring of mechanisms for distributing state resources to schooling an even more important policy consideration than it has been in the past (see Chapters 8 and 9).

Flat grant and foundation programs of state aid to school districts, particularly when they permit large local leeway, are inequitable to students and taxpayers in property-poor districts which need to spend beyond established aid levels. Unfettered percentage equalizing schemes remove the inequitable effects of variations in the distribution of property wealth; but they do not remove the inequitable effects of variations among school districts in the priority given to education and, therefore, the willingness to tax themselves to provide educational services. Full state funding is equitable in that it treats all alike. But the cost to liberty is high, and the difficulty of determining what level of support is adequate may impinge upon efficiency.

Of all financing strategies, full state funding most clearly recognizes that providing for the basic educational needs of citizens is a responsibility of the state as required by state constitutions. Full state funding does not necessarily eliminate the possibility of decentralized decisions about matters of curriculum and how the schools are organized and operated. Further, full state funding does not preclude the recognition that some children require more expensive sets of educational services than do other children (see Chapter 9).

The greatest difficulty with full state funding arises in defining the level of funding, that is, determining how much is enough. It assumes that state legislatures are fully competent to determine unilaterally what an "adequate" standard of finance for education is—a role currently filled by independent school districts. Equal inadequacy is of little value to anyone and would certainly precipitate the abandonment of public schools by all who are able. On the other hand, no state can afford equal opulence.

Full state funding replaces many independent decisions of local districts about the level of financial adequacy for schools with a single state-level decision. On the surface, this appears to be the height of efficiency—if state legislatures were infallible; unfortunately, they are not. School districts are not infallible either, but the decisions of each district affect only a small portion of a state's population except for major city districts; the law of averages works to dilute the bad decisions—and we learn from both good and bad decisions.

The pattern of finance operating in most states assumes a partnership between state and local authorities. Local authorities define financial requirements based on constituent demands for schooling, educational program needs, and the availability of resources from locally generated revenue and intergovernmental transfers. State aid to education represents a series of political compromises within the economic constraints inherent in a state's tax-collecting capacity. The compromises are forged by legislators and governors in response to pressures generated by advocates of the public schools, advocates of the many other functions of state government, and advocates of reduced public services and taxes.

Since, in most states, the state level of support lags far behind actual expenditures by school districts, the definition of an adequate level of financial support is actually made by each school district through its regular planning and budgeting processes, which involve primarily school-related groups and individuals. In seeking funds at the state level, the effectiveness of arguments by advocates of high-quality educational services has been greatly enhanced in the past by the ability to draw upon data generated by independent decisions of many school districts. To remove all local discretion in establishing expenditure levels would remove a very important experience test in determining the adequacy of state support levels, perhaps leaving resource allocation decisions to be made largely on political rather than educational grounds. It was noted in Chapter 8 that the highest-expenditure states in the nation tend to be those that rely equally on state and local sources of revenue.

Permitting variation in local expenditures enhances the ability of school districts to accommodate local preferences. With no absolute pedagogical principles to guide educational decision makers, valuable empirical evidence may be gained through the encouragement of a variety of educational programs and expenditure levels. From a political standpoint, such a procedure holds the potential for reducing social stress as long as local resource bases are equalized in that the interest groups which must be satisfied within any given school district are fewer than for the state as a whole. A limited amount of local discretionary authority in setting expenditure levels permits districts to meet higher costs because of unique local conditions and/or aspirations without unduly complicating a state aid formula with technical corrections (see Chapter 9).

Growing out of this discussion, the following are recommended as guides for structuring a state school finance program.

1. The state has the overall responsibility for the provision of educational services.
2. The state may define expenditure constraints for school districts in the light of state resources, but it should not make all decisions relative to expenditure levels of school districts.
   a. Wide variation among districts in educational expenditures cannot be justified, given societal interest in equality of educational opportunities.
   b. Economic, social, and environmental variations within most states preclude the establishment of a single expenditure level for the entire state. Local authorities are in the best position to make finite expenditure adjustments and need some degree of leeway to do so.
   c. Since there is no absolute standard of an adequate educational program, limited local discretion provides state authorities with data critical to the establishment of realistic expenditure ranges.
3. Within established constraints, the taxing ability for each school district should be equal to the taxing ability of the whole state; that is, a given tax rate in any school district should produce as much, but no more, revenue per pupil as the same tax rate levied against all the property in the state. State revenue should guarantee the yield at this valuation level, and the state should recapture amounts above this production.
4. State governments should gradually increase the proportion of educational costs they provide through nonproperty taxes up to about 60 percent of all local districts' spending levels combined.
5. Any aid formula should automatically adjust to changes in educational costs, educational needs, and local taxing ability.
6. The relationship between state aid and state objectives should be apparent. The implication is that more than one formula may be required to accomplish the objectives of present operating aid formulas.
7. Aid for meeting extraordinary educational needs should be separate from aid to correct for the uneven distribution of wealth among school districts and to relieve the burden on the property tax.
8. The cost of meeting extraordinary educational needs should be financed solely from state and federal funds.

These guides could be made operational with a state finance program that includes the following characteristics:

a minimum support program, below which no district may spend, financed from the state's general fund and a state-levied property tax;

a discretionary range of expenditure (not to exceed 20% of the base) that is supported by state and local funds according to one of the alternative methods for implementing the percentage equalizing concept, including a recapture provision; and

special aids for extraordinary educational needs.

The objectives of the minimum support program, the discretionary range of expenditures, and the maximum support level are to make available to every child in the state educational services adequate for meeting the needs of a typical child, to equalize the property tax ability at chosen levels of effort, and to distribute schooling costs equitably between property and nonproperty taxes. The objective of special aids is to provide adequate educational services for children with extraordinary needs.

DETERMINING THE MEANS BY WHICH EDUCATIONAL SERVICES ARE PROVIDED

For over a decade, reports of national assessments of educational progress have provided strong evidence that the public schools, in general, are not living up to societal—or individual—expectations. Part IV of this text deals with issues of restructuring to bring schooling outputs in line with societal expectations. Chapter 11 looks at the issues of equality and efficiency from the perspective of judicial review. Chapter 12 examines the issues of equality and fraternity from the perspective of policy analysts. Chapter 13, using economic paradigms, concludes that schooling inadequacies developed more from the inefficient use of economic resources already available to schools than from the inadequacy of available resources. Personnel matters are the focus of Chapter 14 including remuneration and professional growth strategies for teachers which would increase the efficiency by which labor resources are used. Also to promote efficiency, Chapter 15 argues for the integration of electronic and communication technologies into the instructional process, the restructuring of the role of teacher, and the total reorganization of the school. The possibilities of injecting marketlike incentives into public school organizations through school-based management and through family choice of schooling are examined in Chapters 16 and 17, respectively.

Throughout those chapters, there is a consistent theme that the school, rather than the district or classroom, is the basic unit of instruction and that the major decisions of operation should be placed at that level. School-based management (SBM) provides teaching professionals with the authority to make decisions of production which require technical expertise, enabling schools to adapt to unique local and individual circumstances. Given the lack of knowledge about the causal relationships between schooling inputs and outputs, SBM enables organizations to use a variety of instructional delivery systems. Careful evaluation of the diversity of schools should contribute to a better understanding of what educational practices work best under specific circumstances, contributing to improved operational efficiency. But, to ensure equity, SBM must function within a state and federal framework which permits professional discretion while allowing prudent monitoring by higher levels of authority.

Increasing the authority of schools at a time when states are assuming greater responsibility for defining curriculum and setting achievement standards for pupils raises serious questions about the future viability of school districts as they are currently organized. In Chapter 13, it is suggested that large city school districts will gradually take on the characteristics of service units, similar to those of intermediate districts serving rural and suburban areas in a number of states, but with the added responsibility of acting as a funding conduit for schools. This is already happening in Chicago.

In rural areas, pressures for the consolidation of small districts are likely to subside because, in many respects, rural school districts already embody many of the characteristics of school-based decision making. On the other hand, county or regional units may more efficiently assume responsibilities currently exercised by rural districts for providing services to schools like levying taxes and furnishing financial and personnel support. In some states there may be attempts to dissolve suburban school districts, dividing their current responsibilities between regional or county units and school-level authorities.

Recent studies of economies of scale show that there is a certain beauty in small schools. Small schools provide for sustained contact among all members of the learning community, which serves as a safeguard against the alienation found in many large schools. Compared to large schools, small schools provide greater opportunity for student participation and greater educational support, which appear to be especially beneficial for at-risk students. The primary advantage of large schools is in their enriched curricular options, but advances in electronic and communications technologies are rapidly bringing such options to small schools also. A challenge of the 1990s is to design arrangements which combine the advantages of big schools and small schools in one setting while eliminating their disadvantages.

As suggested, technological advances can assist in correcting some of the shortcomings of present-day schools. Computers facilitate individualized instruction and provide a mechanism for continuously and patiently monitoring drill and individual progress. CD-ROM and other video technologies provide for instructional enrichment which cannot be matched by words alone—written or spoken. Communication technology can make the world's information resources available to any person at any place.

Integrating technology into the instructional process facilitates the reduction of the number of professionally trained personnel needed and enables the more extensive use of lower-cost paraprofessionals. This, in turn, enables the upgrading of the teaching profession, permitting teachers to concentrate on activities for which professional discretion is required. Differentiated staffing allows for more professional career options; and because of their fewer numbers, salaries of those professional teachers remaining could be competitive with other professions.

Putting all these factors together, we see that reforming the structure of schools through the integration of technology into instructional processes permits a redefinition of the role of teaching and its rewards in a way that makes the profession more attractive to persons with exceptional skills. Available technology can improve the efficiency of schooling by enabling students, teachers, and support personnel to use their time and talents more productively and by upgrading the competence of those attracted into the teaching profession. Further, production decisions are best made at the school building level with support services provided at district, intermediate, and state levels and through the private sector.

DETERMINING FOR WHOM EDUCATIONAL SERVICES ARE TO BE PROVIDED

Except for those few who are able to exercise private options, determining for whom educational services will be provided has been largely a societal decision. And over the years, society has expanded the availability of schooling until virtually all people between the ages of 6 and 18 now have access to some form of publicly funded instruction. Expansion is frequently the result of intensive lobbying on the part of special interest groups such as those promoting educational opportunities for children with handicapping conditions. But although there is a general recognition of the value of education to the individual, there are differences of opinion about the philosophy, content, and context appropriate for specific individuals.

Differences in educational tastes increase social tensions, especially when the choices available through the public sector are narrowed, as they have been in recent years. As the implementation of SBM spreads, more schooling options will exist, but this will not reduce tensions unless the options are freely available to family clients. As a matter of fact, options without choice will further frustrate family clients, increasing social tension.

Once the bureaucratic uniformity among schools is broken, it is difficult to justify district assignment of pupils to schools. Family choice of schooling permits the matching of a child's characteristics and family preferences with the school's characteristics. It also provides a monitoring mechanism which assures society that each public school is satisfactorily providing a service desired by a sufficiently large clientele. Choice enhances the policy objectives of liberty and efficiency. Unfettered choice could violate the objectives of equality and fraternity, however. This can be avoided with social controls such as those exercised through the magnet school concept or the regulated compensatory voucher model described in Chapter 17.

SBM frees the "producers" of educational services to use their professional knowledge, experience, insights, and imagination to design instructional systems to fit specific situations as they assess them. Family choice of schooling permits clients to select among available options the ones that they feel are best for their children and family circumstances. When a "money follows the child" strategy is used for allocating resources to schools, marketlike forces are generated which make producers more sensitive to the needs of clients and potential clients. Producers also become more aware of alternative uses of available resources in order to maximize their positive impact. A dissatisfied client who leaves takes with him or her resources from a school; likewise, each new client attracted brings additional resources.

DETERMINING THE LEVEL OF INVESTMENT IN POPULATION QUALITY

In Chapter 13, we reviewed a number of studies of the external efficiency of expenditures for education. This is an important consideration in determining what proportion of a society's resources should be allocated to the provision of educational services. Because of the heavy involvement of government in the provision of elementary and secondary education, the level of investment in schooling has become a largely political decision, supplemented marginally by decisions made by individuals through the market.

We noted that level of education is directly correlated with an individual's expected earnings. Education increases the value of one's labor by increasing the cache of knowledge at one's command and honing one's occupational skills. Anticipation of higher incomes causes individuals to be willing to invest some of their own resources in their further education, especially at the postsecondary level. By the same token, the more sophisticated the technological development of a country, the greater is the demand for highly skilled workers. Thus, we see that the proportion of a nation's resources allocated to education increases along with the sophistication of its technology.

Rate of return studies have shown that the United States, along with most other developed countries, is investing in education at an appropriate level given the current organization of elementary and secondary schools. If there is any area where greater investment might be justified, it is at the primary, and possibly the preschool, levels. The percentage of GNP allocated to precollegiate education during the 1990s may continue to fluctuate modestly along with the proportion of the population engaged in schooling. Expenditures per pupil can be expected to increase in real terms, but at a slowing pace.

During the late 1970s and early 1980s, the rate of return for postsecondary education dropped below the yield for other types of investments, particularly for persons considering careers in education. By the close of the decade of the 1980s, however, the postsecondary rate of return had risen to acceptable levels and may now be on the verge of rising to a point justifying larger relative investments.

Privatization of elementary and secondary education would probably increase the investment of upper-income persons in the education of their children at the expense of less investment for children from lower-income families. On the other hand, further centralization would probably result in less investment by upper-income individuals and somewhat more for low-income children. Some voucher plans may encourage greater investment on the part of upper-income families while protecting the level of investment available to children from poorer families, resulting in a net increase in investment for education.

SUMMARY

The greatest problem facing policymakers during the 1990s in the field of public school finance is designing systems for financing schools which encourage improvement in their efficiency. The second most important problem is the improvement of the equity of the distribution of resources to schools whereby all children may have access to good facilities, competent instruction, and state-of-the-art learning materials.

The primary barrier to the implementation of reforms directed toward making the educational system more efficient appears to be the bureaucratic nature of its current organization. Federal and state categorical aids along with court interventions and state regulation have contributed significantly to this condition. To counter schooling's bureaucratic nature, decision making concerning the organization and operation of schools and the allocation of resources within schools needs to be devolved to persons at the school level. To provide incentives for making school personnel more sensitive to the demands of family clients and more concerned about the quality of service provided, the assurance of school funding needs to be removed and linked to the quality of school performance. This can best be accomplished by permitting parents to select the schools their children are to attend and linking the flow of resources to the flow of children. School finance strategies facilitating such arrangements are school-based decision making, open enrollment among public schools, and educational vouchers. The last are appropriate only if private schools are to be brought into the purview of the publicly supported system.

To safeguard legitimate societal concerns, including concern for equal educational opportunities, school-based decision making and family choice among public schools must function within a framework of state and federal finance and supervision. Societal controls may well include a required basic curriculum, mandated admission of minorities and children with handicapping conditions who want to attend particular schools, monitoring of standards and progress through formal systems of evaluation, and a system of information and counseling available to parents to assist them in enrolling their children in the most appropriate schools. The proportion of school funding from state resources is likely to continue to increase through the 1990s, and it is entirely conceivable that some states may formally take over the taxation of property for school purposes.

Equity demands that states require the maintenance of a minimum level of support at the school level commensurate with the cost of an adequate basic educational program and that a cap, fractionally above the required minimum, be placed on spending. The current linkages must be broken among per pupil expenditure levels, the wealth of school districts, and the priorities given to education by constituents of school districts. With the centralization of some decisions at the state and federal levels and with the decentralization of many decisions to school personnel and to parents, the future viability of school districts as currently organized is in question.

The 1990s will see dramatic changes in the financing of elementary and secondary schools, reflecting the organizational changes that will take place within them. The problems are sufficient to challenge the best and the brightest policy analysts.

ACTIVITIES

1. Discuss the prognosis of school finance policy for the 1990s presented in this chapter. Identify the issues with which you agree and those with which you disagree. Present your rationales in both instances.
2. Develop your own scenario of the evolution of school finance policies during the 1990s. How does your prognosis differ from that of the authors? How do you account for any disagreements?

REFERENCE

Easton, D. A. (1965). *A framework for political analysis*. Englewood Cliffs, NJ: Prentice Hall.

Index

Figures and tables are indicated by italicized page numbers.